ST ANDREWS STUDIES
IN PHILOSOPHY AND PUBLIC AFFAIRS

Founding and General Editor:
John Haldane, University of St Andrews

Values, Education and the Human World
edited by John Haldane

Philosophy and its Public Role
edited by William Aiken and John Haldane

Relativism and the Foundations of Liberalism
by Graham Long

Human Life, Action and Ethics: Essays by G.E.M. Anscombe
edited by Mary Geach and Luke Gormally

*The Institution of Intellectual Values:
Realism and Idealism in Higher Education*
by Gordon Graham

Life, Liberty and the Pursuit of Utility
by Anthony Kenny and Charles Kenny

Distributing Healthcare: Principles, Practices and Politics
edited by Niall Maclean

Liberalism, Education and Schooling: Essays by T.M. Mclaughlin
edited by David Carr, Mark Halstead and Richard Pring

The Landscape of Humanity: Art, Culture & Society
by Anthony O'Hear

*Faith in a Hard Ground:
Essays on Religion, Philosophy and Ethics by G.E.M. Anscombe*
edited by Mary Geach and Luke Gormally

Subjectivity and Being Somebody
by Grant Gillett

Understanding Faith: Religious Belief and Its Place in Society
by Stephen R.L. Clark

*Profit, Prudence and Virtue:
Essays in Ethics, Business & Management*
edited by Samuel Gregg and James Stoner

Practical Philosophy: Ethics, Society and Culture
by John Haldane

Sensibility and Sense: Aesthetic Transformation of the World
by Arnold Berleant

*Understanding Teaching and Learning:
Classic Texts on Education*
edited by T. Brian Mooney and Mark Nowacki

Truth and Faith in Ethics
edited by Hayden Ramsay

From Plato to Wittgenstein: Essays by G.E.M. Anscombe
edited by Mary Geach and Luke Gormally

*Natural Law, Economics, and the Common Good:
Perspectives from Natural Law*
edited by Samual Gregg and Harold James

The Philosophy of Punishment
by Anthony Ellis

Social Radicalism and Liberal Education
by Lindsay Paterson

Logic, Truth and Meaning: Writings by G.E.M. Anscombe
edited by Mary Geach and Luke Gormally

The Moral Philosophy of Elizabeth Anscombe
edited by Luke Gormally, David Albert Jones and Roger Teichmann

Art, Morality and Human Nature: Writings by Richard W. Beardsmore
edited by John Haldane and Ieuan Lloyd

The Life and Philosophy of Elizabeth Anscombe
edited by John Haldane

Ethics, Politics and Religion: Essays by Michael Dummett
edited by John Haldane

The Life and Philosophy of Elizabeth Anscombe

Edited by
John Haldane

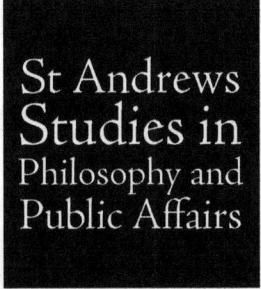

imprint-academic.com

Copyright © this collection Imprint Academic Ltd., 2019

Individual contributions © the respective authors, 2019

The moral rights of the authors have been asserted.
No part of this publication may be reproduced in any form
without permission, except for the quotation of brief passages
in criticism and discussion.

Published in the UK by Imprint Academic
PO Box 200, Exeter EX5 5YX, UK

Distributed in the USA by
Ingram Book Company,
One Ingram Blvd., La Vergne, TN 37086, USA

ISBN 9781788360043 paperback
ISBN 9781788360036 cloth

A CIP catalogue record for this book is available from the
British Library and US Library of Congress

Cover Photograph:
St Salvator's Quadrangle, St Andrews by Peter Adamson
from the University of St Andrews collection

For Mary Geach and Luke Gormally

Contents

J. Haldane, Preface	ix
Contributors	xiii
J. Haldane, Elizabeth Anscombe: Life and Work	1
A. Kenny, Elizabeth Anscombe at Oxford	12
A. Gibson, Anscombe, Cambridge and the Challenges of Wittgenstein	23
U. Hlobil & K. Nieswandt, On Anscombe's Philosophical Method	42
J. Finnis, Anscombe on Human Immateriality, Spirituality and Dignity	62
J. Haldane, Anscombe and Geach on Mind and Soul	77
G. Rohrbaugh, Anscombe, Zygotes and Coming-to-be	107
J. Zeis, Anscombe and the Metaphysics of Human Action	133
R. Wiseman, The Intended and Unintended Consequences of *Intention*	148
C. Vogler, Nothing Added: *Intention* §§19 & 20	173
T. Cavanaugh, Anscombe, Thomson and Double Effect	195
S. Broadie, Anscombe and Practical Truth in Aristotle	216
A. Müller, Truth as Eternal Norm: Anscombe on Anselm's *De Veritate*	238
C. Diamond, Asymmetries in Thinking about Thought: Anscombe and Wiggins	266
R. Teichmann, The Identity of a Word	286
Index	308

John Haldane

Preface

The publication of this book is part of a project begun over fifteen years ago with the preparation for a volume of Anscombe's essays on action and ethics edited by Mary Geach and Luke Gormally. That appeared in 2005 under the title *Human Life, Action and Ethics*, since when Geach and Gormally have edited three further volumes of writings by Anscombe: *Faith in a Hard Ground* (2009), *From Plato to Wittgenstein* (2011) and *Logic, Truth and Meaning* (2015). It has been my privilege to work with Luke Gormally on the process of selecting and preparing material and a special benefit to have had each volume introduced by a short essay by Mary Geach. With the original project completed it then seemed apt to include in the same general series of books two partner collections of essays on aspects of Anscombe's work. The first of those, *The Moral Philosophy of Elizabeth Anscombe* (2016), was concerned mostly with themes from *Human Life, Action and Ethics*, while the present volume is more addressed to issues in mind and metaphysics. Details of these and of writings by and about Elizabeth Anscombe appear in the bibliography below.

Eleven of the following fifteen essays (chapters 1, 2, 3, 6, 8, 9, 10, 11, 12, 14 and 15) appeared previously in a special issue of the *American Catholic Philosophical Quarterly* (vol. 90 (2) 2016) but with the permission of that journal and of the authors they are made available again here. There are in addition two other previously published essays:

U. Hlobil and K. Nieswandt, 'On Anscombe's Philosophical Method', *Klesis*, 35, 2016 and
G. Rohrbaugh, 'Anscombe, Zygotes and Coming-to-be', *Noûs* 48 (4) 2014.

I am grateful to the editors and publishers of these journals for granting permission to reprint these items. I am also grateful for assistance in the preparation and production of this volume to Adam and Sarah Myers, Benjamin Rusch, and Graham Horswell.

G.E.M. Anscombe Bibliography

A. Books

1. *Intention* (Oxford: Basil Blackwell, 1957; 2nd edition, 1963); (Cambridge, MA: Harvard University Press, 2000).
2. *An Introduction to Wittgenstein's Tractatus* (London: Hutchinson, 1959; 4th revised edition, 1971); corrected text appears as part of *Logic, Truth and Meaning: Writings by G.E.M. Anscombe* (see below).
3. [With Peter Geach] *Three Philosophers: Aristotle, Aquinas, Frege* (Oxford: Basil Blackwell, 1973).

B. Translations

1. L. Wittgenstein, *Philosophical Investigations* (Oxford: Blackwell, 1953).
2. [With Peter Geach] *Descartes: Philosophical Writings* (Edinburgh: Nelson, 1954).
3. L. Wittgenstein, *Remarks on the Foundations of Mathematics* (Oxford: Blackwell, 1956).
4. L. Wittgenstein, *Notebooks 1914–1916* (Oxford: Blackwell, 1961).
5. L. Wittgenstein, *Zettel* (Oxford: Blackwell, 1967).
6. [With Dennis Paul] L. Wittgenstein, *On Certainty* (Oxford: Blackwell, 1967).

C. Pamphlets

1. [With Norman Daniel] *The Justice of the Present War Examined: A Criticism Based on Traditional Catholic Principles and on Natural Reason* (Glasgow: John S. Burns, 1939); Part I: Anscombe, 'The War and the Moral Law.'
2. *Mr Truman's Degree* (Oxford: Oxonian Press, 1956).
3. *On Transubstantiation* (London: Catholic Truth Society, 1974).
4. *Contraception and Chastity* (London: Catholic Truth Society, 1977).
5. *Causality and Determination: An Inaugural Lecture* (Cambridge: Cambridge University Press, 1971).

D. Collections of Essays

1. *From Parmenides to Wittgenstein: The Collected Papers of G.E.M. Anscombe Volume 1* (Oxford: Blackwell, 1981).
2. *Metaphysics and the Philosophy of Mind: The Collected Papers of G.E.M. Anscombe Volume 2* (Oxford: Blackwell, 1981).

3. *Ethics, Religion and Politics: The Collected Philosophical Papers of G.E.M. Anscombe Volume 3* (Oxford: Blackwell, 1981).
4. *Human Life, Action and Ethics: Essays by G.E.M. Anscombe*, ed. Mary Geach and Luke Gormally. St. Andrews Studies in Philosophy and Public Affairs (Exeter: Imprint Academic, 2005).
5. *Faith in a Hard Ground: Essays on Religion, Philosophy and Ethics*, ed. Mary Geach and Luke Gormally. St. Andrews Studies in Philosophy and Public Affairs (Exeter: Imprint Academic, 2009).
6. *From Plato to Wittgenstein: Essays by G.E.M. Anscombe*, ed. Mary Geach and Luke Gormally. St. Andrews Studies in Philosophy and Public Affairs (Exeter: Imprint Academic, 2011).
7. *Logic, Truth and Meaning: Writings by G.E.M. Anscombe*, ed. Mary Geach and Luke Gormally. St. Andrews Studies in Philosophy and Public Affairs (Exeter: Imprint Academic, 2015).

E. Secondary Studies
Monographs

1. C. Diamond, *Reading Wittgenstein with Anscombe, Going On to Ethics* (Cambridge, MA: Harvard University Press, 2019).
2. J. Doyle, *No Morality, No Self: Anscombe's Radical Scepticism* (Cambridge, MA: Harvard University Press, 2018).
3. P. Rayappan, *Intention in Action: The Philosophy of G.E.M. Anscombe* (Bern: Peter Lang, 2010).
4. D. Richter, *Anscombe's Moral Philosophy* (Lanham, MD: Lexington, 2010).
5. R. Teichmann, *The Philosophy of Elizabeth Anscombe* (Oxford: Oxford University Press, 2008).
6. R. Wiseman, *Routledge Philosophy Guidebook to Anscombe's* Intention (London: Routledge, 2016).

Collections of Essays

1. V. Aucouturier, ed., *Lectures contemporaines de Elisabeth Anscombe* (Contemporary Essays on Anscombe), *Klēsis* 35, 2016.
2. C. Diamond and J. Teichman, eds., *Intention and intentionality: Essays in Honour of G.E.M. Anscombe* (Brighton: Harvester, 1980).
3. A. Ford, J. Hornsby and F. Stoutland, eds., *Essays on Anscombe's Intention* (Cambridge, MA: Harvard University Press, 2011).
4. L. Gormally, ed., *Moral Truth and Moral Tradition: Essays in Honour of Peter Geach and Elizabeth Anscombe* (Dublin: Four Courts Press, 1994).
5. L. Gormally, D.A. Jones and R. Teichmann, eds., *The Moral Philosophy of Elizabeth Anscombe*. St. Andrews Studies in Philosophy and Public Affairs (Exeter: Imprint Academic, 2016).

6. J. Haldane, ed., Special Issue on Elizabeth Anscombe, *American Catholic Philosophical Quarterly*, 90 (2) 2016.
7. J. Mizzoni, ed., *G.E.M. Anscombe and Human Dignity* (Aston, PA: Neumann University, 2016).
8. J. Mizzoni, P. Egan and G. Karabin, eds., *G.E.M. Anscombe and the Catholic Intellectual Tradition* (Aston, PA: Neumann University, 2016).
9. A. O'Hear, *Modern Moral Philosophy*. Royal Institute of Philosophy Supplement 54 (Cambridge: Cambridge University Press, 2004).
10. R. Teichmann, *Logic, Cause and Action: Essays in Honour of Elizabeth Anscombe*. Royal Institute of Philosophy Supplement 46 (Cambridge: Cambridge University Press, 2000).

Contributors

Sarah Broadie is Professor of Moral Philosophy and Wardlaw Professor at the University of St Andrews.

Tom Cavanaugh is Professor of Philosophy at the University of San Francisco.

Cora Diamond is Kenan Professor of Philosophy Emerita at the University of Virginia.

John Finnis is Biolchini Family Professor of Law in the Notre Dame Law School and Emeritus Professor of Law and Legal Philosophy at Oxford University.

Arthur Gibson is a research member of the Department of Pure Mathematics and Mathematical Statistics, University of Cambridge.

John Haldane is J. Newton Rayzor Sr Distinguished Professor of Philosophy at Baylor University and Professor of Philosophy at the University of St Andrews.

Ulf Hlobil is Assistant Professor of Philosophy at Concordia University in Montréal.

Anthony Kenny is Emeritus Fellow, St John's College, Oxford University.

Anselm Winfried Müller is Visiting Professor of Moral Philosophy at the University of Chicago and Emeritus Professor of Philosophy at the University of Trier.

Katharina Nieswandt is Assistant Professor of Philosophy at Concordia University in Montréal.

Guy Rohrbaugh is Associate Professor of Philosophy at Auburn University.

Roger Teichmann is Lecturer in Philosophy at St Hilda's College, Oxford.

Candace Vogler is David B. and Clara E. Stern Professor of Philosophy and Professor in the College at the University of Chicago.

Rachael Wiseman is Lecturer in Philosophy at the University of Liverpool.

John Zeis is Professor of Philosophy at Canisius College in Buffalo, New York.

John Haldane

Elizabeth Anscombe: Life and Work

1

1919 was the year of the birth of three exceptional British women philosophers: Elizabeth Anscombe, Mary Midgley and Iris Murdoch; a fourth, Philippa Foot, who was a contemporary student of theirs at Oxford, was born the following year. Foot, Midgley and Murdoch were undergraduates together at Somerville College, while Anscombe studied at St Hugh's, but she and Foot were later academic colleagues at Somerville for almost a quarter of a century. Women were not formally admitted to Oxford as members of the University until 1920 and at the time when these four came up (between 1937 and 1939) there was still a sense that female undergraduates were a novelty. It is remarkable, therefore, that within a decade of beginning their studies Anscombe, Foot and Murdoch held Oxford college fellowships. (Midgley settled into a university career later). Not only that but they came to prominence within professional philosophy and are seen individually and collectively as having reoriented ethics away from the emotivism and subjectivism that had begun to take hold at Oxford during their student days through the influence of A.J. Ayer and been developed in the decade following the end of the Second World War by R.M. Hare.

What accounts for the rise, confidence and success of this female quartet so soon after the formal admission of women into the University and in a period when Oxford philosophy was associated with a group of brilliant and powerful men: A.J. Ayer, J.L. Austin, Isaiah Berlin, Stuart Hampshire, H.L.A. Hart and Gilbert Ryle? Four factors suggest themselves: backgrounds, personalities, abilities and opportunities. Anscombe, Midgley and

Murdoch all attended private girls schools that aimed to build their pupil's confidence—the motto of Anscombe's was 'fear nothing'—while Foot was educated by private tutors. All four had a strong sense of their own identities and were resistant to condescension or intimidation. Again, all four were awarded first class honours degrees.

While these factors may have contributed much to their self-assurance, there were two special circumstances that provided significant opportunities for them to develop as philosophers. First, there was the fact of their mutual companionship, and second, the onset of World War Two and especially the period from the German invasion of Belgium, Luxembourg and the Netherlands in May 1940 when men began to enlist or be conscripted into the military thereby shifting the balance of the sexes in the undergraduate population at Oxford and removing a number of the leading younger dons and fellows including Austin, Hampshire, Hart and Ryle which collectively changed the style, tone and subjects of discussion. Mary Midgley has made this point on several occasions, as in the following:

> [T]he reason [why quite well-known female philosophers emerged from Oxford soon after the war] was indeed that there were fewer men about then. The trouble is not, of course, men as such—men have done good enough philosophy in the past. What is wrong is a particular style of philosophising that results from encouraging a lot of clever young men to compete in winning arguments. These people then quickly build up a set of games out of simple oppositions and elaborate them until, in the end, nobody else can see what they are talking about. All this can go on until somebody from outside the circle finally explodes it by moving the conversation on to a quite different topic, after which the games are forgotten ... By contrast, in those wartime classes—which were small—men (conscientious objectors etc) were present as well as women, but they weren't keen on arguing. It was clear that we were all more interested in understanding this deeply puzzling world than in putting each other down. That was how Elizabeth Anscombe, Philippa Foot, Iris Murdoch, Mary Warnock [who came up to Oxford in 1942] and I, in our various ways, all came to think out alternatives to the brash, unreal style of philosophising—based essentially on logical positivism—that was current at the

time. And these were the ideas that we later expressed in our own writings.[1]

There is a further fact which was the precocious philosophical ability and passion of Anscombe, who was acknowledged among them as being the most natively brilliant of the group and who influenced them all philosophically but particularly in the rejection of moral scepticism and subjectivism.

2

Elizabeth Anscombe was certainly a remarkable and formidable woman, and an outstanding philosopher. Orders of intellectual greatness are hard to assign, particularly when the subject in question belongs to one's own time, but there is no question that Anscombe was one of the most gifted and accomplished philosophers of the twentieth century. Her work will continue to be read long into the future, and a place for her in the history of philosophy is assured.

Her contemporary peers include the Americans Roderick Chisholm, Donald Davidson, Van Quine and Wilfred Sellars; the British Austin, Ayer, Ryle and Peter Strawson; and the Europeans Hannah Arendt, Maurice Merleau-Ponty, Paul Ricoeur and Simone Weil. Given the dense and complex character of her work and its often unorthodox conclusions it has not received the same attention as most of these others, but as study of her writings increases it is likely the estimate of her can only increase and I would say that she is at least the equal of the best of those listed. She was not a genius of the order of her teacher and friend Wittgenstein, but he may be the only twentieth-century figure securely in that category; and he does not qualify as a contemporary peer, having been born in the nineteenth century and only barely survived into the second half of the twentieth.

Considering her place in the category of women philosophers she is the clear leader, marked out by her creativity, imagination, industry, insight, range and rigour. There is also a kind of singularity about her work: she proceeds directly to the topic of her investigation, makes few references to contemporaries or to

---

[1] 'The Golden Age of Female Philosophy', Mary Midgley letter to the *Guardian*, 28 November 2013. See also her *Owl of Minerva: A Memoir* (London: Routledge, 2005).

current trends, writes in a concentrated and often indirect manner, eschews academic jargon, generally avoids footnotes and sometimes ends with an expression of perplexity. Again, unlike most philosophers of her standing, she engaged in philosophical analysis and argumentation before non-academic audiences. In this connection, while she proportioned the depth of her thinking to their likely knowledge and comprehension she never resorted to glibness or misleading oversimplification.

Wherein lies her greatness? Among the elements composing this were her intellectual commitment, stamina and toughness. Of themselves these do not make for brilliance, but without them there tends only to be, at best, unsustained cleverness. In addition she had tremendous powers of analysis and argument. She also had a "nose" for fakes and mistakes, not the superficial yet pervasive sort that characterize the work of most philosophers in any period, but the deeper kind that give rise to ways of thinking that seem inescapable until the error and the escape routes are pointed out. Into this category fall Descartes' and Locke's accounts of mind as co-extensive with consciousness, and of thought as only causally related to the world; Hume's arguments regarding fact, value and practical normativity, and causality; and Kant's disconnection of reason from nature. Moving down a league, there are Bentham's obliteration of the intended/foreseen consequence distinction, Quine's double standard as regards extensional/scientific and intensional/everyday discourses, and Hare's description/prescription gap. All of these were the subject of insightful and destructive Anscombean critiques.

The *Philosophical Lexicon* in one of its less clever and less witty entries gives two definitions of the verb "Anscombe":

> v. (1) To gather for safe-keeping. 'She anscombed with all the notes and letters.'
>
> (2) To go over carefully, with a fine-tooth comb, in an oblique direction.

The first refers to her work as editor and translator of Wittgenstein; the second to her philosophical style. More apt, and deserving of the noun form "Anscombes", would have been what Dennett writes in definition of Bernard Williams: "The dream-sensation of running for one's life while wearing diving boots. 'His comments on my paper gave me the [Anscombes].'" Such were her analytical powers that the idea of being a focus of

Anscombe's critical attention might occasion nightmares. She was invariably frank, often brusque and sometimes harsh. I am not sure whether she intended to be rude, though something perceived as such might be in evidence where she regarded what had been said as stupid or vacuous, or suspected vainglorious pretension. In any event, the simple fact of her applying her intelligence to claims and arguments would be enough to occasion anxiety, though she was also a supportive tutor and supervisor.

Elizabeth Anscombe died on 5 January 2001, within days of the passing of Quine with whom, through her husband Peter Geach, she had formed a personal friendship. While they were united in their attachment to rigour, to a belief in the importance of logic and to a conviction that philosophy had been transformed by the work of Gottlob Frege, their own philosophical outlooks and conclusions could not have been more different: he being one of the foremost proponents of scientific materialism, she a teenage convert to Roman Catholicism and a lifelong advocate of theological orthodoxy. Additionally, while Quine thought of philosophy as closely aligned with science and due to develop as the latter progressed, Anscombe, while respectful of science *per se*, was anti-scientistic and sceptical of attempts to solve philosophical questions by appealing to empirical theories. She also had no inclination to suppose that contemporary philosophy was in general an improvement on the thought of the past. In general, perhaps because there were more great figures there, and because Wittgenstein had dismantled the philosophy of Descartes which separated modern thought from its predecessors, she tended to look to earlier times rather than to the present or recent past. She had a particular feeling for philosophers from the pre-modern period, particularly Plato, Aristotle, Anselm and Aquinas, but also, though she studied them less, Spinoza and Kierkegaard. Of her contemporaries and juniors, she appreciated the work of her friends Georg Von Wright, Philippa Foot and Arthur Prior, and that of Saul Kripke.

3

Gertrude Elizabeth Margaret Anscombe was born on 18 March 1919, the youngest of three children and only daughter of Alan Wells Anscombe, a science master at Dulwich College in South London, and of his wife Gertrude Elizabeth, a classics teacher, after whom she was named. Her father was an atheist and her mother a nominal Anglican. Before she entered her teenage years and up to the middle of them Elizabeth discovered Roman Catholicism by reading a book on the lives and work of Elizabethan English recusant priests, and read her way into the Catholic faith; but her parents were strongly opposed to her wish to become a Catholic and it was only on leaving Sydenham High School for Girls and getting to St Hugh's College Oxford that she felt free to receive instruction preparatory to admission to the Church.

At Oxford she studied "Greats" (Classics and Philosophy) and in her first year became a Roman Catholic. Shortly thereafter she met Peter Geach, another philosopher convert, while both were in a Corpus Christi procession at the Servite Priory of St. Philip a few miles north of Oxford. Like her, he had been receiving instruction from the Dominican Fr. Richard Kehoe of Blackfriars, Oxford. They became engaged shortly thereafter and married at the Brompton Oratory in London on St. Stephen's Day (December 26) 1941. Earlier in the same year Anscombe had graduated with First Class Honours, secured by the brilliance of her philosophy scripts and in the face of her apparently comprehensive ignorance of ancient history.

"Miss Anscombe", as she continued to be called, even by Geach (and through the course of having seven children), crossed in 1942 to Cambridge to take up the Sarah Simpson post-graduate research studentship at Newnham College. It was in Cambridge that she met Wittgenstein, who then held the Chair of Philosophy and whose lectures she attended, becoming increasingly enthusiastic about his revolutionary ideas. Writing in 1945 to Myra Curtis, Principal of Newnham, Wittgenstein refers to her as "Mrs G.E.M. Geach", saying that "She is undoubtedly the most talented female student I have had since 1930 when I began to lecture ... There is very good reason to expect that she will produce sound and interesting work in Philosophy". By 1946 she had returned to Oxford as a research fellow at Somerville College, where she remained in one or another capacity (as college lecturer 1951, university lecturer 1958, and official college fellow from 1964) until her appointment to the Chair of Philosophy at Cambridge in 1970.

Between first meeting him and returning to Oxford, Anscombe maintained contact with Wittgenstein, travelling to Cambridge once a week to meet with him. In the course of that year 1946-1947 they became close friends. Wittgenstein was obsessive about the originality of his own thought and somewhat misogynistic; she was one of the few academics he ever trusted, and he would address her affectionately as "old man". Although he is quoted by Norman Malcolm as saying of Anscombe and of another philosopher convert, Yorick Smithies, that he "could not possibly believe all the things they believe", in his final year, when he knew he was dying, Wittgenstein asked Anscombe to put him in touch with a "non-philosophical priest". That she did, calling upon Fr. Conrad Pepler, O.P., of Blackfriars, Cambridge. Notwithstanding that she effected the introduction, however, Anscombe never presumed that Wittgenstein had resumed the faith of his childhood, and speculations to that effect are fanciful. Early versions of these may have been encouraged by the following facts: (1) Fr. Pepler did administer the last rites while Wittgenstein was still alive (though he had fallen into unconsciousness by then), (2) he was given a Catholic burial, and (3) members of his family subsequently arranged for the printing and distribution of an *in memoriam* card which in Catholic circles would normally be taken to indicate that the person remembered, and for whom prayers were sought, had died a practising Catholic. Anscombe regretted any encouragement that may have been given by these facts to the belief that Wittgenstein had returned to the Catholic faith.

Preparation for the task of translating Wittgenstein's work (written in German) had begun while he was still alive, but now she and the other two literary executors and editors (G. von Wright and Rush Rhees) set about the project of bringing material to publication. Anscombe took the lead in this, and the appearance in 1953 of her translation of Wittgenstein's masterpiece *Philosophical Investigations* was, without any question, one of the major turning points in twentieth-century philosophy.

This was followed by her translations of other works: *Remarks on the Foundations of Mathematics* (1956), *Notebooks 1914–1916* (1961), *Zettel* (1967) and (with Denis Paul) *On Certainty* (1969). She also concerned herself with Wittgenstein's earlier philosophy, publishing *An Introduction to Wittgenstein's Tractatus* (1959), and together with Geach translated *Descartes' Philosophical Writings* (1954).

Anscombe's appreciation of philosophers with whom she disagreed profoundly (principally Descartes and Hume) was marked, as was her range. She could write authoritatively, using her own translations, of Plato, Aristotle, Anselm, Aquinas, Descartes, Frege and Wittgenstein. But first and foremost she was neither an historian, a translator, nor an editor, but an original philosopher. Her short book *Intention*, first published in 1957 and republished by Harvard University Press in 2000, is universally regarded as a classic account of the nature of intentional behaviour, and as the founding text of the theory of action. In it she argued that intentional actions are ones to which a particular sense of the question "why?" applies: one which seeks a reason that is provided either by identifying a backward-looking factor, such as that the agent is rectifying a failing or wrong, or a forward-looking one such as an immediate aim or further objective. Additionally, the performance of such actions is known to the agent non-observationally.

Anscombe's motive in investigating intention included her perplexity and frustration at attempts to excuse or minimize culpability by saying that an agent only ever intends *immediate* acts and that further desired consequences are something distinct for which he is not directly morally responsible. Thus she forged a link between philosophical and moral psychology which was further adverted to in her 1958 article "Modern Moral Philosophy", which introduced the term "consequentialism" into the English language. The writing of this had resulted in part from the desire to see what moral philosophers had to say about the determinants of the value of actions, and in part from the practical need to read ethical texts in preparation for tutoring the subject in Oxford which she had agreed to do in order to allow her Somerville College colleague Philippa Foot to take a period of study leave. Yet it is rightly credited as being the principal cause of the revival of an ethics focussed on virtue rather than on rule or outcome. However, Anscombe never supposed that the whole of ethics could be done in terms of the concept of virtue and on that account she cannot correctly be termed a "virtue ethicist".

Similarly, "Causality and Determination", her inaugural lecture as Professor of Philosophy at Cambridge, subverted — and some believe refuted — a centuries' old orthodoxy about the nature of causation: namely, that it is essentially necessitarian and/or lawlike. Instead she treated the notion of "causality" as an abstraction formed on the basis of particular verbal descriptions such as "cutting", "pushing", "tearing" and so on, which are deployed in everyday observation and explanation. To the extent that there is a unifying core to these and hence to the notion of causality more generally, it is, she suggested, that of derivativeness, of one thing "coming from" or "being due to" another. This approach connects with other themes in her work on epistemology and metaphysics, where she subverts empiricist accounts and in the process blocks one route to scepticism. For Anscombe, here developing ideas from Wittgenstein, concepts which are specific instances of ones of substance, causation and value are not got by abstraction from experience but brought to it through the grammar of language. It is not a discovery that gold is a substance for "gold" is a substantival term.

As indicated here, Anscombe's work was for the most part highly academic, usually difficult to comprehend, and often combative in expression. It sometimes took readers years to see the point of what she was arguing, but this was because she always took on the hardest problems and had no time for slick presentation. Rush Rhees quoted Wittgenstein as often saying "go the bloody hard way"; this is a direction Anscombe appears to have taken to heart. She is reported to have said to A.J. Ayer, "if you didn't talk so quickly, people wouldn't think you were so clever" — though, in fairness his reply should also be quoted: "if you didn't talk so slowly, people wouldn't think you were so profound."

From her student days, however, she had discussed and written about issues of moral, political and religious interests. In 1939 she co-authored a then highly controversial pamphlet predicting that Britain's conduct in the Second World War would be unjust, and in 1956–1957 she protested the award by the University of Oxford of an honorary degree to President Truman, charging that he had commanded the murderous use of nuclear weapons against innocent Japanese civilians. Troubled by how people found it easy to defend Truman, she came to the conclusion that they failed to understand the nature of his actions, and showed in *Intention* that in doing one thing (moving one's hand) one may intentionally be doing another (directing the death of human beings).

In 1948, in debate with C.S. Lewis at the Socratic Club in Oxford, she demolished his favoured argument for "the self-refuting character of naturalism". Where some apologists viewed this as giving comfort to the enemy (atheism), Anscombe characteristically saw herself as simply exposing bad argumentation. Her own verdict on the event "that it was an occasion of sober discussion of certain quite definite criticisms, which Lewis's rethinking and rewriting showed he thought were accurate" seems the correct one. In any event, no one could seriously doubt her belief in the value of Christian apologetics if they read the likes of her pamphlets *On Transubstantiation* (1974) and *Contraception and Chastity* (1977), where she argued passionately in favour of traditional Catholic teachings.

In 1967 Anscombe was elected Fellow of the British Academy. She subsequently received a number of other distinctions, including foreign honorary member of the American Academy of Arts and Sciences. In 1982 she was awarded the Aquinas Medal by the American Catholic Philosophical Association, and in 1999 (along with Peter Geach) the papal medal *Pro Ecclesia et Pontifice*. Three volumes of Anscombe's *Collected Papers* were published in 1981: *From Parmenides to Wittgenstein; Metaphysics and the Philosophy of Mind;* and *Ethics, Religion and Politics*. Two collections of papers were dedicated to her: *Intention and Intentionality* (1979) and *Logic, Cause and Action* (2000), and together with Geach she was the recipient of a volume of essays, *Moral Truth and Moral Tradition* (1994), published to honour their fifty years of marriage.

Since Anscombe's death four further collections of her writings have been published in the same series as the present volume: *Human Life, Action and Ethics* (2005), *Faith in a Hard Ground* (2009), *From Plato to Wittgenstein* (2011) and *Logic, Truth and Meaning* (2015), and several collections of essays and studies of her work have appeared. The current book adds further to the growing library of writings by and about Anscombe (the main items of which are specified below) which is built upon and is further contributing to the renaissance of interest in her work. This promises to have several good outcomes. First, we will understand better the work of hers that was already known. Second, we will gain further insight into areas and developments within her philosophy through engaging with hitherto unknown or neglected material. Third, we will be able to bring this knowledge to the ongoing effort to understand and resolve, so far as that is ever possible, some of the central questions of philosophy.

One of Anscombe's last pieces of philosophical writing was characteristically quirky but likewise also suggestive of hitherto unseen lines of enquiry. In "Russelm or Anselm?", *Philosophical Quarterly*, 43 (1993), she defended the thesis that Anselm's argument of *Proslogion* 2 could be saved "from the stupidity of an Ontological Argument" by deletion of a comma. This rests on the claim that in "*Si enim in solo intellectu est, potest cogitari esse et in re, quod maius est*" the second (later editorial) comma ought to be omitted; in which interpretation ("if that than which nothing greater can be thought of exists only in the mind, something which is greater can be conceived to exist also in reality"), the argument does not treat existence as a property of objects and so does not fall foul of Kant's objection. Writing of her defence Anscombe remarked:

> [I have] thought harder about Anselm's argument than I did before. But I still think that I haven't thought hard enough. I don't know whether Anselm's argument is valid or invalid — only that it is a great deal more interesting than its common interpretation makes it.

The scholarship, imagination, boldness and honesty evident in this essay characterized her work as a philosopher and may serve as an inspiration to her admirers.

Anthony Kenny

Elizabeth Anscombe at Oxford

The first lecture series I attended when I went to Oxford as a graduate philosophy student in 1957 was a course on Thought and Action given by Stuart Hampshire, who published a book of the same title two years later.[1] He began by telling us all to read Miss Anscombe's recently published *Intention*.[2] It was indeed the publication of this short book of fewer than one hundred pages which established her as an influential philosopher in her own right. Her account of the nature of one's knowledge of one's own intentional actions and her development of Aristotle's discussion of practical reasoning set the terms of several debates that continue to the present day.

Anscombe had already become famous in Oxford, but not for theoretical philosophy. In 1956 the University offered an honorary degree to the U.S. President who had authorized the bombing of Hiroshima and Nagasaki. Anscombe opposed the proposal, arguing in a pamphlet, *Mr Truman's Degree*, that it was monstrous to honour a man responsible for two massacres. She set out the doctrine of the just war, as developed long ago by Catholic theologians such as Suarez and Protestant jurists such as Grotius. According to that doctrine nothing could justify the deliberate killing of non-combatants in war.

Anscombe did not succeed in persuading her fellow dons: only four people voted against the conferment of the degree, and the inside cover of *Truman's Degree* bears the words "Dedicated with respect, but without permission, to the others who said 'Non

---

[1] Stuart Hampshire, *Thought and Action* (London: Chatto and Windus, 1959).
[2] *Intention* (Oxford: Blackwell, 1957); second edition 1963.

placet'". Surprisingly, however, the theory of the just war—which had been almost totally forgotten during the 1939–45 war—has gradually become accepted not only in ecclesiastical circles but also in official and military ones. In the last decade, for instance, several of the cardinal principles of that doctrine were enunciated in the counter-insurgency manual issued by General Petraeus to the U.S. forces under his command, which declares, among other things, that "Soldiers and Marines are not permitted to use force disproportionately or indiscriminately" and goes on to state that:

> 7.31 The principle of proportionality requires that the anticipated loss of life and damage to property incidental to attacks must not be excessive in relation to the concrete and direct military advantage expected to be gained.
>
> 7.34 Discrimination requires combatants to differentiate between enemy combatants, who represent a threat, and noncombatants, who do not. In conventional operations, this restriction means that combatants cannot intend to harm noncombatants, though proportionality permits them to act, knowing some noncombatants may be harmed.[3]

The revival of the theory, I believe, is due more to Elizabeth Anscombe than to any other individual.

Intention was followed up by an influential paper of 1958, "Modern Moral Philosophy".[4] Its first paragraph proclaims a resounding thesis:

> The concepts of obligation and duty—moral obligation and moral duty, that is to say, and of what is morally right and wrong, and of the moral sense of "ought", ought to be jettisoned if this is psychologically possible; because they are survivals, or derivatives of survivals, from an earlier conception of ethics which no longer generally survives, and are only harmful without it.[5]

According to Anscombe, Aristotle, though he has much to say about the virtues and vices, has no concept answering to our term

---

[3] *Counterinsurgency* (Washington, DC: Headquarters Department of the Army, December 2006), Chapter 7.5 'Ethics', 7-5 & 7-6.
[4] First published in *Philosophy*, 33(174) 1958: 1–19, and reprinted in G.E.M. Anscombe, *Ethics, Religion and Politics, Collected Philosophical Papers Vol. III* (Oxford: Blackwell, 1981) and again in *Human Life Action and Ethics: Essays by G.E.M. Anscombe*, eds. M. Geach & L. Gormally (Exeter: Imprint Academic, 2005). Page references are to the 1981 publication.
[5] *Ibid.*, p. 26.

"moral". It was, she says, Christianity, taking its moral notions from the Torah, that introduced a law conception of ethics. Conformity to the virtues and avoidance of the vices henceforth became a requirement of divine law.

> Naturally it is not possible to have such a conception unless you believe in God as a lawgiver; like Jews, Stoics and Christians. But if such a conception is dominant for many centuries, and then is given up, it is a natural result that the concepts of "obligation", of being bound or required as by a law, should remain though they had lost their root; and if the word "ought" has become invested in certain contexts with the sense of "obligation", it too will remain to be spoken with a special emphasis and a special feeling in these contexts. It is as if the notion "criminal" were to remain when criminal law and criminal courts had been abolished and forgotten.[6]

Anscombe agreed with the then current shibboleth that one cannot infer an "ought" — a moral "ought" — from an "is"; but that was because this special *moral* "ought" has become a word of mere mesmeric force, once the notion of a divine lawgiver has been dropped.

The notions of duty, and of moral right and wrong, Anscombe proposed, should be discarded in favour of the notions of justice and injustice, which had a genuine content. Even of these notions it remained difficult to give a clear account, until we had a satisfactory philosophical psychology. For one cannot analyse the concepts of justice and virtue unless one has a satisfactory account of such terms as "action", "intention", "pleasure" and "wanting".

Anscombe had already herself made a monumental contribution to this area of philosophy in *Intention*, a book which was taken as a model by many later investigators. There was little explicit moralizing in the text, but the clarification of the notion of intention enabled her to play a significant part in fundamental philosophical and legal debates.

Moral philosophers, according to Anscombe, could be divided into absolutists and consequentialists. Absolutists believe that there are some kinds of action that are intrinsically wrong, and should never be done, irrespective of any consideration of consequences. Consequentialists believe that the morality of actions should be judged by their foreseen consequences, and that there is

---

[6] *Ibid.*, p. 30.

no category of act which may not, in special circumstances, be justified by its consequences. Prior to Bentham most philosophers were absolutists, because they believed in a natural law, or natural rights. If there are natural rights and a natural law, then some kinds of action, actions that violate those rights or conflict with that law, are wrong, no matter what the consequences. But Bentham scorned the notions of natural law and natural rights.

In the 1950s many moral philosophers rejected Bentham's utilitarianism, accusing it of committing a naturalistic fallacy.[7] Nonetheless, most of them were consequentialists (as became abundantly clear in the discussions of Truman's use of the atom bomb). Every one of the best known English academic ethicists, Anscombe claimed, "has put out a philosophy according to which, e.g. it is not possible to hold that it cannot be right to kill the innocent as a means to any end whatsoever and that someone who thinks otherwise is in error". She pointed out that this put them at odds with the Hebrew and Christian moral tradition, which was absolutist.

In *Intention* Anscombe presented a concept of intention as an operation of the will rather than of the intellect. One intended one's chosen ends, and the means selected to those ends. At the time she wrote, however, the concept of intention dominant in the thinking of legal academic writers and in the judgments of the courts was a Benthamite one in which whatever an agent foresaw as the result of his action was something that he intended. H.L.A. Hart wrote that "for the law a foreseen outcome is enough, even if it was unwanted by the agent ... the law does not require in such cases that the outcome should have been something intended in the sense that the accused set out to achieve it, either as a means or an end, and here the law diverges from what is ordinarily meant by expressions like 'he intentionally killed those men'".[8]

---

[7] In this they were following G.E. Moore who introduces the expression, and the analysis it represents, and deploys it against Bentham in *Principia Ethica* (Cambridge: Cambridge University Press, 1903), chapter 1, §14: "The naturalistic fallacy illustrated by Bentham." In the 1950s Moore's claim was further elaborated by Oxford moral philosophers including R.M. Hare in *The Language of Morals* (Oxford: Oxford University Press, 1952) and P. Nowell-Smith in *Ethics* (Harmondsworth: Penguin, 1954) with both of whom Anscombe soon found herself in public disagreement.

[8] H.L.A. Hart, *Punishment and Responsibility* (Oxford: Clarendon Press, 1968), p. 120.

A number of legal decisions in the 1950s and 1960s appeared to enshrine the Benthamite interpretation of intention into the definition of murder as killing with malice aforethought. However, some legal writers, influenced by Anscombe, argued for a voluntarist interpretation of the notion of intention. Foremost among these was John Finnis, who in a paper of 1991, "Intention and Side Effects", claimed that the confusion concerning intention in the English law of homicide had been cleared up by a number of recent decisions.[9] The courts, he claimed, had begun to make a sharp distinction between intention and foresight: the fact that one foresees a certain result as likely or even certain to follows from one's action(s) does not entail that one intends that result. Sadly, legal decisions in murder cases since 1991 have not reflected the acute philosophical distinctions championed by Anscombe and Finnis.

In the late 1950s the dominant figure in Oxford moral philosophy was R.M. Hare, then a tutor at Balliol. In reaction to the previously fashionable emotivism, Hare was anxious to make room in ethics for logic. In *The Language of Morals* he pointed out that there is a logic of imperatives no less than a logic of assertion, and he drew on this to expound a theory of moral reasoning. He distinguished between prescriptive and descriptive meaning. A descriptive statement is one whose meaning is defined by the factual conditions for its truth. A prescriptive sentence is one which entails, perhaps in conjunction with descriptive statements, at least one imperative. To assent to an imperative is to prescribe action, to tell oneself or others to do this or do that. To make a moral judgment is to issue an imperative which applies universally, to oneself as to all others in similar situations.

Hare distinguished between ethics and morals. Ethics is the study of the general features of moral language, of which prescriptivity and universalizability are the most important; moral judgments are prescriptions and prohibitions of specific actions. In principle, ethics is neutral between different and conflicting moral systems. But this does not mean that ethics is practically vacuous:

---

[9] John Finnis, "Intention and Side Effects", in *Liability and Responsibility: Essays in Law and Morals*, eds. R.G. Frey and C.W. Morris (Cambridge: Cambridge University Press, 1991), pp. 32–64; reprinted with additional notes in J. Finnis, *Intention and Identity: Collected Essays Vol. II* (Oxford: Oxford University Press, 2011).

once an understanding of ethics is combined with the desires and beliefs of an actual moral agent, it can lead to concrete and important moral judgments.

Anscombe detested Hare's moral philosophy, which in its practical results, she believed, differed little from utilitarianism — a judgment which his own later writings confirmed. But the academic assault on Hare she left to her husband Peter Geach and her Somerville colleague, Philippa Foot. Foot, I believe, was the only Oxford philosophy colleague with whom she was entirely comfortable. That did not mean that there were no differences between them — most obviously, Foot was an atheist and Anscombe a Catholic — but each had complete respect for the other. (From time to time Elizabeth would lament to me that she felt quite unable to offer Philippa a proof of the existence of God.)

The senior Oxford philosophers at this time were Gilbert Ryle (Waynflete Professor of Metaphysics), John Austin (White's Professor of Moral Philosophy), H.H. Price (Wykeham Professor of Logic) and Herbert Hart (Professor of Jurisprudence). Price was by that time generally regarded as superannuated and his tenure as Wykeham Professor was moving to an end. Ryle and Anscombe were kept aloof from each other by their differing relationships to Wittgenstein. (Elizabeth told me that while reading Ryle's *Concept of Mind* shortly after it appeared in 1949 she went to meet Wittgenstein off a train, and felt obliged to conceal the book under a wrapper. This did not prevent the great man from snorting with disapproval when he discovered what she was reading.) In his book *Mental Acts* (1957) Peter Geach had criticized Ryle severely — but Ryle was not overprotective of his works and seemed to me to bear no grudge.

Anscombe and Austin, however, detested each other cordially. Austin would refuse to discuss Anscombe's writings when invited to do so by students attending his informal instruction; she, in her turn, would say scornfully that she expected any day that some student would report to her that Austin had discovered a difference between "enough" and "sufficient". Anscombe had, on the other hand, a qualified respect for Hart. She gave me his *Causation in the Law* [10] to read — but praising it on the specific grounds that

---

[10] H.L.A. Hart and Tony Honoré, *Causation in the Law* (Oxford: Clarendon Press, 1959).

its preface exhibited clearly the complete bankruptcy of contemporary philosophical ideas of causality.

As a graduate student, I was never officially supervised by Anscombe. It was she, however, who suggested to me the topic of my dissertation, namely the intentionality of psychological verbs. The topic was approved by the philosophy sub-faculty, and I was assigned Antony Quinton as my supervisor—the beginning of a lifelong friendship. Anscombe gave me access to appropriate unpublished papers of Wittgenstein, and Quinton was a wonderful guide to contemporary philosophical literature.

Anscombe was extremely welcoming to graduate students who had a serious interest in philosophy. She kept open house in 27 St. John Street—one could drop in at any hour of day or night and start a discussion of a philosophical problem. She had a houseful of children, to whom she would attend from time to time, but that did not interrupt the flow of philosophy. She was also in those days a chain smoker, dropping her butts into a huge wooden bowl. It was only in later years, as a tutor myself beset with the enthusiasms of young graduate students, that I came to appreciate fully the generosity with which she made herself available.

Among my many memories of these discussions, one stays in my mind. A fellow student who also enjoyed discussions with Anscombe was Tom Nagel. One evening, trying to understand the Catholic opposition to artificial contraception, Tom put the question, "Elizabeth, would it be sinful if I were to play the piano with my penis?" There was a long pause, and then Anscombe said slowly, "An und für sich, No".

Another contemporary graduate student was John Searle. He was too close to Austin to become an Anscombe groupie, but he did visit 27 St. John Street from time to time, since for a while his doctoral dissertation was supervised—on Austin's recommendation—by Peter Geach. In a 2015 article in *Philosophy* Searle has given a vivid and hilarious account of the family's unorthodox methods of parenting.[11] However, in my view, he seriously under-

---

[11] John Searle, "Oxford Philosophy in the 1950s", *Philosophy*, 90(2) 2015: 173-93. At p. 181, he writes, "Elizabeth once gave a lecture on the evils of the modern world and cited three enormous evils: ... the one that sticks in my mind was the National Society for Prevention of Cruelty to Children. Apparently she had a lot of problems with this organization. They would

estimates Anscombe as a philosopher. He ends his portrait of her by saying, "I do not wish to give the impression that Austin and Anscombe were somehow equal figures in stature in Oxford, not at all".

Those of us who in those days attended Austin's lectures (which later became *Sense and Sensibilia* and *How to do Things with Words*)[12] remember with gratitude many happy hours of instructive philosophical entertainment. But I believe that, to those who were willing to learn from her, Anscombe had much more to offer than ever Austin gave to his disciples. Certainly, in the long term, she has had a much greater influence on philosophical thinking worldwide.

Publicly, Anscombe offered the lectures which became *An Introduction to Wittgenstein's Tractatus*.[13] More important were the evening seminars in a run-down annex of Somerville in which she inducted us into Wittgenstein's argument against private ostensive definition. From time to time she would single me out as a spokesman for the private language, and then gradually demolish everything I could say in its defence. It was a painful experience — the intellectual equivalent of defoliation by wax — but immensely rewarding. I gradually came to understand what Wittgenstein meant and to see why it was important. As a result of her seminars I found my whole mindset altered, so that every philosophical problem looked different from the new perspective I acquired.

"D'you know, Tony," Elizabeth once said to me, "I don't have a single idea in my head that wasn't put there by Wittgenstein." The remark was revealing, but wholly inaccurate. In the first place, there were the ideas that were put there by her husband,

---

innocently send some hapless social worker out to lecture Elizabeth on how to raise her children and one can only imagine what Elizabeth would do to this unfortunate. Once in the presence of Susan Sontag a child came to her and said, 'Can I go out in St. Giles and play?' and Elizabeth said, 'No dear the police just don't understand.'"

[12] Austin died of lung cancer at the young age of 48 in 1960 and both books were published posthumously two years later: *Sense and Sensibilia*, ed. G.J. Warnock (Oxford: Clarendon Press, 1960) and *How to do Things with Words*, ed. J.O. Urmson (Oxford: Clarendon Press, 1962).

[13] G.E.M. Anscombe, *An Introduction to Wittgenstein's Tractatus* (London: Hutchinson, 1959). The revised 4th edition is reprinted in *Logic, Truth and Meaning: Essays by G.E.M. Anscombe*, eds. M. Geach & L. Gormally (Exeter: Imprint Academic, 2015).

Peter Geach, who had been teaching her long before she met Wittgenstein. Obviously, Geach and Anscombe had a great influence on each other; but as philosophers they operated quite differently. Anscombe was the better tutor, Geach the better lecturer and much the better writer. Geach was more influenced by Aquinas and by Frege than he was by Wittgenstein. He could take offence when people asked him what his wife thought on a philosophical topic, and assumed that he knew, and agreed with, whatever it might be. "As her husband," he used to say, "I have privileged access to her body, but not to her mind." In the second place, Anscombe's head was full of Catholic thoughts that were at some distance from the ideas of Wittgenstein. At a different time she said to me, "On the topic of religion, Wittgenstein is sheer poison". A few years before publishing her *Introduction* to the *Tractatus* she wrote:

> I do not think a Catholic could accept Wittgenstein's *Tractatus* if he understood it, because of its teaching on ethics. ("The world is independent of my will" — so I cannot be morally responsible for anything that happens; and similarly: "The facts all belong to the task and not to the performance.") This is, I think, quite closely connected with all the rest; so the whole must be wrong. Of his later work Wittgenstein said: "Its advantage is that if you believe, say, Spinoza or Kant, this interferes with what you can believe in religion; but if you believe me, nothing of the sort." I do not know whether he was right about this.[14]

In 1959 Price retired. After a stormy meeting which led both Austin and Ryle to resign from the electoral board in protest at the way the Vice-Chancellor had conducted the election, A.J. Ayer was appointed to the Wykeham Chair of Logic. Anscombe was disgusted. "We've already had Ayer in Oxford," she said to me, "we don't need him again." In public discussion they were willing to be quite rude to each other, as in the legendary exchange:

> "Professor Ayer, if you didn't speak so fast, people wouldn't think you were so very clever,"
> "Miss Anscombe, if you didn't speak so slowly people wouldn't think you were so profound."

---

[14] G.E.M. Anscombe, "Misinformation: What Wittgenstein Really Said", *The Tablet*, 203 (5942) 1954: 13.

In 1959 I left Oxford for four years, returning briefly in 1961 to defend my dissertation on intentionality. The thesis was examined by David Pears and Patrick Gardner. *Viva voce* examinations are theoretically public in Oxford but rarely attract an audience. Surprisingly, Elizabeth turned up to listen to mine. Her presence seemed to disconcert the examiners no less than myself. Fortunately they retained enough composure to accept the dissertation, which was then published as *Action, Emotion, and Will*.

In 1961, Anscombe and Geach published a book called *Three Philosophers*. It consisted of three projected encyclopaedia articles — on Aristotle, Aquinas and Frege — that had been rejected as idiosyncratic by the editors of the encyclopaedia. A few years later I reviewed it at length for *Mind*. The review was full of admiration, but contained some substantial criticisms. When it was published Elizabeth wrote to me: "I am glad that Peter and I don't have the kind of friends who think they have to give us favourable reviews." In later years, when I published other books myself, she returned the compliment with interest.

When I returned to Oxford as a don in 1963, Austin had been succeeded by Kneale as Professor of Moral Philosophy. When, in 1966, Kneale retired through ill-health, Anscombe applied for the chair. She was not successful; the victor was R.M. Hare. However, there was a consolation prize. Hare's promotion left a vacancy for a philosophy fellow at Balliol, and it was filled by Arthur Prior from Manchester, whose work on modality Anscombe had long admired.

In those years, while I was a philosophy tutor at Balliol, I gave a number of joint classes with Anscombe, and we benefited from the flexibility of Oxford tutorial arrangements to exchange pupils. I sent some of my most promising Balliol undergraduates to her, and she allowed me to give tutorials to some of her brightest Somerville pupils, such as Lesley Wallace (now Brown), Kate Mortimer (since deceased) and Emma Rothschild. Anselm Müller, a monk from the Benedictine abbey in Trier, already author of a distinguished work on Wittgenstein's *Tractatus*, came to Oxford to be supervised by Anscombe for an Oxford doctorate. As she was on sabbatical for part of his residence I temporarily took her place, and thus began one of my most rewarding philosophical friendships. Anselm is currently working on a personal and intellectual biography of Anscombe, to which all her former colleagues and pupils look forward with keen anticipation.

Anscombe's second application for a chair was more successful than her first. In 1969 she succeeded Wisdom as Professor of Philosophy at Cambridge, and thus brought to an end her Oxford career. Her inaugural lecture, however, on "Causality and Determination",[15] was a brilliant attempt to fill the gap in current philosophical understanding of causality, which had troubled her for so many years. So the lecture, as well as an inauguration to Cambridge, was a most appropriate valedictory to Oxford.

---

[15] Reprinted in G.E.M. Anscombe, *Metaphysics and the Philosophy of Mind, Collected Philosophical Papers Vol. II* (Oxford: Blackwell, 1981).

Arthur Gibson

Anscombe, Cambridge and the Challenges of Wittgenstein[1]

1. Introduction

Elizabeth Anscombe arrived in the midst of wartime Cambridge. WWI had been, and WWII was, taking their toll on Wittgenstein. Their consequences for him, alongside his additional difficult past and present influences, indirectly engaged Miss Anscombe. Wittgenstein's contrasting relationships with his former amanuensis and conversant—namely, Francis Skinner—and with Miss Anscombe are pertinent both to understanding the burden that she thereby successfully took on and to modulating individual strengths in her own philosophy. Wittgenstein's choice of Elizabeth Anscombe as translator and literary heir speaks for itself, not least since he did not altogether like Rush Rhees's earlier attempt at translating a partial draft of his main work. How do we position the importance of Anscombe's own emerging creativity when placed alongside contemporaries competing for Wittgenstein's attention? Subsequent to Wittgenstein's death, Anscombe's insights matured into a distinct philosophy, which is deeply systematic yet avoids being a system. Its potential for generating insights into some scientific subjects and the humanities is largely untapped yet ripe to emerge.

Professor Anscombe's period in Cambridge is already so well documented by distinguished publications that it would be superfluous to repeat many aspects of the history. Nevertheless, as their

---

[1] With thanks to John Haldane for helpful comments and suggestions.

authors recognize, further matters await attention. Being taught for three undergraduate years by Professor Anscombe, with subsequent discussion in Cambridge over thirty years, continues to yield for me insights into various aspects of her life, some of which were antecedent agents of influence.[2]

I had arrived as a "mature" student, aged twenty-seven, replete with a family of four young children, lately emerged from an underclass background, having been taught logic privately for three years by Professor Geach in Leeds. Very soon after our arrival in Cambridge, both Anscombe and Geach arrived in a car to invite us to Sunday lunch. This was the first of many visits in which they showed fine hospitality and gave other kindly support. The event also hallmarked many future visits on my own to discuss philosophy with Miss Anscombe at home, in addition to being taught in her faculty office. On occasions Peter Geach was also present in their home and joined in.

Due to a medical condition, it was arranged for me to take my university examinations at their home in a first floor study. During these proceedings (I realized only a long time afterwards something untoward had happened), I had some fits and lost consciousness which caused my body inadvertently to distribute a bowl of soup over a recently re-upholstered silk sofa. Having regained consciousness, I dimly noticed that there was a line of cushions oddly placed along the sofa, which subsequently I discovered was to hide the effects of my accident so as not to disturb my completing the remainder of the exam. Meanwhile downstairs on that day, to add to the occasion, my college tutor, who was there to obey university rules while I sat the examination, was shocked to be confronted by "a wild alcoholic tramp" bursting in through the French windows—threateningly demanding drink. The tutor was quite frightened, since his engagement with such a world heretofore had been restricted to its occurrence

---

[2] For those who are new to Professor Anscombe, there is a valuable account in J. Teichman, "Gertrude Elizabeth Margaret Anscombe 1919-2001", in *Proceedings of the British Academy, Biographical Memoirs of Fellows*, 115, ed. F.M.L. Thompson (January 2013): 31–50, doi: 10.5871/bacad/9780197262788.003.0002; for the briefest outline see R. Teichmann, *The Philosophy of Elizabeth Anscombe* (Oxford: Oxford University Press, 2008), pp. 1–9. Although short, the especially sensitive focus of the following article is valuable: David Jones, "About Elizabeth Anscombe", *Anscombe Bioethics Center* (2006), [Online], http://www.bioethics.org.uk/page/about_us/about_eliza-beth_anscombe.

in comic irony in plays of Molière, of which he was a master. By way of contrast, Professors Anscombe and Geach had formerly commanded this hitherto homeless gentleman to live in their shed at the end of the garden as a means to insist on his rehabilitation. Three years before, when they came to invite my family to lunch, this same homeless man had tried to break into their parked car. On that occasion they had forcefully locked him in the car; and later, upon leaving our house, they took him home with them. Some people in Cambridge seemed to have limited awareness of Anscombe and Geach: only as a bizarre Socratic couple; such kindness as the above was entirely characteristic of their working together for the common good, however.

2. The Absence of Skinner and the Presence of Miss Anscombe

Elizabeth Anscombe's engagement with Wittgenstein is partly a function of events in his Cambridge life prior to her arrival there at Newnham College in 1942. These were presaged by vexed pressures on and within Wittgenstein, which in 1941 were exacerbated and framed by the Luftwaffe's bombing targeting Wellington Bombers and other aircraft at various RAF airfields outside of Cambridge.[3] The bombing indirectly led or contributed to his companion's death.[4] Ponder the variously imploding lives of Wittgenstein and Francis Skinner in 1941, as he nursed a dying Francis, deposited in hospital but left neglected and untreated due to the arrival of wounded RAF personnel at the hospital.[5] Skinner's death certificate confirms that he died of acute anterior poliomyelitis; it also records that Wittgenstein was present at his death. The certificate reports that the attending physician's name

---

[3] E.g. Oakington, Lakenheath, Waterbeach, Newmarket Race Course (converted to an airbase); sites around the edges of the city, such as Newmarket Road, Mill Road through to Trumpington Road—near Addenbrookes old hospital, and Huntingdon Road were periodically subject to massive incendiary bombs.

[4] Wittgenstein's knowledge indirectly adds to his distressing alienation: in the 1938 Austrian elections, 99.73 percent of his now-former countrymen voted for Hitler (whom Wittgenstein denied would ever enter to rule Austria). By 1941 there were many ace Austrian pilots in the Luftwaffe.

[5] See L. Wittgenstein, *Dictating Philosophy to Francis Skinner: The Wittgenstein Skinner Manuscripts*, ed. A. Gibson [forthcoming].

is Dr. Henry E[dward] Nourse,[6] to be noted especially because, as Brian McGuinness[7] points out, Dr. Nourse was Wittgenstein's doctor. Nourse had been recommended to Wittgenstein by Lord Adrian of Trinity before WWII.[8] This somewhat underscores the intricate personal care of and involvement in Wittgenstein's grieving attention to Francis. We can also recognize an immediate impact of Skinner's death on Wittgenstein. On the day of Francis's death he sent a letter to the Cambridge VC attempting to resign his Professorship, aiming to work at Guy's hospital, which had earlier had been a joint plan with Skinner.

Subsequent to Francis's death, Elizabeth Anscombe's arrival in Cambridge amounts to a marked contrast with him, yet furnished an oblique partial precedent for her future engagement with Wittgenstein. When Skinner graduated in 1933, he was of similar age (twenty-one)[9] to Anscombe (twenty-two) upon her first meeting with Wittgenstein in the 1940s. Even with a Trinity research award to pursue his own mathematical investigations, Skinner had already discarded them and fallen under Wittgenstein's spell. In his biography of Wittgenstein, *The Duty of Genius*, Ray Monk writes that Skinner "became utterly, uncritically, and almost obsessively devoted to Wittgenstein".[10] Anscombe was not so easily led; whilst fulsomely absorbed by Wittgenstein's talent, she was making her own way into her original philosophy. After Skinner died, insofar as he could be replaced, or displaced, by an identity at variance with his, Miss Anscombe came to emerge in rapport within Wittgenstein's own final phase, though not as an amanuensis. She was an exception to Wittgenstein's customary

---

[6] Not based in hospital, but called in from his practice at 3 Trinity St (where he practised from 1927–1972). Dr. Nourse and his medical family were of some distinction; he had patients such as Dadie Rylands, the 13th Earl Ferrers and his family. Dr. Nourse later became Freemasonic Cambridge Provincial Grand Master. Wittgenstein, who was frequently ill in bed during this period under the care of Dr. Nourse, surrounded Skinner with his own personal community of care.
[7] B. McGuinness, *Wittgenstein in Cambridge* (Oxford: Blackwell, 2008), p. 351n2 and p. 302n2.
[8] It was only at the end of Wittgenstein's life that Dr. Bevan became his doctor.
[9] David Pinsent was also of similar age when he came to know Wittgenstein before WWI.
[10] R. Monk, *Ludwig Wittgenstein: The Duty of Genius* (London: Cape, 1991), p. 331.

practices concerning women. Fania Pascal noted, "Wittgenstein dictated the *Brown Book* to Skinner ... But would we not be wrong to assume that Skinner acted only as an amanuensis? ... It appeared as if Wittgenstein tested and perfected his thoughts in his endless talks with Francis and a few other young men. They were somehow essential to the formulation of his thought".[11] Research on Skinner's (hitherto unpublished) handwritten copy of the *Brown Book* attests to the importance of Skinner's contribution, not least the thousands of revision details in Francis's hand that appear to be under the direction of Wittgenstein, alongside Wittgenstein's own handwritten revisions in the manuscript.[12] This witnesses to a complex interplay in drafting and refining, which exposes some of the anatomy of Wittgenstein's creative originality, and Francis's functions in it. Pascal, who taught Wittgenstein and Francis Russian together from early 1934, adds that they "were inseparable", "and knew [Francis] to have been the constant companion of Wittgenstein throughout most of the 1930s, till his early death in 1941".[13] Professor Anscombe possessed Skinner's dated letters to Wittgenstein—presumably given to her by Wittgenstein himself, which embodies a sense of his sharing a facet of his life, and past, with her. Wittgenstein's exceptional attitude to Anscombe is captured in the story that he occasionally addressed her (affectionately) as "old man".

Unlike Francis, Miss Anscombe came to be a profound and original philosopher. Perhaps Wittgenstein's engagement with her presupposed an inkling of her qualitative gifts later attested to by Donald Davidson, who estimated her short monograph *Intention* to be "the most important treatment of action since Aristotle".[14] It is impressive that living amid the throes of WWII, giving birth to a

---

[11] F. Pascal, "Wittgenstein: a Personal Memoir", in *Ludwig Wittgenstein: Personal Recollections*, ed. R. Rhees (Totowa: Roman & Littlefield, 1981), pp. 26-62, at p. 40.

[12] See A. Gibson, "Francis Skinner's Original Wittgenstein *Brown Book* Manuscript", in *Language and World Part One: Essays on the Philosophy of Wittgenstein Publications of the Austrian Ludwig Wittgenstein Society*, ed. V. Munz, K. Puhl and J. Wang, New Series 14 (Heusenstamm: Ontos Verlag, 2010), pp. 351-66; A. Gibson, "The Wittgenstein archive of Francis Skinner", in *Wittgenstein: After his Nachlass*, ed. N. Venturinha (New York: Palgrave Macmillan, 2010), pp. 64-77.

[13] Pascal, "Wittgenstein: a Personal Memoir", pp. 26, 27.

[14] See the cover of the Harvard edition of her *Intention* (Cambridge, MA: Harvard University Press, 2000).

large family, often engaging with forces surrounding Wittgenstein, and holding her own with him, Elizabeth was simultaneously crafting her own philosophical progress.

As Miss Anscombe later prepared to translate the *Philosophical Investigations*, she would meditate upon Wittgenstein's own 1945 preface to that work and the relevance of its chronological details, well framed by the epigraph, which he quoted from Nestroy: "*The trouble about progress is that it always looks much greater than it really is.*" Below this, Wittgenstein's Preface commences:

> The thoughts that I publish in what follows are the precipitate of philosophical investigations, which have occupied me for the last sixteen years.
>
> Four years ago, however I had occasion to reread my first book…
>
> For since I began to occupy myself with philosophy again, sixteen years ago, I could not but help recognize grave mistakes.

The repetition of "sixteen years" in an otherwise austere prefatory landscape may seem a bit over-rich, but sixteen years before the preface's date of 1945 was the year in which Skinner and Wittgenstein met for the first time and engaged with each other.

Wittgenstein's "four years ago, however, I had occasion to reread my first book" leads us from 1945 back to the date of 1941 — the year of Francis Skinner's death.[15] The turmoil in Wittgenstein's mind immediately after Skinner's tragic demise, and before meeting Anscombe, was so great as to amount to a nervous breakdown, and for him to press for an attempt to resume his and Francis's desire to work in medicine was perhaps an atoning memorial. Why atonement? Evidence of a direction in Wittgenstein's distress is to be found in the doom-filled poems by Pushkin, which Wittgenstein copied out in Russian immediately subsequent to Skinner's death — poems that he and Francis

---

[15] Skinner himself was a counterpart with a previous parallel: David Pinsent was, leading up to WWI, a sometimes cantankerous dialogee and close friend with Wittgenstein. In contrast, in the years leading up to WWII, Skinner was more compliant than was Pinsent. Both died as a consequence of wars, though not directly by means of military battle. Partially as a result of following Wittgenstein's counsel, both worked with fine machine tools related to aircraft. This counsel seems to have a basis in Wittgenstein's pre-WWI Manchester flight experiments and design of his patented aero engine — adopted and modified by the Nazis in 1937, which perhaps troubled him as war carried on overhead.

learned. In his writing these down, he seems to regard himself as an incarnation of their subjects—variously a devil possessed to destroy, a false prophet and a poisonous tree.[16]

Highlighting some threads in the history hovering in and behind Wittgenstein's route to composing a more final form of his *Philosophical Investigations* will also benefit our grasp of Anscombe's challenges engaging with Wittgenstein. When she arrived in Cambridge, the young Elizabeth faced many of its complex facets, one cluster of which was some effects of the Wittgenstein/Skinner/Piero Sraffa triangle. Later she had to judge its connections with the emerging *Philosophical Investigations* and his other writings. Although this is very specific in time and theme, a reason for focussing on the period is that, as Anscombe settled down with Wittgenstein, it was one of those pivotal periods in the crystallizing of his thoughts.[17]

The *Investigations* preface includes an acknowledgement of indebtedness to the Italian Cambridge economist Piero Sraffa for critical discussions. On the evenings leading up to Skinner's death, Wittgenstein repeatedly left Skinner's bedside only to go to Sraffa's side for support (as Sraffa's diaries indicate).[18] Behind this is the legacy of using Skinner as a go-between for Wittgenstein and Sraffa. Brian McGuinness isolated one piece of evidence for this practice: there is a 1934 document in Skinner's handwriting, which is dictation from Wittgenstein, to be sent to Sraffa.[19] It is attached to a reply in Sraffa's handwriting, with the latter's reply

---

[16] See N.A. O'Mahony's research, "Russian Matters for Wittgenstein", in *Doubtful Certainties*, ed. J. Padilla-Galvez and M. Gafal (Heusenstamm: Ontos), pp. 149-80.

[17] Such learning curves for Anscombe included mastering Wittgenstein's Austrian German and its attendant complex subtleties; cf. a sample of Schulte's investigations into this sphere in relation to Anscombe: G. Kahane, E. Kanterian and O. Kuusela, eds., "Ways of Reading Wittgenstein", in *Wittgenstein and His Interpreters* (Oxford: Blackwell, 2013), pp. 145-68, especially pp. 148, 154 and 164.

[18] Sraffa's diaries are held in Trinity College Library; catalogue: Sraffa: E13. To illustrate the above note see entries for October 10 and 11, 1941 (the latter entry adds 8:45p.m.).

[19] McGuinness, *Wittgenstein in Cambridge*, documents 171 and 172, pp. 225-28. As Brian McGuinness notes, the separate letter (number 173, p. 228) is from Wittgenstein addressed to Sraffa about this matter. Additionally Wittgenstein talks of his making a rough draft, but in the form that reaches Sraffa it is a neat draft in Skinner's hand.

both disputing and agreeing with Wittgenstein. A part of this is incorporated as a portion of the text in the *Brown Book*.[20]

3. Skinner and Anscombe as Literary Heirs and Editors

These tensions embrace other presuppositions behind Wittgenstein's own will and various dedicatory tributes both to Skinner and to Anscombe. Readers rightly think of Miss Anscombe as a leading literary heir, trustee and editor as well as translator of Wittgenstein's works, yet prior to November 1941 — and until well after WWII — that was not the situation. We should position the fact that in some German manuscripts in the 1930s there are dedications to Francis Skinner in Wittgenstein's handwriting and in code which specify that in the event of Wittgenstein's death those manuscript volumes should be passed to Skinner to handle, presumably as sole heir and/or trustee and editor. Here is one dedication, whose original form is partly in code but here translated:

> In the event of my death before the completion or publication of this book my writings are to be published in fragments under the title "Philosophical Remarks" and with the dedication: "for FRANCIS SKINNER." He, if this remark is read after my death, is in a position to know my intention, at the address: Trinity College, Cambridge.

Wittgenstein's willingness to place such works in the hands of Skinner speaks volumes, as does his much later decision to make Miss Anscombe a literary heir and to choose her as his translator. This somewhat raises the stakes in giving due consideration to the comparisons and contrasts between Wittgenstein's choice of the two in different conceptual worlds, dislocated by the beginnings of WWI and WWII.

A further matter should occupy us here: Wittgenstein had — perhaps transiently, in dark depression — expressed a wish for Skinner's death, in his diary entry for 4 January 1938, written in

---

[20] Furthermore, a full copy of the *Brown Book* has been discovered in Skinner's handwriting — with a somewhat more refined opening and seventy pages longer than the hitherto extant version. See chapter 1, L. Wittgenstein, *Dictating Philosophy*, ed. A. Gibson, forthcoming.

one of his philosophical manuscripts, as was sometimes his practice.

Such thinking and its fulfilment strike a stark contrast, perhaps confrontation, with the newly married devout Roman Catholic woman convert, who retained the title "Miss" Anscombe, with the only seeming light touch being his ascription to her of the status of an honorary "chap". Wittgenstein's own self-troubled psychology and his serious entertainment, only a few years before, of possibly marrying a woman, even while Skinner was with him in Norway, reflects his internal crises amid a complex period of interplay with other people and forces around and beyond Francis's death.

4. Elizabeth Anscombe's Tenacity

It is too easy to accord Miss Anscombe's tough skin and bullish manner to explain (away) her success in engagement with Wittgenstein, considering past and present strata of pressures condensed into his difficult yet highly skilled, complex personality — a person who sometimes cast himself variously as mad, mentally unstable or suicidal. We need not dwell on the other ineluctable influences to which he was subject, such as the suicides of family members. Rather, witness later observations of his sympathetic former pupil, subsequently a psychiatrist, M.O'C. Drury, who deemed Wittgenstein unsuitable (to express it politely) to train as a psychiatrist because of his significant mental problems. In this respect it is worth reading accounts of Drury's time with Wittgenstein when the latter went to live near the former in and beyond Dublin.[21]

So Miss Anscombe was not going to be able to stay on the right side of Wittgenstein, and become his literary heir and gain tenure at Somerville College Oxford, merely by some mannish pose. Immediate, as well as long-term, wisdom and fine-tuned balancing judgments were constantly required. Any mere actorly poses would be spotted, and any prospect of work together thus doomed. Wittgenstein, in certain states, was a man dangerous to himself, and especially to much younger people, despite or perhaps because of his genius. His well-intended counsel ruined, or inappropriately redirected, a number of lives, including Skinner's. Of course, he was kind as well, as Peter Geach testified

---

[21] M.O'C. Drury, *Ludwig Wittgenstein: Personal Reflections*, ed. R. Rhees (Totowa: Roman & Littlefield, 1981), pp. 91–189.

to in print on several occasions including in his "Philosophical Autobiography":

> Personally Wittgenstein was a trusty and generous friend. His practical advice was sound and often helpful; he wrote references for me and for Elizabeth, when we were looking for academic work ... He helped us financially when our second child was born, and devoted a lot of trouble to removing our young daughter's helpless perplexity over elementary arithmetic, both acts were in character.[22]

Elsewhere he writes to repudiate a view of Wittgenstein as "a total egotist" expressed by Michael Dummett in a review of Ray Monk's biography. Geach says, "Wittgenstein treated Elizabeth Anscombe and me with habitual kindness, and indeed on occasion with financial generosity when we were poor".[23] Even so, such kindness can complicate non-fiscal deviations surrounding such kindness. For Anscombe to hold a moderate position against such mental instability and imbalance inherent in his sincere help, which often turned to dominating manipulation, amounts to a major — and perhaps not fully recognized — achievement. Wittgenstein's deep penetration of people's language and weaknesses left no loose space to dodge being the prey, if such "weakness" existed.

5. Wittgenstein, Anscombe and Georg Kreisel

Because of features subsumed in the history sketched above, an entirely positive decisive early assessment by Wittgenstein of Anscombe seems not to have been evident. In a letter to Rush Rhees (28 November 1944), Wittgenstein mentions his classes and the attendees, noting that they include "a woman, Mrs so and so who calls herself Miss Anscombe, who is certainly intelligent, though not of Kreisel's caliber [sic]".[24]

From the tone or aspects of this view, it is easy to come away from it sensing that presuppositions hover offstage: Miss Anscombe is a woman, and tagged as such, matched against a

---

[22] P. Geach, "Intellectual Autobiography", in *Peter Geach: Philosophical Encounters*, ed. Harry A. Lewis (Dordrecht: Kluwer, 1991), p. 14.
[23] "Views of Wittgenstein", letter to *The Tablet* (21 November 1992), p. 15. Dummett's review appeared in the same periodical on 10 October 1992, p. 9.
[24] B. McGuiness, "Letter 321", in *Wittgenstein in Cambridge* (Oxford: Blackwell, 2008), p. 371.

person who is not marked as male but is very much a dominating one. It's an odd matching for criteria of contrast: how does one measure "calibre" between a marked woman philosopher and an unmarked male logician, called by Wittgenstein a "philosopher" and a "mathematician". As Ray Monk's splendid biography reports:

> In 1944—when Kreisel was still only twenty-one Wittgenstein shocked Rush Rhees by declaring Kreisel to be the most able philosopher he had ever met who was also a mathematician. "More than Ramsey?" Rhees asked? "Ramsey?!" replied Wittgenstein. "Ramsey was a mathematician."[25]

Given Wittgenstein's negative contrast of Anscombe with Kreisel, in what follows next we should account for the subsequent and quick disappearance of Kreisel from Wittgenstein's life, in contrast with Wittgenstein's almost immediate absorption of Anscombe into his intellectual creative life in such a way that permanently fixed her into Wittgenstein's publishing future as his literary heir.[26] So there is no need to apologize here for the somewhat detailed digression into Kreisel's history, for it relates to Anscombe in more ways than one might surmise.

Wittgenstein's then-opinion was that Kreisel was a "philosopher"; but Kreisel never published any philosophy, except for occasional remarks that anyone who is not a philosopher yet has philosophical opinions as an amateur might draft. Wittgenstein is not reported above as saying Kreisel was a "philosopher of maths", though maybe this was what he intended. Contrariwise, Kreisel's subsequent writing was largely on narrow technical aspects of logic, without extensive or original writing on specific topics in philosophy of mathematics. So some reassessment is in order, not least since Kreisel was notorious for attacks on other

---

[25] Monk, *Ludwig Wittgenstein: The Duty of Genius*, p. 498. The endnote for this page (631) refers to Rush Rees as source.
[26] It is puzzling, if Kreisel was so good in Wittgenstein's view at the time, why Wittgenstein did not appoint Kreisel as a literary heir or translator instead of, or in addition to, Anscombe. Furthermore, neither she nor the other literary heirs professionally knew the mathematics Wittgenstein used; also, Anscombe was learning German while Kreisel was Austrian. Of course, there may be plausible reasons why he was not chosen; but the question is, do they include ones that would indicate a change in Wittgenstein's assessment of Kreisel? And if there were no such reason, why was he not brought on board given Wittgenstein's high estimate of him?

people's ideas rather than spending time producing any lengthy original philosophical or mathematical writings.[27]

In a notorious review of Wittgenstein's *Remarks on the Philosophy of Mathematics*, Kreisel savagely attempted to demolish Wittgenstein's reputation, concluding: "It seems to me to be a surprisingly insignificant product of a sparkling mind."[28] Upon hearing this and being asked about the worth of Kreisel's own research, the very significant mathematician Sir Peter Swinnerton-Dyer, who knew Kreisel well, asserted: "Kreisel's life-long research contribution was small and insignificant. This output is a striking contrast to his boastful manner and destructive attitude to other mathematicians, not least young ones whom he on occasion eviscerated in public, clearly attempting to ruin their careers."[29] In an unpublished letter written many years later Kreisel wrote: "In a sense I might be said to have made fun of Wittgenstein in a review I wrote in the [19]50s of his *Remarks on the Foundations of Mathematics*."[30]

Recall the foregoing reference to Kreisel and Ramsey in the quotation from Wittgenstein: "'More than Ramsey?' Rhees asked? 'Ramsey?!' replied Wittgenstein. 'Ramsey was a mathematician.'" Professor Martin Hyland, who knew Kreisel well, precisely remembers Kreisel having stated that he had just read a study by Ramsey presenting his original results on logic and intuitionism. Kreisel then roundly denounced them and stated: "Ramsey clearly did not understand them at all and did not have the faintest idea about the subject."[31] Ramsey's work in this arena greatly outpaced Kreisel and now stands as having historic significance. Furthermore with his Ramsey's Theorem, and the extraordinary deep Ramsey Theory, which took up some strands of Ramanujan's

---

[27] "Mathematical" (to accord with Wittgenstein's use of "a mathematician" – with, e.g., Littlewood as a typical example) is here used in a professional sense of pure and applied maths, to indicate their domains that do not include logic though it is a narrow domain with maths.

[28] G. Kreisel, "Remarks on the Foundations of Mathematics", *The British Journal for the Philosophy of Science*, 9 (34) August 1958: 35–158.

[29] Quoted with permission from Professor Swinnerton-Dyer, former Cambridge University VC and Professor of Pure Mathematics.

[30] I thank Mathieu Marion for providing me with a copy of Kresiel's handwritten letter. Martin Hyland verified Kreisel's handwriting.

[31] Quoted with permission from Professor Hyland, Cambridge University.

research and greatly advanced it, Ramsey was a mathematical giant, in contrast with Kreisel. In his review of Wittgenstein's book mentioned above, Kreisel denounces Wittgenstein's use of Gödel. The renowned specialist on Gödel and related matters Solomon Feferman, a long-time colleague of Kreisel at Stanford, was greatly troubled by Kreisel's attacks on Gödel's mathematical writings,[32] which are in the same arena as Kreisel's criticism of Ramsey above. For example, Kreisel asserted, "Gödel used crude, hackneyed formulations". Feferman's analysis of Kreisel's remarks concludes: "This tells us more about Kreisel than about Gödel."[33] We have enough warrant with these above cases about Kreisel — and there are others — to generalize Feferman's conclusion: many of Kreisel's vehement attacks are his own inadvertent autobiographical disclosures, rather than extensionally valid critiques. Feferman believes that Kreisel's wartime work with applied mathematics encouraged a casual disregard for mathematical fastidiousness.[34] This might signal one of the reasons for a change in Kreisel, which could suggest that the Kreisel whose calibre Wittgenstein contrasted with Miss Anscombe's was by then a soul lost to any great research. And this is the most charitable construction.

Feferman also pinpoints how Kreisel made mistakes and failed in his published attempt to advance research on Littlewood's 1914 theorem. This may explain why Littlewood and Hardy did not rate Kreisel as a significant mathematician. They did not fulfil Kreisel's wish that he be considered for a Trinity fellowship. There is no evidence that Wittgenstein proposed him for a Trinity philosophy fellowship or any other post. This is odd, assuming the report by Rush Rhees that Wittgenstein rated him the best.

---

[32] Kreisel, "Gödel's Excursions Into Intuitionistic Logic", in *Gödel Remembered: Salzburg, 10-12 July 1983*, ed. Paul Weingartner and Leopold Schmmetterer (Naples: Bibliopolis, 1987), pp. 65–186; cf. p. 161.

[33] S. Feferman, "Lieber Herr Bernays! Lieber Herr Gödel! Gödel on Finitism, Constructivity, and Hilbert's Programme", *Dialectica*, 62, 2008: 179–203. Feferman quotes Rosser's very critical review of Kreisel's technical work in the *Journal of Symbolic Logic*, 18, 1953: 78–79, where "there are too many errors to permit a complete listing". *Notre Dame Journal of Formal Logic*, 31(4) 1990: 602–641, doi: 10.1305/-/ndjfl/1093635594.

[34] For those who wish to research the matter further, explorations of Kreisel's associations with Iris Murdoch and Philippa Foot (from their viewpoints), and these two women's friendships with Elizabeth Anscombe, amount to a worthy challenge.

Possibly, soon after Wittgenstein made his judgment to Rush Rhees, there arose grounds for him to change his mind about Kreisel's calibre.

6. Kreisel and Anscombe's Editing

The previous section sets the scene for a fresh account of Kreisel's later notorious demolition of Wittgenstein's *Remarks on the Foundations of Mathematics*.

It appears that Anscombe and/or Rhees sought Kreisel's view, or he campaigned for it, concerning what to select from the extensive families of archives that resulted in the book *Remarks on the Foundations of Mathematics*. It is generally acknowledged that the published book, especially after part one, is somewhat of a jumble, which is not faithful to the distribution of material and conceptual relations in the original manuscripts, which are drawn from in an ad hoc way. Only about 40 percent of the relevant archives appear to have been chosen, and at least partly, or substantially, on the basis of Kreisel's views. It appears that this was also accompanied by a claim on Kreisel's part that somehow certain of Wittgenstein's compositions were a form of joint authorship or dialogue with Kreisel.[35] There is no manuscript or historical evidence for this. The two Notebooks, which comprise a

---

[35] For example, Kreisel's discussions with Wittgenstein in 1943. There are two sequential Notebooks (MSS 126 and 127), items from which were taken up into the *Remarks on the Foundations of Mathematics*. It has been proposed, perhaps at Kreisel's instigation, that MSS 126, 127 should be deemed a dialogue, or based on a dialogue, between Wittgenstein and Kreisel, resulting in joint authorship. In the relevant Notebook manuscripts 126 and 127 there is no indication at all about a joint dialogue or second-party co-author. There is only Wittgenstein's handwriting in continuous composition. Nothing else. There are also others in discussions with Wittgenstein on the same topics at the same time. For example, Rhees records that he—Rhees—is involved with Wittgenstein discussing logic—a subject in the Notebook in the same month (April 1943) as Wittgenstein is writing Notebook 127. What there is, which is distinct from this Wittgenstein manuscript, is a typed version produced by Kreisel at a later date after Wittgenstein's death in response to a request by Wittgenstein's trustees to furnish them with a selection to be included in the *Remarks of the Foundations of Mathematics*. Further reading on the assessment of this and its wider contexts can found in J. Floyd and F. Mühlhölzer, *Wittgenstein's Annotations to G.H. Hardy's A Course of Pure Mathematics: Wittgenstein's Non-extensionalist Understanding of the Real Numbers*, Nordic Wittgenstein Studies (Chaum: Springer; forthcoming).

continuous narrative, are only in Wittgenstein's hand, and have no annotations or indication that anyone had a role in their composition; we should conclude that Kreisel as co-author is a delusion which has no basis in any of Wittgenstein's manuscripts.

Had Kreisel been a co-author or dialogee, he would have been destroying aspects of his own work in his review of *Remarks on the Foundations of Mathematics*. Strangely, Kreisel states in it: "Of course I do not know what I should have thought of it fifteen years ago." Contrariwise, he expressed a parallel viewpoint some years before on one of Wittgenstein's manuscripts on the foundation of mathematics—an unpublished version that has only recently been discovered. So we seem to have a complex contrary situation which Kreisel forgot to mention in the review: he was a source who chose part of the selection that he criticized—and on grounds that it is not a balanced treatment or in error. This raises the question of the extent to which his selection and interpretation of it queers the pitch. Also whether, if the omitted parts from Wittgenstein's manuscripts were included, this would remove or mitigate the grounds for Kreisel's criticism of Wittgenstein. The whole arena needs entirely fresh investigation. There is also the obvious question: why should a continuous composition entirely in Wittgenstein's hand not have been published as a separate publication, rather than be dismantled into elements for separated and different publications?

There are two other types of type of concern about Kreisel's approach to Wittgenstein briefly announced here. The first is his claim that Wittgenstein continually made crucial mathematical mistakes. Secondly, Kreisel attacked at least one of Wittgenstein's manuscripts by writing on it under the heading "NONSENSE" ("UNSINN"), which then marks alleged mistakes, and they turn out to be false allegations by Kreisel. As far as I can discover, this has not been noticed before nor mentioned in publications.[36]

---

[36] A study on this matter is due to be published on a later occasion, by A. Gibson, I.B. Leader and J. Smith, "Kreisel's mistreatment of Wittgenstein's mathematical philosophy and manuscripts", forthcoming. Some of these are in Kreisel's review: for example, supposed misuse of Euler, finite series seemingly falsely derived from infinite series, and errors of calculation. Upon analysis of these supposed errors, the authors of this study discovered that Wittgenstein's calculations are sound, whereas Kreisel's criticisms are mathematically erroneous and misread both Wittgenstein and Euler.

Elizabeth Anscombe, and perhaps the other literary heirs, not knowing such mathematics, trusted Kreisel to guide her objectively. If there are any defects due to the absence of balance in examples in *Remarks on the Foundations of Mathematics*, it is not due to the editors or trustees. I believe they are largely the result of Kreisel's industry.[37]

7. Sharing Minds

Whilst Elizabeth Anscombe's mind and spirit did not seem easily to reside in the contemporary halls of academia, there is a typical "Wittgensteinian" picture of her, which reputedly hangs around in some of these halls. This present essay is not concerned to dawdle there, nor is there a motive to craft adoration.

Rather, the concern is to dwell on her capacity for thinking outside the box while still inside it and her ability to compose blue skies thinking on a cloudy day—thinking that is also of value outside of academic philosophy. True, her manner was somewhat oracular—at times as if hardly aware of her audience, so much was she concentrating. Her students needed to press beyond the theatrical. Hers was not an attempt to imitate Wittgenstein's style, except in emulating his quality—encouraging the student into battle with and against her, as a friend yet foe, to reach the heart of new thought. Her mannered trappings were mere devices to eliminate the arthritic professional philosophical spirit encased in some established traditions. Anscombe was against the effect of conventional academia and the too-polished customs which reward conforming eloquence that is superficially laced with overly respectful nuances.

Professor Anscombe's presuppositions displayed the writing of original philosophy as a direct residue of one's thought. An archivist might say the same thing when contrasting a book derived from its manuscripts. The gap between thinking and expression remains a considerable one, which Anscombe succeeded in narrowing. Clever academic writing, though not always a specious sphere, is not infrequently a mode of

---

[37] I made a number of attempts to meet Kreisel about this matter, but without any success. So as to formulate a broader perspective about Kreisel, it is instructive to read P. Odifreddi, ed., *Kreiseliana: about and around Georg Kreisel* (Wellesley, MA: A.K. Peters, 1996). Notice S. Feferman's chapter, "Kreisel's Unwinding Program".

communication that widens the gap via polished surfaces whilst seeming to close it. As she saw it, the risk of manufacturing a counterfeit of philosophy was a great threat within faculties of philosophy.

In a certain narrow sense Elizabeth Anscombe's manner of philosophical thinking was an attempt to be presuppositionless. It is obvious that she had certain presuppositions that some readers may find excessive or unacceptable, and which sharply impacted her thinking and writing to the extent of limiting some of the express qualities of her consciousness while doing philosophy. Even so, such readers will do well to characterize her originality in other ways: think of Socrates' strangeness.[38] At times her writing and oral discussion were at such a depth that they were mistaken for obscurity. Of course when thinking at great depth obscurity can go with the territory, but that is different from incoherent obscurity defacing an otherwise transparent surface. Her language was often plain. Conceptually it could at times be misconstrued as too plain or impossible. As Kolmogorov stated of mathematics: "At any moment there is only a fine layer between the 'trivial' and the impossible. Mathematical discoveries are made in this layer."[39] It is noteworthy that this quotation is used as an epigraph in John Conway's biography, so as to render explicit the narrow and unexpected conjunction of conditions that occasion deep originality.

Wittgenstein's view was that a philosopher is not a member of a society. Although in some senses Anscombe was firmly within a society, her way of being a philosopher included living Wittgenstein's remark. It was this abstract focus, its relentless pursuit of fresh insight, and only seeming unconcern with applications, that yields insights for subjects outside of philosophy.

I sometimes challenged her teaching by asking a question such as: "So you want me to tackle understanding intention; all very well, but how does your research on it relate to intention's use in, say, criminal law?" Her reply began by explaining how Glanville Williams had "got it wrong" in his *Mental Elements in Criminal*

---

[38] See Gregory Vlastos, *Socrates, Ironist and Moral Philosopher* (Cambridge: Cambridge University Press, 1991); and T.H. Irwin, "The Strangeness of Socrates", in *London Review of Books*, 13 (22) 1991: 14–15.

[39] This quotation is from Conway's biography, in S. Roberts, *Genius at Play: The Curious Mind of John Horton Conway* (New York: Bloomsbury, 2015), p. 83.

Law.⁴⁰ I read it, and argued how his case might be rectified to sidestep some of her objections, as well as suggesting he had sensed for himself a feature or two of her insights. She responded with one of her typical organizational moves. I had sprung on me (as a first year undergraduate) an invitation "requiring" my attendance at Professor Glanville Williams's to address his third-year student seminar on why he was wrong about criminal intention, in his rooms at Jesus College, with his chairing the session as if in court.

As a philosopher with a great sense of tradition, Elizabeth Anscombe was deeply aware, sometimes instinctively, of a neglected or repressed area in a subject arena about which she had thought, even if it might be a scientist's specialty. For example, when she was in dialogue with John Polkinghorne, her open and probing manner exposed in him some autocratic rigidity, familiar on some scientific committees, rather than open-minded thinking. (Although Professor Polkinghorne was a generation after Paul Dirac, Dirac's manner, though somewhat autistic, was always the "younger" pioneering style in contrast with Polkinghorne, one of his last students.) In dialogue with Anscombe, Polkinghorne was pushing traditional mid-twentieth-century physics, as if it were there to eradicate some newer directions. The debate was centring on his view of physics in contrast with her position on causality and determination.⁴¹ He incorrectly assumed that her views were based on an elementary view of Newton. Mathematically more informed than she he certainly was, but conceptually he was not in this case. After noting that Newton's question of what was "force" was still unanswered, Anscombe introduced the question of fundamental forces of nature *and* how they relate to interference and prevention of a certain type of causal function. For good measure, she included how new models of elementary particles might link up to combine with ideas about quantum gravity, which would yield exotic notions that disturb causality. It was only specialists in the audience who would realize that, either knowingly or instinctively, Miss Anscombe had taken Polkinghorne directly into the area of the second half of Dirac's life's work

---

[40] Glanville Williams, *Mental Elements in Criminal Law* (Jerusalem: Magda Press, 1976).
[41] Cf. G.E.M. Anscombe, "Causality and Determination", in *The Collected Works of G.E.M. Anscombe II: Metaphysics and the Philosophy of Mind* (Minneapolis, MN: University of Minnesota Press, 1981), pp. 133–47.

that Polkinghorne had typically avoided, was not convinced of, or did not adequately understand.[42] The result was a sense that Anscombe's thought had explanatory potential for emerging science, whereas Polkinghorne was inflexible to some fresh developments in his own subject.

8. Lasting Memory

The last time I met Professor Anscombe was one of a typical shared private treasure. It was the occasion of the informal celebration in his rooms in Trinity of the publication of John Marenbon's book on the philosophy of Peter Abelard.[43] There were only a few present, Elizabeth and Peter Geach making the numbers up to seven. On arrival, Peter aimed for the back of the room to talk to John, while Elizabeth settled at the front on the small sofa, indicating that I should sit beside her. Although ill, she was her acute philosophical self, tackling new territory. The seeming absence of others was a function of her concentration, cutting deep. Part of the time she was in tears, variously beaming with joy, but also at times in mental anguish deeply trying to grasp the point. We exchanged words, interspersed with silent meditation. That was Elizabeth Anscombe.

---

[42] For example, in his book *Quantum Theory* (Oxford: OUP, 2002) there is no mention of quantum gravity or monopoles. A one-sided appreciation of Dirac also appeared in Polkinghorne's London *Times* obituary of Dirac (http://www-history.mcs.st-and.ac.uk/Obits/Dirac.html). He had left out much of the deep pioneering research that characterized the second half of Dirac's life, which is on a par with his earlier work on quantum mechanics. P. Goddard and J.C. Taylor pressed this omitted perspective into *The Times*, to rectify this omission by publishing their Addendum (for which see http://www-history.mcs.st-and.ac.uk/-Obits/Dirac_2.html). I thank my colleague Gary Gibbons for these *Times* references.

[43] John Marenbron, *The Philosophy of Peter Abelard* (Cambridge: Cambridge University Press, 1997). A reason for my presence was that John had asked me before publication to read and examine the manuscript that was the draft of it, especially in the areas of future conditionals; he had also asked me to write the Ockham chapter for the Routledge *History of Philosophy*, which I think Peter Geach had a hand in suggesting.

Ulf Hlobil and
Katharina Nieswandt

On Anscombe's Philosophical Method[1]

While many of Elizabeth Anscombe's philosophical views are well-known (e.g. her views on practical knowledge or consequentialism), little has been written on her philosophical method, i.e. on her way of doing philosophy. This is unfortunate, for two reasons. First, the failure to understand Anscombe's method is a major stumbling block for many of her readers. Second, and more importantly, we can still learn a lot from Anscombe's way of doing philosophy: her view differs considerably from current alternatives in metaphilosophy. Here we want to begin to fill this lacuna.

The chapter is organized as follows: in Section 1, we describe an argumentative pattern that can be found in many of Anscombe's essays. This pattern is not the only one in her methodological toolkit, but it is particularly important. In Section 2, we isolate this pattern in three of Anscombe's essays. In Section 3, we locate Anscombe's implicit "philosophy of philosophy" relative to some rival metaphilosophies.

1. A Recurring Pattern in Anscombe's Work

The method on which we shall focus can be described as a four-step pattern. Anscombe applies this template to a large variety of topics, and her arguments at each step vary accordingly, but the general pattern can be described in the abstract.

---

[1] Previously published in *Klesis*, no. 35, 2016, in a special issue on Anscombe.

Step 1: Philosophically Puzzling "What is x?"-Questions

Anscombe uses this four-step pattern in cases where questions of the form "What is x?" or "What does 'x' mean?" seem philosophically important. These questions are her starting point. Often, the first step involves a move from "What is x?" to "What does 'x' mean?" Note that in asking the latter, Anscombe is not interested in questions regarding a particular language or a particular conception of x. She is interested in how we can understand and talk about x at all, i.e. what it is to understand and talk about x. Here "about" is used in a thin sense that is roughly one of the senses that Ryle famously groups together under the heading of "about-linguistic".[2] After all, we cannot presuppose that x exists and that we are not confused about what our words refer to, etc.

Anscombe usually starts by asking "What is x?" The x in question typically plays (or seems to play) an important role in our practical or theoretical lives, and we take ourselves to have some grip on what x is. On reflection, however, puzzling questions regarding x arise, and we end up with a peculiar kind of puzzlement that we might call "philosophical puzzlement". We somehow feel that we should know the answers to the puzzling questions regarding x and that empirical investigations will not help us answer them. But when pressed to answer them, we either don't know what to say or we are inclined to give answers that Anscombe reveals to be trivial, incoherent or highly implausible.

Step 2: A Translation or Analysis of "x" is Impossible

Anscombe's next step with respect to these puzzling cases is to argue that there can be no straightforward answer (as we shall call it) to the question what x is or what "x" means. Anscombe sometimes calls the type of answer she has in mind here a "translation or analysis";[3] sometimes she calls it a "definition".[4] The idea is that the questions "What is x?" and "What does 'x' mean?" can be

---

[2] See G. Ryle, "About", *Analysis*, 1 (1) 1933: 10–12. Thanks to an anonymous referee for prompting this clarification and further helpful comments.
[3] See G.E.M. Anscombe, "The Reality of the Past", in *Metaphysics and the Philosophy of Mind: Collected Philosophical Papers, Volume II* (Oxford: Blackwell, 1981), p. 116.
[4] See G.E.M. Anscombe, "On the Source of the Authority of the State", in *Ethics, Religion and Politics: Collected Philosophical Papers, Volume III* (Oxford: Blackwell, 1981), p. 138.

answered by providing an expression "*y*" such that the answer "to be an *x* is to be a *y*" or "'*x*' means the same as '*y*'" respectively is informative and satisfying. Examples of such (alleged) straightforward answers may be the following: "Knowledge that *P* is a justified, true belief that *P*" or "The word 'I' means the same as 'the speaker/thinker of this'". Such a "translation or analysis" must be non-circular; we must be able to understand "*y*" without any prior understanding of *x*. Furthermore, the equivalence of "*x*" and "*y*" must help us to resolve our puzzlement regarding *x*. The connection between *x* and *y* might be a conceptual connection, or it might be some kind of metaphysical entailment or some kind of reductive explanation.

In many philosophically puzzling cases, Anscombe thinks, no such "translation or analysis" is to be had. For some of these, she argues that any straightforward answer must run in a circle, for others, that all possible candidates for a "translation or analysis" must be rejected. In any event, our philosophical puzzle regarding *x* cannot be solved by giving a "translation or analysis" of "*x*".

In this situation, we must find a different way of answering the questions "What is *x*?" or "What does '*x*' mean?" We need an explanation of *x* or the meaning of "*x*" that is not a translation, analysis or definition in Anscombe's sense. She says: "definition is not the only mode of explanation".[5] This is not the platitude that some explanations are not definitions. She claims that there are illuminating answers to the questions "What is *x*?" or "What does '*x*' mean?" that do not provide informative and non-circular necessary and sufficient conditions for something being an *x* or meaning the same as "*x*" — and that in the philosophically puzzling cases at hand the right answers are of this kind.

Step 3: Descriptions of Our Practices or Abilities Provide an Answer
Anscombe's own solutions for philosophically puzzling cases rest on accounts of how we think about, talk about and act with respect to *x*. Such an account usually takes the form of a description of a practice or an ability.[6] This has two advantages.

---

[5] *Ibid.*, p. 138.
[6] Anscombe often sees such practices as grounded in or justified by something that, in contrast to the practice itself, does not depend on human conventions, e.g. a universal human need. This is particularly important in the normative domain.

First, it allows Anscombe to use "*x*" in her description of our abilities and practices, where no "translation" is possible. After all, she is giving an account that situates our thinking and talking about *x* in the world, and the relevant worldly facts may involve *x*. In "The Reality of the Past", for instance, it allows her to use the past tense in an explanation of how our talk about the past connects with the actual past.[7]

A second advantage of Anscombe's descriptive approach is that it puts sufficient distance between us and our common thought, talk and action regarding *x*, so as to see it as something that plays a non-mysterious role in the overall fabric of our practices and abilities.

Step 4: How this is a Solution

Anscombe's final step is to demonstrate how the resulting account can resolve the philosophical puzzle with which we began — even though we still don't have a "translation or analysis" of "*x*". As we will see below, Anscombe at this point often presents results that have a therapeutic or deflationary aspect. Thus, her resolution often seems less "substantive" than one might have expected. Nevertheless, Anscombe's results are often not exclusively concerned with thought or language, and they often constitute surprising theses about *x*.

2. Three Examples

The above is an abstract description of Anscombe's four-step pattern. In the current section, we shall show how this pattern occurs at crucial passages in her writing, using as our examples arguments from three important essays: "Rules, Rights and Promises", "The First Person" and "The Intentionality of Sensation". The same pattern can also be found in other places, e.g. in "The Reality of the Past". But the three cases we are going to discuss strike us as important, representative and diverse enough to be helpful examples.

We cannot do justice to any of these rich and difficult papers, and we don't want to discuss — let alone defend — the substantive philosophical theses put forward in them. Our point is that they share a common argumentative structure.

---

[7] Anscombe, "The Reality of the Past", p. 118.

1. "Rules, Rights and Promises"

In "Rules, Rights and Promises" Anscombe asks: what is a rule, a right or a promise? Hume already posed this question for promises, and he answered that promises are not "naturally intelligible", i.e. we cannot understand what promises are without understanding human practices and social conventions.[8] Anscombe thinks that the same holds for rules and rights as well. Let us go through the four steps of her pattern, as it occurs in that paper.

Step 1: Rules, rights and promises can be defined as entities that make certain actions necessary for us. Sometimes we *must* do something because a rule says so, because somebody else has a right that we do it or because we have given a promise. What is this necessity that rules, rights and promises generate? What does it mean to say that doing something is "necessary" in this sense?

Step 2: A straightforward answer to these questions would take the form: "the relevant kind of necessity is …" or "the expression 'necessary' as used in the context of rules, rights, and promises means …" respectively — where what goes into the place of the dots can be understood without already understanding the necessity. We say in what sense it is necessary to perform the action by saying in what sense it is impossible not to perform it, where this explanation of the impossibility is independently intelligible. Anscombe argues that no such independently intelligible explanation can be found; all answers that take the above form are ultimately circular. The only plausible answer is that one cannot perform the necessary act without being guilty of something: doing a wrong, making a mistake, being unjust, etc. As it turns out, though, we cannot understand the relevant kind of guilt, wrongness or injustice without already understanding the necessity that rules, rights and promises generate. (This problem is sometimes called "Hume's Circle".)[9] Our x — the necessity that rules, rights and promises generate — thus is one of these philosophically puzzling cases. We must look for an answer that does not take the form of a "translation or analysis".

---

[8] David Hume, *A Treatise of Human Nature*, eds. D.F. Norton and M.J. Norton (Oxford: Oxford University Press, 2007), 3.2.5, §1.

[9] For a discussion of this see K. Nieswandt, "Do Rights Exist by Convention or by Nature?", *Topoi*, 35, 2016: 313-25.

Step 3: Anscombe suggests: "What we have to attend to is the use of modals."[10] Instead of offering a "translation or analysis" of *necessity-generated-by-rules-rights-or-promises*, Anscombe offers a description of our practices and of our ability to use certain modal expressions — in particular a class that she calls "stopping modals". She illustrates what these modals are as follows: "If I say 'You can't wear that!' and it's not, e.g., that you are too fat to get it on, that's what I call a stopping modal."[11]

Anscombe gives a description of how children learn to use these modal expressions and what role they play in our lives. In particular, Anscombe points out that stopping modals often occur with "what sounds like a reason", although it turns out that it is not a reason in the sense of an independently intelligible fact that could serve to ground the stopping modal. She calls such reasons "*logoi*".[12]

> [What we mention] appears to be a reason. And it *is* a 'reason' in the sense of a *logos*, a thought. But if we ask what the thought is, and for what it is a reason, we'll find that we can't explain them separately. We can't explain the "You can't" on its own; in any independent sense it is simply not true that he can't (unless 'they' physically stop him). But neither does "it's N's ..." have its peculiar sense independent of the relation to "you can't".[13]

Using stopping modals together with certain *logoi* is the paradigmatic way to express the necessity generated by a rule, a right or a promise.

> Now, this form: "you can't ..., its N's ...", though it has other applications as well, is also the form *par excellence* in which a *right* is ascribed to N.[14]

Anscombe goes on to suggest that "rule", "right" and "promise" indicate *logos*-types; "they tell us the formal character of the stopping modal."[15]

---

[10] G.E.M. Anscombe, "Rules, Rights and Promises", in *Ethics, Religion and Politics: Collected Philosophical Papers, Volume III* (Oxford: Blackwell, 1981), pp. 97–103 at p. 100.
[11] *Ibid.*, p. 101.
[12] *Ibid.*, pp. 101–02.
[13] *Ibid.*, p. 101.
[14] *Ibid.*
[15] *Ibid.*, p. 102.

Step 4: Anscombe's description of our practices helps us understand what a right (a rule or a promise) is, even though we still lack an independent explication. In the last paragraph of the paper, Anscombe summarizes her account thus:

> These 'musts' and 'can'ts' are the most basic expression of such-and-such's being a rule; just as they are the most basic expression in learning the rules of a game, and as they are too in being taught rights and manners. But they aren't, in Hume's phrase, 'naturally intelligible'. The mark of this is the relation of interdependence between the "you can't" and the 'reason' where this is what I have called the theme or logos of the "you can't". These musts and can'ts are understood by those of normal intelligence as they are trained in the practices of reason.[16]

This is a resolution of our philosophical puzzle because it (a) explains why we cannot give a straightforward answer to the question "What is the necessity generated by rules, rights, and promises?" and (b) it allows us to see how our thought and talk about this necessity is grounded in an entirely non-mysterious practice. Stopping modals form part of larger social games, in which we are trained as we grow up. This is why rules, rights and promises on the one hand and the necessity they generate on the other depend on each other conceptually (but in a pragmatically grounded way). Anscombe has argued that the request to fill in the dots in: "The necessity that rules, rights, and promises give rise to is ..." with something independently intelligible asks for something that cannot exist. Nevertheless, she has given us an informative alternative answer, namely that rules, rights and promises can only exist within social practices, more precisely practices that involve the use of a particular kind of modal expression. This answer is not a "translation or analysis" because we cannot explain what a practice is without relying on the idea of a rule. We haven't broken out of Hume's Circle; rather, we have situated rules, rights and promises from within the circle by attending to the broader context in which they have their home.

To summarize: we ask what that is, a rule, a right or a promise (step 1), and discover that any attempted definition or analysis ends up in a circle (step 2). An alternative, Anscombe suggests, is to look at how we think of and talk about rules, rights and promises. As it turns out, all three form part of larger social

---

[16] *Ibid.,* p. 103.

practices, in which we are trained as we grow up (step 3). How does this answer our original question? It tells us why the type of answer we originally sought cannot exist, and it gives us insight into rules, rights and promises by relating them to a broader context of social practices. It furthermore contains a surprising thesis about the ontology of rules, rights and promises: they only exist as part of human practices (step 4).

2. "The First Person"

In "The First Person", Anscombe argues that "'I' is neither a name nor another kind of expression whose logical role is to make a reference".[17] This thesis, she thinks, is an important step on the way to an adequate understanding of self-consciousness. Let us try to discern our pattern again.

Step 1: Anscombe starts with the question: what does "I" mean? She is clear that she does not mean this as a question about reference but as a question regarding the sense of the word "I". She asks what grasping the concept expressed by "I" amounts to.

Step 2: Anscombe explores different straightforward answers, all of which are proposals for how to pick out the referent of "I" so as to employ the concept expressed by "I". That is, they are accounts of the form: grasping the meaning of "I" is to be able to pick out object O in way W. None of these straightforward answers works. To see this, let's first assume that the way W of picking out O must involve sensory stimulation. Now, "I" cannot be a name for oneself, nor a demonstrative, nor any other kind of indexical that is such that we need sensory stimulation to determine its referent. After all, sensory deprivation does not prevent us from using "I" in the usual way. In a situation of sensory deprivation, "I have not lost my 'self-consciousness'; nor can what I mean by 'I' be an object no longer present to me".[18] If way W does not involve sensory stimulation, then the referent of "I" must be given to me in some non-sensory way. It thus seems that "I" must mean something like "my Cartesian Ego" or "the thinker/speaker of this". However, neither of these "translations or analyses" works. The first "translation" cannot explain why we cannot make mistakes in identifying our Cartesian Egos; the

---

[17] G.E.M. Anscombe, "The First Person", in *Metaphysics and the Philosophy of Mind: Collected Philosophical Papers, Volume II* (Oxford: Blackwell, 1981), p. 32.
[18] *Ibid.*, p. 31.

second cannot guarantee that there is really only one thinker/ speaker and not many. So all our attempts to say what "I" means by specifying how the user of "I" must pick out its referent fail. An understanding of "I" must consist in something other than the ability to pick out a certain referent.

Step 3: Anscombe suggests that to grasp the meaning of "I" is to possess a certain ability. It is to be able to express and use-in-thought the unmediated, reflective consciousness of states, actions, motions, etc. of our body. Uses of "I" must be appropriately related to this "subjectless"[19] consciousness of states, actions, motions, etc. This constitutes the meaning of "I".[20]

> [...] "I" is not a name: these I-thoughts are examples of reflective consciousness of states, actions, motions, etc., not of an object I mean by "I", but of this body. These I-thoughts (allow me to pause to think some!) ... are unmediated conceptions (knowledge or belief, true of false) of states, motions, etc., of this object here, about which I can find out (if I don't know it) that it is E.A.[21]

Step 4: Anscombe concludes her paper by saying: "The (deeply rooted) grammatical illusion of a subject is what generates all the errors which we have been considering."[22] She thinks that what lies at the bottom of the puzzles about "I" is that we are looking for a conception of oneself, a way of picking out oneself, that one must have in order to use "I" correctly. If Anscombe is right, however, then there is no need for such a conception. Instead, the unmediated conceptions that allow us to have I-thoughts are "subjectless". "I" is, as it were, marking a particular status of a conception as acquired by reflective consciousness, rather than picking out the subject of the conception. So, our ability to use "I" neither depends on sensory stimulation nor on our ability to identify a Cartesian Ego or a thinker. As in the case of rules, rights and promises, our problems are dissolved in that we realize we have been looking for the wrong kind of answer all along. The question "What does 'I' mean?" receives a deflationary answer, in the sense that, on Anscombe's view, there is no such thing as an

---

[19] *Ibid.*, p. 36.
[20] Anscombe spells out why she can still accept the principle that if X asserts something with "I" as subject, her assertion is true just in case it is true of X.
[21] *Ibid.*, p. 34.
[22] *Ibid.*, p. 36.

"I" or a "self". Although this reaction of Anscombe has a "deflationary" aspect, it is also a substantive metaphysical thesis.

3. "The Intentionality of Sensation"

In "The Intentionality of Sensation", Anscombe asks: what are the immediate objects of sensation? She focusses on the sense modality of sight and argues that we must distinguish what she calls "material objects" of sight from "intentional objects" of sight. Intentional objects are not objects in the sense of entities. Rather, the idea of an intentional object should be understood on the model of a grammatical object. Let's go through our pattern again.[23]

Step 1: Anscombe asks: what are the "proper" and "immediate" objects of sight? Some people think that these are the ordinary physical objects around us; others believe that we immediately only see sense-data or something the like. This disagreement reflects a puzzle that naturally arises. On the one hand, it seems commonsensical to think that you sometimes see things like tables, chairs or dogs. On the other hand, in cases of illusions and hallucinations, we can sometimes truly say of someone that she sees, e.g., a pink elephant although there is no such elephant anywhere near her. In such cases, we might be inclined to say that what the subject sees is a sense-image or something the like. If that is what one sees in cases of illusions and hallucinations, however, then it seems implausible to think that we don't see such sense-images in cases of veridical perception, too — thus rejecting common sense regarding tables, chairs and the like. And from that position it is not far to scepticism about the external world.

Step 2: A straightforward answer to the question "What are the objects of sensation?" would take the form "The objects of sensation are ...", where "..." is some description of a particular kind of object. Anscombe argues that no account of this type works. After having explained the general structure of her own solution (to which we'll turn below), Anscombe opens the second part of her essay thus:

> In the philosophy of sense-perception there are two opposing positions. One says that what we are immediately aware of in

---

[23] The order of the steps of our pattern does not match the order of exposition in Anscombe's essay.

> sensation is sense-impressions, called "ideas" by Berkeley and "sense-data" by Russell. The other, taken up nowadays by "ordinary language" philosophy, says that on the contrary we at any rate *see* objects (in the *wide* modern sense which would include e.g. shadows) without any such intermediaries ... I wish to say that both these positions are wrong...[24]

Hallucinations speak against the ordinary language view. In such cases, we can truly say that someone *sees* something, without there being any object (in the relevant sense) that is seen and without using the verb "to see" in a derivative or secondary sense. Against the sense-data view, Anscombe points out that there really is a sense in which one cannot see what isn't there and that this sense is epistemologically prior and fundamental.

> [W]e ought to say, not: "Being red is looking red in normal light to the normal-sighted," but rather "Looking red is looking as a thing that *is* red looks in normal light to the normal-sighted."[25]

The sense-data theorist cannot easily accept this explanation of "looks red" — at least not for things other than sense-data. Furthermore, the idea that someone who hallucinates is really seeing a sense-image is analogous to the idea that someone who is worshipping a god that does not exist is really worshipping an idea — and the latter claim is clearly false. Thus, the sense-data theorist's solution to the problem of non-existing objects of sensation does not carry over to cases to which it should, at least *prima facie*, carry over.

One might try to find a third kind of straightforward answer by suggesting that the things seen in hallucinations are unreal or non-existing objects. But Anscombe thinks that this suggestion succumbs to the same objection that was raised against sense-data theories. Drawing an analogy between seeing and thinking, she says:

> [T]he mere fact of real existence (is this now beginning to be opposed to existence of some other kind?) can't make so very much difference to the analysis of a sentence like "X thought of—". So if the idea is to be brought in when the object doesn't exist, then equally it should be brought in when the object does exist. Yet [in

---

[24] G.E.M. Anscombe, "The Intentionality of Sensation", in *Metaphysics and the Philosophy of Mind: Collected Philosophical Papers, Volume II* (Oxford: Blackwell, 1981), pp. 3–20, at p. 11.
[25] *Ibid.*, p. 14.

such cases] one is thinking, surely, of [e.g.] Winston Churchill [the man himself].[26]

It seems that no account of the form "the objects of sensation are …" can be successful. After all, neither "ordinary objects", nor "sense-images" or the like, nor "unreal objects" can fill the place of the dots. And there seems to be no further plausible candidate.

Anscombe thinks that it is a mistake to look for an answer of the form: "the objects of sensation are …" In the first part of her essay, she discusses this issue with view to the more encompassing class of what she calls "intentional objects", and she says:

> The question [of what an intentional object is] is based on a mistake, namely that an explanatory answer running say "An intentional [...] object is such-and-such" is possible and requisite. But this need not be so. Indeed the only reasonable candidates to be answers are the ones we have failed.[27]

How can the question what kind of entity the objects of sensation are be a mistake? This will become clearer in the next step.

Step 3: Anscombe thinks it is helpful, in this situation, to compare our ability to think and talk about objects of sensation to our ability to think and talk about grammatical objects. (And here the "about" is again of Ryle's linguistic variety.) For a similar, but less puzzling, situation arises there. We find out, for example, what the direct object of the sentence "John sent Mary a book" is by asking: "What did John send Mary (according to the sentence)?" And we answer: "A book." However, there might not be any book that John sent Mary. And even if such a book exists, we cannot substitute *salva veritate* co-referring terms in our answer. This seems to suggest that our answer should really be "'a book'", i.e. that we should mention and not use the word "book". However, the question "What did John send?" cannot be answered correctly by saying, "The words 'a book'". Put differently, although there is a sense in which the grammatical object of a sentence is clearly a word or a phrase, you cannot understand what a grammatical object is unless you know how to answer questions like: "What did John send?" And in the answer "a book" you are using the word "book" in a special way that is analogous to the way in which we use words that describe objects of

---

[26] Ibid., p. 5.
[27] Ibid., p. 8.

sensation. The question "What kind of thing is this book that you are talking about?" does not have any reasonable answer—nor does it need one. Anscombe thinks that this also holds for (a particular use of) questions like this: "What kind of thing is the pink elephant that you say you are seeing?" Thus, a description of our ability to think and talk about grammatical objects gives us some insight into our ability to think and talk about objects of sensation.

Step 4: Our puzzle was that it seems that the objects of sensation are either ordinary objects or sense-images (or the like) and that neither of these options is acceptable. Anscombe's solution is this: we must distinguish between intentional objects and material objects of sensation. An expression that gives an intentional object of sensation is like "a book" in the answer to "What did John send?" in the following way: (a) the thing it mentions might not exist, (b) where the thing exists we cannot always substitute a co-referential expression for our expression *salva veritate,* and (c) what is named can be indeterminate or vague (in a way that ordinary objects cannot be). With the analogy to grammatical objects in mind, we can say all that. And we can say it without being forced to say that we see sense-images (which would be the sense-data theorist's way of explaining these three features).[28] Turning to the other side of the distinction, the material object of a sensation is given by any expression that is co-referential with an expression that gives an (existing) intentional object of the sensation.

We can use the verb "see" with an intentional or a material object. Those who think that the objects of sensation are ordinary objects treat "to see" as if it could only occur with a material object. That is the use of "see" in which we can say "You cannot see what isn't there". Anscombe acknowledges that there really is this use of "to see", but she thinks that there is also another use, namely the use with an intentional object. By distinguishing these, we can do justice to the correct motivations behind sense-data theory and those behind direct realism; and we can do so without having to posit anything like sense-data. Thus, Anscombe's

---

[28] A sense-data theorist's explanation of the three features would go like this: (a) Images can show things that do not exist. (b) We cannot substitute parts of images that picture the same object for one another without changing the identity of the overall images. (c) There can be an image of, e.g., a tree that does not picture the tree as having a particular number of leaves.

account resolves our philosophical puzzle, without giving a translation or analysis of "object of sensation".

One upshot of Anscombe's view is that perception must have content. We always perceive things "under a description", as it were. This comes out in the fact that descriptions of what one perceives are intentional in the sense of having features (a)–(c) above. So in spite of rejecting the question "What are the immediate objects of sensation?", Anscombe puts forward a substantive thesis about perception.

3. Anscombe's Implicit Metaphilosophy

All three papers we have looked at follow the structural pattern described in Section 1. In all three, Anscombe argues for a novel and interesting solution to the respective philosophical puzzle. One might take issue with many of her arguments and theses. Our aim in this last section, though, is not to defend them. Whatever the merits of Anscombe's particular claims in the three discussed papers, we think that Anscombe's argumentative pattern provides a useful approach to philosophical puzzles. And we want to put this approach on the map of current alternatives in metaphilosophy.

3.1. Her Deflationary Method Produces Substantive Metaphysical Claims

Anscombe's method typically leads to metaphysically deflationary accounts, very broadly construed. Either the puzzling "entity" turns out to be of a different metaphysical kind from what one has been looking for at the outset or the very question after its metaphysical status turns out to be a mistake. In "Rules, Rights and Promises", the necessity that arises from all three is found to be the necessity of a move within a certain practice. There is no "deeper" explanation of this necessity than simply putting the relevant practice in plain view. In "The First Person", we start by looking for a way of picking out a subject. This results in the need for an explanation of what egos, "selves", or "I's" are. Anscombe instead argues that "I" does not refer to any such entity; it marks a certain perspective on objects and events. And in "The Intentionality of Sensation", Anscombe argues that our talk of the "object" of a perception lets us forget that perceptions are intentional; they don't have an "object" whose metaphysical status we could then further investigate (except a material object). (Is it a sense datum? A real table?)

Notice, however, that the kind of "deflation" Anscombe offers in the three papers differ in important respects. It does make sense, for example, to ask after the metaphysical status of a right, at least in the sense in which this question is answered by saying: a right is something "whose existence does depend on human linguistic practice".[29] This is a substantive metaphysical thesis about rights, since it amounts to a denial of the idea of natural rights. The answer is not a "translation or analysis" because we cannot understand what a practice is without relying on the idea of a rule and, hence, on an antecedent understanding of the necessity that is imposed by rules, rights and promises. But the result is reached by showing that the relevant kind of necessity cannot be explained in a non-circular fashion.[30] The "deflation" consists in the ungrudging recognition that we cannot dig deeper than an account of our practices of using certain modal expressions. By contrast, Anscombe rejects the question after the metaphysical status of intentional "objects" of perception as a mistake. Here the "deflation" consists in the claim that the puzzle rests on our impulse to find an entity wherever there is an intentional object. Anscombe "deflates" the object of sensation to something that is not an entity. The "deflation" in "The First Person" is similar to this. After all, "I" does not have a referent. As in the case of rules, rights and promises, however, there is something informative that we can say in response to our initial question. We asked: what does "I" mean? That is, what is it to grasp the meaning of sentences in which "I" occurs? And we can say at least this much: "I-thoughts [...] are unmediated conceptions [...] of states, motions etc., of this object here", i.e. of my body.[31]

Notice also what Anscombe does not do. (a) She does not presume that philosophy consists in analysing concepts. In fact, she typically begins her philosophical investigations where the

---

[29] G.E.M. Anscombe, "The Question of Linguistic Idealism", in *From Parmenides to Wittgenstein: Collected Philosophical Papers, Volume I* (Oxford: Blackwell, 1981), p. 118.

[30] Here we leave out the important step from the claim that the necessity involved in rules, rights and promises cannot be explained without circularity to the claim that rules, rights, and promises exist by convention.

[31] Anscombe, "The First Person", p. 34.

possibility of providing analyses gives out. (b) She does not pay disproportionate respect to the ordinary use of expressions and concepts.[32] When Anscombe argues that there is no straightforward solution to a problem, she is not restricting herself to solutions that are in accordance with the ordinary use of words. In "The Intentionality of Sensation", for example, she also discusses the usual suspects in the philosophical tradition, which are often clearly revisionary. Where her arguments are successful, we could hence not evade the conclusion that there is no straightforward answer by changing our way of talking or thinking. She does not stubbornly refuse to consider the possibility that ordinary thought and talk need reform, as some philosophers in the Wittgensteinian tradition are sometimes accused of doing. (c) For the same reason, Anscombe's appeals to our ordinary practices of using certain expressions and concepts as a solution to a puzzle is not aimed at critiquing alternative philosophical theories. She brings in our practices and abilities only after having rejected alternative views. (d) She is not claiming that all philosophical problems rest on confusions. Rather, she merely holds that some important philosophical problems don't have straightforward solutions. And that is something very different.

3.2. Anscombe's Metaphilosophy in Relation to Current Alternatives

The conception of philosophy implicitly at work in the discussed papers can be summarized thus: (A) Many philosophical problems take the form of "What is x?" or "What does 'x' mean?" (B) Solutions to such problems need not take the form of a "translation or analysis". (C) When the method of analysis gives out, it is often helpful to look at the practices and abilities underlying our talk, thought and action regarding the puzzling phenomenon. Descriptions of these practices and abilities often provide us with an indirect solution to our problem.

To be sure, these three points vastly underspecify Anscombe's conception of philosophy. Nevertheless, it will be helpful to locate the resulting metaphilosophy relative to other metaphilosophies.

---

[32] As Anselm Müller puts it, Anscombe "is not an advocate of 'ordinary language philosophy', which she thinks pays undue respect to colloquial speech and its nuances" — Müller, "G.E.M. Anscombe: Entdeckung einer philosophischen Entdeckerin", in *Anscombe: Aufsätze* (Berlin: Suhrkamp, 2014), p. 361.

To this end, we can adapt Kevin Sharp's helpful classification of philosophical methods.³³ Sharp distinguishes six of these. In the list below we have changed Sharp's ordering and added a few names. (For each of the named philosophers, some might question whether they actually fall into the respective category, but our point here simply is to sketch a map.)

1. *Methodological naturalism* claims that philosophy is continuous with the sciences and should be pursued as the most abstract and theoretical part of the sciences (W.v.O. Quine).
2. *Experimental philosophy* suggests we should investigate our intuitions and concepts empirically (J. Knobe, E. Machery).
3. *Conceptual analysis* tries to solve philosophical puzzles through finding illuminating *a priori* or analytic connections between concepts (A.J. Ayer).
4. *Reductive explanations* try to explain philosophically puzzling phenomena by means of some kind of reduction to less puzzling phenomena via translation, *a priori* entailment or metaphysical constitution/grounding/identity relations (or a combination thereof) (J.J. Smart, F. Jackson on ethics).
5. "Quietism" about phenomena "avoids proposing and defending philosophical theories, and instead sees philosophical problems as the result of confusions that are often caused by misunderstanding language"³⁴ (J. McDowell is often named as a proponent, but he sometimes protests against this label).
6. "Analytic pragmatism", which, "[i]nstead of emphasizing the relations between sets of concepts on which conceptual analysis or reductive explanation focuses", looks "to relations between how words are used and the concepts those words express"³⁵ (W. Sellars, R. Brandom).

Anscombe's view clearly differs from methodological naturalism and experimental philosophy in that, for her, philosophical problems are typically problems that cannot be fruitfully addressed by empirical means. The method of conceptual analysis, too, has limited applicability for her. After all, she holds that, in some important cases, there are principled reasons to think that we

---

³³ K. Scharp, *Replacing Truth* (Oxford: Oxford University Press, 2013), Section 0.1.5.
³⁴ *Ibid.*
³⁵ *Ibid.*

cannot give a "translation or analysis" of the crucial concepts. For the same reason, Anscombe must think that there are cases where no reductive explanation is possible. For we cannot find the translations or *a priori* entailments or metaphysical relations that would be needed for such an explanation. Note that Anscombe's descriptions of practices are not (attempted) reductive explanations. It is clear, e.g., that Anscombe does not think that we can give a reductive explanation of what a rule is—doing so would mean to escape Hume's Circle.[36]

Anscombe is also not a quietist. She believes that philosophy can yield interesting and surprising results. She clearly does not think, for example, that her claims that the normative force of rules, rights and promises depends on human practices or that "I" is not a referring expression are unsurprising or not substantive. Furthermore, she is not reluctant to put forward philosophical theses and theories.

Analytic pragmatism seems closer to Anscombe's way of doing philosophy than any of the other methods. Like Sellars and Brandom, Anscombe believes that a large part of the philosopher's task is to describe the use of terms that are crucial for a given philosophical topic (such as the terms "promise" or "I"). For the analytic pragmatists, however, most philosophically interesting concepts, on reflection, turn out to be "covertly metalinguistic". The role of these concepts is to "make explicit", describe, convey or express fundamental and universal features of our talk and thought. These concepts may, for example, allow us to express ideas regarding the conceptual framework that we are using. Or they "convey" the same ideas as overtly metalinguistic claims.[37] For Anscombe, on the other hand, the mere fact that there is no "translation or analysis" of a concept and that we must understand it through describing the practices in which it is used, does not imply that this concept has the role of expressing, conveying or making explicit something about these practices (although

---

[36] Anscombe's attitude towards "purely metaphysical reductions" that do not claim to give any explanation of, e.g., the concept of a right is complex. She has her own, very special, version of "nothing over and above"-theses. See G.E.M. Anscombe, "On Brute Facts", in *Ethics, Religion and Politics: Collected Philosophical Papers, Volume III* (Oxford: Blackwell, 1981).

[37] See R.B. Brandom, *From Empiricism to Expressivism: Brandom reads Sellars* (Cambridge, MA: Harvard University Press, 2014), Ch. 1 and 7, for a helpful discussion of this.

some of the concepts in which Anscombe is interested might be of this metalinguistic type).

The pattern we have described does hence not fit nicely into any of the six categories that Sharp helpfully distinguishes. We think that Anscombe's view deserves careful consideration and its own place on the map of current metaphilosophy.

3.3. Anscombe Values T-Philosophy

In Anscombe's writings, we can see a version of the conceptual turn (broadly construed) at work that does not treat philosophical problems as pseudo-problems, as resting on confusions that are particular to the philosopher or as problems that are in an important sense merely about thought and talk and not about the world.[38] In the papers we discussed, for example, Anscombe argues that rules, rights and promises depend for their existence on social practices, that there are no such things as Cartesian Egos or the like, and that perception has content. These are not just claims about the way we think or talk, nor are these claims responses to pseudo-problems or something that is obvious to everyone who is not in the grip of some confusion induced by philosophy. Thus, Anscombe must think that putting forward substantive and surprising philosophical theses about the world can be rational. (Naturally, reflecting on our conceptual abilities and practices can be a crucial step on the way to such a thesis.) This sets Anscombe's view apart from metaphilosophies like the one Paul Horwich attributes to Wittgenstein.[39]

Of course, Anscombe's way of doing philosophy is heavily influenced by Wittgenstein. In "The Reality of the Past", e.g., she says: "Everywhere in this paper I have imitated his [i.e. Wittgenstein's] ideas and methods of discussion."[40] And Anscombe, just like Wittgenstein, "is infuriatingly prone to take each case on its merits"[41] rather than to apply a general theory.

---

[38] For a defence of conceptual analysis against Timothy Williamson's criticism in *The Philosophy of Philosophy* (Oxford: Blackwell, 2007), that makes some related points, see M. Balcerak Jackson & B. Balcerak Jackson "Understanding and Philosophical Methodology", *Philosophical Studies*, 161 (2) 2012: 185–205.
[39] See P. Horwich, *Wittgenstein's Metaphilosophy* (Oxford: Oxford University Press, 2012).
[40] Anscombe, "The Reality of the Past", p. 114n.
[41] Teichmann, *The Philosophy of Elizabeth Anscombe*, p. 1.

However, she is equally influenced by the views of Aristotle, Aquinas, Hume and Frege—at least some of which Horwich would presumably classify as "T-philosophy". Anscombe does not share Horwich's conviction that "T-philosophy is indeed irrational".[42] Rather, her philosophy is an attempt to synthesize analytic philosophy with the ancient and medieval tradition.

4. Conclusion

We hope to have accomplished two things. First, we hope that our description of the pattern we identified in Anscombe's work helps in understanding that work. Seeing the pattern can help to identify the crucial claims of a given paper as well as Anscombe's general stance on what philosophical problems are and how to tackle them. Second, we hope to have shown that Anscombe's method—or at least the part we have described here—does not fit easily into any preconceived metaphilosophy. Perhaps we have even convinced the reader that Anscombe's implicit conception of philosophy is worth exploring and deserves a place in current debates in metaphilosophy.

---

[42] Horwich, *Wittgenstein's Metaphilosophy*, p. 66.

John Finnis

Anscombe on Human Immateriality, Spirituality and Dignity[1]

1

Elizabeth Anscombe's work was, and is, a paradigm of Christian intellectual life, carried out in the belief that since everything that can be inquired into is what it is by virtue of God's actuality, one's inquiries and every other element in one's intellectual life can be pursued with confidence that they will not contradict the faith and if successful will have brought one a little closer to understanding what is really so. Such is the free and diligent way in which she carried out the work that is widely and reasonably judged the twentieth century's outstanding English Catholic philosophical achievement. While the point is general, the fact and form of the paradigm are more apparent in some writings than in others. Here I consider some of her discussions of the nature of human beings as rational animals.[2]

---

[1] The following draws material from J. Finnis, *Intention and Identity: Collected Essays Volume II* (Oxford: OUP, 2011): "Introduction" and "Anscombe on Spirit and Intention" – the latter originating in a review article "Anscombe's Essays" published in *National Catholic Bioethics Quarterly*, 9, 2009.

[2] The sources of these, and of related, discussions are essays gathered in G.E.M. Anscombe, *Metaphysics and the Philosophy of Mind: Collected Philosophical Papers Volume II* (Oxford: Blackwell, 1981) hereafter *M&PM*; *Ethics, Religion and Politics: Collected Philosophical Papers Volume III* (Oxford: Blackwell, 1981) hereafter *ER&P*; and in the first three of the four volumes of her writings edited by Mary Geach and Luke Gormally in St Andrews Studies in Philosophy and Public Affairs: *Human Life, Action and Ethics: Essays by G.E.M. Anscombe* (Exeter: Imprint Academic, 2005) hereafter *HLA&E*; *Faith in a Hard*

2

The way we find we are, the kind of being we find ourselves to be in a world of diverse kinds of being, distinguishes us from every other kind of being of which we have experience, and is both utterly familiar yet deeply strange compared with simply physical realities. One aspect of this strangeness concerns the immaterial, the spiritual — the kind of reality which we find manifested in words, where material marks or sounds are freighted with meaning, which on the one hand cannot be communicated without materiality (signs, visible marks, audible sounds, etc.) but on the other hand can be detached from any particular material reality whatsoever and be precisely the same in meaning, be the same proposition or expression, constant through indefinitely many different material realities (different signs, sounds, marks) and sharable across vast distances of time and space.

In writing about the philosophy of Wittgenstein she quotes a place where he distinguishes between the order of thought and that of materiality. She writes:

> In *Zettel* 608–610 we have a passage where Wittgenstein says: "No supposition seems to me more natural than that there is no process in the brain correlated with associating or with thinking", and further on asks "Why should there not be a psychological regularity to which no physiological regularity corresponds?" He remarks "If this upsets our concepts of causality, then it is high time they were upset."[3]

Anscombe's own sinewy explorations of thinking clear the ground for getting Wittgenstein's point here. She shows, example after example, how far and how ordinarily it is the case that thinking something, or thinking of something, or associating something with something else, is not a matter of having a kind of experience. In "Events in the Mind", for example, she begins with the case of realizing one has not sent someone a Christmas card as intended, and argues

---

Ground: Essays on Religion, Philosophy and Ethics by G.E.M. Anscombe (Exeter: Imprint Academic, 2008) hereafter *FIHG*; *From Plato to Wittgenstein: Essays by G.E.M. Anscombe* (Exeter: Imprint Academic, 2011) hereafter *FPTW*; and *Logic, Truth and Meaning: Writings by G.E.M. Anscombe* (Exeter: Imprint Academic, 2015).

[3] Anscombe, "Ludwig Wittgenstein", in *FPTW*, p. 169.

> May it not be that there was absolutely nothing which occurred in one and meant "Oh heavens I haven't yet sent that card", but that one simply had the thought in a flash, which would be expressed by those words, and that is what one remembers: it's no use asking what it consisted in because it didn't consist in anything or have any vehicle, it was only the thought itself. Yet, deprived of a vehicle, of the slightest flicker which should signify it, the naked thought seems like a nothing when one tries to recall what it was — which in another sense one can say perfectly well: one simply gives the words which express it.[4]

And, she might have said, those could be any words, in any language, that express it. Later she writes of such cases:

> There is [a kind mental report] of thought *of*, or *that*, such and such [as in] "There's a snowy landscape", "I haven't sent the card I meant to send to John", or "If Kennedy pressed the button, then luckily someone interfered with the connections between Kennedy and the thermonuclear missiles". [What is reported] is an event, but not an experience; what we call its content is given by words which do not describe an inner experience (unless that is what the thought was about) but which have their primary application [not the secondary application the words can have when what is considered is an image or experience ("I see a snowy landscape in my mind's eye", "I had a sudden image of Kennedy pressing the button"].[5]

And the same is true of intending, which "after all needn't be a thought, for one can intend what one is not thinking of, as when one intends over a whole period to make a certain journey, but in fact seldom thinks of it, and when one even thinks of it, one's thoughts aren't to the effect that one is going to make that journey";[6] rather, they are thoughts about whether, for example, inexpensive transport will be available or the destination country will have granted a visa, and so forth. But always one could, if asked or if reflecting, say (and think!) what one intends — and thus tell just what one is up to, is doing. Not spying, or fleeing, or touring, but emigrating (and with the ultimate intention of raising a family there).

---

[4] "Events in the Mind", in *M&PM*, p. 59.
[5] Ibid., pp. 63 and 57.
[6] Ibid., p. 59.

3

Another instance of the strangeness of what is familiar as part of human nature concerns freedom of choice which can be expressed starkly in the passage from Aquinas which Anscombe doubtless had in mind to test, and support, in her explorations of causality and freedom,[7] the passage in *De Veritate* where he says (a) that to actively think about something requires an *intention* of one's will (a wanting and trying to think about it, to focus on the matter and order or set about (re)ordering or amplifying one's ideas about it), and (b) that such "movements of [human] will are not dependent on or connected with any natural cause".[8]

As to (a): though such an intending to think about X does not entail that there was either deliberation or choice (for one can and often does just spontaneously set about thinking something out), it does involve the freedom which Aquinas will starkly assert in (b), and which becomes freedom of choice whenever some alternative possibility, incompatible with thinking (or thinking about) such-and-such, comes to mind and seems attractive, so that one needs to choose whether or not to think about X. As to (b): Aquinas here asserts what Anscombe also argues for but Wittgenstein only suggests. None of these philosophers holds that our thinking has no natural causal and indeed physical (chemical, electrical, etc.) preconditions—a well-functioning brain—any more than any of them thinks that we can communicate without marks or sounds, which are brutely physical. They are pointing out, after searching reflections on the phenomena of thought (and of intention), that what is decisive about our thoughts (and intentions)—that they make sense, are relevant, are argumentatively sound, are true and so forth—simply transcends, escapes, surpasses the natural, material causality that we sum up as "physiological" and the like: the criteria of intelligibility, soundness and so forth are entirely

---

[7] See Anscombe's inaugural lecture in Cambridge, "Causality and Determination" and "Soft Determinism" both in *M&PM*, especially pp. 145–47 in the case of the former and at p. 172 of the latter where she writes "...the soft determinist ... does think freedom compatible with physical impossibility ... since, being a determinist, he thinks that everything except what actually happened was always impossible ... I am at liberty to say that I believe a 'can of freedom' which holds in face of physical impossibility is pure nonsense".

[8] *De Veritate* q.8 a.13c: "*motus autem voluntatis non habet dependentiam nec connexionem ad aliquam causam naturalem.*"

distinct from, and could not be improved by knowledge of, any natural, material causes.

The immaterial reality in play in one's meaning something, publicly or privately, is the reality we call mental or spiritual. The freedom from natural causality in free choices, when we make them, is only the most obvious manifestation of the difference in kind between the spiritual and what one might call the rest of creation, or the nature and natural causality with which natural sciences (including neurophysiology and empirical psychology) are concerned.

Less specialized than the meaning of "nature" that is in play in the natural sciences is the metaphysical sense of "nature" that is implicit in the epistemological axiom deployed by Aristotle and, more extensively, by Aquinas: a being's nature is what you understand by understanding its capacities, which you understand by understanding its activities, which you understand by understanding their objects (objectives). The axiom is epistemological because it sets out the order in which we come to know. In that order, nature comes last, because real knowledge of something's nature is the end of a process of inference. In the ontological order—that is, the structure of reality (being)—the order is the opposite: it is because something has the nature it has that it has the capacity to act in the way it does for the objects its activity has.

One of the implications of this axiom, as it bears on human free choices and intentions, is that we will not understand what kind of being human persons are unless we take with full seriousness the capacity for free choice, a capacity which we become aware of, intimately and securely, both in being aware of attractive alternative incompatible options (objects shaped up in deliberation) each fully available for our choosing, and in the choosing itself, whether experienced as a distinct event or identified only in retrospect. That awareness is awareness that nothing—not reasons, not internal forces, nor any external pressures—settled our choice except the choosing itself.

4

Engaging with an empiricist philosophical culture in which it was widely assumed that progress would be made in understanding human understanding by scrutinizing "I see a red patch before me", Anscombe's challenges to materialist, behaviourist and other reductivist misapprehension of reality deploy examples like someone's pointing to something's shape rather than its colour. The strategy has its efficacy, but spirit's forming up of the simply material and simply animal into the human is exemplified more extensively in the vastly more elaborate and refined ways of intending and meaning that are found in human conduct of the realistically complex kind which provides matter for dramatic and/or poetic (re)presentation. Both the simple and the complex are reminders of the heavy freight of meaning in the traditional tags: we are rational animals and each of us is, in Boethius's succinct definition, an individual substance of a rational nature.

For, as Aquinas says in his mature treatment of the phrase *individua substantia* in the Boethian definition of a person, there are individual substances of many kinds but if the substance is not merely organically developing, as animals do, but has the self-mastery that is entailed by being able to make free choices, choices made and carried out not by one's being acted upon but on one's own initiative and intention and responsibility, then we have that more special and perfect kind of substance that we call a person.[9] The full significance of this excellence of the person, compared with all that is sub-personal in the animal and organic realm, is only understood when account is taken of its manifestations in intentional action of every kind, including acts expressing irony, commitment, shame, hope, love, deception, fidelity and so forth.

This judgment must have guided the editors' decision to head up the essays in the first of the four posthumous collections of Anscombe's essays *Human Life, Action and Ethics* with seven papers under the heading "Human Life", and to open with three remarkable lectures given at the University of Navarre in Pamplona in 1979, 1985 and 1988. There could have been no better beginning than the first of these, given by Anscombe under the title "Analytical Philosophy and the Spirituality of Man", the great interest of which is only enhanced by the inclusion in the second volume, *Faith in a Hard Ground*, of a paper from two decades earlier, "The Immortality of the Soul", wrestling with much the same matters. With these four essays, one should also take "The Causation of Action", from *HLA&E*'s second section (Action and Practical Reason).

---

[9] *Summa Theologiae* Ia q.29 a.1c; cf. *Sent.* I d.25 q.1 a.1. On being master of one's own acts, and its strategic place in his ethical thought, see J. Finnis, *Aquinas: Moral, Political, and Legal Theory* (Oxford: OUP, 1998), p. 20.

All these five essays attack the delusion, called by Anscombe "Cartesian", that thinking and willing (say, intending) are to be taken to be events in an immaterial (spiritual) substance or medium: soul or spirit. Explicitly or implicitly, they all affirm the reality of the human soul and the spiritual nature of that human life, a spirituality that belongs to man's substance. They defend, that is, a "metaphysics of the spirituality of man's nature".[10] They do so with great resource: attentiveness alike to the history of philosophy and the contemporary physiology of movement, brain states, etc.; and a close-in and sinewy phenomenology, holding one closely to an awareness of what one's thinking and intending is really like, really is. But their point and thrust is always to instil and enforce an awareness, and some theoretical grasp, of just how radically different the immaterial and spiritual is from the material, including brain states, sensing and mental imaging and other kinds of imagining. Of just how strange—relative to cause and effect in natural events, and to all that we can picture—our everyday thinking and intending (say, pointing to something's shape as opposed to its colour) really is, when analysed philosophically.

The proto-treatment "Immortality of the Soul", never published by Anscombe, proposes that "the spirituality of the human soul is its capacity to get a conception of the eternal, and to be concerned with the eternal as an objective ...",[11] and notes that from a certain point of view this non-reliance [only] "on sensible things, physical probabilities, and purely conventional procedures", this "acting as if something unseen were there", is a kind of "insanity".[12] The later treatment ("Analytical Philosophy and the Spirituality of Man") holds that "the immateriality of the soul consists at bottom in the fact that you cannot specify a material character or configuration which is equivalent to truth".[13] Anscombe immediately adds, rightly:

> This thought is more like a chapter heading for many thoughts, the fruits of many investigations, than a conclusion of one. But it is already implicit in the consideration that the physical act of pointing, considered purely as a material event, is not even an act

---

[10] *HLA&E*, p. 6; likewise *FIHG*, p. 76.
[11] *HLA&E*, pp. 15-16.
[12] *FIHG*, p. 82.
[13] *HLA&E*, p. 15.

of pointing—it is just the fact that a finger, say, has a certain line. We may say that we cannot find a bodily act of pointing which in respect of its physical difference has to be an act of pointing to the shape as opposed to the colour. That is to say, in the sense in which pointing to this colour as opposed to that one must be pointing in a different direction. For the colours must lie in different places.

Now if that is so we can say that man *qua* body can't be described as pointing to the colour rather than the shape. For his act of pointing is certainly a bodily act; but it is not *qua* bodily act that it is determined as pointing to the colour. This does not mean that we have to postulate a different, *another* act of pointing by a *different* sort of substance, an immaterial one—that path to the concept of "spirit" which Wittgenstein implicity criticizes. But we can say that this bodily act is an act of a man *qua* spirit.[14]

In these and various other respects the later paper is better, as well as being in its own right a superb introduction to Anscombe's thought, to its relationship to Wittgenstein's and the ancients', and to the strangeness that is at the root of human dignity.

Still, the earlier essay provides a valuable clue to one of the several diverse springs of her thought, of her way of doing philosophy. The essay's one authorial footnote remarks that Christians, unless superstitious, do not believe that spirits (the angels) hear them, *nisi in Verbo*.[15] This is one of the relatively few references the editors have not identified, but it is certain that it alludes to Aquinas's argument in *De Veritate* q.8 a.13c that angels cannot know the secrets of our hearts, "unless one or another *cogitatio* is revealed to an angel in the Word [*nisi in Verbo ei reveletur*]". Nowhere else does Aquinas use the phrase she quoted; and this place in Aquinas, which Anscombe thus surely read with attention, is one which most strikingly asserts what I am calling this "strangeness" of commonplace human thinking and willing. For in the three sentences preceding the one she quotes from, Aquinas gives his reasons for taking angels to be naturally unable to read our thoughts; and the two key reasons are (1) that to think about something requires an *intentio* of one's will (so as to focus on the matter and one's ideas about it), and (2) that such "movements of [human] will have no dependence on or connection with any natural cause". True, one's acts of will, as Aquinas explains

---

[14] *Ibid.*, pp. 15-16.
[15] "The Immortality of the Soul", *FIHG*, p. 80.

here and in later writings,[16] are not independent of or unconnected with divine causality operating both as the creative and sustaining cause of everything and as the truly universal good that is the good to which one is responding when one['s will] responds to particular intelligible goods. But no chain of causality in the created world known to science and experience embraces or accounts for them.

In "Sin: Voluntariness and Sins of Omission" (a lecture she gave in 1989), Anscombe resumes her critique of the "quasi-Cartesian" "doctrine of an act of the will, which is willing".[17] She worries that Aquinas may hold this doctrine, but in the end is doubtful that he differs so widely from her about all this.[18] Be that as it may, this late lecture is one of the very rare occasions when she raises the question how far she agrees with or dissents from Aquinas. Overall, the influence of Aquinas on her thought was greater, I believe, than she made clear. In her introduction to *Faith in a Hard Ground*, Mary Geach says that Anscombe "devised a method, which she recommended to me, of mining Aquinas for helpful philosophical points" and "philosophically usable bits in the *Summa Theologiae*" by "considering to what Catholic doctrine her particular philosophical problem was relevant".[19] Still: Anscombe set her own philosophical problems for herself, and even when her conclusions approximate to Aquinas's fairly closely, as in *Intention* and the essays I have mentioned, her argumentation is her own. It's just that she thought of Aquinas as "a strikingly good philosopher",[20] from whom help is always on the cards albeit, like everything else in philosophizing as such, never guaranteed.[21]

---

[16] See *De Malo* q.16 a.8; *Summa Theologiae* Ia q.57 a.4; q.105 a.4; q.106 a.2; I–II q.9 a.6; *Summa Contra Gentiles* III. 88–91 (e.g. c.88 n.2: "No created substance can act on the will, or be a cause of our choice, except by acting as a suasive [*nisi per modum persuadentis*]").

[17] *FIHG*, p. 129.

[18] Ibid., pp. 137–38.

[19] *FIHG*, p. xiv.

[20] *FIGH*, p. 135.

[21] Much of Anscombe's philosophical effort is directed, at least implicitly, towards thinking through what is needed from philosophy in relation to faith, and the faith. In a 1975 address to seminarians and their teachers she said that "the only possible use of a learned clever man is as a *causa removens prohibens*. There are gross obstacles in the received opinion of my time and in its characteristic ways of thinking, and someone learned and clever may be able to

5

The bearing on human dignity and worth of Anscombe's position about the radical difference between, on the one hand, one's thinking and willing, and on the other one's sensing, feeling, imagining, digesting, etc. is not extensively articulated. It seems in a sense clear: to possess dignity is to be somehow raised above a common level, and the considerations she brings out so well do show how each human being, just as having the capacity for the thinking and willing that are quite above the brain states and other natural processes that are this spirituality's human substrate, is raised above the other animals and creatures of every kind of which we have experience. We have all the levels of reality they have, and much more. In a sense, infinitely more, as knowers and choosers. Yet, if we ask how this dignity is also a worth, a matter of intrinsic and generic value, we reach considerations that Anscombe, especially perhaps in her writings from the mid-1970s and after, was wont to call "mystical".[22]

In "Knowledge and Reverence for Human Life" she explores the ways in which knowing this worth is "connatural". As she says, this is not how St. Thomas uses "connatural"; rather, it is a scholastic application of the term, and one whose source she does not claim to know.[23] It denotes a kind of knowledge that "is not unavailable to those of us who are not virtuous but may be restrained by shame from misusing people we have the power to misuse[, but] is strong only in good people".[24] I heard her deliver that address in 1981 and thought then, as now, that this sort of taxonomizing of knowledge, while it has its truth, does little to

---

dissolve these" (*FIHG*, p. 18). For an example of such obstacle-clearing, one may take not only the explications of human spirituality but also her devastating critique of Hume's very influential arguments against the possibility of miracles and prophecies: "Hume and Miracles", in *FIHG*, pp. 40–48.

[22] In "Contraception and Chastity" she speaks of the mystical directly: "Sexual acts are not sacred acts. But the perception of the dishonor done to the body in treating them as the casual satisfaction of desire is certainly a mystical perception. I don't mean, in calling it a mystical perception, that it's out of the ordinary. It's as ordinary as the feeling for the respect due to a man's dead body: the knowledge that a dead body isn't something to be put out for the collectors of refuse to pick up. This, too, is mystical though it's as common as humanity" (*FIHG*, p. 187).

[23] See *HLA&E*, p. 60, and *FIHG*, p. 200.

[24] *HLA&E*, p. 66, and *FIHG*, p. 100.

convey the truth at issue, even when the categorizing is given the vigorous workout she does. She doesn't go in for it much.

"Mystical", though formally a category, and one taken from another context, has the advantage that it directs the mind to what I have called the strangeness of the spiritual, its radical difference from the material which nonetheless it forms and animates. This strangeness Anscombe also profitably calls wonderful. In doing so, she deliberately appropriates the prayer from the canon of the Tridentine mass: "*Deus, qui humanae substantiae dignitatem mirabiliter condidisti* ... [O God, who didst wonderfully create/establish the dignity of human substance/nature ...]."[25] In her most full-dress treatment of the issue, in "Murder and the Morality of Euthanasia" she links this dignity to both origin and end:

> But men, being spirit as well as flesh, are not the same as the other animals. Whatever blasphemes the spirit in man is evil, discouraging, at best trivializing, at worst doing dirt on life ... It is irreligious, in a sense in which the contrasting religious attitude — one of respect before the mystery of human life — is not necessarily connected only with some one particular religious system ... A religious attitude may be merely incipient ... Or it may be more developed, perceiving that men are made by God in God's likeness, to know and love God ... Such perception of what a human being is makes one perceive human death as awesome, human life as always to be treated with a respect which is a sign and acknowledgement of what it is for.[26]

6

Anscombe's profoundly and rightly influential book *Intention* came from a course of lectures given as a result of her stand, in June 1956, against Oxford University's conferral of an honorary degree on the man who ordered the massacres at Hiroshima and Nagasaki. But (in line with one of the theses or prescriptions in her most famous piece of writing, "Modern Moral Philosophy") that book rigorously eschews any concern with moral reasoning or with the question what bearing the fruits of her analysis of intention would or should have for ethical analysis or moral judgment or assessment. The book ascribes a descriptive and

---

[25] See *FIHG*, p. 197; and *HLA&E*, p. 72.
[26] *HLA&E*, pp. 269–70.

explanatory priority to the description(s) which behaviour has in the practical reasoning (the deliberations) by which the acting person shaped up the proposal he or she adopted by choosing to behave (act or forbear) in this way. This shaping of description(s) in practical reasoning and deliberation is not a matter of finding a description under which the behaviour one is determined to carry out will be acceptable to oneself or others. Rather, it is settled by what one considers a necessary or helpful means to achieving an objective (usually a nested set of objectives) that one considers desirable, in view of the factual context as one understands its bearing on both one's end(s) and the means that one judges serviceable for achieving such end(s). In summarizing her book's main thesis in this way, I use terminology (for example, "proposal", "adopt") which is not altogether hers. But her favourable albeit informal and oral response to an exposition and analysis of intention which I gave in her presence in 1990 served, in my mind, to confirm my opinion that her main thesis was, or was in line with, what I have just set out.

However, her essays' discussions of intention in an ethical context tend to depart somewhat from that account. Characteristic is what she says (c. 1978) in judging immoral ("simoniacal") the action of certain Catholic priests in Africa who have made it a condition of adult baptism that the convert first make a payment to the Church, their good motive or further intention in making this demand being to require the convert to "show his good disposition", that is, his willingness to support the Church financially. She writes:

> ...what determines what the intention is? Can you determine it by telling yourself and others "I am not doing this, I am doing that"? No, you can't: the facts of the case, the conditions and consequences of one's act are mostly enough to determine what intentional act you are performing, they often declare it very loud and clear, and you cannot make it not be so by a story you tell or by inviting people to perform some little semantic exercise and call something a different name from the name that belongs to it from the facts of the case.[27]

This passage offers two alternative candidate-determinants of the action-defining intention-in-the-act: (1) telling yourself something, performing a little semantic exercise, etc.; and (2) the conditions

---

[27] "Simony in Africa", in *FIHG*, pp. 242-43.

and consequences of your act, "the whole context that fixes and determines the further description of the kind of act you are performing".[28] But these alternatives omit what *Intention* had treated as decisive: your real practical reasoning, in which you identified the behaviour as a satisfactory means to the end(s) you were concerned to attain. Conditions, consequences and context are surely determinants as they figure in one's practical reasoning, one's deliberating towards choice (not to be confused with some story one tells oneself or others in order to escape or attract some moral characterization of the act).

Nor does it matter what words one uses in this reasoning. If, to take the case in hand, one judges that it would be good to make payment to the Church a condition of baptism, it doesn't matter whether one uses (thinks in terms of) the words "payment" or "condition" or their equivalent in any other language. Still less, of course, does it matter to the relevant description of what one is doing whether one knows the term "simony" or is aware that hereabouts there is a class of acts judged by the Church to be seriously wrong.

In criticizing Anscombe's ethics-oriented analysis here for overlooking the act-analysis (intention-analysis) employed in her non-ethical writings,[29] I am resuming a criticism I have made before, especially in relation to her essay "Action, Intention and

---

[28] *Ibid.*, p. 243.
[29] This distinction is not tight: in "Practical Inference" (*HLA&E*, pp. 109–47), mostly a revisiting in 1974 of *Intention*, Anscombe says by way of illustration: "The British ... wanted to destroy some German soldiers on a Dutch island ... and chose to accomplish this by bombing the dykes and drowning everybody." This she says is an instance of a decision "to kill everyone in a certain place in order to get the particular people one wants". But equally it may have been an instance of a decision to kill German soldiers by bombing the dykes, accepting the deaths of any Dutch civilians as a side effect, perhaps fairly, perhaps with vicious unfairness depending on the context and the planners' reasoning about its bearing on all affected. In her earlier (1956) account of this event, in "Mr Truman's Degree", she recounts it in a way somewhat more open to the second version, in which there simply is no intent to kill everyone as a means to killing some but "unscrupulousness in considering the possibilities" (in *ER&P*, p. 66). One can agree with her that such unscrupulousness in considering side effects can "turn it into murder", since "murder" extends beyond its central paradigm—killing with intent to kill—to secondary cases such as intent to seriously wound, or recklessness about the lethal side effects of one's acts (especially, but not necessarily, unlawful acts).

'Double Effect'".[30] But I do not dissent from her conclusion in relation to the clergy's well-motivated but wrongful demand in the African missions. And as Mary Geach remarks, the essay shows how far Anscombe was from being a party-line woman. One can add that it also shows that her interest in ethics was not simply apologetical, and like her essay on usury's injustice ("Philosophers and Economists: Two Philosopher's Objections to Usury") and her notable papers on promising and on political authority it[31] witnesses that her interest was in no way limited to the ethics of sex and of killing.

7

In the 1989 McGivney Lectures delivered in Washington DC on the general subject "Sin", Anscombe revisited in a remarkable way some of the prior themes. As her lectures end, she says that one of her purposes in giving them was "to heighten my awareness of the amazing character of some of the things that we believe",[32] a purpose in line, as I have said, with much of her work in pure philosophy, too. Her final reflections are on the possibility of living here and now in the presence, the constant consciousness, of God. But here, too, part of her purpose is to wean us away from imagining some mental experience, some Cartesian *cogitatio* within a "Cartesian consciousness".[33] No, it is a matter of keeping in mind that God sees and hears us, and that there are divine commandments. And this keeping in mind is no more, in turn, than this: that a truthful account by us of the ultimate reasons for what we are at any time doing would mention those facts about divine knowledge and will. A reasonable mind ought always to have this form of divine presence to it. She writes "The absence of it, which is all but universal in the human race, is what I call 'God's Exile'", to which she adds, disclosing an amazing depth in all that she had elsewhere written about human spirit:

> Exile from what exists, even in Hell, is impossible for God. The exile of which I have been trying to speak is not an exile from our

---

[30] For Anscombe's essay see *HLA&E*, pp. 207–26, and for my criticism "Intention and Side-Effects", in J. Finnis, *Intention and Identity*, pp. 189–93.
[31] "On Promising and its Justice", "Rules, Rights and Promises" and "On the Source of the Authority of the State" all in *ER&P*.
[32] *FIHG*, p. 155.
[33] *Ibid.*, p. 148.

physical or mental existence: that too is impossible. It is an exile from our spiritual existence ...[34]

---

[34] *Ibid.*, p. 149.

John Haldane

Anscombe and Geach on Mind and Soul

1. Introduction

Reflecting on his intellectual life and his relationship as a philosopher with Elizabeth Anscombe, Peter Geach observed:

> Although we have both followed a philosophical career, and have sometimes formally collaborated and often critically read one another's works, we think about different though overlapping topics, and in a noticeably different style; and either of us, when questioned about the thought of the other, will often not know the right answer. I am surprised that people find this surprising.[1]

Elizabeth Anscombe (1919–2001) and Peter Geach (1916–2013) met in Oxford in 1938 and married three years later on Boxing Day 1941 at Brompton Oratory in London. They retired from full time professorial positions in the 1980s: he from Leeds in 1981, she from Cambridge in 1986. Thereafter they continued to read papers and to publish for a decade or more. We may say, therefore, that they shared lives as productive philosophers for over half a century; they also occasionally referred explicitly to one another in print, mostly citing particular items. In part this essay addresses three biographical-cum-interpretative questions: to what extent did they work together? What themes emerge from any significant collaboration? Is their mutual influence evident in their individual writings? I am also concerned, however, with two philosophical issues: first, what is the nature of their resistance to the idea of a

---

[1] Peter Geach, "Intellectual Autobiography", in *Peter Geach: Philosophical Encounters*, ed. Harry A. Lewis (Dordrecht: Kluwer, 1991), p. 10.

surviving, subsistent, immaterial soul? Second, how might one respond to the objections they raise?

2. Collaboration and Mutual Influence

So far as "working together" might mean contributing to a joint project, which is what, I think, Geach had in mind in speaking of having "formally collaborated", the answer to the question "To what extent did they work together?" is "very little". It is worth mentioning at the outset, however, that in the four- to six-year period between their meeting in Oxford and marrying, and Anscombe later beginning to attend Wittgenstein's classes as a post-graduate in Cambridge first in 1941–1942 and then when he resumed lecturing in 1944, Geach acted as something of a philosophy "tutor" to her. In his "Philosophical Autobiography", quoted from above, he writes:

> Elizabeth had a lot of philosophical teaching from me. I could see that she was good at the subject, but her real development was to come only under the powerful stimulus of Wittgenstein's lectures and her personal conversations with him. Naturally she then moved away from my tutelage; I am afraid that I resented that, but I could recognize this feeling as base and irrational, and soon overcame it.[2]

Geach had graduated from Balliol with a First in *literae humaniores* in 1938 and been awarded a Gladstone Research Studentship (at Gladstone's Library at Hawarden in North Wales), for which he chose the topic of John McTaggart's idealist metaphysics. The subject was one about which he was already quite knowledgeable, having been directed to read McTaggart's *Some Dogmas of Religion* at about the age of twelve by his father George Geach, who had been a student with C.D. Broad and Wittgenstein at Trinity College, Cambridge, studying there with G.E. Moore, Bertrand Russell, John Neville Keynes and McTaggart himself.

George Geach had come back to England having been a professor of philosophy in the Indian Educational Service, but, being unable to secure a professorship in England, he devoted himself to teaching his son from Keynes's *Formal Logic* proceeding to *Principia Mathematica*. Then, while the younger Geach was still at school, he set the foundation for him to make a serious study of

---

[2] *Ibid.*, p. 11.

McTaggart's *The Nature of Existence*. Two points arising from this precocious background are relevant to his influence on Anscombe and may bear upon their most nearly joint academic project, which I will describe in detail in a moment. First, when they met and took up with one another, and during the period of her undergraduate studies also in *literae humaniores*, Geach was already well-read, publicly acknowledged to be exceptionally gifted and desirous of sharing the fruits of his studies. Second, his familiarity with and liking for McTaggart's spiritualist idealism, which maintained the reality of souls in loving communion with one another, made him unresponsive to the Cartesian problems of egocentrism and other minds; it also made him ripe for the idea, which he and Anscombe would later get from Wittgenstein, that participation in shared forms of life is necessary for human intellectual activity—and that on this account there is no question of doubting that others think, or indeed in many cases what they think, given that language manifests thought and that meaning is public.

Two books are attributed to Anscombe and Geach jointly. First, *Descartes Philosophical Writings*,[3] in which they translated and edited selected texts: the *Meditations*, most of the *Discourse on Method*, parts of the *Principles*, extracts from *Rules for the Direction of the Mind* and *Notes on a Certain Program*, and a few other items. Second, they co-authored *Three Philosophers*,[4] consisting of three chapters on Aristotle, Aquinas and Frege, respectively.

These two works are different in composition. The first was a collaborative effort in which they discussed translations, selections and a note to readers, though most of the work was done by Geach.[5] The volume carries an introduction by the historian and philosopher of modern science Alexander Koyre, which is celebratory of Descartes' work but makes no reference to the translation. Anscombe and Geach themselves present only a "Translators' Note", yet this is of some significance, for it explains a rendering decision that represents a particular interpretation of Descartes'

---

[3] G.E.M. Anscombe and P.T. Geach, *Descartes: Philosophical Writings* (Edinburgh: Thomas Nelson, 1954).
[4] G.E.M. Anscombe and P.T. Geach, *Three Philosophers* (Oxford: Blackwell, 1961).
[5] See Anthony Kenny, "Peter Thomas Geach (1916–2014)", *Biographical Memoirs of Fellows of the British Academy*, vol. 14 (London: British Academy, 2015), pp. 185–203, at p. 191.

account of the nature of mind — an interpretation that would feature prominently in later writings by each[6] and influence others in thinking about Cartesian philosophy of mind.[7]

Up to that point, and until the publication in 1985 of the Cambridge University Press two-volume edition of *The Philosophical Writings of Descartes* translated by John Cottingham, Robert Stoothoff and Dugald Murdoch, the standard English rendering of Descartes' texts was the Elizabeth Haldane and G.R.T. Ross translation, *The Philosophical Works of Descartes* (1911, also published by Cambridge), which does not introduce interpretative emphases into the translated text. Anscombe and Geach explain the significance of their translation decision as follows:

> The most important problem of a Descartes translation is the rendering of the verbs *cogitare* and *penser* and their derivatives. Since Locke, the traditional English renderings have been the verb *think* and the noun *thought*. We have decided to abandon this tradition, which seems to us to run the risk of seriously misrepresenting what Descartes says ... Descartes himself defines the words as applying not only to intellectual processes but also to acts of will, passions, mental images, and even sensations ... The words think and thought will sometimes do ... We have, however, often found it advisable to use more general terms, such as the noun and verb *experience* and the adjective *conscious*; we have fairly consistently used *conscious being* as a rendering of *res cogitans*.[8]

The point is evidently connected with the fact that Aristotle, his medieval followers and later scholastic-trained philosophers,

---

[6] See Anscombe, "Events in the Mind", in *The Collected Philosophical Papers of G.E.M. Anscombe*, vol. 2 (Oxford: Blackwell, 1981), pp. 21–36, dating from 1963 but first published in 1981 in *Metaphysics and the Philosophy of Mind*. See also Anscombe, "The First Person", in *Collected Philosophical Papers*, vol. 2, pp. 56–63, which was first published in 1975 in *Metaphysics and the Philosophy of Mind*. In this article, she attacks Descartes' argument for dualism. In a rare reference to the Descartes volume, Anscombe writes in footnote 1 of the latter essay that "*Principles of Philosophy*, I, LX contains Descartes' best statement [of his argument]" and then quotes the passage from her and Geach's edition of Descartes *Philosophical Writings*, p. 21. For Geach see *Mental Acts: Their Content and Their Objects* (London: Routledge & Kegan Paul, 1957), section 26.

[7] As indicative see Anthony Kenny, *Descartes, A Study of his Philosophy* (New York: Random House, 1968) and Saul Kripke, "The First Person", in *Philosophical Troubles, Collected Papers, Volume I* (New York: Oxford University Press, 2011), ch. 10.

[8] Anscombe and Geach, *Descartes: Philosophical Writings*, pp. xlvii–xlviii.

including Descartes' own Jesuit teachers at La Fleche, distinguished between sensory experience and thought, attributing the former to the sense powers and the latter to an intellectual power which, together with the will, comprises the rational mind. Descartes departs from this tradition by bundling all psychological states into a single broad category "mind" (*mens*) and in treating consciousness as being the criterion of inclusion within this. Anscombe and Geach do not include the *Second Set of Replies to the Meditations* where Descartes says as much but they do begin the selection from *Principia Philosophiae* with section nine, where (in their translation) he writes:

> By the term *conscious experience* (*cogitationis*) I understand everything that takes place within ourselves so that we are aware of it (*nobis consciis*), in so far as it is an object of our awareness (*conscientia*). And so not only acts of understanding, will and imagination, but even sensations, are here taken as experience (*cogitare*).[9]

It is worth emphasizing how innovative was Descartes' use of *cogitatio* or *pensée* to cover any kind of mental item. His contemporary readers initially supposed that he meant acts of judgment, and so objected that in characterizing human psychology in terms of these he was seemingly omitting much else. One such was le Père Mersenne to whom Descartes replies by writing, "You argue that if the nature of man is solely to think, then he has no will. I do not see that this follows; for willing, understanding, imagining, and sensing and so on are just different ways of thinking, and all belong to the soul".[10]

There is a further, and arguably more important, feature of their translation that Anscombe and Geach do not mention but which is also part of their interpretation of the distinctiveness of Descartes' position. It concerns the object of self-awareness as rendered through the first-person reflexive pronoun "I". In their translation of *Meditation* II which contains Descartes' famous argument that his conscious/thinking self (*ego ipse cogitans*) is distinct from his body, they italicize "I" (*I*) or put it into single inverted

---

[9] Ibid., p. 183.
[10] Descartes, "Letter to Mersenne End of May 1637", in *The Philosophical Writings of Descartes: Volume 3, The Correspondence*, trans. John Cottingham, Robert Stoothoff, Dugald Murdoch and Anthony Kenny (Cambridge: Cambridge University Press, 1991), p. 56.

commas ('I'). The first measure might be read simply as giving emphasis, but both are intended to capture a kind of usage that they are thereby attributing to Descartes. One might wonder whether this is a question-begging intrusion, for in the original text when he writes of wanting to know what it is of which he is conscious when he is aware that he exists, Descartes does not seem to mark out *ego* in any distinctive way ("*Novi me existere; quaero, quis sim ego, ille, quem novi*"). In fact, however, there is a peculiarity here, for he applies the demonstrative "that" (*ille*) to the first-person pronoun (*ego*) thereby putting the latter into the category of a generic term just as much would the use of a definite or indefinite article.

Since Anscombe and Geach provide no philosophical commentary and do not advert to the treatment of "I" in the prefatory note, my attribution of an interpretative purpose might seem conjectural. In fact, however, it became an important feature of their criticism of Descartes' argument for mind/body dualism that they read him as introducing in the *Meditations* a special use of "I" in the reporting of thoughts and utterances and as presenting an associated special mode of reflection. This diagnosis is a feature of Anscombe's famous essay "The First Person", in which she argues that Descartes' proof of the non-identity of himself with the human being involves a special indirect reflexive use of "myself" which is parasitic upon an understanding of a use of "I" that is presupposed in Descartes' self-addressed reflections.[11]

Anscombe holds that in the context of these reflections, which include doubts as to whether subjective experience presents any material existent, this use involves an illegitimate transposition of an ordinary reflexive indicator into the category of a referring expression, which, because of seeming immunity to error through misidentification, calls for a special kind of referent distinct from Descartes the man. She writes:

> [If the referent of "I" is not this body] nothing but a Cartesian Ego will serve ... Thus we discover that if "I" is a referring expression then Descartes was right about what the referent was.

Then later she writes:

---

[11] Anscombe, "The First Person".

> With that thought: 'The I was subject, not object, and hence invisible,' we have an example of language itself being as it were possessed of an imagination, forcing its image upon us.
>
> The dispute is self-perpetuating, endless, irresoluble, so long as we adhere to the initial assumption, made so far by all the parties to it: that "I" is a referring expression ... And this is the solution: "I" is neither a name nor another kind of expression whose logical role is to make reference, at all.[12]

Anscombe's conclusion about "I" not being a referring expression has been widely rejected and even treated as evidently absurd,[13] but it is important in evaluating it to take full account of the Cartesian context which provides the setting and to note that the use of "I" with which she was concerned was one taken to be such that it could not fail of reference. Part of the widespread dismissal of her case is also attributable, however, to her characteristically dense and non-linear style of argumentation. It is valuable, therefore, to compare her criticisms with the briefer, clearer and more engagingly presented reasoning to a similar conclusion given by Peter Geach in *Mental Acts* and again in "Reincarnation".[14] The first was published in 1957 (the same year as Anscombe published *Intention*), and the second in 1969 in *God and the Soul*, but, as the preface to the latter reports, *Mental Acts* borrowed material from an earlier version of "Reincarnation", so we may suppose that the relevant part was written quite close to the period of the Descartes translations. Here then is a passage from "Reincarnation" which anticipates the publication of Anscombe's "First Person" argumentation by twenty years:

> If I enunciate propositions containing the word "I" to hearers or readers, they will be given certain information, true or false, about the speaker or writer: they will be truly informed if and only if the corresponding proposition is true that they would enunciate using "Peter Geach" where I use "I" and making the requisite grammatical changes ...

---

[12] *Ibid.*, pp. 31–32.
[13] One salient consideration is that any inference in which "I" is treated referentially is valid—e.g. "I have a headache" entails "someone has a headache"; "neither I nor anyone else was present" entails "no one was present", and so on.
[14] See Geach, *Mental Acts*, section 26, especially pp. 118–20, and Geach, "Reincarnation", in *God and the Soul*, pp. 1–16, especially pp. 6–9.

> The only interpretation of "I" for which [empirical] first-person propositions would not be straightforwardly [confirmable] or refutable is a certain soliloquistic use of "I." By way of illustrating this, consider a Descartes brooding over his German stove and saying, "I'm getting into a frightful puzzle—but what then is this 'I' that is puzzled?" ...
> ... The use of "I" here is essentially soliloquistic; the idea is that each man who has mastered the use of "I" could in solitude use these lines of argument to convince himself.
> ... But what is it that is indubitable? What are the soliloquistic utterances "I am in horrible pain" and "I am frightfully puzzled" supposed to supply over and above the soliloquistic utterances "This pain is horrible" and "This is frightfully puzzling"? ...
> ... It appears to me that this use of "I" in soliloquy is a degenerate use, and there is no question of it referring to anything.[15]

What emerges from the Descartes translations and the writings that follow and implicitly refer back to it[16] is a shared view of Descartes' revolution: which, in effect, introduces what proved to be a compelling conception of the human person and of the primary tasks of philosophy—namely, relating the conscious immaterial self, epistemologically and ontologically, to non-mental reality. So far as evaluation of Descartes' philosophy is concerned, they might be described as holding that he was a genuinely creative but misdirected thinker (an opinion they also shared regarding David Hume). In particular, in their estimate, Descartes reoriented philosophical thinking about mind and knowledge by introducing a particular form of seemingly self-directed thought and by extending the notion of thought itself from a restricted range of intellectual operations to consciousness in general.

The second book bearing their names as authors—*Three Philosophers*—did not assign chapters to writers individually, and this might have led some to suppose they were co-authored. They were not. Anscombe wrote the Aristotle chapter and Geach those on Aquinas and Frege. This is clear enough from the prose styles

---

[15] *Ibid.*, pp. 6–7.
[16] Geach, "Reincarnation", p. 8, writes: "Was it, perhaps, by a Freudian self-betrayal that Descartes wrote in his private notebook '*lavartus prodeo*,' 'I come forward in a mask'?" Here he recalls the opening paragraph of the first selection in *Descartes: Philosophical Writings*, 3.

and preoccupations, but it is testified to by the fact that the Aristotle chapter evidently derives from Anscombe's 1952 Joint Session paper, "The Principle of Individuation",[17] while the Aquinas chapter reproduces elements from Geach's "Form and Existence",[18] and the Frege chapter reiterates points made in several of his *Philosophical Review* articles from the 1950s (later gathered in *Logic Matters*[19]).

In summary, these chapters argue (1) that the core of Aristotle's philosophy is his metaphysics, more particularly his theory of substance; (2) that Aquinas was wide-ranging, prudent and insightful, especially with regard to the nature of causation and cognition, with again metaphysics being the key to understanding his ideas; and (3) that Frege's theory of functions serves to illuminate both semantics and Aquinas's account of essence and existence. The last point is not presented in the Frege chapter but in the Aquinas one, while the Aristotle chapter refers us to that on Aquinas for a development of the idea proposed in the *De Anima* — namely, that cognition involves receiving the form of the object into the cognitive faculty as a determining structure: what in the thing was a substantial or accidental nature is in the sense or in the intellect a perceptual or conceptual structure.

While there is some acknowledgment of the presence of other chapters, there is no special effort to relate them. Here the two authors were pursuing their individual enthusiasms, and it is clear from later writings that in general either tact was exercised in not taking exception to points made by the other, or else it was only on later reflection that differences came to be acknowledged. One example may be mentioned which is also relevant to points made below. The theory of thought as sharing the same form (*in esse intentionale*) as its worldly correlate (*in esse naturale*) is expounded approvingly by Geach in "Form and Existence" and later defended in the course of replying to an essay by Anthony Kenny.[20] Anscombe, however, in a paper which does not refer to Geach entitled "Thought and the Existence of Objects" (of

---

[17] Reprinted in *From Parmenides to Wittgenstein: The Collected Philosophical Papers of G.E.M. Anscombe*, vol. 1 (Oxford: Blackwell, 1981) pp. 57-65.
[18] Geach, *God and the Soul*, pp. 42-64.
[19] Peter Geach, *Logic Matters* (Oxford: Blackwell, 1972).
[20] See Anthony Kenny, "Form, Existence and Essence", and Peter Geach's reply in *Peter Geach: Philosophical Encounters*, pp. 65-75 and pp. 256-57.

unknown date and only recently published) claimed to be able to make little of this idea,[21] and elsewhere, as will be seen, she seems close to actual criticism.

In that connection it should also be noted that she was a more spontaneous, less systematic and less literary writer than he. Both were highly creative, introducing a number of important ideas into contemporary philosophy, several of which are referred to by the expressions they gave them, such as, in Anscombe's case, "brute fact", "consequentialism", "non-observational knowledge" and "under a description", and in Geach's "Cambridge change", "intentional identity", "personal vs. impersonal reference" and "relative identity". But whereas Geach's work appears well-composed and well-stocked with philosophical, theological, historical and literary references, Anscombe's writings usually give the sense of starting afresh each time in response to some newly discovered, or freshly returned to, puzzle — not writing to a plan but setting down the movement of thought and only occasionally referring to contemporary philosophers, even more rarely quoting particular texts. These differences contribute to the common experience of his work as being a delight to read and of hers as inducing the sense of being dragged through a dense forest by a powerful solitary animal as it simultaneously evades predators and pursues prey. In the passage from his "Philosophical Autobiography" that heads this essay Geach writes: "we think about different though overlapping topics, and in a noticeably different style." I have said what part of that difference consists in, but there is something else, I suggest, that explains this: Geach had the thinking and writing manner of a literary don even when he was young; Anscombe had those of a spirited student even when she was old. His prose style is continuous with that of Bunyan, Johnson and Chesterton while hers is often Socratic, sometimes colloquial, and occasionally inclines to the satirical modes of Juvenal and Swift. It is tempting to add that hers also reflects the vocabulary and style of Wittgenstein as it appears in the *Philosophical Investigations*, but while her thought and mode of expression certainly were influenced by Wittgenstein, it also has to

---

[21] Anscombe, "Thought and the Existence of Objects", in *Logic, Truth and Meaning: Writings by G.E.M. Anscombe*, ed. Mary Geach and Luke Gormally (Exeter: Imprint Academic, 2015), pp. 198–205.

be noted that the translation of that work is by Anscombe, and no doubt something of her style influenced that of the published text.

Before proceeding to the next section, in which I consider what Anscombe and Geach singly have to say on their own accounts about the nature of mind and soul, I want to suggest that these early books are very significant in revealing something of their approach to philosophy and in shaping the concerns of their subsequent work.

First, there is the obvious fact of them engaging with historical figures—Aristotle, Aquinas, Descartes and Frege—but in ways that bring them into relation with contemporary philosophy, even though the latter is often not adverted to. Anscombe's first three papers in professional academic journals were "The Reality of the Past" (1950), "The Principle of Individuation" (1953) and "Aristotle and Sea Battle" (1956);[22] Geach's (other than logical/semantic pieces) were "Form and Existence" (1955), "Good and Evil" (1956) and "The Third Man Again" (1956);[23] Aristotle was drawn on directly in the first, second, third and fifth, Aquinas in the fourth, and Plato in the sixth. This engagement with the past is certainly not antiquarian, nor just an artefact of classical education. Rather, Anscombe and Geach responded to figures who appeared to them as great philosophers rather than to contemporaries who seemed, like themselves, gifted students and teachers of an academic discipline. Second, however, is the fact that they were engaged by large issues: metaphysics, thought, language and reality, human nature, and the debate between materialism and spiritualism (the latter in a non-occultist sense that will be clearer shortly). It is to that last theme that I now turn.

3. Geach on the Soul

Anscombe and Geach both made important contributions to philosophy of psychology: she through *Intention* (1957)[24] and

---

[22] The first is reprinted in *Metaphysics and the Philosophy of Mind: The Collected Philosophical Papers of G.E.M. Anscombe*, vol. 2 (Oxford: Blackwell, 1981), pp. 104–19, and the second and third in *From Parmenides to Wittgenstein: The Collected Philosophical Papers of G.E.M. Anscombe*, vol. 1 (Oxford: Blackwell, 1981), pp. 57–65 and pp. 44–55, respectively.

[23] Geach, "Good and Evil", *Analysis*, 17, 1956: 33–42; "The Third Man Again", *Philosophical Review*, 65, 1956: 72–82.

[24] G.E.M. Anscombe, *Intention* (Oxford: Blackwell, 1957).

subsequent writings on action and practical reasoning; he through *Mental Acts* (1957) and a number of essays related to the theme of his third and unpublished series of Stanton Lectures (entitled *Freedom and Prediction*).[25] Neither, however, gave a great deal of time to the "mind–body problem", and it is hard to construct definite general theories from their writings. Part of the explanation for this is their shared belief that the usual ways of formulating mind-body questions involve the kind of Cartesian distinctions and inferences they had come to think confused and fallacious. More positively, they subscribed to the Aristotelian view that the soul is the principle of life, organization and activity of the living human body, and that "mind" is not a *thing* (material or immaterial) but a set of capacities for thought of various kinds. Even so, they believed that the exercise of this capacity, while it might be expressed in bodily activity, is not itself a material process, and they thought that this conclusion could be argued for. I will consider some of those arguments shortly, but I want to anticipate their shared conjecture—held very firmly by Anscombe and somewhat less firmly by Geach—namely that little, if any, natural sense can be made of the idea of a subsistent immaterial soul. Again, they thought that this sceptical conclusion could be argued for, and I will also summarize those arguments before responding to them on behalf of the claim which they both knew that Aquinas, for whom they had great respect, advanced: that the existence of an immaterial subject follows from the fact of immaterial acts and that this subject is separable from the human body.

In *Mental Acts* Geach first argues against the view of Ryle that ascriptions of psychological events and activities are equivalent to semi-hypothetical statements about behaviour.[26] His objections include the observation that the attempt to distinguish between two individuals' different mental states exhaustively in terms of

---

[25] Geach proclaimed himself unsatisfied with what he had managed to produce, but parts of the series were drawn upon in published essays, such as that contributed to a volume on Anscombe; see Peter Geach, "Intention, Freedom and Predictability", in *Logic, Cause and Action: Essays in Honour of Elizabeth Anscombe*, ed. Roger Teichmann (Cambridge: Cambridge University Press, 2000), pp. 73-82.

[26] Both Geach and Anscombe take exception to Ryle's view and show errors in the attribution of similar views to Wittgenstein. For Geach see *Mental Acts*, pp. 2-4. For Anscombe, see "Analytical Philosophy and the Spirituality of Man", discussed below.

different behavioural dispositions gets things backwards. We explain differences in behaviour by reference in part, but ineliminably, to mental acts and not by hypothetical differences in the agents concerned. Furthermore, where two subjects did not differ in behaviour, it is intelligible to suppose that they may yet have been in different mental states without having any view regarding the truth of different counterfactuals about what each would have done if things that did not happen had occurred. On this basis, Geach maintains that at least some psychological ascriptions, those attributing mental acts and events, are categorical and not hypothetical in character.

That fact, however, would be compatible with the events themselves being physical, as in type or token versions of materialism, but Geach rejects this possibility by reference to aspects of thinking and to the character of descriptions of human thought, language and action. The latter argument (which is also to be found in passing in Anscombe[27]) is first given in "Faith", which is chapter two of *The Virtues*, where Geach discusses the question of how original sin might be inherited and observes:

> The modes of description needed for human intellectual activities, language and institutions are logically different from those that will serve to describe the facts and laws of sub-human nature. If so, then no logic can derive from the facts and laws of sub-human nature an explanation of human nature.

Later he continues,

> I cannot here develop the logical difference I have alluded to; Quine has anyhow done the work for me in *Word and Object* and other writings. He insists that there is no logical bridge from the propositions of natural science to the language involving indirect speech constructions that we naturally use to describe our own and our fellows' attitudes and meanings.[28]

The logical difference in question is between descriptions that are intensional and those that are not, in the former case (among other features) resisting substitution of co-extensive expressions *salva veritate*. "Edinburgh" and "The capital of Scotland" are co-

---

[27] See G.E.M. Anscombe, "On Wisdom", in *Faith in a Hard Ground*, pp. 258-66.
[28] Geach, *The Virtues* (Cambridge: Cambridge University Press, 1977), pp. 26-27.

designating such that "Edinburgh has a population of more than 250,000" is true if and only if "The capital of Scotland has a population of fewer than 250,000" is true; but "John believes that Edinburgh has a population of fewer than 250,000" may be true while "John believes that the capital of Scotland has a population of fewer than 250,000" may be false—likewise for *orationes obliquae* such as "John says that ..." etc.

While I am sympathetic to arguing from the intensionality of descriptions of human activity to the falsity of materialism,[29] this style of argument is open to two kinds of objections. First, that implied by Quine's strictures against "intensional idiom"— namely, that it is a *façon de parler* and should not be treated as factive. Second, that the logical non-derivability, or reducibility, of intensional descriptions and explanations to extensional ones is a linguistic or conceptual phenomenon and does not settle the question of the ontological character of thoughts, utterances and actions. More precisely, they could be physical even if certain ways of specifying them are non-scientific or otherwise do not imply their materiality.

This is not the occasion to engage those responses,[30] but in any case Geach has a more directly ontological argument against materialism. This is presented and in his essay "What Do We Think With?" and relevantly it draws upon a distinction made by Anscombe in her essay "On Brute Facts".[31] There Anscombe distinguished between levels of description illustrated by the fact that (1) in a certain context bringing vegetables to one's house might be (2) supplying foodstuffs, which given further contextual features might amount to (3) fulfilling a contract. She describes the relationship between the facts described in (1), (2) and (3) as one of "brute relativity", in which (1) is brute relative to (2) and (2) brute relative to (3). Geach adopts this logical analysis, re-terming it one

---

[29] For an extended argument in this vein see John Haldane, "Naturalism and the Problem of Intentionality", *Inquiry*, 32, 1989: 305-322, and "A Return to Form in the Philosophy of Mind", *Ratio*, 11, 1998: 253-277.

[30] See *ibid*.; Haldane, "Folk Psychology and the Explanation of Human Behaviour", *Proceedings of the Aristotelian Society*, 62, 1988: 223-254; and Barry Stroud, "Quine on Exile Acquiescence", in *Meaning, Understanding and Practice* (Oxford: Oxford University Press, 2000), pp. 151-69.

[31] *The Collected Philosophical Papers of G.E.M. Anscombe: Ethics, Religion, and Politics* (Oxford: Blackwell, 1981), pp. 22-25.

of "relative basicness". His argument against materialism is then based on the following premises:

I. Thinking is an activity.
II. Thinking is a basic activity (there is nothing else more basic the occurrence of which in a context constitutes thinking).
III. The activity of thinking does not have the kinds of time-relations that physical processes have.

Given the identity of indiscernibles or its contrapositive, which Geach following McTaggart termed "the diversity of dissimilars",[32] it follows from III that thinking is not a physical process. This is an interesting argument, and it is surprising that until recently it barely received any attention beyond mention in reviews of *God and the Soul* in which it was published.[33] Its first premise follows upon what Geach had argued in *Mental Acts* and is independently plausible. The third premise is the most complex in its grounds, and it could perhaps be accepted by a non-reductive token-physicalist who might distinguish relations between events *qua* physical and *qua* elements in phenomenal consciousness. It is, however, the second that a defender of physicalism is most likely to head for and about which Geach himself writes: "This, I think, is the point at which my argument should be most closely scrutinized. But so far as I can see, thinking is a basic activity."[34] His judgment might be further supported by reflecting on the hyper-intensionality of thought, though here I am not concerned to defend Geach's argument but instead to focus on its conclusion. He writes, "Materialism then is false but it does not follow that immaterialism is true". These contraries, as he conceives them, agree that a person thinks with a part of themselves; what they disagree over is whether that part is a material or an immaterial one. Regarding the latter thesis Geach writes:

---

[32] See Peter Geach, *Truth, Love and Immortality: An Introduction to McTaggart's Philosophy* (London: Hutchinson, 1979), p. 51.
[33] Recent discussion is more concerned with premise III considered not as contradicting materialism but as concerning the character of consciousness. See Matthew Soteriou, *The Mind's Construction: The Ontology of Mind and Mental Action* (Oxford: Oxford University Press, 2013), chapter 2, and Elijah Chudnoff, *Cognitive Phenomenology* (London: Routledge, 2015), pp. 90–99.
[34] Geach, *God and the Soul*, p. 37.

> It is a savage superstition to suppose that a man consists of two pieces, body and soul, which come apart at death; the superstition is not mended but rather aggravated by conceptual confusion, if the soul piece is supposed to be immaterial ... In truth a man is a sort of body, not a body plus an immaterial somewhat; for a man is an animal, and an animal is one kind of living body; and thinking is a vital activity of a man, not of any part of him, material or immaterial. The only tenable conception of the soul is the Aristotelian conception of the soul as the form, or actual organization, of the living body; and thus you may say that a man thinks with his soul, if you mean positively that thinking is a vital activity of a living human being, and negatively that thinking is not performed by any bodily organ.[35]

In light of this, and of remarks made in an ancestor of the time-relations argument in *Mental Acts* where there is no mention of an anti-materialist conclusion,[36] the paragraph immediately succeeding the one just quoted, as well as a later paragraph, may come as something of a surprise:

> In our present experience we encounter thought as an activity of organisms. But since thought is in principle not locatable in the physical time continuum, as the vegetative, and I think also the sensitive, activities of organism are, there is a logically open possibility that thought should occur independently, not as the activity of a living organism.[37]

Then later, he writes:

> And some continuing disembodied thought might have such connexion with the thoughts I have as a living man as to constitute my survival as a "separated soul." To be sure, such survival must sound a meager and unsatisfying thing; particularly if it is the case, as I should hold, that there is no question of sensations and warm feelings and mental images existing apart from a living organism. But I do not want the prospect to be anything but bleak; I am of the mind of Aquinas about the survival of "separated souls," when he says in his commentary on I Corinthians that my

---

[35] *Ibid.*, p. 38.
[36] He writes: "What I have just said about the 'loose' relation of judgements to physical time is a logical point about applying time-specifications in our discourse about judgements; it does not imply, e.g., that judgements are really performed in a super-physical realm ... and for judgements to be tied loosely to physical time is still for them to be tied" (Geach, *Mental Acts*, p. 106).
[37] *God and the Soul*, p. 38.

soul is not I, and if only my soul is saved then I am not saved and nor is any man.[38]

A fairly clear tension exists between the paragraph beginning, "It is a savage superstition to suppose that a man consists of two pieces, body and soul, which come apart at death", and that occurring on the facing page regarding "my survival as a 'separated soul'". The explanation of this, I suggest, is that Geach is indeed conflicted, trying to hold on with one hand to a Wittgensteinean view and with another to a Thomistic one.

4. Anscombe on the Soul

I will come to Aquinas's position in due course, but next I turn to consider Anscombe's discussions of associated issues. Here, additionally to items previously cited, four essays and an interview are relevant: (a) "The Immortality of the Soul" (1950s), (b) "Analytical Philosophy and the Spirituality of Man" (1979), (c) "The Causation of Action" (1983), (d) "Has Mankind One Soul?" (1985) and (e) "The Existence of the Soul" (1990s).[39]

In the third of these, Anscombe is concerned with rejecting (as she had done in *Intention* §§9–11) an approach to the nature and explanation of action according to which actions are events caused by reasons typically conceived of as belief/desire pairings. In "The Causation of Action", she presses the point that this way of thinking, conjoined with natural assumptions about the causation of bodily movement, leads to the identification of both the having and the mental expression of reasons with states of the brain. Against this, she argues that the content of beliefs is fixed externally:

> There can be no such brain-state as the kind of brain-state corresponding to such-and-such a belief in the sense of being a sufficient condition of it. "Why not? There are untold millions of possible states of the brain. So it may well be that among these is a set of states which all are, and which are the totality of, states of a brain whose owner for example believes that such-and-such." But even

---

[38] *Ibid.*, pp. 39–40.
[39] These are published as follows: (a) G.E.M. Anscombe, *Faith in a Hard Ground*, pp. 69–83; (b), (c) and (d) in *Human Life, Action and Ethics: Essays by G.E.M. Anscombe* (Exeter: Imprint Academic, 2006), pp. 1–16, 17–25 and 89–108, respectively; and (e) in *Great Thinkers on Great Questions*, ed. Roy Abraham Varghese (Oxford: Oneworld, 1998), pp. 52–56.

on that supposition the brain state is not a sufficient condition for the belief. Why not? Because the belief might be say a belief about banks, and a human being whose brain might get into that state might never have heard of a bank ... Nor is any other state of the person [a sufficient condition for the belief] ... we cannot ascribe a belief about the bank's opening hours to someone not living in a world of banks and clocks.[40]

This sort of argument is more familiar from the writings of Hilary Putnam, Tyler Burge and Donald Davidson, and Anscombe's presentation combines (or elides) considerations of object (banks) and concept ("bank") dependence, which Putnam and Burge tended to treat separately, as in their examples of "water" and "arthritis". The general idea, however, is clear enough: thoughts cannot be identified with brain states, since the character of the latter is fixed independently of questions of intentional content, which depends either conceptually or referentially upon aspects of the subject's environment. As with the Geach temporality proof, this is not the occasion to explore the cogency of this externalist, anti-materialist argument. But like the earlier argument concerning intensionality I am sympathetic to this type of proof, yet again there are lines of reply available to the materialist, one of which is to claim that all this shows is that content is not determined intra-cranially and that insofar as thoughts are world-dependent, they may be identified with brain-environment complexes.[41]

Elsewhere, Anscombe argues differently against materialism. In "The Immortality of the Soul", she reasons that in the case of actions that are explicit expressions of intellectual processes, such as working out a mathematical problem using pen and paper, "[while] a purely physical description of this procedure could be given ... that description would not characterize it as thinking or calculating".[42] At the same time, however, she rejects the idea that what is missing is a description of an internal immaterial activity: "that is not to say it is an act of an immaterial, or spiritual,

---

[40] Anscombe, "The Causation of Action", pp. 98–99.
[41] For further argumentation see John Haldane, "The State and Fate of Contemporary Philosophy of Mind", *American Philosophical Quarterly*, 37, 2000: 301–321. The line of reply I envisage above for the materialist may be countered by claiming that it confuses contingent causal and spatial relations with non-contingent intentional-constitutive ones.
[42] Anscombe, "The Immortality of the Soul", p. 69.

substance."[43] To the extent that she is willing to allow something to the idea that thinking is "immaterial", it is only in the negative sense that it is not a material activity. This echoes Geach's observation in "What Do We Think With?" quoted above, "materialism then is false but it does not follow that immaterialism [its contrary] is true", and like him she takes the contradictory of materialism to be anti-materialism.[44]

This negative conclusion is liable to prompt questions about what follows positively from the falsity of materialism. Anscombe takes up that issue in "Analytical Philosophy and the Spirituality of Man", which is an uncharacteristically expository essay, perhaps owing to it being the text of a lecture delivered to an audience in Spain that could not be assumed to be familiar with Anglophone philosophy of mind. I suspect, however, that she was also dissatisfied with the earlier essay's negative character; for a close reading of the two texts shows that she had it, or a strong memory of it, before her when writing the latter. Here her anti-materialist argument occurs in the context of expounding Wittgenstein (focussing on *Philosophical Investigations* Part I, 35 and 36) and placing his views in relation to a familiar three-way distinction between philosophies of mind: Cartesian dualism, identity-theory and reductive behaviourism. She writes:

> In describing the options that seem to the present day analytic philosopher to be open for consideration, I have left out Wittgenstein ... Wittgenstein and those who attempt to follow him closely deny that he is a behaviourist. To others the matter perhaps seems to be obscured by a sort of evasiveness: a failure to come out in the open and plump for any one of what seem to be all the alternatives. Does Wittgenstein, do Wittgensteinians, believe that mental events are material events? No. Do they believe they are events taking place in an immaterial substance? Certainly not. Then, if not behaviourism, what do they believe?[45]

---

[43] Ibid.
[44] The resemblance between conceptual elements of these two essays, the independent dating of which places them both in the late 1950s (close to the period of the Descartes translations), and the fact that Anscombe's "Immortality" was delivered to the Philosophical Enquiry Group that met at a Dominican venue in England (Spode House) of which Geach was also a member, suggests a degree of mutual influence in these writings, if not "formal collaboration".
[45] Anscombe, "Analytical Philosophy", p. 7.

Anscombe was familiar with the charge of evasiveness and with the suspicion that Wittgenstein and perhaps she also were behaviourists, be they of a non-reductive kind; for regarding mind she *was* a kind of Wittgensteinian,[46] and she was closer than Geach to Wittgenstein's own anti-immaterialism. Her argument against materialism begins with reflections on Wittgenstein's remarks about the practice of identifying or drawing attention to some object or feature. Imagine someone doing so and saying "look at this". Nothing in the physical orientation of the body, even including the direction of the finger, serves to determine the content of the thought, including its formal object (whether substance, shape, colour, texture, location, etc.). What makes it the case that a person had in mind the shape rather than the colour, say, is not something passing through consciousness but the context, including what was said and done before and what follows later. Anscombe is concerned to set aside various kinds of reductive interpretations of this account but has little to say about its precise ontological implications.

There are clear connections between this line of argument from ostension and that concerning the impossibility of reducing calculating to the physical process of making marks on a piece of paper. Again, though, the content of the non-materialist account of mind is spare. She writes:

> The immateriality of the soul consists at bottom of the fact that you cannot specify a material character or configuration which is equivalent to truth [or she might have said "to meaning"] …
>
> We can say that man *qua* body can't be described as pointing to the colour rather than the shape. For his act of pointing to the colour is certainly a bodily act; but it is not *qua* bodily act that it is determined as pointing to the colour. This does not mean that we have to postulate a different, *another* act of pointing by a *different sort* of substance, an immaterial one—that path to the concept of "spirit" which Wittgenstein implicitly criticizes. But we can say this bodily act is an act of man *qua* spirit.

---

[46] This essay is one of the few places where by implication she identifies herself as such. Anthony Kenny reports her as once saying to him, "I do not have a thought in my head that does not come from Wittgenstein". He rightly describes this as inaccurate, and in her later years she once took the opportunity to emphasize in conversation with me that her "greatest teacher" was Frege.

What does it do for us to say this? Is it an explanation? I mean an explanatory hypothesis? No. It might indeed in certain circumstances help to explain the concept of spirit.[47]

It is tempting to say that the view being presented is a kind of hylomorphism where the meaning or intentional content of an action stands to the physical movement (or lack of movement in the most obvious case of a refraining) as form to matter, and tempting to then generalize from this so to say that the relation between a minded agent and her body is that of a substance to its matter. Certainly, like Geach, Anscombe avows an Aristotelian conception of the soul. He writes:

> The only tenable conception of the soul is the Aristotelian conception of the soul as the form, or actual organization, of the living body.[48]

While she writes:

> There is a primary principle of the life of any kind of material thing ... This primary principle I call its soul ... The vegetative functions are performed in animal life too. But except for growth they are transposed to a new key. And similarly the remaining vegetative functions and the animal activities and powers are transposed in the life of man. For here there is something new: the intellective principle is the differentia of the human soul.[49]

There being something new does not in itself imply any supervening or emergent immateriality; after all, there is something new in the transition from the vegetative to the sensitive functions. Given the foregoing, however, we may grant that she credits to the human kind of life a specific form of non-materiality as indicated by the non-reducibility of calculating to making marks or of intending an object to extending one's finger. But even if the differentia of human life is reason (broadly conceived), Anscombe seems intent on denying that the subject of this is anything other than the living human being, which is a kind of body. She is insistent, and consistent, in resisting any reifying inclination to interpret the idea of an intellectual principle as an intellectual subject unto itself; and there is nothing like Geach's concession to the possibility of "disembodied thought; thought unconnected

---

[47] Anscombe, "Analytical Philosophy", pp. 15–16.
[48] Geach, "What Do We Think With?", p. 38.
[49] Anscombe, "Has Mankind one Soul?", pp. 18, 22.

with any living organism". She even writes in a way that might seem directed against the sort of thing that Geach had proposed. Immediately following the previously quoted sentence, he wrote, "And some continuing disembodied thought might have such connexion with the thoughts I have as a living man as to constitute my survival as a 'separated soul.' To be sure, such survival must sound a meagre and unsatisfying thing ... Even if Christians believe there are 'separate souls,' the Christian hope is the glorious resurrection of the body, not the survival of a 'separated soul'". Meanwhile, she wrote,

> There is no reason whatever for believing in a temporal immortality of the soul apart from the resurrection; above all there is no "natural immortality of the soul" that can be demonstrated by philosophy ... I take the Christian doctrine of immortality to be the doctrine of an unending human life, happy or unhappy, after the resurrection and not the doctrine of an immortal sort of substance, the soul, to which is appended the doctrine of the resurrection because a disembodied soul is not a complete man, though I know that in apologetics the matter is often presented like that.[50]

One might make the case that the issue is one of emphasis and cite in support of this that Anscombe seemingly allows the same possibility as Geach envisages when she writes elsewhere, "If the principle of rational human life in E.A. is a soul (which perhaps can survive E.A., perhaps again animate E.A.) that is not the reference of 'I.' Nor is it what I am. I am E.A. and shall exist only as long as E.A. exists".[51] Her "perhaps" may correspond to his concession introduced by the phrase "there is a logically open possibility". My sense, though, is that her scepticism or resistance was the stronger, and I offer a final piece of evidence in support of this assessment. Presented with the observation that Aquinas held that the spiritual, i.e. immaterial, nature of the human was grounds for affirming the possibility of it surviving death, she replied:

---

[50] Anscombe, "The Immortality of the Soul", p. 77.
[51] Anscombe, "The First Person", p. 35. Kripke points out that her use of her initials "E.A." to distinguish "I" from a genuine referring expression follows Wittgenstein's use of "L.W." in similar contexts and that in *Mental Acts* Geach does likewise, distinguishing "I" and "P.T.G."; see Kripke, "The First Person", p. 311.

> Well, he investigated it. It was for him a serious problem precisely because he believed the Aristotelian principle — the soul is the form of the body ... Probably he did [think this]. I would say to him it was a problem and it is not clear that he solved the problem. I don't think I know his writings well enough to say, but I would expect that he thought he had solved the problem. What I do note is that for him it was a problem and that is the right approach to this matter which should be a problem.[52]

Anscombe knew Aquinas's writings pretty well, and I think that here she is being charitable not wanting to say that Aquinas believed he had given a coherent account of how the form of the body may also be a subsistent that can survive the death of the body because she thought that if he had believed that, then he would be in error.

Geach wrote, "We think about different though overlapping topics, and in a noticeably different style; and either of us, when questioned about the thought of the other, will often not know the right answer". Here we have seen them thinking about closely aligned topics and in ways that suggest a fair degree of familiarity with what each had written. There are differences of style but also of emphasis and perhaps of substance. They both believed that materialism is false and argued against it, but Geach's arguments are more directly and obviously metaphysical in manner and implication. Both deny that human beings think with immaterial parts of themselves (their souls), but Anscombe also labours to distinguish sharply between immateriality and spirituality, not just with respect to substance but with respect to activities. For her the "spirituality" of the human being is not a matter of some immaterial ontological component but is shown most clearly in the human orientation towards value. Men are drawn towards truth, towards the good, and towards the eternal: not just as formal objects of speculative and practical thought but as ends (*fines*) of life, which not being naturally attainable stand as transcendental ends that might yet be given — by God, in the life of the world to come. That, however, for Anscombe and Geach, is the resurrected world.

---

[52] Anscombe, "The Existence of the Soul", pp. 53, 55.

5. Rejection of Materialism and Immaterialism

What then to make, philosophically, of their rejection of materialism and of immaterialism (save that in the sense in which the latter is equivalent to non-materialism). As regards the former, I have expressed appreciation of their arguments, and while acknowledging likely directions of reply, particularly on behalf of token physicalism, I think there are further grounds for rejecting both reductive and non-reductive materialism and that the envisaged lines of response can themselves be countered. One set of such grounds are those appealed to by Aquinas in his arguments for the immateriality of intellectual acts, which I will consider in a moment.

First, however, there is the issue of Anscombe's and Geach's scepticism regarding, or rejection of, the idea of an immaterial subject of thought such as might continue following the death and destruction of the human body. Geach's concerns are clearly set out in *Mental Acts* and in *God and the Soul*. They are of two sorts. First, that concepts of mental events, processes and dispositions, such as seeing, hearing, being in pain, being angry, having a belief or a desire and so on, apply primarily to human beings, and in some cases by extension to other animals; but that we can make no sense of applying them to an immaterial subject. The contents of these concepts are acquired and given through language, and the application of the associated terms is non-contingently linked to features of the natural environment, to conditions pertaining to that and our interactions with it, and to the behaviour of those whom such mental events, processes and dispositions are predicated.

Disconnecting the use of psychological terms and concepts from these physical and bodily ones drains away the sense of the former. The conditions necessary for ascribing "seeing" to a subject involve (a) the presumption of visual experiences, but also certain kinds of behaviour such as focussing and responding, (b) the visibility of the objects seen which is in turn connected with various physical features of subject and object, such as the conditions of the eyes, and (c) the causal links between these and perceived objects (and further enabling conditions). Remove (b) and (c) and it is no longer clear that one can coherently ascribe "seeing" or hold on to the idea of visual experiences.

The second set of concerns relates to the identity or continuity of a disembodied subject with a previously existing human being, and to the individuality of an immaterial entity. The issues are the familiar ones of personal identity and individuation. Sameness or difference in respect of characteristics do not constitute the individuality, continuity or identity of a substance but presuppose them. In the case of physical substances, being one and being the same involve quantities of designated matter (*materia signata quantitate*), but on the hypothesis under consideration there is no such matter.

Geach's overall assessment of these two kinds of considerations is that the first rules out as unintelligible the idea of sentient immateriality while the second implies the impossibility of what I will term "intrinsic" individuality and identity. Consistent with his reluctant concession to the idea of a separated soul, however, he introduces the possibility that while such an entity could not be a subject of experience, it might be identifiable extrinsically, or relationally, via its historic and prospective (via resurrection) connection to living human bodies. He writes:

> So the upshot of our whole argument is that unless a man comes to life again by resurrection, he does not live again after death. At best some mental remnant of him would survive death; and I should hold that the possibility even of such survival involves at least a permanent capacity for renewed human life.[53]

Returning to Anscombe, I find two arguments directed against the idea of an immaterial subject of human thought, both of which relate to the idea of substance. The first is explanatory and debunking of considerations taken to favour postulating an immaterial subject; the second challenges the coherence of the very idea. The former restates reasoning by Wittgenstein expounded by her in "Analytical Philosophy and the Spirituality of Man". Here it will be useful, therefore, to have these original Wittgensteinian passages before us:

> To repeat: in certain cases, especially when one points "to the shape" or "to the number" there are characteristic experiences and ways of pointing—"characteristic" because they recur often (not always) when shape or number are "meant." But do you also know of an experience characteristic of pointing to a piece in a game *as a piece in a game*? All the same one can say: "I mean that this piece is called the 'king,' not this particular bit of wood I am pointing to."

---

[53] Geach, "Immortality", p. 28.

> 36. And we do here what we do in a host of similar cases: because we cannot specify any one bodily action which we call pointing to the shape (as opposed, for example, to the colour), we say that a *spiritual* [mental, intellectual] activity corresponds to these words. Where our language suggests a body and there is none: there, we should like to say, is a *spirit*.[54]

In brief, the argument is that while an intentional action (expressive of, or manifesting, a mental state) cannot be identified with a physical movement or, importing the earlier externalist conclusion, with movement plus some associated brain states, it is a mistake to move from the non-materiality of action in this sense to the idea that it derives from a "spiritual" activity and thereby to conclude that the agent is some immaterial entity associated with the body. The explanation of what encourages this move involves the (misleading) grammar of ascription, and in showing that no such inferences are warranted, the analysis thereby also debunks the idea that non-materiality implies immateriality of activity and thereby of agent.

There are, I think, two main things to be said about this. First, while there may appear to be an ontological leap in moving from the *non-materiality* of an activity to the immateriality of the actor, it is not obvious that such a leap is involved in proceeding from the *immateriality* of an act to that of the agent. Of course, if by "an immaterial act" one simply *meant* "act of an immaterial agent", this would invite the charge of *petitio principii*. But this need not be definitional. Anscombe thinks that the considerations she endorses only tell against materialism but not in favour of immaterialism, but this assumes a distinction between the falsity of the former and the truth of the latter. If anti-materialism is simply a negative claim, then that may be the case, but only if "non-materialism" with respect to an activity can be given determinate content short of immaterialism regarding it. Put another way, if anti-materialism is non-materialism, and this is more than, say, a claim about incommensurable descriptions of one and the same thing, then it looks as if the least that Anscombe is committed to is property dualism — and that seems to amount to immaterialism regarding attributes, i.e. to the claim that there are real non-material features. Alternatively, if she would deny this,

---

[54] Ludwig Wittgenstein, *Philosophical Investigations*, trans. G.E.M. Anscombe (Oxford: Blackwell, 1953), part 1, pp. 35–36.

then it is hard to see that her non-materialism amounts to an ontological position rather than a form of conceptual pluralism.

At the outset of "Analytical Philosophy" Anscombe writes, "I can't help thinking that the Platonic substance, the Idea or Form, is of importance in the tradition whereby intellect came to be thought of as immaterial substance. For that which could grasp those immaterial beings, the Forms, had itself to be immaterial: the soul, Plato said is akin to the Forms".[55] Then in conclusion she returns to this idea now seeming to endorse it: "The pre-Cartesian, indeed originally Platonic conception is right ... The immateriality of the soul consists at bottom in the fact that you cannot specify a material character or configuration which is equivalent to truth."[56] It is unclear how close to equivalent Anscombe takes the affinity of thought to the forms and to truth to be, though one might suppose that the reasoning is that in both cases the objects of thought are immaterial and that whatever can "grasp" either must share that nature. But the conclusion mentioned in each case concerns not just *thinking* but the *thinker*, and this raises a question about how to reconcile Anscombe's sympathy to these Platonic views with her antipathy to the idea of an immaterial soul.

A cluster of object-act affinity arguments is to be found in Aquinas, most pertinently that which reasons from the nature of the contents of intellectual cognition, which are universals rather than particulars and hence exist apart from matter:[57] but he is also explicit in providing the further act-agent link. In his *Commentary on Aristotle's De Anima* he writes:

> The type of every act or operation is determined by an object. Every operation of the soul is the act of a potentiality, either active or passive ... The objects of the active capacities are related to these as the final terms attained by the activities; for in this case the object is what each of these activities effectively realises ... The objects in question are such things as sensible being and intelligible being with respect to the sensitive and intellectual faculties.

---

[55] Anscombe, "Analytical Philosophy", p. 4.
[56] *Ibid.*, p. 15.
[57] See *ST* I, q. 75, a. 5.

... So we proceed from objects to acts, from acts to faculties, and from faculties to essence.[58]

The character of the argument is clear enough: the cognitive objects of intellectual acts are immaterial forms; acts are specified by their objects, hence intellectual acts are themselves immaterial; but faculties are specified by acts, hence immaterial faculties; and the bearers of faculties are specified by the nature of the faculties, hence immaterial subjects.[59] Another way of approaching the same conclusion is by thinking about the attribute–bearer relation and the plausibility of a metaphysical compatibility principle to the effect that a fundamental attribute of kind K can only be possessed by a bearer of kind K. This would explain why an immaterial bearer could not have material properties and, by parity of application, why a material bearer could not have immaterial ones.

Such considerations, in conjunction with earlier argumentation, favour the idea that there is an immaterial subject of thought. But still standing against this is Anscombe's second argument, which challenges the coherence of an immaterial substance. Her claim is that the very notion is a delusive conception. The argument is somewhat obscure, but it is connected with the fact that substance concepts are introduced in answer to certain kinds of "what" questions—specifically, those that ask, "What is the nature of that (thing)?" and are answered by specifying what the nature or whatness is *quod quid est* (hence *quidditas*, "what-it-is-ness"). Her point, if I understand it, is that whereas such questions are in order so far as natural (material) substances are concerned, they lapse, or fail to find application, or make no sense in connection with, the idea of immaterial substance. Perhaps another way to put the point would be to say that there are no such natures as those of kinds of immaterial entities, no "whatnesses" of them.

This deserves an extensive discussion in place of which I can only offer a series of brief observations serving as headings for further enquiries.

---

[58] Aquinas, *Commentary on Aristotle's De Anima*, trans. Kenelm Foster O.P. and Silvester Humphries O.P. (London: Routledge & Kegan Paul, 1951), book 2, lectio 6, 208–209.

[59] For further discussion see John Haldane, "Kenny and Aquinas on the Metaphysics of Mind", in *Mind, Method and Morality*, ed. John Cottingham and Peter Hacker (Oxford: Oxford University Press, 2010); and Haldane, "Is the Soul the Form of the Body?", *American Catholic Philosophical Quarterly*, 87, 2013.

First, and following Aquinas, we might note that the nature of a thing may be specified from its powers, as indicated by its acts, as specified by their objects. Arguably such a procedure lies behind the formulation of concepts of natural substances, but in the case of the agent of intellectual activities it might be granted that since only its operations and effects are cognizable, notions of what-it-is are somewhat obscure.

Second and connected to this is the thought, again advanced by Aquinas, that the intellectual soul as agent of thought is not directly apprehended even in the consciousness of one whose soul it is but is only ever inferred.[60]

Third, such a scheme ought to be familiar from another case of a seemingly ineffable subject, namely God. In *Summa Theologae* I, q. 2, considering whether the existence of God can be demonstrated, Aquinas notes that inferences may proceed either *a priori* from cause to effect or else *a posteriori* from effect to cause, and he explains that where a cause is not directly known, it may yet be inferred from observed effects as a necessary condition of them. As in the case of a transcendent immaterial cause, so perhaps in that of an immanent immaterial one. Again in questions four and thirteen, and elsewhere (as in *De Potentia* VII, 5), Aquinas advances the idea of primary and secondary applications of concepts to creatures and to God, which one may take as an instance of a more general pattern of analogical predication that might be invoked in the case of the agent of intellectual acts. In the case of affirmative (*via analogica*) predications, he observes that because of the different mode of signification of terms applied to creatures and to God, "the affirmation of them is described as vague as being not altogether fitting". Again one may suppose something similar in the transfer of descriptions of the effects of mental activity, such as speech, to the source of it.

In relation to the terms "makes" and "made" as applied, ordinarily, to the work of cooks or sculptors whose making consists in modifying some pre-existing stuff and, extraordinarily, to the creative activity of God *ex nihilo*, Anscombe writes, "As soon as 'out of nothing' is introduced we are using 'makes' in a new way,

---

[60] The fact that there may be no introspective awareness of the subject of one's mental acts should be distinguished from whether there is reflexive knowledge of such acts. On the latter, see John Haldane, "(I am) Thinking", *Ratio*, 16, 2003: 124–139.

which paralyses critical questions based on the implications of the former way: but the fact that it is a new way is not itself a criticism; it would not be possible to erect a principle of never using words in a new way without paralysing language".[61]

This observation comes, however, just a few pages after writing about the delusiveness of the conception of an immaterial substance. My sense is that Anscombe was not willing to grant to talk of "spiritual substance" the same scope for innovation and development, and that the reason for this was less a convincing case against the possibility of a separable intellectual subject, the soul, than a conviction that any philosophical argument for such a thing had been scuppered by Wittgenstein and any religious concern for future life was fully met by the hope of bodily resurrection. Geach thought the latter too, but he was willing to concede more to the immaterialist possibility, not for want of appreciation of Wittgenstein's arguments against Cartesianism but in recognition that what Aquinas argued for was something sparer. I think a coherent possibility lies thereabouts and that the case for it begins with arguments against materialism,[62] including those advanced by Anscombe and Geach, but I am happy to accept that until much more work has been done an appropriate attitude might be one of agnosticism — certainly with regard to the whatness, if not so certainly to the thatness, of the human intellectual soul.

---

[61] Anscombe, "Immortality", p. 70.
[62] See John Haldane, "The Examined Death" and "Philosophy, Death and Immortality", in Haldane, *Reasonable Faith* (London: Routledge, 2010), chs. 11 and 12.

Guy Rohrbaugh

Anscombe, Zygotes and Coming-to-be[1]

There are hard questions surrounding what is called "the beginning of life", but "When did I begin?"' has never seemed like a particularly difficult one. If one is asking an ordinary biological question—when did it begin for this organism, this living thing, this creature?—then what other sensible answer could there be than "at conception"? The union of sperm and egg marks the beginning of a new living thing, one that is the subject of a perfectly continuous succession of life-processes from zygote to me here now. We are one, and what "we" are, and have always been, is a human being. It seems simple enough.

The question will seem much less simple if we are not careful to distinguish it from various pressing moral questions in the neighbourhood, as well as sundry quasi-moral questions about persons. So too, our having put the question in first-personal terms might be thought to muddy the waters. But a moment's reflection shows *our* question to be removed both from any broadly normative issues and from epistemological subtleties of the first person. We could equally have asked, "When did he begin?" and it would only have been a change of topic, and not a shift in the kind of question, to have asked, "When did it begin?" where "it" was a fish or an armadillo and not a man.

Let our question be thus distinguished from its neighbours and thereby do away with confused sources of resistance to the simple answer. Even so, there are those who say the simple answer is quite wrong and that a zygote, or subsequent early embryo, is not

---

[1] Previously published in *Noûs*, 48 (4) December 2014: 699–717.

a human being. Rather, we only have a human being on hand at some later point in the developmental story, leaving us to make some other kind of sense of what was there beforehand. The source of this view, one held by philosophers as otherwise far apart as Lynne Rudder Baker[2] and Peter van Inwagen,[3] is an argument given by Peter Geach and Elizabeth Anscombe concerning identical twins. All say that the possibility of twinning shows that what can twin, the early embryo, is not a human being. Of particular interest here is the promise of an argument that rides on purely logical or metaphysical considerations and circumvents the familiar, criterial disputes over the necessary conditions of being human.

Whether the simple view must give way before this argument depends on what, exactly, it is supposed to be. Geach mentions the issue only in passing,[4] but Anscombe develops the thought at greater length in two papers,[5] and it is her version of the reasoning that is usually credited. But you will not be surprised to learn either that Anscombe's text is difficult to make out or that her readers have come away with very different impressions of how her argument runs. I will argue that some versions of the argument, those due to Baker and A.A. Howsepian,[6] are obviously flawed, that van Inwagen's understanding, while more plausible as interpretation, is not yet compelling as argument, and that a very different understanding yields a more interesting, stronger argument against the simple view.

---

[2] L.R. Baker, *The Metaphysics of Everyday Life* (Cambridge: Cambridge University Press, 2007), pp. 72-73.
[3] P. van Inwagen, *Material Beings* (Ithaca, NY: Cornell University Press, 1990), pp. 140-57.
[4] P. Geach, *The Virtues* (Cambridge: Cambridge University Press, 1977), p. 30.
[5] G.E.M. Anscombe, "Embryos and Final Causes", in *Human Life, Action, and Ethics*, eds. M. Geach and L. Gormally (Exeter: Imprint Academic, 2005), pp. 45-58, and G.E.M. Anscombe, "Were You a Zygote?", in *Human Life, Action, and Ethics*, eds. M. Geach and L. Gormally (Exeter: Imprint Academic, 2005), pp. 39-44.
[6] A.A. Howsepian, "Four Queries Concerning the Metaphysics of Early Human Embryogenesis", *Journal of Medicine and Philosophy*, 33, 2008: 104-157.

1. Baker on Identity

Let us begin with Baker's understanding of the argument. Baker shares Anscombe's thought that the possibility of twinning shows an important difference between a zygote and me, that the zygote is not yet a human being and, thus, that conception does not mark the moment at which a human being comes to be.[7] For Baker, this is fundamentally a question about identity, whether the zygote is identical with the adult human being it becomes. She argues that it is not.

> If it is physically possible for a fertilized egg to produce twins (whether it actually does so or not), a fertilized egg cannot be *identical* to an organism. As long as it is possible to twin, a zygote is not a human anything, but a cell cluster.[8]

This is said to follow from the logic of identity, in particular its transitivity. Consider a zygote, Z, and twins, B and C, into which it might have split. Given that B and C are distinct, Z cannot be identical to both of them. Baker concludes that, "neither of the twins is identical to that fertilized egg, on pain of contradiction".[9] This is too quick, as the identity of Z with only one of B and C is perfectly consistent, but surely Baker sets aside these cases for the same reason others do. Given the symmetry in the way B and C come from Z, there seems nothing that could make it the case that it is one, rather than the other, that is Z. Anscombe herself points out that we know it is not a case in which one grows out of the other like a sprout, the sort of consideration that would give sense to its being one or the other. Baker goes on to conclude that since Z is neither of the human beings B and C, Z must not itself be a human being, even in the actual case in which it does not split.

The argument is invalid. One, more minor, problem is that the distinctness of Z from the human being it becomes does not, by itself, demonstrate that Z is not another, short-lived human being. This gap can probably be ignored. It would be a peculiar doctrine that every human life, in the ordinary way of counting these, is really a sequence of two human beings, one of which cannot ever

---

[7] Not the zygote, really, but the ensuing cell cluster, early embryo, or 'blastocyst', as the splitting involved in twinning is not a split in a single cell, but in a cluster of them.
[8] Baker, *The Metaphysics of Everyday Life*, p. 72.
[9] Ibid., p. 73.

mature. Without trying to identify this peculiarity more clearly, I will assume that showing Z to be distinct from any potentially adult human being is as good as showing that Z is no human being at all. There is, however, a second, more fatal invalidity in the argument.

Baker's reasoning is directed at the counterfactual situation in which Z splits into B and C, but her conclusion concerns the actual situation in which Z does not so-split. To see the problem clearly, let it be A into which Z actually develops without splitting. Baker is arguing that if it is possible for Z to have split, then Z is not A. The possibility of Z's splitting gives us the world of B and C, and she has argued that B and C are distinct from Z. But what matters here is the distinctness of A from Z and this does not follow from the distinctness of B and C from Z. It is perfectly consistent with the logic of identity to maintain that A is Z as long as one insists that A is also distinct from B and C. In pictures, the situation could be this:

$$w_1: Z \neq B \neq C$$
$$\| \quad \nparallel$$
$$w_0: Z = A$$

Nor is it immediately implausible to think that A is neither of B and C. One need only accept that one would not have survived had one's zygote split, for neither of the resulting twins would have been you. There is, again, nothing to make it the case that you would have been one rather than the other. Without excluding this scenario, the mere possibility of twinning fails to establish the distinctness of me and my zygote, and nothing about the logic of identity alone excludes it.

It might seem that we could reinstate the original argument by the addition of another premise, albeit one that Baker and Anscombe do not mention. Suppose that one insisted on the truth of the claim that I could have been a twin, and thus on the identity of A with one of B and C. Many will find this *prima facie* plausible, and there are ways of holding on to it even after reflection. One would simply have to deny that there need be some basis for my being one twin or the other, and there are haecceitist philosophical views of modality that would allow just this. Once we have identified A with, say, B, won't we then have to deny A's identity with Z on the basis of B's distinctness from Z?

$w_1: Z \neq B \neq C$
$ \| \|$
$w_0: Z \neq A$

Not just yet, for it appears that we have also given up the very grounds for insisting that Z would be neither of B and C which we had earlier granted Baker in passing. If A's being B rather than C needs no ground, then perhaps Z's being B rather than C needs no ground either. This new argument must contend with invalidating possibilities in which it is true that I could have been a twin but in which the other twin is treated like a sprout despite the lack of qualitative difference in the way it comes from Z.

$w_1: Z = B \neq C$ $\qquad w_1: Z = C \neq B$
$ \| \| \qquad \| \|$
$w_0: Z = A \qquad\quad w_0: Z = A$

Matters are now beyond easy adjudication. Perhaps one could insist that identity over time must have a basis in a way that cross-world identity need not; perhaps that would be difficult. What is clear is that uncontroversial theses about the logic of identity alone will not validate this argument for the distinctness of me and my zygote. While it is true that some basic considerations about identity must form the background of any discussion of twinning cases, it is reasonably clear that it is the special nature of living things that gives rise to Anscombe's puzzlement over the possibility of twinning and not the logic of identity in general.

2. Howsepian on Indeterminacy

We find a considerably different account of Anscombe's reasoning in a paper by A.A. Howsepian.[10] On Howsepian's reading, Anscombe denies that zygotes are human beings, not because they are distinct from the human beings they become, but because zygotes are indeterminate with regard to the number of human beings they are. This kind of indeterminacy, what we might call "count indeterminacy", is incompatible with being *a* human being.

> First, perhaps a human zygote is neither a *single* human thing nor a multiplicity of human things; rather, perhaps a human zygote is an *indeterminate* number of human beings. If this were the case,

---

[10] Howsepian, "Four Queries Concerning the Metaphysics of Early Human Embryogenesis", pp. 104–57.

there simply would be no numerical answer to the question, "How many human things is the human zygote?" Assuming that all human beings *are* essentially a determinate number of things, namely, one and only one human thing, no indeterminate human thing could possibly be a human being.[11]

Let us pass over the question-begging nature of this last assumption in the larger argument and instead consider the argument Howsepian finds for the count indeterminacy of the zygote in Anscombe's reasoning about the twins. Here, Howsepian stays closer than Baker to the letter of Anscombe's text, which lays out four possibilities, arguing for the fourth by rejecting the first three.

(1) Z is already both B and C
(2) Z is identical to only one of B and C, the other being like a sprout
(3) Z splits into, and is replaced by, B and C, in the style of amoeba
(4) Z is a whole substantial human entity, but not a human being

where Howsepian glosses this last phrase of Anscombe's as

[A]n entity that is human, but neither a single human nor a multiplicity of humans. In other words, according to Anscombe, a human zygote is an indeterminate number of humans.[12]

Howsepian's understanding of the argument is that if we reject all the "conceivable identity relations" among Z, B and C, then "what remains is that Z is neither a single human nor a multiplicity of humans", and thus that Z is an indeterminate number of human beings.[13]

What he seems to have in mind is this. There are four combinatorial possibilities for Z, B, C and "=", taking $B \neq C$ as given, viz.

$Z = B$	$Z = B$	$Z \neq B$	$Z \neq B$
$Z = C$	$Z \neq C$	$Z = C$	$Z \neq C$

---

[11] Ibid., p. 142.
[12] Ibid., p. 143. I ignore Howsepian's second gloss of the phrase, i.e. "By which she means that although prior to its first mitotic division materially Z had been B and $B1$, Z had not at that time also been B and $B1$ 'in form and existence'" (p. 143). Anscombe uses this language to describe the backward-looking relation between the zygote and the two gamete cells whence it came, not the forward-looking relation between Z and the ensuing twins.
[13] Ibid., p. 143.

He takes Anscombe's rejection of (1) to be the rejection of the first combination, her rejection of (2) to be the rejection of the second and third combinations and her rejection of (3) to be the rejection of the last combination. If none of the four combinatorial possibilities hold, then we are to conclude that Z is identical with no fixed number of humans and is, itself, an indeterminate number of humans.

This is all patent nonsense, both as free-standing argument and as interpretation. Most obviously, rejecting all four combinations does not get us some fifth possibility called "indeterminacy" but bare incoherence, for the combinations are exhaustive. If anything, an argument here should take the form, not of rejection, but of being forced to *accept* more than one of the combinations, so that we end up having to say Z is simultaneously both and only one of B and C. It is also ludicrous to suppose that the first combination, a logical impossibility, even needs ruling out or that that is what Anscombe's rejection of (1) is doing, especially given that the rejection is said to be on empirical grounds. What Anscombe has is mind with (1) is a situation in which Z already has B and C as proper parts. This is not a situation in which Z somehow manages to be identical with distinct things but is another case in which Z is strictly distinct from both B and C, though in a way one can well describe as "already being both B and C" as long as one does not take the verb for the "is" of identity. This is all made quite clear in Anscombe's subsequent discussion of a case in which we lack empirical grounds for rejecting (1), that of armadillos. Their fertilized ova always split into four embryos which can thus be understood as already "in" the fertilized ovum as parts.

Setting all this aside, it is clear enough what Howsepian is groping for in the case of the twins. What is indeterminate, Anscombe is supposing throughout, is how many human beings will eventually come from any one zygote. Whether it be one, two, more or zero is not, we think, fixed at the time when there is one, or only a few, cells. If it were fixed, then human zygotes would be more like armadillo zygotes. What will twin would already be two or more humans from the get-go, as in (1), and what does not twin could not twin and would already be one human being. Anscombe's worries would cease to apply. But seeing this, it is also clear enough what basic confusion drives Howsepian's interpretation: that the indeterminacy supposed must somehow be understood in terms of the zygote itself being an indeterminate number of humans. This is surely an optional, and inadvisable, way of thinking about the situation. It is not Anscombe's view, for she thinks the number of human beings Z is is determinately zero. Nor is it the simple view, on which Z is determinately one human being before the split. What is indeterminate, on both views, is whether there will be such a split.

Howsepian is not wrong to think determinacy issues are in the air here. A clear indication comes in Anscombe's later paper, which contains an abbreviated version of the same argument from twinning. Just before rehearsing it, she says,

> The argument for [the simple view] I think, the *serious* argument, is that the whole programme for the coming to be of a human being out of this one cell is there; indeed it is a programme in each case for a quite particular and unique human development.[14]

It is no accident that the twins are mentioned immediately afterwards, for the possibility of twins undermines this argument at its first step. The number of possible genetic combinations is surely astronomical and provides a practical guarantee that each union of gametes provides a unique genetic profile, but "arising from this union", simply fails as a sufficient condition for being identical to a particular individual precisely because the result of this union sometimes splits in two. Forgetting this, it is easy to think that the question, "Which individual is in the offing?" already has an answer just because the question "What will it be like?" does already have one. But even if twinning cases undermine this argument, it would be a mistake to read Anscombe as confining the case to this role. The ensuing argument is described as one that, "seems to operate against the thesis that here you already have a human being", and this is to think the twins are not merely an objection to an argument for the simple view, but a positive argument against it in its own right.[15]

3. Van Inwagen

The twins also make an appearance in Peter van Inwagen's rejection of the simple view in his *Material Beings*. Although the interpretation of Anscombe is not van Inwagen's concern — he cites only the brief passage from Geach — his way with the case offers a more viable understanding than what we have seen. We

---

[14] Anscombe, "Embryos and Final Causes", p. 52.
[15] *Ibid.*, p. 53.

need, however, to take account of the context that van Inwagen's own project imposes on the discussion. The topic of *Material Beings* is the search for the conditions under which composition occurs, and van Inwagen's famously distinctive answer to this question—that things compose an object when and only when their activity together constitutes a life—is already on the table when the simple view is broached.

Van Inwagen's primary argument against the simple view does not concern twinning, but instead how we are supposed to understand the mitotic transition from the zygote, a single cell, to the two-celled cluster which succeeds it. The usual choices are on offer. Either Z goes out of existence and is replaced by two new cells, or Z continues on alongside its newly minted replica, or Z continues on now composed of two (new) cells instead of one. He favours the first option, which has as a consequence that you are not identical with your long gone zygote. The second option is set aside because it would be "arbitrary and implausible" to take either of the cells present after division to be identical with the cell present beforehand. The third option, the only one on which you are identical with your zygote, is rejected because van Inwagen thinks there is no two-celled organism there for Z to be identical with. The two cells are there, for each is a living thing composed by the cooperative activity of its sub-cellular bits, but the two cells do not together compose another thing, a multi-cellular organism, because their joint activities do not amount to a life. They are merely stuck together, and being stuck together is not, in his view, a way of composing a new thing. At some point, there are enough cells in the cluster interacting in complex enough ways to constitute a life, and it is then that a multi-cellular organism appears on the scene. When this occurs is left as an open, empirical question.

Straight away, though, van Inwagen introduces a familiar constraint on answers to this question, that a developing embryo cannot yet be an organism if twinning is still possible. What follows is clearly intended as a *reductio* of the thought that such a mere cell cluster is an organism, let alone a human being.

> It seems to me to be most implausible to suppose that the developing embryo is yet an organism if it is still at a stage at which monozygotic twinning can occur. Suppose I was once a mass of adhering cells that was still capable of splitting into two masses, each of which would have developed into an organism that was genetically exactly like me. Suppose, then, that this had happened. What would have become of me? Only one answer is even

superficially coherent: I should have ceased to exist, and two new organisms would have been generated out of the cells that had composed me. I prefer to think that if an embryo is still capable of twinning, then it is a mere virtual object.[16]

Although the reasoning is compressed, van Inwagen is essentially saying that the supposition that the cell cluster amounts to an organism leads immediately to Anscombe's (3), where Z, a cluster of cells composing a genuine object, splits into and is replaced by B and C. But to admit Z as an object in the first place is to allow the question, "What becomes of Z?" and then to be forced to admit that Z would have ceased to exist. Van Inwagen rejects this description of the situation and concludes that there must be no Z in the first place.

Although van Inwagen's conclusion here differs from Anscombe's (4), that Z is "a whole substantial human entity" but "not a human being", his reasoning surely tracks Anscombe's in a way Baker's and Howsepian's do not. What is central to the reassessment of Z's status is the rejection of (3). But what is most remarkable about this passage is that no reason is offered; the error of (3) is treated as evident. In this, too, van Inwagen's dismissive attitude resembles Anscombe's, for she says,

> The third possibility, namely that one human splits into two, I am disposed to reject out of hand.[17]

which is precisely what van Inwagen does. Even so, van Inwagen's framing of the issue in terms of organic unity takes us further along by suggesting that the impossibility in question is not logical but somehow biological.

Now, one could make good sense of the proposed *reductio* if one held that there is a direct conceptual connection between cooperation sufficient to constitute a life and a unity too strong to admit of fission: if the cells in a cell cluster can come apart to form two new cell clusters with the same status, then they cannot possibly be cooperating in a manner sufficient to constitute a single life. The problem here is that, once stated baldly, the proposed connection seems groundless. Unless one is just stipulating a meaning for "alive" here, there is no *a priori* connection between the two notions and no contradiction in the thought of a living

---

[16] Van Inwagen, *Material Beings*, p. 154.
[17] Anscombe, "Were You a Zygote?", p. 41.

individual constituted by the cooperative activity of parts that would tolerate being split into two such individuals. Nor, of course, do we even need to imagine merely possible creatures to convince ourselves of this. Van Inwagen's own discussion of cell division already violates the supposed connection, as do a variety of earthworms, hydra and starfish at the multi-cellular level. The rejection of (3), even understood as merely biological, remains unexplained.

Whatever grounds van Inwagen's preference here, we already have reason to think that it can, at best, serve as a partial guide to Anscombe's. She does not share his assessment that the joint activity of the early embryonic cells do not amount to a genuine composite living object. Her papers are full of vital descriptions of, e.g., how the cells "marvelously work together in multiplying and becoming differentiated", and she goes so far as to say "that the zygote is *alive* no one can rationally doubt", where is it clear enough that "zygote" here refers not just to the single, initial cell, which van Inwagen would allow, but to the ensuing collection of cells as well.[18] Nor, even if this weren't true, does Anscombe share van Inwagen's bold thesis about the exclusivity of composition to the living. Either way, she is not in the business of denying existence to Z or undermining the description of the case as one in which a living thing splits into two. We are left with puzzles about why (3) is unacceptable and how taking Z to be less than a human avoids the trouble.

4. Is "Human Being" a Phase Sortal?

Perhaps another look at Anscombe's conclusion is in order. One virtue of the simple view is, of course, its simplicity. It is, in contrast, a conspicuous feature of Anscombe's discussion that no clear view of the zygote's status emerges. She tries on a good half dozen descriptions, none canonical. The zygote is, variously, "a carrier of human life", "human but not *a* human", "a whole substantial human entity", "a new beginning of human life" and "the *proxymate matter* of a human being". One aspect of these descriptions does seem clear enough. The zygote is being compared to other

---

[18] Anscombe, "Embryos and Final Causes", p. 54. Howsepian (A.A. Howsepian, "Who or What Are We?", *Review of Metaphysics*, 45 (3) 1992: 483–502) provides more empirically-minded evidence for vital relations amongst the cells.

living items or organic unities that are biologically human but are not themselves human beings, things like human cells, organs and blood. The zygote is not quite like these because the zygote is not a part of a human being. She counts it as "a substance", as she does not count the examples of parts, and so holds the zygote to be a whole, independent and autonomous living thing. Human sperm and eggs cells are said to have a similar status, whole living human things which are not parts of humans nor humans themselves. None of the three are members of our species, for "the way in which the human kind determines its way of developing is not a matter of a species to which it already belongs as a member".[19]

But the oneness of the zygote raises a question which sperm and egg do not. Is the zygote identical to the paradigmatic human being who later develops? Anscombe is less univocal than might be hoped.

> If a zygote was the beginning of a new human substance, and I (singly) was that zygote, then wasn't that zygote the beginning of *this* human being? Yes; but if there can be a human substance without its being a human, then either *this* individual human substance did not begin then or at one time *this* individual human substance did indeed exist but wasn't yet a human. So I wasn't yet *a* human? That seems correct.

Here, she appears to lean toward the view that Z is A when A does not split and this forces her view in a particular direction. If one and the same thing is not-F at some earlier time and later becomes F (where F is a predicate associated not just with criteria of application but of identity), then F cannot be a proper sortal but must be a phase sortal, one that only applies to an individual during a certain stage of its development or history. On this view, a zygote is not a human being in much the same way that it is not a fetus, adolescent or senior citizen. It has not reached the stage of development which these terms correctly describe. Surprisingly, Anscombe would not be pressing the metaphysical claim she is usually read as making—that something new comes to be after the possibility of twinning has passed—but a semantic one.

There are disadvantages to reading Anscombe in this way. Some concern the interest of her argument. If "human being" turns out to be a phase sortal, then there must be some other,

---

[19] Anscombe, "Were you a Zygote?", p. 43.

genuine sortal which applies throughout the existence of what is temporarily a human being, a sortal of which "human being" is a restriction. Let it be "human organism" which does this job.[20] One's immediate suspicion must be that "human organism" is now the genuine biological notion in play—the species notion—so that zygotes would turn out, contra Anscombe, to be members of the species after all, just at an earlier part of a human organism's life cycle. But now Anscombe's denial that "zygotes are human beings" would turn out not to address the "ordinary biological question" with which we began. Instead, Anscombe would have joined the list of those who suggest that counting as a human being requires something more than being a biological human. The promise of an argument which pre-empted familiar but vexed criterial disputes over what more is needed would escape us.

The phase sortal interpretation threatens not only the interest of her conclusion, but also the quality of the argument for it. It can now seem that her rejection of (3) rests on little more than the charge that saying "Twinning destroys a *human being*" is poor diction. If what she means by "human being" is "human organism which has achieved developmental stage D", then the claim that "Zygotes aren't human beings" was already true without resting on considerations about twinning and the whole thing might easily be denied or set to the side by someone who meant something else by "human being". Nor is there anything here to satisfy one like van Inwagen, who wants to resist saying that "I would have ceased to exist had my zygote undergone twinning", for that is just what would have happened on this view, though I would not yet have been a human being when death took me. And there is some indication that Anscombe shares this resistance, for she ends her initial rejection of (3) by asking, to my ear incredulously, "Has he—or it—simply ceased to exist, as we might say the parent amoeba ceases to exist on splitting?" It will be worth looking further into these papers for a different sort of interpretation.

---

[20] The terminology is Warren Quinn's. On this reading, Anscombe's view would be identical to the "stage view" explored by Quinn (W. Quinn, "Abortion: Identity and Loss", in *Morality and Action* (Cambridge: Cambridge University Press, 1993), pp. 20–51, at pp. 23–29).

5. Three Interpretive Principles

There is, I think, no getting clearer on what is going on here without taking account of two themes, the importance of which to Anscombe ought to be manifest to any reader of these papers. I will suggest that their combination with a third idea—an interpretive suggestion not so obviously grounded in the text—brings a different philosophical picture into view.

5.1. Organic Unity

One theme running through the papers is a clear concern for "a real problem about the unity of a multi-cellular organism", a concern she obviously shares with van Inwagen.[21] How is it that a collection of individual cells manages to constitute or compose a single living thing, one that is itself the subject of biological predicates for various states and activities properly attributable to the whole organism. Not any old collection of cells amounts to another living thing, nor, she indicates, is there any room here for the kind of conventionalism she associates with artefacts as opposed to some objective unity brought off in some cases and not others. The sort of unity in question is an active one, something that is literally brought about by the collaborative efforts of the things thereby unified and one that goes beyond mere social cooperation in a way that it is the heart of a certain philosophical puzzle to characterize.

Her concern for this question shows itself clearly in her discussion of amoebas. All would agree that the possibility of splitting in amoebas should be treated as having the logical profile of (3); what continues on could, instead, split into two and thereby cease to be. Type-(3) cases are thus possible, both logically and biologically. But Anscombe points out that we cannot simply assimilate the case of zygotes to that of amoebas, precisely because this issue of organic unity arises for multi-cellular organisms in a way it does not for amoebas. In the human case, what splits is a cluster of cells, and the results are also each a cluster of cells. Whether or not we can treat the human case as having this same

---

[21] Anscombe, "Embryos and Final Causes", p. 49. She would not, it is equally obvious, share his thought that this sort of unity is the key to answering his Special Composition Question or that such a question is even worth posing.

profile turns precisely on the questions at issue, viz. whether these cells in fact constitute a further individual and of what kind?

5.2. Kinds of Life, Kinds of Unity

The second theme animating her papers concerns the developmental processes by which animals come to be. Where it is possible to see only an undifferentiated and continuous succession of life-processes between zygote and adult, Anscombe holds that there is a qualitative difference between what is going on at various points in development, a difference in kind of activity and in kind of life lived. She contrasts "a life of growth and nutrition" at the "earliest stages" with "the animal life of movement and sensation" which comes later and requires such things as hearts, brains, sense organs and limbs, as well as more complex kinds of cooperation among such parts.[22] There is here no commitment to a sharp cut-off between these stages or a denial of empirical continuity at the level of parts, only an insistence that the phenomena at the level of the whole be understood as a transition between two different sorts of activity. Because that active unity of living things is a matter of what they do, Anscombe also thinks the early and later stages thus enjoy different sorts of unity and are, in some sense, different kinds of thing.

What most concerns Anscombe is not the imposition of these specifically neo-Aristotelian biological categories, but that we recognize the presence of a teleological relationship between these stages, however described.

> Cell differentiation is for the sake of the kind of structured, organized living thing that gets formed through it. The kind of living thing that gets formed as a result of multiplication and differentiation of cells determines the differentiation and organization of them to the extent that this happens in a normal manner.[23]

She is saying that the activities of the early embryo, those properly ascribed to it as a whole in virtue of the kind of unity it enjoys, can only be understood as what they are in terms of what they are for, specifically in terms of those later activities, the infrastructure for which this early growth provides. Or again, in a different register, her thought is that the sorts of chemical or low-level biological

---

[22] Anscombe, "Embryos and Final Causes", p. 57.
[23] Anscombe, "Were You a Zygote?", p. 43.

activity ascribed to the various parts here amount to, say, growth of the embryo only because they are understood in terms of their making possible a different sort of life, a different set of distinctly animal activities. It is these activities-to-come that fix the range of what counts as normal development or as development at all. In a different biological context, in a different kind of organism, these same processes might add up to a different sort of activity with different norms, or to nothing at all.[24]

Here we must observe that the status of genuine, non-reductive teleological explanations in biology is philosophically controversial. For some, the presence of robust teleological notions in the argument will be a deal breaker, but these worries would take us too far afield. I will simply acknowledge their presence and then take them for granted in an attempt to see what Anscombe is up to.

5.3. Particularity and Processes of Creation

As a way of bringing a different interpretation into view, I propose to fix on just one element in her descriptions of the zygote, the denial that it is a *particular* human being. This will have the advantage of making Anscombe out as concerned with a *logical* issue, and not simply that of identity and distinctness. The sense of "non-particularity" that will be at issue is most familiar in its uncontroversial role in characterizing creative desires and intentions. If I want to write an essay, bake a pie or build a tandoor in my backyard, the relevant desire is not directed at some particular individual of these kinds but only at a more or less specific *sort* of thing. One cannot profitably ask in these cases, "But *which* pie do you want to bake?" unless one is enquiring after the variety of pie to be baked, with "cherry" and "buttermilk" among possible answers. Insistence on identifying an individual here, unlike the case of buying or eating a pie, would be senseless, not least because "the" pie in question does not yet exist, indeed, might never exist.

In contrast, if I desire to own a Rolls-Royce, this may be either a matter of wanting a particular token automobile, Elvis's 1966 Silver Cloud, say, or merely a matter of wanting some Rolls or other, mere relief from Rolls-less-ness, as Quine might have had it.

---

[24] On this register and its presence in Anscombe, cf. M. Thompson, *Life and Action* (Cambridge, MA: Harvard University Press, 2008), Part I.

Reports of Rolls-wanting make available these two readings, non-specific and specific, where reports of creative desires have only one reading, the non-specific. The non-specific reading here, again, fails to support *which* questions, unless understood as addressing the sort of thing sought. And what goes for creative desires goes for creative intentions as well. My intention to bake you a pie is not an intention to bake some particular possible- but-not-yet-existent pie, but something of the kind *pie*. Obviously, the success of such intentions and the satisfaction of such desires demand a pie which is a particular pie, as all pies are, but the particular identity of the eventuating pie is no part of the content of these states, no part of what is wanted or aimed at.

What is more controversial is the extension of this same thesis to processes of coming-to-be: actually ongoing creative processes do not have a particular object as their subject any more than the correlative desires or intentions have one as their object.[25] When I am writing an essay, there is no particular essay that I am in the process of writing. I may be writing an essay of a very specific sort—it has a topic, outline, uses certain arguments, makes certain moves, has a certain title—but not a particular essay, one among the inventory of extant individual essays. And similarly for the pie. As I sift, mix, beat and bake, I am in the process of making pie, but no specific individual pie (or pies) is itself underway. Again, there is no denial that particular essays and pies are the outcome of successful efforts, only that the efforts themselves aim at or already effect the very individuals that (sometimes) result.

In support of the doctrine, we might notice that the *which-*questions which lacked application in prospect continue to lack application in development. If these processes fail or are abandoned prior to their successful completion, then there simply is no particular F the identification of which could serve as an answer to the question. This is not to say that the form of words in the question cannot be used to elicit useful information of some kind,

---

[25] A model for the view is already present when Prior (A. Prior, "Identifiable Individuals", in *Papers on Time and Tense*, 2nd ed., eds. Per Hasle, Peter Øhrstrøm, Torben Braüner and Jack Copeland (Oxford: Oxford University Press, 2003), pp. 81-92) suggests that possibilities of coming-to-be are not particular *de re* possibilities. The view receives direct expression, in the service of Aristotle interpretation, in Owen (G. Owen, "Particular and General", in *Logic, Science, and Dialectic* (Ithaca, NY: Cornell University Press, 1986), pp. 279-294), as do the considerations about whichness-questions.

for one can issue a variety of descriptions, even definite descriptions, of the *sort* of thing that is in the offing: I'm making the pie you ordered yesterday; I'm writing the essay commissioned for your anthology. But the application of these descriptions, and whether their definiteness is proper, remain contingent matters. Nothing might come of my efforts, and if I come up with two, "the" right one is whichever one I give you. At bottom, the truth of "I am making a pie", is compatible with the falling away of all answers to the "Which pie?" question, and in a way categorically unlike "I am eating/buying/slicing a pie", the truth of which license a demand for the identification of a particular pie. Nor, to be clear, is the phenomenon restricted to intentional action. The points hold equally of my claim that a storm is forming or that a certain protein is being synthesized.

The doctrine is compatible with a recognition of the fact that, at some point, we do have a particular, but undercooked, pie in the oven, a first draft on the computer. There is clearly a continuum of cases with regard to the question, "To what degree is an unfinished F an F?" If I am digging an escape tunnel or proving a theorem, then "unfinished" is surely an alienating adjective. But if I am just digging a hole in the ground or raking together a pile of leaves, then I have a hole from the very first shovelful of dirt, a pile from the first stroke of the rake. Most cases are probably between these extremes.[26] I have to dig a while in order to dig a grave, but at some point what I have is a shallow one and not just a hole, even if I keep digging or ought to. Before that point, no grave has been dug nor is any particular grave or other underway. It will also be agreed on all hands that these transition points are often imprecise, and indeed may not be susceptible of further, useful precisification. What is important is the thought that, prior to these points, there is no particular F that is coming to be even if it is already true that an F is coming to be. The thought is opposed both to the claim that (i) a particular individual is already existent and is the subject of what is really a process of perfection, and to the weaker claim that (ii) a particular not-yet-existent individual is the object, or target, of the process.

---

[26] These examples parallel a useful discussion in A. Galton, "On the Process of Coming into Existence", *The Monist*, 89 (3) 2006: 294–312.

6. Anscombe's Picture

While there is, I want to grant, little direct textual evidence that this last view is at work in Anscombe's thinking, taking it on board provides a natural understanding of her attempts to describe something which is human but not *a* human and the role of the twins in her thinking. Understood in this fashion, her conclusion could be better put by saying that when we have a zygote, it is true that a human being is coming to be, but false that there is any particular human being that already exists or is on the way.[27] We do, of course, have an empirically determinate instance of the kind "zygote", a particular one even, but this is held not to be a phase of some longer lived human organism but only that which makes it true to say that a human being is then coming to be, that a human-being-making-process is underway. While this understanding would force Anscombe to retract her tentative identification of Z and A, it would also square better with her denial that the zygote is a member of our species but is, instead, a sort of intermezzo entity like sperm or egg, distinct from what is to come. It would also allow her to join van Inwagen in denying that twinning would have killed me had my zygote split.

The possibility of twining is then supposed to demonstrate the veracity of this picture because it shows the inapplicability of *which*-questions. While twinning is still a possibility for the zygote, there seems to be no matter of fact about which human being, if any, will eventuate or is now eventuating. If no split occurs, we will be in a position to say that A came to be. If the zygote splits, we will be able to say that B and C came to be, each presumably distinct from A. If the process fails altogether, as in a case Geach mentions of development into a lump of tissue or "mole", no human being ever came to be.[28] At this early stage, the question, "Which human being is now coming to be?" appears to lack a determinate answer, but this in no way undermines the truth of, "A human being is coming to be", for this claim only reports the existence of a human-being-making process, that embodied in the zygote's activities.

---

[27] Here it is crucial to appreciate the imperfective aspect of these predications, for what is being suggested is an instance of the so-called "imperfective paradox" and an affirmation of the idea that an intensional context accompanies a verb of creation.
[28] Geach, *The Virtues*, p. 30.

I think it must be granted that this is an appealing, and widely overlooked, alternative picture of the beginnings of life. It nicely handles both the given facts of biological continuity and the possibility of twinning, while also acknowledging, at a metaphysical level, the tentativeness and contingency surrounding these earliest stages. Furthermore, it does so by assimilating the case to what is said to be a widespread metaphysical phenomenon which we have good, independent reason to recognize.

Even so, we are still a good bit short of being able to say the picture is compulsory and not just because one might reject the wider metaphysics of becoming on offer. Even within this framework, there is a straightforward way in which the simple view might be consistently couched. Recall that we have allowed that there are some sortals for which an unfinished F itself counts as an F, and further that there are some, those like "hole in the ground", which apply from the very beginning of a creation process. The proponent of the simple view should maintain that "human being" is one of those latter, those for which "unfinished" is never an alienating adjective and that we have a particular human being on hand as soon as the process of development is underway, i.e. at conception. Processes of development that transpire in the womb would not count as processes in which a human being is coming to be, but instead as processes of finishing or perfecting what is *already* a human being. Alternatively, all this could be said of the "human organism" with "human being" again treated as a phase sortal. Either returns us to a view that accepts the possibility of (3) and the lethal nature of twinning. A novel metaphysics of becoming will be beside the point.

It is here that Anscombe's other themes become relevant to her reasoning. Let us begin by asking what it is about a sortal like "hole" or "pile" that permits it to get a grip so immediately in the process of digging or raking. Presumably, it is a matter of the kind of unity such things possess, a unity that is easily achieved because it is a simple matter of spatial continuity. Rake a couple of leaves together and, voilà, you immediately have a pile. So too, these unities tolerate splitting into things of the same kind because such splitting requires only spatial division and results in two unities of the same sort. If the unity of a zygotic cell cluster were like this, then the simple view would be home and dry. But the unity of a living thing, even one like the zygote, is not like this. There is the matter of cooperation of the right kinds between the parts. One might even wonder, as Anscombe and van Inwagen do, whether the initial single cell could itself count as such a further unity. If cooperation requires at least two, then there is an extra difficulty about the first cell's being a human being. Even so, Anscombe allows, as van Inwagen implausibly does not, that by the time we have a divisible cluster on our hands we also have cooperation sufficient for some kind of living organic unity.

But we have also to take account of her second theme, the teleological relations between what the zygote is and is doing and that for the sake of which it is doing these things. The growth of a zygote is not like the growth of a cell culture or a cancer, and what makes the repeated division and differentiation of cells a case of the former and not the latter is the goal-directed character and context of the former. In its growth, a zygote is laying the foundations for a being with a different sort of life and unity, that of an animal. What matters crucially here, for the sake of the argument, is the nature of the object of these early goals. This is not, of course, a matter of any psychological, intentional or representation states possessed by the zygote, but only "garden variety" biological teleology correctly attributable—we are assuming— from the outside. On the one hand, Anscombe wants to hold that "what is governing here is the principle of unity of a new and coming life", and that it is a teleology of becoming.[29] On the other, the simple view will maintain that these things are done for the sake of what it already is, i.e. for its own sake, and that the teleology is that of perfection. What's to decide this question?

What should jump out at us, given our previous discussion, is that the two pictures differ precisely in the specificity of the goals attributed to the zygote. On Anscombe's picture, the kind of process underway isn't aimed at any particular instance of animal life but only at the production of *an* animal. The goal is non-specific. In contrast, the perfective goal attributed by the simple view is specific in nature. The point of Z's activities is Z's own completion and perfection. This difference, in turn, induces a difference in their respective accounts of twinning. The goal Anscombe would attribute to the zygote is "splittable", i.e. when Z splits in to B and C, they inherit Z's non-specific goal unchanged in content. Each "acts" for the sake of *an* animal but no particular one. Twinning would thus involve, not just a physical division, but a division in goals as well. In contrast, the specific goal of perfection is

---

[29] Anscombe, "Embryos and Final Causes", p. 57.

unsplittable. Where Z activities are for Z's sake, B and C's activities are for their respective sakes and the contents of their goals must be understood as having changed.[30]

What would complete the argument is a demonstration of the claim that the goals do not, in this sense, change in twinning. If B and C inherit Z's goal, then it cannot be a specific, Z-directed goal of perfection, but only a non-specific goal like that of "making *an animal*" which Anscombe's picture attributes. Let us examine the prospects. It might seem hard to see any basis for attributing such a change. The cells in B, none the wiser, continue to do just what they were doing when they were the left half of Z. This thought, however, concerns the activities of individual cells and not the activity of the wholes which are what matter. In the potentially parallel case of amoebas, we might say just the same of the various sub-cellular bits. Before division, the activities of the "left-hand" bits contribute to the specific, self-directed goals of one amoeba; after division, they contribute to the new goals of another. The splitting of amoebas is a Type-(3) case and clearly involves a change in specific goals. As long as these two cases share a profile, no demonstration will be forthcoming.[31]

7. Substantial Life

Anscombe clearly holds these cases to be relevantly different, but understanding why is the most challenging aspect of these papers. I believe she would say that the difference turns on the fact that splitting in amoebas is a genuine case of reproduction while splitting in zygotes is something fundamentally different. Let us begin with a reminder of some concrete differences between the cases. Zygotes enjoy a multi-cellular unity where amoebas do not. These cellular clusters are largely homogeneous during the period in which twinning is possible. A little too much differentiation, that present by about the thirteenth day, produces only conjoined twins. More than that, two days later, prevents it altogether. In contrast, amoebas have much more differentiated internal structure. For amoebas, splitting is only the final stage in a longer,

---

[30] This is concealed by thinking of the goal as one of "self-perfection", for all three share that goal, but what self-perfection comes to in each case is a distinct, specific and unsplittable goal.

[31] Thanks are due to an anonymous referee for raising this and several other helpful points.

more complex process, one starring the earlier mitotic doubling and division of the genetic material in the nucleus. One cannot simply saw an amoeba in two and get two more of them, but something like this is true of zygotes. Indeed, Anscombe remarks that, "[h]ere, the division *is* like the division of a lump of clay in two".[32]

But, perhaps surprisingly, what Anscombe says is divided here is not the material, as in the case of the clay, nor the cluster of cells, as you might expect, but "*the life*". It is worth trying to understand this talk as more than figurative. What is puzzling is that she talks of "life" here and elsewhere as if it were a thing or kind of stuff. Our first philosophical instincts are, of course, to parse away the seeming substantiality here in favour of the underlying adjectival use. Among the sober, "x's life" comes to no more than "x is alive", with no obligation to make sense of the sameness and distinctness of lives beyond the sameness and distinctness of what live them. But there are those who have not taken it this way. Think, in this connection, of Locke's use of the phrase "same life" in his account of the identity and distinctness of animals.[33] His use curiously seems to presume a similar grip on "same life" that is prior to and independent of "same animal".

One thing Anscombe is marking here is the thought that the identity of a zygote, the unity of its parts at and over time, is not a matter of material identity. It is a unity that permits replacement, deletion and addition of parts. Living things grow, metabolize and waste away. Dividing a lump of clay is material division and no more. Dividing a zygote involves material division, but is primarily a division of the living unity into two such unities. Recall, however, that this is a unity she takes to be a matter of their joint activity. It is something that the parts do and do together.

> How is a set of cells *an* individual living thing? Well, they marvelously work together in multiplying and becoming differentiated, so as to be the matter of a living thing which is nourished and grows. That they do this essentially by dividing and so multiplying, means that they are governed by a principle of unity as constituting a developing living thing, and this I call a soul.[34]

---

[32] Anscombe, "Were You a Zygote?", p. 44.
[33] J. Locke, *An Essay concerning Human Understanding* (Oxford: Oxford University Press, 1975), pp. 330–32.
[34] Anscombe, "Embryos and Final Causes", p. 52.

Her talk here of "principle" and "soul" stands with (or near) her talk of "life", for we might say that these joint activities are those in virtue of which it is an individual. But we also might say, by way of metaphysical categorization, that a "life" belongs to the ontology of events, or better actions, i.e. something drawn from the category of concrete, temporally extended particulars. While there are many distinct acts a living thing engages in, we might cobble them all together into longer, more encompassing act, the life it is living. This, at least, is the sort of thing we might understand to divide in a literal sense, as, perhaps, our search for a missing camper might split into the activities of two search parties or as our road trip to Vegas in caravan gets separated into two journeys.

What is interesting, or potentially scandalous, is that Anscombe, unlike Locke, contemplates the possibility that this sort of life is shared by numerically distinct living beings. It is clear that she thinks that zygote and adult human being share a life in the no-split case, for she says, "Here something comparatively large and much developed is one and the same living thing with the zygote". While it is tempting to read this as supporting her identification of Z and A, one cannot square this reading with her subsequent claim that, in the splitting case, Z shares a life with numerically distinct B and C, for she continues here by saying, "Or, if there should be twins, they are two living things and jointly the same with the zygote".[35] The thought comes out somewhat more clearly in the closing lines of her earlier paper.

> At this stage the life is divided into two only because the living thing is cloven in two; and hence only inasmuch as it is so cloven. We cannot say yet that we have here two distinct animals. But we can say that we have two materially distinct carriers of the life that started with the formation of the zygote.[36]

The suggestion that Anscombe thinks one and the same life is shared by distinct entities also helps explain her resistance to the description of case (3) as one in which Z dies or is killed. In an oddly literal way, splitting turns out to be a case, not of less life, but of more. Even though something goes out of existence, it is no ordinary death because the life of Z does not come to an end but

---

[35] Anscombe, "Embryos and Final Causes", p. 50.
[36] Anscombe, "Were You a Zygote?", p. 44.

continues in B and C. This distinguishes it from other, more ordinary cases of going out of existence in which the life also comes to an end.

This brings us back to the contrast with amoebas. Splitting in amoebas, we said, was a reproductive process, the way in which their kind create offspring. Anscombe would hold that this, and any proper, reproductive process is one that gives rise, not just to a new, distinct entity, but one with a new life, distinct from that of the parent. In contrast, the splitting of a zygote is not a reproductive process despite the fact that two new zygotes result. Even if zygotes are human beings, this is not how human beings reproduce, nor is there a race of zygotes with their own way of doing this. What is importantly different is that their splitting does not result in new life, but in the communication of the very same life already being lived to two new zygotes which continue to live it. In those early days, the unifying, joint activity of the cells is sufficiently simple and homogenous to permit this odd kind of division into new individuals which, nevertheless, continue to prosecute the numerically same activity.[37]

Lastly, we should connect all of this to the question of goals. These lives, on our understanding, are essentially action-like particulars, and on Anscombe's understanding their being the activities they are is a matter of what they are for. Their goals make them the activities they are. We are now in a position to assert that the relevant goal must be non-specific, precisely because the life, the numerically single ongoing unifying activity, is shared by distinct entities Z, B and C. We cannot say here that Z, in living, acts for the sake of perfecting Z because B and C live the very same life even though Z is gone. The only goal that is as sharable as their life is the non-specific goal of making an animal. In contrast, we can attribute a specific goal of self-perfection to an amoeba and then new, distinct specific goals to its offspring because their lives are not one and the same. It is true that these lives must be able to accommodate some shifts of goals, for

---

[37] It is an advantage of Anscombe's view here that it neatly extends to handle cases of mosaicism, those in which two zygotes fuse into a single one. Given that the unities are weak enough to be divided like a lump of clay, it comes as no surprise to find that they are, on occasion, "squished together" as well. The simple view can only multiply the number of ephemeral human casualties of such a process.

"making a human being" is no goal of A's while sharing Z's life, but this transition is accompanied by the transition to a distinct particular. While leaving many questions unanswered, we have, I think, a complete argument on the table.

8. Conclusion

It is time to step back. We are far from the idea that the possibility of twinning, together with some basic logical considerations, shows that the zygote is no human being. Instead, we have found a surprisingly complex metaphysical picture, one involving the non-specific character of creative processes, the teleological character of organic unities, and a notion of particular, substantial life which fails to imply identity. All are controversial theses, to put it lightly. Even so, we have remained true to the idea that the phenomena of twinning presents a challenge for the simple view based only on purely metaphysical considerations, if unorthodox ones. If I am right about what Anscombe is really up to in these pages, there is an interesting and defensible argument against the simple view and for a plausible alternative picture. The argument is not as straightforward and light on premises as most have taken it to be, but it offers a reason to reassess our views about the status of early human life that bypasses the usual and highly vexed criterial arguments about what it takes to be a human being.

John Zeis

Anscombe and the Metaphysics of Human Action[1]

1. Causality and Action

Anscombe's work *Intention* is of course the centrepiece of her theory of human action; but in that work she says very little about the nature of the causality of human action. In fact, in *Intention*,

---

[1] In 1978 and 1979, I had the great fortune of taking courses at the University of Pennsylvania from Elizabeth Anscombe and Peter Geach. Geach offered courses based on his Stanton lectures, *Providence and Evil* (Cambridge: Cambridge University Press, 1977), *The Virtues* (Cambridge: Cambridge University Press, 1977), and *Freedom and Prediction*. Anscombe offered courses on Action Theory and Wittgenstein. I found Anscombe's course on Action Theory particularly perplexing, especially given the discussions of her position on the causality of human action — or what I took to be a flat out rejection of a position on the lack of the causality of human action. I remember vividly a long discussion in class of intentionally raising one's arm. We (students) wanted to know what its cause was; we kept pressing the issue and she kept denying that there was one. We were clueless then as to how that could be so. At that time, I was also unequipped to deal with her work in *Intention* and in her Cambridge inaugural lecture, *Causality and Determination*. In the thirty-five years since, I have laboured to try to understand her general position on the metaphysics of human action, and only wish that I could now discuss with her how I *think* I understand what she was trying to convey to us. There are of course numerous pieces of her position on the general issue throughout her corpus, but as was her style, her work displays an intense focus on the individual topic under consideration in each piece and a lack of a global roadmap guiding the reader to a synthesis of all the individual pieces. In this chapter, I wish to synthesize three elements in her action theory: her positions on the causality of human action, on practical reason and on intentional action.

when she cites examples of causation involved in human acts, they are not cases of human action.[2] Her focus on intention in that work is to some extent a deflection from the way in which the causality of human action had historically been discussed, at least since the period of Descartes, and which would shortly, and in part in reaction to her work, be given a new formulation by Donald Davidson in his argument that reasons for action are (and must be) causes.[3] A stark contrast with the position of Anscombe on the causality of human action is the view of Jonathan Edwards in *A Careful and Strict Inquiry into the Freedom of the Will*.[4]

I choose Edwards' conception of the causality of human action for two reasons. First, Edwards presents a very clear picture of human action which entails a deterministic conception which Anscombe unequivocally rejects. Second, at the time I took Anscombe's action theory course, Geach devoted a significant degree of attention to Edwards' conception when discussing the issues he was dealing with in what he planned for his third Stanton lecture, *Freedom and Prediction*. Geach used Edwards' view as just the sort of view of the will which needed to be refuted. He surely must have discussed his views on Edwards' position with Anscombe and, given her disdain for what she considered to be the "pipedream" of determinism and her rejection of causal explanations of intentional action, I am confident that she would have shared the same sort of assessment as Geach of Edwards' picture of the will.

Edwards' philosophical position on the determinism of the will had, of course, an extra-philosophical motivation, namely, his Calvinism. But in his *Freedom of the Will*, he argues for this deterministic position from a strictly philosophical base. The elements of his positions are quite clear and simple. For Edwards, an act is free if and only if it is caused or determined by an act of the will; but then it follows that, for an act of the will to be free, it too must be caused by an act of the will. However, this would then result

---

[2] On p. 13 in *Intention*, 2nd edition (Ithaca, NY: Cornell University Press, 1976), she gives the example of "the odd sort of jerk or jump that one's whole body sometimes gives when one is falling asleep". She also cites other examples, each of which are involuntary acts and hence are not human actions in her sense.

[3] Donald Davidson, "Actions, Reasons, and Causes", in *Essays on Actions and Events*, 2nd edition (Oxford: Clarendon Press, 2001), pp. 3–20.

[4] Jonathan Edwards, *Freedom of the Will* (Prisbrary Publishing, 2012).

either in an infinite regress of acts of the will determining subsequent acts of the will or an act of the will which is caused or determined by something which is not itself determined by an act of the will. Since an infinite regress of acts of the will is impossible, an act of the will must originally be determined in its causes by something other than an act of the will.

Here is Edwards in his *reductio* of the Arminians' position:

> If the Will determines all its own free acts the soul determines them in the exercise of a Power of willing and choosing; or, which is the same thing, it determines them of choice; it determines its own acts, by choosing its own acts. If the Will determines the Will then choice orders and determines the choice; and acts of choice are subject to the decision, and follow the conduct of other acts of choice. And therefore if the Will determines all its own free acts, then every free act of choice is determined by a preceding act of choice, choosing that act. And if that preceding act of the Will be also a free act, then by these principles, in this act too, the Will is self-determined; that is, this, in like manner, is an act that the soul voluntarily chooses; or, which is the same thing, it is an act determined still by a preceding act of the Will, choosing that. Which brings us directly to a contradiction; for it supposes an act of the Will preceding the first act of the whole train, directing and determining the rest; or a free act of the Will, before the first free act of the Will. Or else we must come at last to an act of the Will, determining the consequent acts, wherein the Will is not self-determined, and so is not a free act, in this notion of freedom; but if the first act in the train determining and fixing the rest, be not free, none of them all can be free ...[5]

Edwards does not shirk from the deterministic position which blocks the infinite regress. Prior to his attack upon the Arminians' position, he details his own view of the matter: the act of the will is determined by the strongest motive which appears before the mind. This is a causal necessity, but not a "natural" causal necessity; it is what he calls a "moral necessity", to which he sees no objection. Well, he may see no objection to this, but I think it is clear that Anscombe would have no truck with such an equivocation. But how would she avoid the *reductio*? There is a hint in another passage from Edwards.

> If to evade the force of what has been observed, it should be said, that when the Arminians speak of the Will determining its own

---

[5] *Ibid.*, p. 587, cf. p. 603.

acts, they do not mean that the Will determines them by any preceding act, or that one act of the will determines another, but only that the faculty or power of Will, or the soul in the use of that power, determines its own volitions; and that it does it without any act going before the act determined; such an evasion would be full of the most gross absurdity.[6]

I think that Anscombe would be "'guilty" of what Edwards calls "the most gross absurdity", and I base this on how she handled the causality of a free human action in class and also on her rejection of Davidson's account in "Actions, Reasons, and Causes".[7] Why she would not think it a "gross absurdity" to deny "any act going before the act determined" when the act is a free action will, I hope, become clear in the next section. If, however, I had been more astute in 1978 when I took her class and Geach's class discussing Edwards' position, I would have asked her about this.

Regarding this "gross absurdity", Edwards also says the following:

> If the meaning be, that the soul's exertion of such a particular act of Will, is a thing that comes to pass of itself, without any cause, and that there is absolutely no reason of the soul being determined to exert such a volition, and make such a choice, rather than another, I say, if this be the meaning of Arminians, when they contend so earnestly for the Will determining its own acts, and for liberty of Will consisting of self-determining power; they do nothing but confound themselves and others with words without a meaning.[8]

What is clear from this passage is that Edwards, like Davidson, conflates reasons and causes. And, in a later passage, he correctly realizes that the reason the Arminians (and Anscombe) wish to deny that free actions are determined in their causes is because they are committed to the fact that free actions are causally

---

[6] *Ibid.*, p. 632.
[7] In her "Practical Inference", in *Human Life, Action and Ethics: Essays by G.E.M. Anscombe*, ed. Mary Geach and Luke Gormally (Exeter: Imprint Academic, 2005), p. 111, she concludes a discussion of Davidson's position by stating that: "Something I do is not made into an intentional action by being caused by a belief and desire, even if the descriptions fit."
[8] Edwards, *Freedom of the Will*, p. 701.

contingent, whereas Edwards denies that any causes can be contingent.[9]

Before proceeding to Anscombe's positive thesis on the causality of human action, we need to clearly delineate the distinction that Anscombe would hold between events which are causally necessitated and causally contingent, and just what causal contingency is supposed to provide for free action. The position of causal determinism I will employ is that given by Alvin Goldman in his *A Theory of Human Action*. It is this:

> Event *e* is determined if and only if a proposition asserting that *e* occurs (at *t*) is deducible from some conjunction of (true) propositions describing laws of nature and events prior to *t* (but not deducible from propositions describing prior events alone).[10]

This view is reflected in Anscombe's view of determinism when she states that "When we call a result determined we are implicitly relating it to an antecedent range of possibilities and saying that all but one of these is disallowed".[11] Causal determinism is a metaphysical position, rather than an epistemological one, so a better definition would be one stated in terms of entailment or implication rather than deducibility. An event *e* is determined at *t* if and only if a proposition that *e* occurs is entailed by some conjunction of true propositions describing laws of nature and events prior to *t*. Causal determinism is then reducible to a thesis of tensed logical necessity.[12] Causal determinism in this sense provides a clear contrast to the indeterminism which Anscombe holds applies broadly in nature and also the way in which she sees practical reason operative in free human action. As she says in "Causality and Determination", "I should explain indeterminism as the thesis that not all physical effects are necessitated by their causes".[13]

---

[9] *Ibid.*, pp. 714 and 743.
[10] Alvin Goldman, *Theory of Human Action* (Saddle River, NJ: Prentice Hall, 1971), p. 172. I am using this definition because it is the one I discuss in my dissertation, *The Paradox of Omnipotence* (University of Pennsylvania, 1980), and to which Anscombe had no objection.
[11] Anscombe, "Causality and Determination", in *Metaphysics and the Philosophy of Mind: Collected Philosophical Papers Vol. II* (Oxford: Blackwell, 1981), p. 141.
[12] This is the way determinism is described by G.H. von Wright in *Causality and Determinism* (New York: Columbia University Press, 1975).
[13] Anscombe, "Causality and Determination", p. 145.

Anscombe begins "Causality and Determination" by denying the identity between causality and the notion of a necessary connection or as an exceptionless generalization.[14] She does not offer anything like a definition of causality, but offers what she considers to be the common core of the notion of causality:

> It is this: causality consists in the derivativeness of an effect from its causes. This is the core, the common feature, of causality in it various kinds. Effects derive from, arise out of, come of, their causes.[15]

One who is focussed on finding necessary and sufficient conditions for what constitutes causality will be dissatisfied with Anscombe's statement of the core of the notion, but I think she has good reason to eschew such an approach. In arguing against Hume that we do indeed observe causality, she offers the following list of causal concepts: "*scrape, push, wet, carry, eat, burn, knock over, keep off, squash, make* (e.g. noises, paper boats), *hurt.*"[16] Let's take a closer look at what she might consider specific examples of the use of some of these concepts:

— I scraped the paint off the window pane with my razor.
— I pushed the sled down the hill.
— I wet my phone when I dropped it in the sink.
— I squashed the slug when I stepped on it.
— I knocked over the glass of milk when I reached across the table for the salt shaker.
— I hurt Olivia when I pushed her hand away from my glasses.

In each of these cases I perform an act which causes a certain effect. In the first, I take my razor and engage in a scraping motion (cause) which removes the paint from the window pane (effect); in the last, I wave my hand, pushing my one-year-old granddaughter Olivia's hand away from my glasses (cause), consequently hitting her in the face (accidentally) and hurting her (effect). Anscombe wants us to consider whether, in all of these cases, there are any good reasons for thinking that, from the laws of nature and the conditions that apply, there is a necessary connection between the cause and its effect. Her position is that

---

[14] *Ibid.*, p. 133.
[15] *Ibid.*, p. 136.
[16] *Ibid.*, p. 137.

there is not; and that the belief that there is such a necessary connection or universal generalization is just a pipedream. Her example of the Galton board creates a scenario where it appears that the laws of nature (gravity) and the relevant condition (the ball hitting squarely on the centre of the pin) should entail, if determinism were true, that the ball should not fall to one side rather than the other. But, of course, the ball *will* fall; and so the believer in determinism must believe that there *must* be some condition or conditions which together with the laws of nature would entail that the ball falls to the side to which it does in fact fall. And what is the evidence for such a belief? It is just the *presumption* that determinism must be universally true—but there is no evidence for that! Newton's laws applied to astronomy do give us a deterministic system, and there are other determining causes, but Anscombe holds that it is just an unwarranted assumption to extend this picture to causality in general; and quantum mechanics gives us positive reason to reject that extension.[17]

The bottom line for Anscombe is that causality is real—effects are brought about from causes—but not always, or not even typically, in a deterministic fashion. This is exemplified in the kinds of causal processes she cites (see above), in the actions of animals (the fox running away from the hounds), and most especially and importantly in human action. Surely, some cases of causality will involve a deterministic end, and all physical processes entail a causality which, once they occur, will be determinate; but there is an openness in nature within which human action can shape the world.[18] Geach, in discussing the distinction

---

[17] In "Causality and Determination", Anscombe says this: "The high success of Newton's astronomy was in one way an intellectual disaster: it produced an illusion from which we tend to still suffer. This illusion was created by the circumstances that Newton's mechanics *had a good model in the solar system*" (p. 143).

[18] In her example of the production of the Coca-Cola message being produced in a bottle no matter what causal process occurs, she gives us an analogue of the way in which she conceives there to be enough openness in natural causality where although those natural processes are operative and follow natural laws, nonetheless, there is also space for our action to shape the world in accordance with our intentions. Every time I raise my hand to pose a question, there is some physical process which occurs in my body, but whatever physical process is operative is also guided by my intention to ask a question (see p. 146).

between the past and the future, spoke of a "forking" of the future. Aquinas, in speaking of the freedom of choice, says this entails that it be contingent, and not follow of necessity.[19] Anscombe, like Geach and Aquinas, holds the same, if not an even more robust conception of indeterminism. As she states in "Causality and Determination":

> My actions are mostly physical movements; if these physical movements are physically predetermined by processes which I do not control, then my freedom is perfectly illusory. The truth of physical indeterminism is thus indispensable if we are to make anything of the claim to freedom. But certainly it is insufficient. The physically undetermined is not thereby "free." For freedom at least involves the power of acting according to an idea ...[20]

Anscombe does not deny that free actions are caused. She holds that there is a physical causality which is conjoined with our bringing about of intentional actions. The way in which this works is nicely illustrated by her Coca-Cola example in "Causality and Determination".

> ...Suppose that we have a large glass box full of millions of extremely minute coloured particles, and the box is constantly shaken. Study of the box and particles leads to statistical laws, including laws for the random generation of small unit patches of uniform colour. Now the box is remarkable for also presenting the following phenomenon: the word 'Coca Cola', formed like a mosaic, can always be read when one looks at one of the sides. It is not always the same shape in the formation of its letters, not always the same size or in the same position, it varies in its colours; but there it always is. It is not at all clear that those statistical laws concerning the random motion of the particles and their formation of small unit patches of colour would have to be

---

[19] This is the way Geach expressed his view in contrasting his position from Edwards in his course discussing freedom and prediction. In the *Summa Theologica* I–II q. 13 a. 6, ad 2, Aquinas states that

> The reason's decision or judgment of what is to be done is about things that are *contingent* and *possible* to us. In such matters the conclusions do not follow of necessity from principles that are absolutely necessary, but from such as are so conditionally; as, for instance, "If he runs, he is in motion."

Summa Theologica, Second and Revised edition, literally translated by Fathers of the English Dominican Province (London: Burns, Oates and Washbourne, 1917).

[20] Anscombe, "Causality and Determination", p. 146.

supposed violated by the operation of a cause for this phenomenon which did not derive it from the statistical laws.[21]

In the example, she imagines a closed container wherein the message "Coca-Cola" always appears, even though the specific causal process changes in each case. Sometimes the message appears in cursive, sometimes not, etc. The causal processes are brought about according to a stochastic relation, not a deterministic one. So that the causal relation is stochastic allows for the openness which free action requires.

Edwards' conception of the causal determinism regarding the will is simple and clear. In Edwards' view, free action is caused by an act of the will. He then questions what could make an act of the will free, and his answer is that it too would have to have been caused by an act of the will. But then the same question would have to be asked about this act of will which caused the act of the will which caused the free action; and either that act of the will, if free, would have to be caused by a prior act of the will. If it were the effect of any other cause, it would not be free. Hence a free act would have to be caused by an infinite regress of acts of the will, which is absurd. Hence there can be no free will.

Anscombe denies that free actions as such are caused, and I have argued that one of her reasons for doing so would have been to avoid the kind of determinism we get in a position like Edwards'. But why deny that they are caused in *any* sense. Can't free actions be caused but in such a way that they are not deterministically caused? Anscombe herself denies that causality is generally a deterministic process. She argues that there is no reason to hold that the physical processes of causation which hold in nature are determined in their causes. So why couldn't free actions have causes which are non-determined?

Well, they *do*! The physical causes of free actions are non-deterministic causes. So doesn't this contradict her position that free actions are uncaused? Well, what I think she means when she denies that free actions have a cause is that she denies that there is a cause which constitutes them as free, as in Edwards' case. For Anscombe there is no act of the will which is the cause that constitutes an action as free. Let us say that there is an act of the will which causes a free action and constitutes it as free. If so, this

---

[21] *Ibid.*, p. 146.

would have to be construed as something like the efficient cause of the free action. But then we could ask if this act of the will were free. Well, if the action is constituted as free because it was caused by an act of the will, wouldn't we have to say, like Edwards, that this act of the will is free because it too had been caused by a prior act of will?

When Anscombe gives examples of mental causation in *Intention*, they are not causes of free actions. They are examples such as being startled by the sight of something, and operating as an efficient cause of some response. For Anscombe, what constitutes intention is that the action is performed under some description. And how is a description supposed to act as an efficient cause? Well, it would have to be the mental state of the agent as the efficient cause. So let us say that my intentional act is the cleaning of my windshield. This act is identical with my exercising my left arm, my dirtying my towel, my killing the fly on the windshield, and my annoying my wife since we are late for leaving for the party. If the mental state is what causes the act, then it causes the act under *all* these descriptions. But then how would this intention be causally distinct from my intention to annoy my wife or to exercise my left arm? It would not be, for all the effects are the same.

If intention A causes p, q and r, and intention B causes p, q and r (all the same states), then what is the distinction of the cause A or the cause B? It seems nothing. But if the intentional act A is distinct from the intentional act B, there would have to be some distinction between them. The only thing which would distinguish them would be the mental event, which would be external to the action. But it is the action which is intentional, and what makes it intentional should be something which is internal to it. In Anscombe's view, the intention would be something akin to a formal cause of the act.

2. Practical Reason

In "The Causation of Action", Anscombe makes it clear that reasons are not causes in the way in which Edwards or Davidson would conceive of them. Reasons for action are not items which fit into a chain of causality to fill a gap in a deterministic system.[22]

---

[22] Anscombe, *Human Life, Action and Ethics*, p. 98.

So fill up that gap how you will. I mean, of course, *suppose* it filled up how you will. No way of filling it up, whether with brain-states or (the fanciful) supposed correlates of expressions of Cartesian *cogitationes*, will fill it up with intentions, beliefs, wants, aims, volitions, or desires. For you are in pursuit of a type of causal history in which those things do not belong *at all*.[23]

In "Practical Inference", Anscombe contrasts the "form" of practical inference from that of the form of theoretical inference in this way. For a practical inference, the form is:

Wanted: that p. (Or let it be that p)
If q then p.
If r then q.
Decision: r!

With the "!" representing a fiat to bring about r. For a theoretical inference, the form is:

r. (Or suppose that r)
If r then q.
If q then p.
Therefore, p.[24]

She points out that the truth conditions for practical inference and for theoretical inference are identical, but what is different in these "forms" is the service of them in application. In the theoretical inference, the propositions r, if r then q, and if q then p, entail p. However, in the practical inference, the propositions p, if q then p and if r then q do *not* entail r. If it were a theoretical inference, this would be a fallacy of the affirming of the consequent, for the conclusion that r does not necessarily follow from the premises.

What is different in the practical inference from the theoretical inference is that the main "premise" is what one wishes to bring about (i.e. p), is the conclusion if it were a theoretical inference. The practical inference is not a logical fallacy; the service of the practical inference is not to affirm the truth of a conclusion from premises, it is to decide on a path of action, which is defeasible. In order to see the defeasibility, take the following instantiation of the form above:

---

[23] *Ibid.*, p. 100.
[24] *Ibid.*, p. 133.

> Wanted: that I meet Steve at Kentucky Greg's at 12:15.
> If I get Gabe to school at noon, I can meet Steve at 12:15.
> If I leave my house at 11:30, I will get Gabe to school at noon.
> Decision: I will leave my house at 11:30.

Given my goal (meeting Steve at 12:15), and the truth of the other premises, my decision to leave my house at 11:30 is a sound practical judgment. However, this decision is not necessitated. For what if I add this to my premises: "If I can get Pam to take Gabe to school, he will get to school at noon"? If I add this premise to my reasons, then I may soundly decide to get Pam to take Gabe to school instead of deciding to leave the house at 11:30. Of course, I may still leave my house at 11:30 and still satisfy my goal (meeting Steve at 12:15), but I may not have to leave by 11:30 since, if I do not have to get Gabe to school, I no longer have as far to drive in order to get to Kentucky Greg's. This example should make the defeasibility of practical reasoning clear. In theoretical reasoning, if an argument is sound, no additional premises will invalidate it: the conclusion still logically follows from the premises—even if the additional premise contradicts the original premises! However, as my example shows, in a process of practical reasoning, the addition of premises can block the original inference. And, of course, there are an unlimited number of additional premises that I could add which block the original inference, even ones that are irresponsible, like "If I leave the house at noon, I can meet Steve at 12:15", where I conclude that I will leave my house at noon, thereby just blowing off getting Gabe to school![25]

The example of a practical inference could always be articulated in a more fine-grained analysis. In the example I gave, I only included the elements which would likely be the result of deliberation, but there are other elements which are included in the operation of the deliberative elements. So, for example, in order for me to pick up my grandson, I will have to drive my car; in order for me to drive my car, I must turn the ignition key; and in order to get the car moving, I must step on the gas. And once I am in traffic, I need to make specific turns, stops and starts in

---

[25] Not all practical inferences will be defeasible, like in Aquinas's example of the continent person who judges that no sin should be done, that this is a sin, and therefore that this should not be done, *de Malo* 3.9, ad 7: see *The De Malo of Thomas Aquinas*, trans. R. Regan, ed. B. Davies (Oxford: Oxford University Press, 2001). This is the case when my end can be satisfied only in one way.

order to pick up my grandson. All of these elements are intentional, but need not be the result of deliberation. My developed driving habits are part of a rational guidance system of my choices.

If this is the case about practical reasoning in general, then we have a lack of necessitation in *both* of the elements necessary for free action in Anscombe's view, i.e. both in natural causality (which provides a *sine qua non*) for free action in Anscombe's position, and in the inferences of practical reason which is the element which distinguishes a free human action from a random event. The element of practical reason in action is what enables Anscombe to avoid Edwards' objection to contingency: "Contingence is blind, and does not pick out and choose for a particular sorts of events."[26] Anscombe's position on practical reason shows the way in which causal contingency, although entailed by action which is free, is *not* blind, but is instead the power of "acting according to an idea".[27]

3. Practical Reason and Actions Intentional Under a Description

In *Intention*, Anscombe introduced the idea of actions being intentional under a description.[28] There are multiple true descriptions of any action, but an action is intentional under only some of those descriptions. For example, as I am waiting for my wife to go to a party, I engage in an action about which all of the following descriptions are true: I am cleaning the windshield, I shoo a fly, I make a squeaking sound with the towel, I dirty the towel, I exercise my left arm, and (when she finally comes out) I annoy my wife. Although all of these descriptions are true of the action, it is intentional only under the description of *washing my windshield*. The question arises: if an action is intentional under only some descriptions, what determines under which description or descriptions the action is intentional?

An intentional action is, of course, the paradigmatic example of a free action. So in the account of free action, it is important to link her position of an action being intentional under a description

---

[26] Edwards, *Freedom of the Will*, p. 799.
[27] Anscombe, "Causality and Determination", p. 146.
[28] Anscombe, *Intention*. See also "Under a Description", *Noûs*, 13 (2) 1979: 219–233.

with the other elements of her metaphysics of human action. In the last section, we saw the way in which she construes the operation of practical reason. Let's go back to my example of a practical syllogism:

> Wanted: that I meet Steve at Kentucky Greg's at 12:15.
> If I get Gabe to school at noon, I can meet Steve at 12:15.
> If I leave my house at 11:30, I will get Gabe to school at noon.
> Decision: I will leave my house at 11:30.

The conclusion of my reasoning process in this first case was my decision to leave the house at 11:30. I left the house at 11:30 in order to pick up Gabe to get him to school by noon; and after getting Gabe to school at noon, I could then get to Kentucky Greg's by 12:15 in order to meet Steve. In the second case, I did not leave the house at 11:30, but at noon, for I was able to get Pam to drive Gabe to school. So in this second case, I asked Pam (who is unfailingly reliable) to pick up Gabe so that I wouldn't have to pick him up so that I could leave the house by noon instead of at 11:30. In the third example, I blew Gabe off: I didn't leave the house at 11:30, I didn't ask Pam to pick him up, and just left Gabe waiting with his Grammie for a ride that was never to come.

In each of these cases, under which descriptions of my action is it intentional, and what determines those descriptions as the ones under which my action is intentional? The answer is the practical reasoning in each case. In the first case, what is intentional is that *I left the house at 11:30* in order to *pick up Gabe and get him to school at noon* in order to *get to Kentucky Greg's by 12:15* in order to *meet Steve*. All of these descriptions are descriptions under which my action was intentional and these descriptions are those which are determined by my practical reasoning. In the second case, what is intentional is that *I asked Pam to pick up Gabe* so that *Gabe would get to school by noon* and I could just *leave the house at noon* and still *get to Kentucky Greg's at 12:15* in order to *meet Steve*. In the third case, what is intentional, and what constitutes my blowing Gabe off? In the third case, I just *left the house at noon* in order to *get to Kentucky Greg's at 12:15* in order to *meet Steve*. This third case was imagined as a result of a practical inference which still included all the conditionals from the first case, but where I just ignore the fact (which I know to be true) that in order to *get Gabe to school by noon* I would either *have to leave the house by 11:30 or make some other arrangement*. If I had just forgotten about getting Gabe to school (after all, I *am* an absent-minded professor), if the conditionals about Gabe's getting to school were in no way involved in my deliberation, then the only descriptions under which my action would be intentional would be that I just *left the house at noon* in order to *get to Kentucky Greg's at 12:15* in order to *meet Steve*. But in the case I am imagining, since I had not just forgotten about Gabe but deliberately ignored the relevant facts and requirements concerning his getting to school, my action also entails that I am intentionally guilty of *not leaving my house on time to pick him up, not making some other arrangements to get him* to school, and *his not getting to school*, and *his and his Grammie's waiting for a ride that would never come*. I am guilty of all these things because I also knew that it was true that if I didn't leave the house at 11:30 to pick up Gabe or make some other arrangement, he would not get to school and I had previously accepted the responsibility of picking him up. This is in contrast to the other true descriptions in my example of washing my windshield, for in that case I had no responsibility for not dirtying the towel or not making a squeaking sound or not shooing the fly or even not annoying my wife when she finally gets in the car. Even in the case of annoying my wife as she waits for me to finish washing the windshield, my annoying her was not in any way part of my deliberation and was a mere side effect of my washing the windshield (for which I had adequate justification). But now we have gone beyond metaphysics into ethics.

4. Conclusion

Anscombe's theory of free action has several elements, some of which were the subject of this investigation. In this investigation, we have examined her position on causality and its implications regarding causal determinism and indeterminism. On the question, Anscombe's position is an unabashed libertarianism. Compatibilism is, for her, not a relevant issue because if nature is not typically a deterministic system, the motivation for determinism is absent. For Anscombe, a nature in which causality is not typically deterministic allows for a place within the world wherein free human actions can really make a difference in shaping that world. And human free action shapes the world, not in a blind way, but in a way which is teleologically directed on the basis of practical reason. Practical reason also delineates what, for any particular agent, constitutes their intentional action. Such a metaphysical view squarely provides the conditions necessary for human responsibility in action.

Rachael Wiseman

The Intended and Unintended Consequences of Intention

1. Introduction

Intention is a text that has frustrated the most sympathetic of commentators from the moment of its publication. Even among those who recognize Anscombe's book as a classic, there is criticism of her style and argument, and confusion about the book's central theme. Nevertheless, from the mid-1960s, there has been a general consensus that *Intention* contains at least three important theses. First, that *intentional action* and not *the mental state of intending to act* is the more basic notion of intention. Second, that an agent's knowledge of the states and motions of her body is "non-observational", in something like the way that her knowledge of the states of her mind is. Third, that actions are individuated—at least primarily—in terms of bodily action; so that if I put my signature on a piece of paper that is an order for a bomb to be dropped, and which brings about the end of the war and blunts my pen nib and gives me cramp, I still only do *one* thing.[1]

---

[1] Though, see *Essays on Anscombe's Intention*, eds. Ford, Hornsby & Stoutland (London: Harvard University Press, 2011) for a number of essays which attempt to disrupt this interpretative consensus. See especially Frederick Stoutland, "Introduction: Anscombe's *Intention* in Context" and Richard Moran and Martin J. Stone, "Anscombe on Expressions of Intention: An Exegesis".

There has been further consensus that *Intention* does not provide adequate argument to establish these theses, nor the sort of theoretical and technical detail needed to sustain them. This verdict has acted as an invitation to others to amend, clarify, develop and correct Anscombe's offering. The legacy of *Intention* has been a continuing debate around these theses, mostly conducted in academic journals, with friends and allies seeking to provide the technical scaffolding Anscombe omits, and foes attempting to show that the scaffolding fails.

In this chapter I argue that this widespread view of *Intention* is fundamentally mistaken. Anscombe does not intend to offer a novel account of action, but something which "isn't a philosophical thesis at all".[2] This becomes clear once we view *Intention* as the product of the ethical debates in which Anscombe was engaged between 1956 and 1958. Through those debates Anscombe came to realize that moral philosophy had lost sight of the distinctive use of the question "What is she doing?", to mark out the class of intentional actions.[3] This question, as she saw it, is essential to identifying the nature and quality of an act, a category without which moral philosophy cannot precede. Once we reframe *Intention* as a corrective to this oversight, it becomes clear that the idea that we need to complete Anscombe's account by providing technical detail or argumentative support is based on a deep misunderstanding of the sort of philosophical undertaking that *Intention* is, and of the status of the statements it contains.

2. The Unintended Consequences of *Intention*

Intention was reviewed in at least seven major English-language philosophical journals: *The Journal of Philosophy*, *The Philosophical Review*, *Philosophy of Science*, *Mind*, *Philosophy*, *The Australasian Journal of Philosophy*, and *Philosophical Quarterly*. The Catholic British weekly, *The Tablet*, also carried a review.[4] Feelings were

---

[2] Anscombe, "Under a Description" in her *Metaphysics and the Philosophy of Mind* (Oxford: Basil Blackwell, 1981), pp. 208–11; originally published in *Noûs*, 13, 1979. This is how Anscombe describes her statement, in *Intention*, that "one and the same action may have many descriptions" (p. 210); my contention in this chapter is that the same can be said of the statements in *Intention* more generally.

[3] Anscombe, *Intention*, §23, p. 37.

[4] Judith Jarvis, "Review", *The Journal of Philosophy*, 56 (1) 1959; Roderick M. Chisholm, "Review", *The Philosophical Review*, 68 (1) 1959; Irving M. Copi,

mixed. Every reader found Anscombe's monograph hard-going. P.T. Heath, the most critical reviewer, accused Anscombe of "indifference to the ordinary standards of literary exposition", and concluded that "the work seems hardly to have got beyond the stage of a first draft".[5] Kurt Baier, whose review is much more sympathetic and insightful than Heath's, reported nevertheless that "the book as a whole is baffling and the outline of its over-all theme not easily discerned", and admitted he would "probably not have persevered in looking for it if I had not undertaken to write this review".[6] A. Phillips Griffiths suggests, rather diplomatically, that "the reader's task would have been lightened if more explicit direction had been given within the text as to the turns the argument is taking".[7]

The difficulty of *Intention*, perhaps, accounts for the fact that — at least in many circles — Anscombe's book came to be seen as something like the "first draft" that Heath suspected it of being.[8] From the 1960s there has been a steady stream of work which aims to move from Anscombe's "first draft" to a complete account of the nature of human action. Much of this work has been focussed around three particularly striking features of Anscombe's treatment of her topic. These features are undoubtedly present, but I will argue that their significance has been misinterpreted.

First, Anscombe is more concerned with *intentional action* than with *the mental state of intending to act*. She denies that "if we wish to understand what intention is, we must be investigating something whose existence is purely in the sphere of the mind", and says that on the contrary the "first thing" we should consider in an enquiry into intention is "what physically takes place, i.e. what a man actually does".[9] This preference for considering intentional action over what goes on "in the sphere of the mind" is reflected in the structure of *Intention*: 46 out of its 52 paragraphs focus on

---

"Review", *Philosophy of Science*, 26 (2) 1959; K.W. Rankin, "Review", *Mind*, 68 (270) 1959: 261-264; A. Phillips Griffiths, "Review", *Philosophy*, 34 (130) 1959: 245-247; P.L. Heath, "Review", *The Philosophical Quarterly*, 10 (40) 1960; Kurt Baier, "Critical notice", *Australasian Journal of Philosophy*, 38 (1) 1960: 71-81; Illtyd Trethovvan, "The Ethics of Intention", *The Tablet*, 11 January 1958.

[5] Heath, "Review", p. 282.
[6] Baier, "Critical notice", p. 71.
[7] Griffiths, "Review", p. 247.
[8] Though, no one says this of Wittgenstein's *Philosophical Investigations*.
[9] Anscombe, *Intention*, §4, p. 9.

the question, "What distinguishes actions which are intentional from those which are not?"[10]

This much is beyond dispute; however, the explanation of the priority that is commonly offered is not. The explanation goes as follows: rather than holding — as is natural — that "intention" first and foremost refers to states of mind, and that bodily movements are described as "intentional" when they bear a certain relation — causal or explanatory — to such a state, Anscombe holds that "intentional" applies first and foremost to a class of bodily movements.[11] Donald Davidson, in his early work, attempted to develop this idea. He argued that when we give the intention with which a person acts — for example, when we say "James went to church with the intention of pleasing his mother" — we do not thereby refer to a state of mind that accompanies his action; rather the function of expressions like "the intention with which James went to church" is to "generate new descriptions of actions in terms of their reasons".[12]

Davidson came to think that his attempt to dispose with the referential use of "intention" — and hence the mental state as referent — ended in failure. The difficulty Davidson found was to account for "pure intending", which he defined as "intending that may occur without practical reasoning, action, or consequence".[13] In short, it is a problem for the view that the mental state of intending can be explained away, or explained by the more basic category of *intentional action,* if the mental state can occur in perfect isolation. Davidson concluded that the intelligibility of pure intending compels a theorist to admit the referential use of "intention" into her theory.[14] And once it has been admitted that

---

[10] I count here paragraphs whose focus is *intentional action* and *intention with which* an action is done. As becomes clear, in giving the *intention with which* an action is done, one also gives a description of the *intentional action.* §§1-3 and 50-52 are the excluded paragraphs.

[11] See e.g. Michael Bratman, *Intention, Plans, and Practical Reason* (Cambridge, MA: Harvard University Press, 1987), pp. 1 and 3. For discussion of this passage, see Moran and Stone, *op. cit.*, pp. 38-39.

[12] Davidson, "Actions, Reasons, and Causes", in his *Essays on Actions and Events* (Oxford: Oxford University Press, 2001), p. 8.

[13] Davidson, "Intending", p. 83.

[14] The case that Davidson describes is extremely odd, and it is not clear to me that it is coherent. Yet, as Anscombe points out, "No reason" is sometimes an intelligible answer to the question "Why?" (*Intention,* §17-18; §51). It is clear, however that Anscombe deals with such cases without taking them to show —

"I intend to X" *sometimes* involves reference to the mental state of intending, "there is no reason not to allow that intention of exactly the same kind is also present when the intended action eventuates".[15] The problem he located would cause problems for Anscombe too—at least on this understanding of the kind of priority she gives to intentional action.[16]

Second, Anscombe says that an agent knows her intentional actions "without observation".[17] This statement has intrigued philosophers of mind. It seems to suggest that one might have immediate, or perhaps groundless, knowledge of the states of one's body, in the way that epistemologists have traditionally thought is possible for states of one's mind. The difficulty is that *Intention* contains no adequate account of the nature of "non-observational knowledge", nor any explanation of how it might be possible to have knowledge of one's movements and actions which is not perceptually grounded. When Anscombe introduces the phrase she does so negatively, via a criterion for speaking of *knowing by observing*:

> where we can speak of separately describable sensations, having which is in some sense our criterion for saying something, then we can speak of observing that thing; but that is not generally so when we know the position of our limbs.[18]

Anscombe has generally been taken to be suggesting that when we have knowledge *without* observation, it is via sensations that are *not* separately describable, but this is itself a very unclear notion, not elucidated in *Intention*. G.N.A. Vesey complained that the "attempt to understand what Miss Anscombe means by 'knowledge without observation' is like a treasure hunt"—the "treasure" being an understanding of "the way in which the mind is embodied"—which, unfortunately "*seem[s]* to lead, not to philosophical treasure at all, but to ... absurdity".[19]

---

as does Davidson—that "there is something there to be abstracted" ("Intending", p. 89).
[15] Davidson, "Intending", p. 89.
[16] For discussion, see Moran and Stone, "Anscombe on Expressions of Intention: An Exegesis".
[17] Anscombe, *Intention*, p. 14.
[18] *Ibid.*, p. 13.
[19] G.N.A. Vesey, "Knowledge Without Observation", *The Philosophical Review*, 72 (201) 1963: 198-212. For other attempts, see C.B. Martin, "Knowledge without Observation", *Canadian Journal of Philosophy*, 1 (1) 1971: 15-24; John

Third, Anscombe seems to suggest that actions are individuated in terms of bodily action; so that if I put my signature on a piece of paper which is an order for a bomb to be dropped and which brings about the end of the war and blunts my pen nib and gives me cramp, I still only do *one* thing.[20] Following Goldman's *A Theory of Human Action*, this view became known as the "Identity thesis" or the "Davidson-Anscombe thesis", formalized as: if a person Fs *by G-ing*, then her act of F-ing = her act of G-ing.[21] Davidson commented that this thesis "immediately raises a number of questions, the first of which is, what are the entities that are identical or different?"[22] The only thing Anscombe has to say on that ontological question is that she has "always balked at [it]".[23]

In the decade following the publication of *Intention*, over 400 articles on its topic were published in peer-reviewed philosophy journals. Reviewing Goldman's book in 1972, Myles Brand lamented the fact that although (or perhaps, because) almost all of the "profitable discussion" had taken place in journals, the result was "piecemeal, often disunified". It was rare, he said, to see views on "act individuation, basic action, reasons as causes ... integrated into a coherent whole".[24] The idea that Anscombe's book contains these three sketched, but inadequately articulated, theses has meant it has been rarer still to see attempts to understand *Intention* as a coherent whole.

I want to take us back to those early reviews, and focus on a puzzle that came up for two reviewers—Judith Jarvis and Illtyd Trethovvan—but which has never really been part of the exegetical literature. In doing so I raise a question that is strikingly absent in work on Anscombe, especially when one considers its

---

McDowell, "Anscombe on Bodily Self-Knowledge", in Ford, Hornsby & Stoutland (eds.), *op. cit.*, pp. 128–46; Andy Hamilton, *The Self in Question* (London: Palgrave Macmillan, 2013), ch. 4.
[20] In fact, this is not Anscombe's view, as we will see below.
[21] Goldman, *A Theory of Human Action* (Englewood Cliffs, NJ: Prentice-Hall, 1970). This formalization is from George Wilson and Samuel Shpall, "Action", in *Stanford Encyclopaedia of Philosophy* (2012). Anscombe responds to Goldman in "Under a Description", *op. cit.*, pp. 211–14.
[22] Davidson, "Aristotle's Action", reprinted in his *Truth, Language and History* (Oxford: Clarendon Press, 2005), p. 284.
[23] Anscombe, "Under a Description", p. 210.
[24] Myles Brand, "Review", *The Journal of Philosophy*, 69 (9) 1972: 249. The "400" figure is Brand's.

prominence in work on her teacher, Wittgenstein: what is the philosophical method of *Intention*?

Neither Jarvis nor Trethovvan characterize *Intention* as a sketch of a theory of action, but instead see it as a contribution toward a descriptive project, designed to clear away misunderstandings and accreted errors about the grammar of the concept of "intention". This is the sort of project that might be associated with Wittgenstein or with the Oxford ordinary language philosophers — Anscombe's colleagues.[25] Jarvis proposes that Anscombe's major achievement is to "cut through a whole mass of philosophical clichés" and "give us a fresh, detailed picture of the concept of an action".[26] Trethovvan says that *Intention* "exposes the inadequacy or the inaccuracy of a good many statements which we might ordinarily let pass on the subject of intention".[27]

These reviewers read *Intention* as looking to provide an accurate description of how we apply the concept of intention, rather than a first sketch of a theory of action. If we look at *Intention*'s opening paragraph, we can bring this contrast into sharper focus.

> Very often, when a man says "I am going to do such-and-such", we should say that this was an expression of intention. We also sometimes speak of an action as intentional, and we may also ask with what intention the thing was done. In each case we employ a

---

[25] The question of the relation between Wittgenstein's grammatical method, and the methods of Oxford ordinary language philosophy — and indeed, the further question of Anscombe's understanding of that relation — is by no means straightforward. In his review, Copi stresses the similarity, saying that

> [Anscombe's] method is the familiar one, now prevalent at Oxford, of considering what one would say, or would accept as significant to say, in this or that particular situation. That method, however, is employed more sensitively and more sensibly by Miss Anscombe than by most of its other practitioners today. (*op. cit.*, p. 148)

However, Mary Warnock recalls that Anscombe was "absolutely furious" at her suggestion that she "thought Wittgenstein would agree with much of what had gone on in [Austin's] things class" (Mary Warnock, *A Memoir: People and Places*, p. 65).

For helpful suggestions on the relation of Wittgenstein and ordinary language philosophy, see Andy Hamilton, *Routledge Philosophy Guidebook to Wittgenstein's On Certainty* (London: Routledge, 2014), pp. 243–45.

[26] Jarvis, "Review", p. 41. It is amazing that there are absolutely no clichés or metaphors in Anscombe's *Intention*, nor indeed, as far as I can tell, in any of her writings.

[27] Trethevvan, "The Ethics of Intention", p. 12.

concept of "intention"; now if we set out to describe this concept, and took only one of these three kinds of statement as containing our whole topic, we might very likely say things about what "intention" means which it would be false to say in one of the other cases.[28]

When Anscombe's book is read as offering a novel theory of action, §1 is understood to make a tripartite division which introduces "philosophical perplexity" and an explanatory task for philosophy.[29] The task is to explain the nature of the connections between the following: the mental state of *intending to act*, *intentional action*, and *reason for acting* (intention with which).[30] In contrast, when read as an application of the methods of ordinary language philosophy, the section does not introduce a puzzle but, as we might put it, the range of statements that are the book's topic. Three sorts of statement employ the concept of intention:

- When she said "I am going to fail this exam", she was expressing her intention.
- She jumped intentionally.
- She left with the intention of fetching him.

The task is accurately to describe the conditions under which such statements are true or significant. We can begin to see the difficulty of that task by considering the three, superficially similar, statements which do not employ the concept:

- When she said "I am going to fail this exam", she was making a prediction.
- She jumped involuntarily.
- The thought "I must fetch him!" caused her to leave.[31]

---

[28] Anscombe, *Intention*, p. 1.
[29] This is Kieran Setiya's phrase in "Intention", *Stanford Encyclopaedia of Philosophy*, 2014.
[30] Indeed, Setiya describes this as the "principal task of the philosophy of intention," (*ibid.*). Moran and Stone call this view "transformed Anscombe", and make an excellent case against reading Anscombe as introducing and undertaking a "connective" explanatory project; for one thing, they point out, Anscombe's first head is "expression of intention for the future" and not the mental state of intending to act (*op. cit.*, esp. pp. 34-35).
[31] As Anscombe stresses in *Intention* (§5 and §§10-15) and in "Intention" (*Proceedings of the Aristotelian Society*, New Series, 57, 1956-7: 321-32), the difference between giving the cause of her leaving and giving a reason is far from straightforward, as these cases show. Consider, "She suddenly thought 'I

In each case, as Anscombe puts it, "the distinction ... *is* intuitively clear" — in the sense that we have no problems with it in our everyday human interactions — but "if ... we ask in philosophy what the difference is ... we are really asking what each of these is", and that is not "something that is intuitively obvious".[32]

At the end of this chapter, I will say something about the way in which this shift in how we think about the task and method of *Intention* changes the way we understand the priority Anscombe gives to intentional action, her statement that we know our actions "without observation", and the passages on action individuation. But first, I want to address a question that immediately arises when *Intention* is viewed as undertaking a descriptive, rather than an explanatory, project. The question is: what is *Intention* for? What is the point of a description of the use of these three kinds of statement? It will not give us a theory of action — at least, not in any traditional sense — and it will not move us beyond the knowledge that is already manifested in our capacity to employ the concept of "intention". As Anscombe acknowledges, these distinctions are already intuitively obvious. Jarvis attempts to reassure those "readers who will say: now that we've been through all of this, what have we?" by explaining that Anscombe has exposed "the sources of a host of philosophical muddles in which one can find oneself in dealing with these concepts".[33] This is the standard defence of descriptive methods in philosophy, but it leaves many unimpressed — especially when what one has to go through is so difficult. Trethovvan articulates his worry more forthrightly:

> Those who are not familiar with this kind of analysis will find it extremely heavy going. Anybody, I suppose, would find it difficult. Miss Anscombe holds that philosophy ought to be difficult, and this is obviously true if it means that philosophy ought not to be banal. The question which arises here is whether, in view of this extreme complexity, the results she has achieved ought to be called banal. This is not to suggest that the book is not worth reading. It provides a mental exercise of a kind which is most valuable in virtue of its very strenuousness; it exposes the inadequacy or the inaccuracy of a good many statements which we might ordinarily

---

must fetch him!' and was so upset by this impulsive idea she left the room in order to get some fresh air".
[32] *Intention*, pp. 1–2 and 6.
[33] Jarvis, "Review", p. 41.

let pass on the subject of intention; and it has an undercurrent, with occasional ebullitions, of quite remarkably caustic wit. But an analysis of intention which eschews all ethical questions seems doomed to reach rather unimportant conclusions.[34]

In the remainder of this paper I want to answer Trethovvan's question: ought *Intention* to be called banal? My suggestion is that Anscombe intended her ethics-free book to make it possible to do ethics; as such, the conclusions are far from unimportant. Though Anscombe eschews ethical questions, she intends the book to have profound consequences for ethics. The content is banal in its etymological sense—"common to all"—but certainly not in its usual English sense of "obvious" or "clichéd".

3. Anscombe on the Public Stage

Intention was published in 1957. Between 1956 and 1958 Anscombe was engaged in a series of public arguments with her colleagues, her university and her compatriots. During these three years, Anscombe came to recognize that the Hebrew-Christian ethic, the moral worldview of her Catholic religion, was utterly at odds with both the "highest and best ideals of the country at large" and with the moral philosophy of her contemporaries.[35] She saw the rejection of the older ethic as deeply corrupting, and as responsible for creating "an actually murderous world".[36] Her Christian ethical outlook, she found, was "hateful to the spirit of the age",[37] not because of its normative content, but because it held that there are some kinds of action for which "it is correct to say 'One doesn't have to consider whether to do this or not, in any circumstances; it is simply excluded'".[38] Anscombe was drawn into bitter public rows because she felt moved to defend that "hateful" truth. Her defence, however, is not of interest only to Christians. Anscombe, we will see, looks to provide a conceptual framework

---

[34] Trethovvan, "The Ethics of Intention", p. 12.
[35] Anscombe, "Does Oxford Moral Philosophy Corrupt the Youth?", *The Listener*, 57 (1455) (London: BBC, 14 February 1957).
[36] Anscombe, "The Dignity of a Human Being", in *Human Life, Action and Ethics: Essays by Anscombe*, eds. Mary Geach and Luke Gormally (Exeter: Imprint Academic, 2005), p. 73.
[37] Anscombe, "Contraception and Chastity", in *Faith in a Hard Ground: Essays on Religion, Philosophy and Ethics by G.E.M. Anscombe*, eds. Mary Geach and Luke Gormally (Exeter: Imprint Academic, 2008), p. 191.
[38] Anscombe, "Does Oxford Moral Philosophy Corrupt the Youth?", p. 349.

within which a secular, as well as theistic, ethics of prohibition could be articulated.[39]

It is against this deeply ethical—and for Anscombe, religious—context that we must see *Intention*. In short, an ethics according to which some actions are excluded simply in virtue of their kind requires a criterion for the *nature and quality of an act*. Anscombe, through these rows, came to recognize that such a criterion was lacking Her intention in *Intention* is to rectify this lack.

In this section we look at that historical context, and at those public debates in which Anscombe participated between 1956 and 1958. In them we witness Anscombe's gradually coming to the view that "it is not profitable for us to do moral philosophy until we have an adequate philosophy of psychology".[40] In the next section I will return to the intended consequences of *Intention*.

On 1st May 1956, Oxford University's Convocation—the University's governing body, comprised of all its academics—considered nominations for honorary degrees, to be awarded the following month. One of the nominations was Harry S. Truman, former President of the United States, and the man who had given the order to drop atomic bombs on Hiroshima and Nagasaki. Anscombe, then a tutor at Somerville College, "caused a small stir" in the House by arguing that the nomination should be rejected on the grounds that Truman was guilty of mass murder.[41] As such, she said, to show him honours was sycophantic and no

---

[39] In this chapter I want to exclude questions about content—about which kinds of acts fall within the prohibition. Here we are concerned with the work that must be done before *any* ethics of prohibition is to be possible. Anscombe coined the label "consequentialism" to describe any philosophical view which denied that it was ever correct to say "One doesn't have to consider whether to do this or not, in any circumstances; it is simply excluded" (Anscombe, "Modern Moral Philosophy", *Philosophy*, 33 (24) 1958: 1–19, reprinted in *Ethics, Religion and Politics: The Collected Philosophical Papers of G.E.M. Anscombe*, Vol. 3 (Minneapolis, MN: University of Minnesota Press, 1981), pp. 26–42, at p. 36). It is worth noting how far the meaning of the label has shifted since Anscombe introduced it (for a helpful discussion, see Mary Geach's introduction to *Human Life, Action, and Ethics*, pp. xvii–iii; and Cora Diamond, "Consequentialism in Modern Moral Philosophy and in 'Modern Moral Philosophy'", in *Human Lives: Critical Essays on Consequentialist Bioethics*, eds. David S. Oderberg & Jacqueline A. Laing (London: Palgrave Macmillan, 1977), pp. 13–38).
[40] Anscombe, "Modern Moral Philosophy", p. 26.
[41] "Limiting War", *Manchester Guardian*, 4 June 1956, p. 6.

different in principle from showing them to Nero or Genghis Khan.

Anscombe's speech did not persuade—though there is reason to suspect that this was less a matter of her argument than of the fact that members had already made up their minds and were not prepared to change them.[42] The House was asked to indicate its attitude towards the nomination, and showed overwhelming support.[43] On 20th June, Truman was awarded his honorary degree. Asked by a journalist about Anscombe's intervention, Truman stated: "I made the decision [to use the bombs] on the facts as they existed at the time, and if I had to do it again I would do it all over again."[44]

The fact that Truman was forced to rebut Anscombe's argument gives an indication of the very public nature of her protest. Reporters from the *Manchester Guardian* and *The Times* were present at Convocation, and both papers carried pieces on her protest, including summaries of her argument. Across the Atlantic, the *New York Times* picked up the story. Anscombe herself contributed to the public dissemination of her view by publishing her speech as a pamphlet. This publication was reported in the *Manchester Guardian*, which told its readers that it "shows that she had a respectable case". Insightfully, the paper also notes that Anscombe's argument "took in far more than Mr Truman" but extended to "all the princes and potentates of the earth—among them the democratic electorates".[45]

The facts that provide the background to Anscombe's intervention are familiar. In July 1945, the Allied forces were engaged in war with Japan, and were seeking the Japanese forces' unconditional surrender. One military option for achieving this end was

---

[42] Anscombe, in her pamphlet, recalls that the "dons of St John's were simply told 'The women are up to something in Convocation; we have to go and vote them down'" ("Mr Truman's Degree", p. 65.)

[43] Just who did and didn't side with Anscombe is a matter of some dispute. At the time, both *The Times* and the *Manchester Guardian* reported that "there were no calls of '*Non placet*' when the proposal was put before the House". However, R.D.M. Foot, who was also present, wrote to the *Manchester Guardian* to inform them that Anscombe's "*Non placet*" had been echoed by some in the House ("Degree for Mr Truman", *Manchester Guardian*, 7 May 1956, p. 6). He does not give names.

[44] "Oxford Don Fights Honor for Truman", *New York Times*, 19 June 1956, p. 3.

[45] "Limiting War".

a land invasion, but there was good evidence that this would have catastrophic consequences. A month earlier, at the battle of Okinawa — the result of Allied forces invading the Japanese island — 90,000 soldiers (US and Japanese) and 150,000 civilians were killed. Mass suicides were reported among the Japanese people. On the expectation that such losses would be repeated if troops were put on the ground, Truman ruled out a land invasion to "prevent ... an Okinawa from one end of Japan to the other".[46] These are among the "facts as they existed at the time".

Alternative means of securing unconditional surrender were sought, and the decision was taken to issue an ultimatum to the Japanese government: if it did not surrender unconditionally, the country would face "prompt and utter destruction". The Potsdam Declaration set out this ultimatum, and was signed by Truman, along with the British Prime Minister Winston Churchill and Chiang Kai-sheck, Leader of the Nationalist Government of China. The Japanese did not surrender and the threat was carried out: on 6th August Truman ordered an atomic bomb to be dropped on Nagasaki. Still no surrender came. On 9th August Truman ordered an atomic bomb to be dropped on Hiroshima. These two bombs killed between 75,000 and 125,000 people on impact, with the same number again dying before the end of the year of injuries and the effects of radiation. On 2nd September 1945 the Allies' end was achieved and the Japanese government surrendered unconditionally.

Anscombe says that Truman was guilty of mass murder. She does not object to killing or to war — Anscombe is no pacifist — but to murder.[47] Murder, Anscombe says, is "one of the worst of human actions" and as such is subject to absolute prohibition.[48] It follows that the predicted or actual consequences of a murderous act are irrelevant to the question of whether or not it should be done; it should not. Thus, when Truman says that he made his decision "on the facts as they existed at the time", he reveals himself to be denying that "it is correct to say [of dropping bombs on

---

[46] David M. Kennedy, *The American People in World War II* (Oxford: Oxford University Press, 1999), p. 410.
[47] Anscombe calls pacifism a false and harmful doctrine ("Mr Truman's Degree", p. 69). See also "War and Murder", in *Ethics, Religion, and Politics*, pp. 51–61; see esp., pp. 55–57.
[48] "Mr Truman's Degree", p. 64.

civilian populations] 'One doesn't have to consider whether to do this or not, in any circumstances; it is simply excluded'".

In her speech to Convocation, Anscombe sets out to show that when Truman ordered the dropping of the bombs, what he did was murder. Killing is murder if it meets two further conditions: it is intentional and the victims are innocent.[49] Her focus is on the second of these conditions and for this reason she devotes much of her speech to distinguishing her view from pacifist opposition to all intentional killing—which would include killing enemy combatants in war—and to considering the application of "innocent" in the context of war. However, our interest is in the first condition: that the killing be intentional. Anscombe, in 1956, supposed that it could not be seriously denied that Truman intentionally ordered the killing of the people of Nagasaki and Hiroshima. After all, he signed the order, and their deaths—their "prompt and utter destruction"—were the means by which Japan's unconditional surrender was to be achieved. In her pamphlet she mentions the speech given by the censor of St. Catherine's college, who spoke in defence of the nomination, and who seems rather inchoately to gesture toward such a denial:

> Mr Truman did not make the bombs and decide to drop them without consulting anybody; no, he was only responsible for the decision. Hang it all, you can't make a man responsible just because "his signature is at the foot of the order".[50]

Anscombe simply remarks that "such a speech does not deserve scrutiny; after all, it was just something to say on such an occasion".[51] She does not take seriously the Censor's suggestion that Truman can be held responsible only for signing his name, and not for all that followed. As we will see, Anscombe soon discovered that this was a misjudgment on her part.

The following year, on 14th February, Anscombe gave a talk on BBC radio's *Third Programme*. Her topic was "Does Oxford Moral Philosophy Corrupt the Youth?" Anscombe argued that it did not, but only because the youth were already exposed to the corrupting ideas of that philosophy in their life before university.

---

[49] Ibid.
[50] Ibid., p. 66.
[51] Ibid.

Anscombe's thesis is that the accusation is unfair because "Oxford moral philosophy is perfectly in tune with the highest and best ideas of the country at large".[52] She cites as evidence six ideas which make up the views of the country at large, and which are reflected in or supported by the moral philosophy of her colleagues.

1) An anti-Platonic view of justice, according to which a just society is one which is well-arranged, rather than one in which individuals act justly.
2) A "high" conception of responsibility for the future, limited only by our capacity to calculate the consequences of our action or inaction. So, a person is responsible for all the foreseen consequences of what she does.
3) A "gentle" conception of responsibility for the past, in which it is unfair to hold someone wholly responsible for what she did, given that it had all sorts of causes. So, causal factors which contributed to her doing what she did, or which were necessary to it having the results that it had, must be taken into account when assessing the extent of her responsibility.
4) A horror of suffering.
5) A flexibility about principles, which allows that one may choose the principles by which one wishes to live, and may change those principles in accord with circumstance.
6) A feeling that the changing nature of the world makes it wrong to impose a rigid moral code on children, who must be allowed to develop their own principles.[53]

In her radio-talk, Anscombe confines herself to "demonstrat[ing her thesis] in a few instances" — that is, to giving examples which show that these ideas are common to her colleague's moral philosophy and the country at large.[54] She conveys her contempt for them through a mixture of mockery and sarcasm — the tone is not so far from Swift's *A Modest Proposal*.[55] For example, she notes

---

[52] "Does Oxford Moral Philosophy Corrupt the Youth?", p. 267.
[53] These can be located in her talk. Anscombe also lists them, in this way, in "Oxford Moral Philosophy", *The Listener*, 4 April 1957, p. 537.
[54] "Does Oxford Moral Philosophy Corrupt the Youth?", p. 267. See also her letter to *The Listener* on 4th April, in which she cites further evidence.
[55] Reflecting on her paper "War and Murder", published in 1961, Anscombe expresses regret that it was "written in a tone of righteous fury" — Jenny Teichman describes Anscombe's tone in that paper as "like the Prophet

that it follows from (1) and (2) that "the correct procedure in making moral [and legal] decisions" is to "calculate the improvement of the general state of affairs", and also "that this is the correct procedure ... is constantly taught in the university". She illustrates its working in the world at large with the following example:

> A frequent occurrence that is much in the same spirit is the removal by authority of elderly widows from their dwelling, which anyone can see they are not keeping in accordance with the standards of hygiene which are desirable for their own and general welfare.[56]

Though forcibly removing widows from their homes on grounds of public hygiene is some way short of eating plump infants to alleviate the suffering of the poor, in presenting the practice Anscombe is clearly aiming for a similar effect on the reader as was Swift.

Among the actions that (1)-(6) make permissible is murder; that is, those ideas have nothing in them which would allow us to say, "One doesn't have to consider whether to commit murder, in any circumstances; it is simply excluded". We can see this if we consider once again the case of Truman. Truman does not act justly, in the Platonic sense, when he orders the killing of Japanese civilians; however, if justice is a matter of the arrangement of society, we may think that insofar as the unconditional surrender that Truman's act brings about is one which is better arranged — peaceful and democratic, for example — we may evaluate his action as promoting justice [1]. It might be said that Truman would have been neglecting his responsibilities if he had refrained from murdering Japanese civilians, given that he was able to predict the relative consequences of dropping the bomb and not dropping it, and to calculate that the former state of affairs was better [2].[57] However, as the Censor indicated, we cannot hold him

---

Jeremiah's" (J. Teichman, "Gertrude Elizabeth Margaret Anscombe: 1919-2001", *Biographical Memoirs of Fellows*, Vol. 115 (Oxford: Oxford University Press, 2002), p. 49. Anscombe laments that "if I was torn by a *saeva indignatio*, I wish I had the talent of Swift in expressing it" (*Introduction to Ethics, Religion and Politics*, p. vii; the Latin phrase is from Swift's self-penned epitaph).
[56] "Does Oxford Moral Philosophy Corrupt the Youth?", p. 267.
[57] In fact, Anscombe quite fiercely denies the claim that Truman saved lives with his act. See fn. 70.

wholly responsible for those murders, given that his order was just one of the many causal antecedents; his order *alone* did not bring about those deaths — he was just one tiny cog in a complex causal machine [3]. One of the reasons why we may think of his action as necessary — though obviously regrettable — is that he prevented even worse suffering than the suffering he caused; anything which decreases suffering is to be admired [4]. Thus, though it is clearly a good rule of thumb that murder is morally wrong, given certain circumstances, other principles, like the principle that one has a moral duty to do what is best for one's country, may replace it [5]. Finally, given that young people are growing into an increasingly complex world, in which the consequences of actions are ever more wide-reaching and interconnected, children should be taught to be flexible in their moral outlook, and to recognize that moral laws are like the Queensbury rules [6].

Anscombe makes absolutely no attempt to disguise her disgust at the ethical outlook embodied in (1)-(6), nor her contempt towards those who propagate it. Her talk outraged her colleagues and peers. Over the seven weeks following her broadcast, the BBC's *The Listener* magazine published fifteen letters to the editor, before announcing the correspondence closed. Four were from Anscombe, defending her thesis and her reputation; the rest were from her Oxford colleagues and other philosophers.

R.M. Hare, one of the Oxford moral philosophers whom Anscombe is attacking, took particular exception. This is no surprise as he is explicitly identified in Anscombe's talk. She begins by referring to a review in *Mind* which reported that "there are people who think that moral philosophy in one of its current fashions 'corrupts the youth'".[58] She refers here to R.B. Braithwaite's review of Hare's *The Language of Morals*. In that review, Braithwaite says that the charge of corruption would be "utterly fantastic in the case of Mr. Hare" due to his "high moral earnestness".[59] Anscombe remarks that earnestness is "not good evidence" for the claim some someone is not a corrupter; on the contrary, she says, "if you really wanted to corrupt people ...

---

[58] "Does Oxford Moral Philosophy Corrupt the Youth?", p. 266.
[59] R.B. Braithwaite, "Review", *Mind*, 63 (250) 1954: 249.

moral earnestness would, in fact, be an important item of equipment".[60]

Hare took Anscombe's opening remarks to imply—which of course they don't—that "if someone seems to be earnest about a moral question, the obvious explanation is that this is 'an important piece of equipment' for corrupting people".[61] Her point is negative: moral earnestness is not evidence that someone is not corrupt.[62] He also represents her as disapproving of "the desire to prevent suffering, especially that of children". What Anscombe says is that what it means to take "preventive measures" in relation to children's welfare (in order to prevent suffering [4]) is to determine to "go into people's homes to push them around, not because they have done anything, but just in case they do"; her point is that suffering ought not to be prevented by unjust action, not that the desire to prevent children from suffering is inappropriate.[63] Anscombe dismisses his accusations as "simple expressions of rage".[64] He attributes to her the view—which he finds incredible—that it is "wrong to judge acts by the foreseen consequences of committing them".[65] But, Anscombe thinks only that it is wrong to think that every kind of act is such that it may be rendered permissible by its consequences.

Antony Flew describes her broadcast as full of "bitter sneers" and "an affront to professional standards and to the decencies of controversy". He accuses her of "characteristically" relying on "the fact that few of her readers will ... check any assertion she

---

[60] Anscombe, "Does Oxford Moral Philosophy Corrupt the Youth?", pp. 266–267.
[61] R.M. Hare, "Oxford Moral Philosophy", *The Listener*, 21 February 1957, p. 311.
[62] That said, she is certainly suspicious of those who appear morally earnest. Compare her discussion of the false view of Christianity: "turning counsels into precepts results in high-sounding principles" ("War and Murder", p. 56). Compare also her third thesis in "Modern Moral Philosophy": "that the concepts ... *moral* obligation and *moral* duty ... ought to be jettisoned if this is psychologically possible." I take it that one of Anscombe's points here is that these words are used to articulate "high sounding precepts" which amount to nothing more than empty expressions of earnestness (p. 26).
[63] Anscombe, "Does Oxford Moral Philosophy Corrupt the Youth?", p. 267.
[64] Ancombe, "Oxford Moral Philosophy", *The Listener*, 28 February 1957, p. 349.
[65] R.M. Hare, "Oxford Moral Philosophy", *The Listener*, 21 February 1957, p. 311.

may find it convenient to make".⁶⁶ Nowell-Smith says she uses "sarcasm, innuendo, and travesty" to spread "misrepresentation about colleagues".⁶⁷ Anscombe replies that her colleagues "aren't angry at me because I misrepresented them, but because I represented them truthfully. Really, their only objection should be that I laughed at them".⁶⁸

The letters display a startling misapprehension of Anscombe's talk. Her style is difficult, it is true, but the lack of understanding looks at times wilful. Her claim is that there is a worldview — prevalent in society and reflected in the work of her colleagues — according to which justice is a matter of how things are arranged, and actions are evaluated by their foreseen consequences. That worldview, she says, may make permissible or preferable courses of action — for example, certain procedures for looking after widows — which are unjust, in the Platonic sense.

Anscombe's strategy of holding up for derision the implications of (1)-(6) was not particularly successful, and not just because it elicited rage rather than critical engagement. She perhaps underestimated the extent to which the actions that she saw as shocking — authorities intervening to prevent cruelty to children by "go[ing] into people's homes to push them around"; bombing civilian populations; removing widows from there homes — would strike her peers as quite sensible policies. A lot of what Anscombe finds shocking fails to shock. What helps to bring out the radical character of (1)-(6) — the familiarity of which can make them seem benign — is to contrast with their negations. This will give us the framework for the ethic Anscombe seeks to recover.

1') A Platonic view of justice, according to which a just society is one in which individuals act justly, rather than one which is well-arranged.
2') A "practicable" conception of responsibility for the future, limited to what we intend or voluntarily bring about.

---

[66] Anthony Flew, "Oxford Moral Philosophy", *The Listener*, 28 February 1957, p. 349; and 21 March, p. 457.
[67] Nowell-Smith, "Oxford Moral Philosophy", *The Listener*, 14 March 1957, p. 405.
[68] Anscombe, "Oxford Moral Philosophy", *The Listener*, 4 April 1957, p. 564.

3') A "severe" conception of responsibility for the past, in which a person is wholly responsible for what he does, intentionally or voluntarily.[69]
4') An acceptance of suffering.
5') An inflexibility about principles, in which principles remain fixed however the circumstances may change.
6') A recognition of parental authority, and parental duty to teach a moral code to children.

Anscombe argues for each of (1')-(6') elsewhere.[70]

Among the letters of protest and outrage is one by Nowell-Smith which identifies the task that needs undertaking if an ethical code based on (1')-(6') is to be possible; he intends this as a rebuke, but Anscombe instead sees it as an invitation:

> The general burden of her criticism of the morality of the country at large is that people tend to judge all acts by their consequences rather than by their "nature and quality" and she implies that Oxford philosophers share this attitude ... Miss Anscombe seems to be (though I can scarcely believe that she is) ignorant of the difficulties involved in drawing a distinction between an act and its consequences. For example, was Mr. Truman's "act" the signing of an order, the killing of a number of Japanese, or the saving of a number of Japanese and other lives? If it was the first only, Miss Anscombe has, on her own principles, as little right to condemn it as Mr. Truman's supporters have to defend it, since both judgments turn on its consequences. But if the killing is to be included in the nature and quality of Mr. Truman's act, why not the saving of lives?[71]

Nowell-Smith's point is worth pause. Anscombe's claim is that when Truman gave the order for the bombs to be dropped, what he did was commit mass murder, and that as such it was an act

---

[69] I take the labels "practicable" and "severe" from Anscombe's description of Christianity in "War and Murder". She says: "The truth about Christianity is that it is a severe and practicable religion, not a beautifully ideal but impracticable one" (p. 56).
[70] See e.g. "War and Murder"; "Murder and the Morality of Euthanasia" in *Human Life, Action and Ethics*; "The Moral Environment of the Child" in *Faith in Hard Ground*; "Authority in Morals" in *Faith in Hard Ground*; "Sins of Omission? The Non-Treatment of Controls in Criminal Trials", in *Human Life, Action and Ethics*.
[71] Nowell-Smith, "Oxford Moral Philosophy", *The Listener*, 21 February 1957, p. 311.

the nature and quality of which render it prohibited. But Nowell-Smith proposes that Anscombe faces a dilemma. If the "nature and quality of an act" is determined by what is done in the moment, then Truman's act is morally neutral (all he did was put "his signature is at the foot of the order"); if it is determined by its foreseen consequences, Anscombe should include as part of the "nature and quality of the act" the lives that Truman predicted his act would save (by its preventing an "Okinawa from one end of Japan to the other"). In which case, what right has she to condemn Truman for murder rather than to praise him for life-saving?

In her letter of response, Anscombe simply acknowledges "the colossal difficulty of making out the character of an act" given that an act may be described in virtue of its foreseen consequences.[72] She goes on:

> The suggestion that one cannot treat "Do not murder" as an intelligible commandment in a broadcast without a preliminary *exposé* of the philosophical problems of defining an action seems to me in a high degree comic. I lecture on such problems in Oxford, in the philosophy of psychology.[73]

During Hilary term (January–March) 1957 — the term in which she gave her radio talk, and wrote that letter — Anscombe was delivering the series of lectures that became the *Intention*.

---

[72] She changes the example because, she says, "a factual example ought to be according to fact", and that Truman's act "saved lives is merely one of the known lies it is permissible to tell"; Truman's act may have spared more lives than would a land invasion, but given that "it is well known … that Truman knew the Japanese were urgently seeking to surrender on terms". Instead, she gives a fictional case, in which the job is to make out the nature and quality of "an act which is at once (*a*) sending chocolates through the post, (*b*) poisoning your aunt, (*c*) securing a legacy". Nowell-Smith takes this to be an act of subversion on her part; he writes to *The Listener* again, complaining that her remark is "sarcastic in that she affects to believe that I would find a 'colossal difficulty' in a case in which there is clearly no difficulty at all". But in this he is quite wrong. There is precisely the same difficulty about Anscombe's fictional case as about Truman's. Are we to condemn the person at the post-box on the grounds that she is murdering her aunt, or commend her for sending chocolates, or think her practical for securing a legacy? That Nowell-Smith fails to see the cases as parallel must reveal a failure on his part to appreciate the nature of the difficulty he himself raises.

[73] Anscombe, "Oxford Moral Philosophy", *The Listener*, 21 March 1957, p. 457.

4. The Intended Consequences of *Intention*

Intention is an answer to the question "how do we tell the character of an act?" This is not a metaphysical question, but a conceptual one. What distinction are we making when we evoke these intuitively clear contrasts: "That was an expression of intention, not a prediction"; "that was involuntary not intentional"; "that was the cause, not the reason"? The central case Anscombe uses to illuminate this question is one of *war* and *murder*:

> A man is pumping water into the cistern which supplies the drinking water of a house. Someone has found a way of systematically contaminating the source with a deadly cumulative poison whose effects are unnoticeable until they can be cured. The house is regularly inhabited by a small group of party chiefs, with their immediate families, who are in control of a great state; they are engaged in exterminating the Jews and perhaps plan a world war. — The man who contaminated the source calculated that if all these people are destroyed some good men will get into power who will govern well ...; and he has revealed the calculation, together with the fact about the poison, to the man who is pumping. The death of the inhabitants of the house will, of course, have all sorts of other effects ...
>
> This man's arm is going up and down, up and down ... Now we may ask: What is this man doing? What is *the* description of his action?[74]

Here is not the place to repeat Anscombe's detailed answer, and there is certainly no space to work through the implications of this shift in our thinking about *Intention*'s task. However, a very quick sketch of Anscombe's answer to the question she poses in §38 will be enough to cast doubt on the idea that her book contains the three theses about action, three theses which need technical and argumentative scaffolding.

Anscombe begins by pointing out that "of course, *any* description of what is going on, with him as the subject, which is in fact true" is a description of what he is doing.[75] When we say what a man is "doing" in this wide sense, we are indifferent to the distinctions that are Anscombe's topic. This list will include descriptions which he *intends* ("operating the pump"), *knows*

---

[74] *Intention*, p. 37.
[75] *Ibid.*, p. 37.

("clicking out a rhythm"), and *does not know* ("generating certain substances in some nerve fibres"); and descriptions in terms of consequences which are *intended* ("poisoning the inhabitants"), *foreseen* ("earning some money"), and *unforeseen* ("causing NN to come into some money through a legacy"). She then notes that her "enquiries into the question 'Why?' enables us to narrow down our considerations of descriptions of what he is doing to a range covering all and only his intentional actions".[76] This range is delimited by the application of the question "Why?", the criteria for which are summarized in §16.[77] Any description that falls within that range will give the "character of [his] act". Next, Anscombe sets out how the descriptions within this range can be arranged into chains of descriptions, and it is this ordering principle that introduces the possibility of asking *how many* things that this man is doing, in that he is moving his arm up and down.[78]

In this context, Anscombe's focus on intentional action—on "what a man actually does"—is explained by the fact that it is there that the criteria for the application of the question "Why?" and the formal order that the question reveals are most easily brought into view. The priority is a matter of method and not metaphysics. The statement that a man knows what he is doing without observation is not an epistemological thesis. Rather, it is the criterion for the application of the question "Why?": a description of what I am doing which I recognize only because I observe that I am doing it is not a description of my intentional action. Anscombe owes no account of the capacity to say straight off how one's limbs are arranged—this capacity, she says, is quite distinct from the capacity to say straight off what one is (intentionally) doing. What *Intention* is concerned with is removing various assumptions about knowledge—and especially about the relation between knowledge and belief—that prevent us from accepting her criterion. She does this by describing the way in which the capacity to reason practically about how to get what one wants can put one in a position to say what one is doing or will do, and then showing that when that reasoning is sound, it is appropriate to characterize this as a case of knowledge. Finally,

---

[76] Ibid., p. 38.
[77] Ibid., pp. 24–25.
[78] Ibid., p. 45.

the "identity thesis", so called, is no part of Anscombe's view. That thesis has ontological commitments, it asserts an identity relation between entities: if a person Fs *by* Ging, then her act of Fing = her act of Ging. Anscombe's, on the other hand, describes an "order that is there whenever actions are done with intentions", an order which shows why a single action may be described in many ways.[79]

The context I have described allows us to reconstruct the intended consequences of *Intention* – consequences which have not come to pass. Had those first reviewers made the connection between Anscombe's "righteous fury" and her philosophy of action, things might have turned out very differently.[80]

The most significant omission from the legacy of *Intention* is an attempt to undertake, using the account of action provided in *Intention*, the ethical task that Anscombe describes in "Modern Moral Philosophy". That paper was published in January 1958, just a few months after *Intention*. In it Anscombe famously defends three theses, the first of which is that "moral philosophy ... should be laid aside at any rate until we have an adequate philosophy of psychology".[81] What is needed, Anscombe says, before ethics can begin, is "an account at least of what a human action is at all, and how its description as 'doing such-and-such' is affected by its motive and by the intention or intentions in it; and for this an

---

[79] *Ibid.*, p. 80.
[80] It is rather surprising that they didn't. Perhaps Alan R. White's rather astounding verdict on the third volume of *The Collected Papers of G.E.M. Anscombe* — the volume on *Ethics, Religion and Politics* — is revealing of a more general prejudice among philosophers:

> The group of articles in the third volume, which I have called personal expressions of opinion, includes such themes as war and murder, the morality of dropping the atom bomb on Hiroshima, the justice of the 1939-45 war ... Since I don't believe that the opinions of a philosopher, however intelligent, are of any more — or any less — value on such themes than those of an equally intelligent non-philosopher, I think they are misclassified under the title *Collected Philosophical Papers*. I shall say nothing about them. ("Review", *The Philosophical Quarterly*, 33 (131) Apr. 1983, p. 192)

Or perhaps the exclusion of overtly ethical questions in *Intention* was enough to push Anscombe's recent forays into questions of ethics to one side. Had *Intention* been published *after* "Modern Moral Philosophy", perhaps the connections would have been more salient.
[81] "Modern Moral Philosophy", p. 26.

account of such concepts is needed".[82] *Intention* provides that piece of "conceptual analysis". Anscombe's intention in doing that work was to provide ethics with a starting point from which it could give an explanation of "how an unjust man is a bad man, or an unjust action a bad one", not a starting point from which philosophers of mind and action could fill out technical details in a metaphysics of action.[83]

---

[82] *Ibid.*, p. 29
[83] *Ibid.*

Candace Vogler

Nothing Added: Intention §§19 & 20[1]

1. Introduction

Suppose that Elizabeth Anscombe gets this much right about intentional action: an action is a means–end-structured process that is intentional under some descriptions, unintentional under others, and an agent's reasons for acting are keyed to those descriptions under which what's done is intentional; these pick out *which* action the agent does.

Let *A*-ing and *B*-ing be types of actions that the agent means to do, and let *A*-ing be a means to *B*-ing. Anton Ford points out that there are three principal varieties of means–end relation.[2] *A*-ing

---

[1] I have had a lot of help with this essay. I am grateful to Will Small, Jonathan Lear, Robert Pippin, David Finkelstein, David Holiday and Charles Todd for early discussion of §§19 and 20 of *Intention*. I am grateful to Olav Gjelsvik and Jennifer Hornsby for an opportunity to give an early draft of the essay in Oslo, and to Patricia Kitcher, Elijah Millgram and Ruth Leys for discussion of my initial revisions while I was at the Wissenschaftskolleg in Berlin. I profited tremendously from comments and questions raised by Eric Marcus (my discussant), Matthew Boyle, Kieran Setiya, Doug Lavin, Agnes Callard, John McDowell, Anselm Müller, Gavin Lawrence, Matthias Haase and Eric Wiland at the conference on Anscombe's *Intention* in Chicago, and to Michael Thompson, Gabriel Lear, Jason Bridges and Anton Ford for their encouragement. Amanda Perreau-Saussine suggested an additional revision, and Jonathan Lear encouraged me to send it off once I had addressed that concern.

[2] Anton Ford, "Handout, Part II: Varieties of Mean–End Relation", Action and Practical Knowledge, Philosophy 51504, University of Chicago, Week 9 (2 March 2009).

can be part of *B*-ing as dissolving yeast is part of baking bread.³ *A*-ing can be, as Anscombe put it in a slightly different context, "brute relative" to *B*-ing, as raising my hand is brute relative to bidding on a horse at auction.⁴ Or *A*-ing can be a species of *B*-ing, as swimming is a species of taking exercise.⁵ There may be other

---

³ See e.g. G.E.M. Anscombe, *Intention* (Cambridge, MA: Harvard University Press, 2000), §23, the poisoning example, on the relation between "moving your arm up and down", "pumping", "replenishing the house water-supply" and "poisoning the inhabitants".

⁴ See G.E.M. Anscombe, "On Brute Facts", reprinted in *The Collected Philosophical Papers of G.E.M. Anscombe, Volume Three: Ethics, Religion and Politics* (Minneapolis, MN: University of Minnesota Press, 1981), pp. 22–25. Anscombe focusses on an example in which, after I have ordered some potatoes, the grocer "brings potatoes to my house" and "leaves them there", in such a way that these acts count as "supplying me with potatoes". Bringing the potatoes to my house and leaving them there are brute relative to supplying me with potatoes, hence, filling my order. The whole — my order, and his filling of my order — are brute relative to my owing him money for the potatoes. In the essay, she is particularly concerned with dispelling crude variations of philosophical faith in the thought that one can't derive an "ought"-claim from a statement of fact. The general point about a variety of means–end relation is this: some act-types — e.g. bidding (while attending an auction, online, through a real estate agent), purchasing, greeting, registering for courses, filing a complaint, making a gift, proctoring an exam, marrying or divorcing — are governed by convention. If I intend to do such a thing, then the means at my disposal are also constrained by convention. For example, if I intend to make a monthly payment on my mortgage, then I need to see to it that some of my funds are *appropriately* transferred to the bank that holds my mortgage. I can do this in any of several ways, but not just *any* way of moving money from my accounts to the mortgage-holder will do. For example, it *won't* count as making a mortgage payment if I withdraw cash in the amount of my monthly payment from my savings account, tie it up in a cloth bag with a red ribbon, and quietly leave the bag in a corner of the lobby of a local branch office of the bank that holds my mortgage. Leaving cash in the lobby is *not* a means to making a mortgage payment. Setting up a repeating payment through my checking account online *is* a means to paying my mortgage, and the various things that I must do in order to set up my payment — e.g. entering different strings of numbers in distinct fields of an online form, entering an address in other fields, checking these entries against information recorded on a billing notice, moving the cursor in order to submit the form to my bank — *are* means to paying my mortgage and so are among the things that I can do that are brute relative to mortgage payment. I am grateful to Amanda Perreau-Saussine for urging me to explain the sense in which "brute-conventional" is a variety of means–end relation.

⁵ See e.g. G.E.M. Anscombe, *Intention*, §22 on the relation between "lying on a bed" and "Resting" or "Doing Yoga".

varieties of means–end relation, but there are at least these three: part–whole, brute–conventional, species–genus.

Anscombe began investigating these matters her 1957 monograph, *Intention*. Partly inspired by Donald Davidson's fondness for that slender volume, Anglophone philosophers of action came increasingly to cite *Intention* with filial piety or substantive approval, and then to attribute theses to Anscombe that she *did not* propound (such as that moral goodness is the constitutive principle of willing,[6] or that psychological states pertinent to action can have exactly one of two directions of fit[7]), to find tendencies in her work that she argued *against* (such as behaviorism[8]) and to provide summaries of her position that are *inconsistent* with her method, arguments and substantive conclusions (such as that she teaches us to see intention under three headings: intending to act, acting intentionally and acting with an intention[9]). Decades of widespread philosophical acclaim marching arm-in-arm with equally widespread philosophical misunderstanding may help to

---

[6] See e.g. J. David Vellemen, "The Guise of the Good", *Noûs*, 26 (1) 1992: 19–20. Anscombe was quick to point out that people knowingly do disgraceful, wicked things for the sake of money, fame, ease, victory in war and so on. The claim that human action aims at good is, for Anscombe, completely compatible with noticing that immorality is common, and need not stir so much as a prick of conscience in the wrongdoer. As she put it,

> It is true that it is usually for the sake of something one thinks advantageous (and so in a sense good) that one consciously misbehaves, but that does not mean that one's will is just for the good and not for the misbehaviour, recognizably such, at all.

[Anscombe, "Sin", in *Faith in a Hard Ground: Essays on Religion, Philosophy and Ethics by G.E.M. Anscombe*, eds. Mary Geach and Luke Gormally (Exeter: Imprint Academic, 2008), p. 125] *Bonum est multiplex*.

[7] See e.g. Mark Platts, *Ways of Meaning* (London: Routledge and Kegan Paul, 1979), pp. 256–57. It is worth noticing, in this connection, that intention in a complex course of action, *qua* cause of what it knows and explains, both changes what is the case (mind-to-world direction of fit) and compasses such matters as taking alternate means to one's end should obstacles arise (world-to-mind direction of fit – intention in action is responsive and answerable to how things are and how they are going). Anscombe gives many examples in her monograph.

[8] See e.g. Michael Bratman, "Davidson's Theory of Intention", in *Actions and Events: Perspectives on the Philosophy of Donald Davidson*, eds. Ernest LePore and Brian P. McLaughlin (Oxford: Basil Blackwell, 1985), p. 14.

[9] See e.g. George Wilson, "Action", *Stanford Encyclopedia of Philosophy* (Spring 2002 edition), ed. Edward N. Zalta, <http://plato.stanford.edu/entries/action/>.

explain why Anscombean practical philosophy is still in its infancy.

In action theory, the standard going alternatives to Anscombean work are indebted to Davidson. In ethics, they are of three sorts: neo-Kantian work, Humean work and the kind of work in virtue theory that rests on the view that, as Philippa Foot puts it, "dispositions, motives, and other 'internal' elements are the primary subjects and determinants of moral goodness and badness".[10] What unites Davidsonian action theory with these approaches in moral philosophy is the conviction that the difference between sound intentional actions and other happenings in a human life is precisely the presence and proper operation of some internal element.

Now, Anscombe has no quarrel with moral psychology. *Intention* is a work of moral psychology. But it is a kind of moral psychology in which we attend to the deliberately making something the case in order to understand having a *mind* to make something the case. The more usual approach takes things the other way around.

The mind-first approach requires locating and giving an account of the internal item or structure that makes an action intentional. When all goes well for an agent, this element will also render her action rational or otherwise good. At the very least, when all goes well, accurate accounting of the internal element will show that agents do *not* paradigmatically take themselves to have overriding reasons to *avoid* doing what they do. The mind-first strategy has been fertile. It turned out, for instance, that an account of intentional action does *not* follow straightforwardly from just any account of having a mind to make something the case. The obvious response was to generate complex proposals in philosophical practical psychology in order to repair the breach.

Anscombe attempted to ward off such approaches in *Intention*. If the arguments of §19 are any good, for example, they ought to tell against the mind-first approach in contemporary Anglophone ethics and action theory. If the arguments of §20 work, then they ought to dispel any sense that Anscombe is prone to behaviourism. Together, the arguments in §§19 and 20 are meant to clear the ground necessary for work on practical knowledge.

---

[10] Philippa Foot, "Rationality and Goodness", in *Modern Moral Philosophy*, ed. Anthony O'Hear (Cambridge: Cambridge University Press, 2004), p. 2, n1.

Both sections are meditations on what happens if we try to develop an account of intention by isolating aspects. In §19, we isolate the doer—"the man considered by himself in the moment of acting"—and in §20 we isolate his deed by asking "is 'intentional' a characteristic of the actions that have it, which is formally independent of" expression of intention for the future and of further intention in acting?[11]

2. Background

Anscombe works from examples. The examples almost always involve a man doing something and an interlocutor asking questions about what he is up to as he goes along. Her arguments build, of course, and she has worked to establish a number of points in the eighteen sections preceding the two I will read. For my purposes, the crucial points emerging from §§1–18 concern intentional actions:

1. You will likely make true statements about what a man intends if you say what he is doing because normally a man intends to do the kind of thing you see him doing, an intentional action [§4].
2. Intentional actions are those datable events in a man's history to which a certain sense of the question "Why are you A-ing?" (where A-ing is a kind of thing that you are doing) has application [§§5–6].
3. The relevant sense of the question can be isolated by considering responses to the question "Why are you A-ing?" that *refuse* its application, crucially, "I merely observed that I was A-ing," "A-ing was involuntary" (in a special sense of *involuntary*) and "I didn't know that I was A-ing" [§§6–17].
4. Since an action can be described in many ways, as A-ing, say, and also as C-ing, "Why are you A-ing?" may be given application while "Why are you C-ing?" is not [§§4 & 6].
5. The question "Why are you A-ing?" is *not* refused application by the answer: "No reason" or "I don't know why I'm doing that" [§17].

---

[11] She has been investigating intention by considering expression of future intention, intentional action and the further intention with which one acts. The question that orients the argument in §20 emerges from this framework.

6. When the question "Why are you *A*-ing?" *has* application, and the response is *not* something on the order of "no reason", the response gives a reason for *A*-ing; such responses are themselves expressions of intention [§§15–16].
7. Finally, a reason for acting, given as a response to "Why are you *A*-ing?" is the kind of statement that you can argue *against* in ways that link the reason with motives and intentions [§15].

All seven points are on the table by the time we reach §19. All are involved in her arguments in §§19 and 20.

3. Reading §19

Begin with a modest reading of §19. The question under consideration is whether an action is made intentional "in virtue of any extra feature which exists when it is performed".[12] Since any such feature will enable a man to give or refuse application of our "Why?"-question, and since that question is couched in terms of the kind of thing we see him doing, his positive responses pick out descriptions under which his action is intentional. The extra feature, then, will have something to do with the man, with what he has in mind in doing what he's doing, and with what kind of thing he is up to.

We suppose such a feature—"*I*"—and claim that a man's intentional actions are all and only those of a man's doings appropriately accompanied by *I*. We know that actions are intentional under some descriptions but not others. We want to account for intentional action. *I*, then, must be "interpreted as a description" or else "as having an internal relation to a description, of an action".[13]

Paradigmatically, intentional actions involve movement—our first clue about a man's intentions came from saying what he was doing—so we at least are supposing that *I* + movement = intentional action, when a man is, say, sawing a plank. We see that he's sawing a plank by watching him. That's not how *he* does it. Since "I didn't know I was doing that" refuses application of the relevant "Why?"-question, he must know something of what he's doing. To distinguish what he knows from what we observe, Anscombe points out that any intentional action we watch will

---

[12] Anscombe, *Intention*, §19, p. 28.
[13] *Ibid.*

involve bodily events — muscle contractions, say. Focussing on *these* movements, then, will likely lead us to focus on his understanding of what he is doing as a species of self-knowledge. And that is just what we hope to do if we hope to understand intentional action by focussing on the man himself isolated at the moment of acting.

Movements like muscle contractions are not *un*intentional, since they are among the bodily aspects of what he is doing. Anscombe calls them *preintentional*. Accordingly, our hypothesis is: preintentional movement + *I* = intentional action. She writes:

> If so, then the preintentional movement + *I* guarantees that *an* intentional action is performed: but which one?[14]

In order to pick out *an* intentional action that the man is performing, *I* must be a description under which what he does is intentional, or else must bear an internal relation to such a description.[15] *Ex hypothesi*, we are beginning from un-interpreted preintentional movements. Our man is charged with assigning a description to them, a description that will place them as bodily aspects of his action. Getting the descriptions right will, in turn, allow us to open the relevant field of new inquiry about what the man is up to and why — "Why are you moving your hand?" for

---

[14] *Ibid.*
[15] Suppose that *I* is a description. Then our situation is the practical equivalent of supposing that I am using the word *white* to name a colour experience — the white-sensation. Now suppose that *I* is internally related to a description. Our situation is analogous to the one in which "The snow *appears* red" expresses the same thought as "The snow *is* white", when the snow is seen under red light. The example is Gottlob Frege's. In §24 of *Die Grundlagen der Arithmetik*, Frege wrote, "When we see a blue surface, we have an impression of a unique sort, which corresponds to the word *blue*; this impression we recognize again, when we catch sight of another blue surface". In §26, he distinguished the "wholly subjective" sensation of, for example, white, from an objective use of the term *white*. The objective use is what is at issue when snow is viewed through a coloured lens or under coloured light: "When we call snow white, we mean to refer to an objective quality, which we recognize, in ordinary daylight, by a certain sensation. If the snow is seen in a coloured light, we take that into account in our judgment and say, for instance, 'It *appears* red at present, but it *is* white.'" I strongly suspect that these passages from the *Grundlagen* were the source of inspiration for Ludwig Wittgenstein's private language argument. See: *Die Grundlagen der Arithmetik* (Breslau, 1884); *The Foundations of Arithmetic*, 2nd Edition, trans. J.L. Austin (Evanston, IL: Northwestern University Press, 1980).

instance, if the muscle contractions are occurring in the course of hand movement.

Suppose that he is moving his hand. Our man could be castling in a game of chess, or displaying the habitual flex that he performs whenever he completes the hostile takeover of a rival firm, or blessing the congregation, or *anything at all*. *Ex hypothesi*, the movements are un-interpreted (hence, *pre*intentional). And "nothing about the man considered by himself in the moment of contracting his muscles, and nothing in the contraction of the muscles, can possibly determine the content of the description: which therefore may be *any* one, if we are merely considering what can be determined by the man by himself in the moment."[16]

This is a modest reading of §19 as an extension of the private language argument in a practical sphere. It's not wrong. It can even accommodate a modest reading of internally related to a description — suppose we ask why he is making a pile of sawdust and he replies that he is sawing a plank. One makes sawdust in the course of sawing.

How will he be able to engage in even *this* simple exchange if we imagine that intentional action is a matter of assigning action-descriptions to un-interpreted, preintentional bodily events? After all, an expression of intention opens a field of inquiry into reasons for acting. Accounts of muscle contractions may invite diagnostic questions, but not questions about practical reason or practical knowledge. Such contractions could occur during fitful sleep or as one lays dying. When Anscombe charges that under the assumption that an extra *I* added to the proceedings makes them intentional action, it "is a mere happy accident that an *I* relevant to the wider context and further consequences *ever* accompanies the preintentional movements", her use of "wider context and further consequences" is meant to remind us of this.[17]

The ambitious reading builds upon the modest reading by enlarging upon the candidates for the intentional-action-making-feature *I*. On the most ambitious reading of §19 that I can sustain, her target is not the view that understanding intentional action requires mapping descriptions onto movements, mind onto world. It is the view that the addition or the proper operation of an internal element — a state, a structure, a disposition, an *I* — makes

---

[16] Anscombe, *Intention*, §19, pp. 28–29.
[17] *Ibid.*, §19, p. 29.

an action intentional, and so makes the difference between intentional action and things like involuntary gestures, muscle spasms or episodes of sleepwalking. And that element could be *any one* that you like. She needs a target this wide and this varied in her sights if she is to justify her claim, "We do not add anything attaching to the action at the time it is done by describing it as intentional", the very first sentence of the section. Showing that we do not get an intentional action by inwardly mapping pre-intentional movements onto action-descriptions is not enough. As far as I know, *none* of her contemporaries thought that an intentional action was bodily events internally mapped to descriptions.

Suppose an account of what a person has in mind when setting out to do something. It doesn't matter what sort of an account you choose. The person has a fully formed, holistic Davidsonian mind and has made all things considered judgments about what she should do as a result of sustained and reflective practical reasoning. Or, the person has an excellent character—he is non-accidentally sensitive to what ought to be done in any circumstances, and disposed to do a good action in the appropriate manner with respect to the appropriate other people under the appropriate circumstances. Or the person has some of the contemporary hallmarks of appropriate self-governance and prudence—he commits himself, takes stands, holds himself accountable. Or the person expects that he will B, and has a standing interest in saying that he means to B on the basis of intimate experience with his own practical tendencies.[18] Or the person has a still more complicated inner stance that registers that he will B, approves B-ing, and directs him to get busy all at once.[19] It does not matter which sort of account you favour of what it is that makes it the case that someone is in good shape volitionally and psychologically as an agent. Call the features stressed in your favourite account "*I*".

Anscombe's question becomes: can any such account show what has to be added to or to accompany an action in order to make the action intentional? Can any such account provide the

---

[18] David Velleman offers such an account in *The Possibility of Practical Reason* (Oxford: Oxford University Press, 2000).
[19] If I understand him, Keiran Setiya offers such an account in *Reasons without Rationalism* (Princeton, NJ: Princeton University Press, 2007).

basis for *distinguishing between* actions and mere behaviour? Can the operation of any such internal element make movement into an intentional action? And her answer is: no.

What we now have in place is a much richer picture of the man in motion. Does building up his psychology do the trick? Well, it depends upon what you take to be the status of the new and improved moral psychology. Many contemporary philosophers of action working on and from moral psychology clearly understand the internal circumstances that they describe as picking out key features of having a mind to make something the case quite apart from what comes of it. For these philosophers, the moral psychology can be folded into an account of "what can be determined about the man by himself in the moment of acting".[20] That puts them in range.[21]

While they do not discuss preintentional movements, each of them is very worried about how to get the reason that is in the man to infuse the action, rendering the action rational or virtuous or prudent or reasonable or in some other way good.

On the one side there is the mind. On the other side there is the action. We want to know what the one has to do with the other — how the mind informs the action. In order to inform the action, the mind has to select those descriptions under which the action will be intentional. How might it do this? Well, the agent can guess. That can't be right, since having a mind to make something the case is supposed to account for changing what is the case. Suppose, then, that the outward act builds upon an inward act. Anscombe makes short shrift of this: it "turns the summoning up

---

[20] Anscombe, *Intention*, §19, p. 29 (echoing p. 28)

[21] The other possible route to go here is a route that Anscombe names "logicism": the theorist adopts the view that the mind to make something the case controls the relevant descriptions of what comes of it through inferential relations obtaining between true descriptions of what is done and the contents of thought and volition. Anscombe's argument against this attempt is to be found in her essay on Von Wright on practical inference. See G.E.M. Anscombe, "Von Wright on Practical Inference", in *The Philosophy of Georg Henrik Von Wright*, eds. P.A. Schlipp and L.E. Hahn (La Salle, IL: Open Court, 1989), pp. 377–404. The essay was reprinted in *Virtues and Reasons: Philippa Foot and Moral Theory*, eds. Rosalind Hursthouse, Gavin Lawrence and Warren Quinn (Oxford: Clarendon Press, 1998), pp. 1–34. I give a reading of her argument in "Anscombe on Practical Inference", in *Varieties of Practical Reasoning*, ed. Elijah Millgram (Cambridge, MA: MIT Press, 2001).

of *I* into an intentional action itself, for which we shall have to look for a second *I*".[22]

Commenting on Anscombe's view, Peter Geach is a bit more helpful:

> A far more influential view [than the view about needing to describe muscle twitches in order to map mind onto action] has been the view that intentions are occurrent acts of the mind. There are immediate grounds for suspicion. It seems absurd that an intention should steal upon one unawares, like a fit of anger or fear. On the other hand, how can there be voluntary acts of intending? ...
>
> People have sometimes identified as acts of intention what are perfectly genuine acts of mind, namely acts of "saying in one's heart" something like "What I am about (to do) is so-and-so." But such performances cannot fulfill the role of intentions. For one thing, in ever so many cases of intentional action, nothing like this is "said in the heart" at the time. Theories of acts of intention cover up such awkward cases by such phrases as "virtual intention" or "habitual intention." ...
>
> Again, as regards what I say in my heart, just as much as what I say aloud, the question may arise whether I really mean it. ... But something as to which we can ask again what was meant and how it was meant cannot fulfill the role of determining the way an outward action is meant.[23]

But surely we are no longer this crude about moral psychology! Surely, at this point, we are more inclined to work on *structural* aspects of having a mind to make such-and-such the case! Geach raises the possibility of asking whether I was sincere, and what I meant in saying something in my heart. That is the sort of difficulty that opens onto whole ranges of issues about what psychoanalysts might classify as unconscious motivation, reminding us that there is no end to the interpretive questions we might ask about the significance of what I tell myself about what I'm doing. But there is a more general problem looming.

As long as complex accounts of the structure and inner workings of having a mind to *A* as a means to *B*-ing hold fast to the point that we no longer have the concept of intentional action

---

[22] Anscombe, *Intention*, §19.
[23] P.T. Geach, "Intention, Freedom, and Predictability", in *Logic, Cause, and Action*, ed. Roger Teichmann (Cambridge: Cambridge University Press, 2000), pp. 73-74.

Anscombe has introduced if "Why are you *A*-ing?" is refused application, such views must hold that I am onto what I mean to do, and that what happens is non-accidentally linked to what I have in mind. But at *any* stage of the proceedings, I can be interrupted.

There are indefinitely many ways that an interruption can disrupt the hinge between what I mean to do and what happens. As Foot might put it, philosophers can arrange it so that the interruption *accidentally produces* an event that seems identical to the act that I mean to do. In stepping off the curb, I take it that I am crossing the street. Suppose that, as I raise my foot, I have a seizure. I stumble into the street, lurch forward, and wind up half-falling onto the sidewalk at the far side of the very road I meant to cross when I raised my foot. All of my reasons for crossing the street are, of course, undisturbed by the seizure, even though what happens next probably involves seeking medical assistance (a thing I never would have dreamed I ought to do immediately upon making it to the other side). And, of course, when I took it I was starting to cross the street I was, as it turned out, starting to cross the street. Nevertheless, it "is a mere happy accident that an *I* relevant to the wider context and further consequences" accompanied "the preintentional movements" involved in stepping off the curb, as Anscombe warned.[24]

The unhappy pedestrian example involves what Davidsonians will treat as "deviant" causal chains. Rather than treat such cases as cases in which *an action* is produced in some unexpected way (calling for a special explanation), Anscombe will treat such cases as one in which *no action occurs*. It's not that an action has a surprising source. It's rather that there *is no action at all* in such cases. The whole tendency to worry about wayward or deviant causation of actions presupposes that a single sort of event—for example, an action (e.g. crossing the street) comes about in an unusual way (e.g. as a result of a seizure). For Anscombe, there is no such thing as an action, *A*-ing (e.g. crossing the street) that could happen in any number of ways—through intention, during a seizure episode, as a result of a mighty wind, through elaborate electrical means involving manipulation of the pedestrian's muscles having paralysed him with a poison dart gun just as he began to cross the street, etc.—such that we might need to explain

---

[24] Anscombe, *Intention*, §19, p. 29.

away many street-crossings as actions that were not properly intentional. The job *isn't* to find the special ingredient that makes some actions intentional. Diagnosing the reasons-for-acting-seeking-question-"Why?" is supposed to illuminate action, intention, and reasons-for-acting all at once. If "Why are you A-ing?" is refused application, then, *prima facie*, A-ing is not among those datable events in an agent's history that count as the agent's actions. If an agent's A-ing is interrupted, then there is, *prima facie*, no reason to suppose that "Why are you A-ing?" will continue to have application even if it looks like it might.

The persistent possibility of *accidentally* being caught up in events that bear superficial resemblance to what I meant to do, Anscombe warns, will haunt mind-first accounts of what has to be added to an action to make it intentional. While the letter of the passage supports the modest reading more directly than it does the ambitious reading, I take it that the spirit of the complaint has wider application.

The general problem with the suggestion that I + action = intentional action is that it fails to take into account the order of descriptions under which an action is intentional. Normally, I A in order to B, B in order to C, C in order to D. I move my arm while holding the saw and steadying the plank with my other hand in order to saw the plank; I saw the plank in order to obtain two shorter lengths of wood; I produce two shorter lengths of wood in order to take the next step in my bookshelf-building project, which I do in order to complete the bookshelf. The whole process has an internal order. That order is in what I do as I go along. Checks on an expression of intention—the sort of thing that we *don't* have in the case of the "saying-in-one's-heart" account of intention—come in the first instance from the end-governed order of events paradigmatic of intentional action, which likewise supports taking alternate means when the initial means fail.

4. Turning to §20

The move in §19 turned on lopping off such aspects of the future as unfolded intentionally in the immediate proceedings, that is, in the intentional action. The move in §20 will turn on lopping off such aspects of the future as will go beyond the immediate proceedings—again, the intentional action. This is the force of her opening question in §20: "Would intentional actions still have the characteristic 'intentional,' if there were no such thing as expression of intention for the future, or further intention in acting?"[25]

She clarifies the question by asking whether "'intentional' [is] a characteristic of the actions that have it, which is formally independent of those other occurrences of the concept of intention?"[26] She means: can we get an account of intention strictly in terms of an analysis of intentional actions?

You might think that we could if you were struck by the fact that an expression of intention is, itself, an intentional action, or by the fact that a further intention in acting is having a mind to do more. You might, that is, have a "one thing after another and then another" account of a life, all made up of one-off intentional actions strung like beads on a wire. If that is a good account of a human life, then it ought to be possible to understand intention by focussing on one-off intentional actions.

She investigates her questions by isolating the immediate proceedings (in roughly the way that she set out to cope with the questions in §19 by isolating the man by himself in the moment of acting). I think that it's much easier to make sense of her "curious suppositions" if we remind ourselves what we will have if we succeed in isolating the immediate proceedings. Consider sawing Smith's oak plank in two, thereby making a big pile of sawdust, a lot of noise and two shorter lengths of wood. Call this event "X-ing". We could make no headway with determining the order in the descriptions under which X-ing was intentional by attending to what could be said only about the carpenter considered by himself in the moment of sawing. If we allow ourselves to include what can be said about the sawing, but disallow any account of what he means to do with the wood when he's done (either what he has in mind or how he might explain it), can we understand intentionally sawing a plank in two? Her answer will be: "No."

We have our intentional action. How do we lop off an account of what is supposed to happen next in order to see whether the action all on its own can give us everything we need to understand intention?

Well, firstly we decide not to make *reference* to the future in *our* account. We do this through supposition (*a*): "Suppose that

---

[25] *Ibid.*, §20, p. 30.
[26] *Ibid.*

'intention' only occurred as it occurs in 'intentional action'."[27] That is, don't worry about anything a man might say about what comes next in his project, and don't worry about what *will* happen next, no matter what he says. Secondly, we dramatically limit the kinds of answers that *he* can give to our "Why?" question: "(*b*) suppose that the only answer to the question 'Why are you X-ing?' granted that the question is not refused application, were 'I just am, that's all'."[28]

The extreme restriction on answers to the "Why?" question at the start appears to lop off not only the future but also the past. It becomes clear that the agent will be allowed to make reference to the past (he can tell us something that happened before he started sawing—the point is that his understanding of the past is entirely confined to what he has to say at present about what he is here and now doing). What happens?

5. The First Interpretation of Supposition (*a*)

Under the first interpretation of (*a*), where we do not advert to anything but the immediate proceedings, "intentional" in "intentional action" becomes an adjective picking out how things seem to be going. Our man is over there. He's sawing. It looks deliberate—it doesn't look like somnambulant busy-ness, for example, and it certainly doesn't look like he's on the verge of fainting again and again, and that the near swoon keeps pushing that saw he's holding forward as he is about to collapse. What sense can we give to "deliberate" under this interpretation of our supposition (*a*)—where the supposition means, basically, it looks like he's doing it on purpose?

The one thing we know is that "deliberately" *cannot* have the sense: to some further end. That is the thing that we have left out of account by hypothesis in our decision to isolate the immediate proceedings. So what sense can it have?

Anscombe says that "intentional action" comes to have the sense "intentious action" under this interpretation of our supposition. She summarizes our situation this way:

---

[27] Ibid.
[28] Ibid.

Intention, on this interpretation of our supposition (*a*), has become a style-characteristic of observable human proceedings, with which is associated the question "Why?"[29]

Exactly the same proceedings are being discussed when we discuss any aspect of Jones's sawing of Smith's oak plank:

- Why are you sweating?
- Why are you raising a blister on your hand?
- Why are you making that racket?
- Why are you making a pile of sawdust on the woodshop floor?
- Why are you sawing?
- Why are you sawing a plank?
- Why are you sawing an oak plank?
- Why are you sawing Smith's plank?
- Etc.

That is, provided that all of these are true descriptions of what is taking place, and we can tell as much, any of these questions might arise. *Ex hypothesi*, Jones is doing all of these things at once, and, by the look of things, he means it. But our questions are doing no more than latching onto any of the indefinitely many true things that might be said about what he's doing. The activity looks deliberate in the way that a facial expression looks sad. And, because the *observers* (rather than the carpenter) are in the position of privilege, this removes the possibility of refusing application of our "Why are you X-ing?" question. Here's how.

On this first interpretation of supposition (*a*), there are two options for the sense of our "Why?" question, neither of which preserves what we have learned about intention.

Option One:
Any true description of the proceedings can become the legitimate subject of the "Why are you X-ing?" question. Here, it does not matter whether the proceedings are intentional *qua* A-ing and unintentional *qua* B-ing, C-ing or D-ing, since all of them are true of exactly the same happenings in the woodshop. This in turn suggests that there is no such thing as refusing application of the question. Since the way that we isolated the sense of our question was precisely by considering the responses that refused it application, we no longer have our

---

[29] *Ibid.*

sense of the question "Why?" and, hence, no longer have a grip on intention.

Option Two:
In order to get around this result, we could try suggesting that Jones's sawing is intentional-under-the-description-"sawing-a-plank-in-two". If we ask Jones why he's sawing *Smith's* plank, Jones can say, "*Am* I? Golly..." Since the *observers* are in the position of privilege here, once the question is posed—"Why are you sawing Smith's plank?"—Jones is now apprised of the fact that the plank belongs to Smith. This, alone, is enough to *extend* the range of descriptions that Jones knows to be true of the sawing. He knew that he was sawing. He now also knows that he was sawing Smith's plank. That is why Anscombe writes, "If we try to make it retain this characteristic by suggesting that proceedings-in-a-given-description are what bears the stamp of intention, we shall have to suppose that a man who, having been seen clearly, is asked 'Why are you X-ing?' can never profess unawareness that he was X-ing except on pain of being a liar if in fact he was X-ing".[30]

We have *given* Jones a *new description* of what he is doing.

What has become of the "Why are you X-ing?" question? Well, now *every* time it is asked of some aspect of the proceedings, the very *asking of the question* introduces the embedded description as a description under which sawing is occurring. Anscombe concludes: "And this supposition would involve such radical changes that it becomes impossible to say whether we could still see a place for the concept of intention at all, or diagnose the question 'Why?'"[31]

Recall that such headway as we've made with intention we made by "diagnosing" the question "Why?" Recall that our diagnosis turned on finding the limits of the field of new inquiry it opened by looking at the points where it was refused application. On this interpretation of supposition (*a*), we no longer have a

---

[30] Ibid.
[31] Ibid., §20, p. 31. (As Will Small once put it in conversation on this interpretation: having a mind to make something the case involves states that are "intensional-with-an-'s' but not yet intentional-with-a-'t'".)

situation in which the question can be *refused* application. So we'll need a new interpretation of supposition (*a*).[32]

---

[32] In conversation, John McDowell urged a different reading of:
If we try to make it retain this characteristic by suggesting that proceedings-in-a-given-description are what bears the stamp of intention, we shall have to suppose that a man who, having been seen clearly, is asked "Why are you X-ing?" can never profess unawareness that he was X-ing except on pain of being a liar if in fact he was X-ing. (*Intention*, §20, p. 30)

If I understand him, McDowell takes it that the restriction to "proceedings-in-a-given-description" is, in effect, a restriction to undeniable descriptions, descriptions such that, provided that our man has his wits about him and came to reason in the same world as we, the observers, did, he *must* accept as descriptions of what he is doing. I think that there are problems with McDowell's reading. In the first place, Anscombe will reject this interpretation of supposition (*a*) because it "would involve such radical changes that it becomes impossible to say whether we could still see a place for the concept of intention at all, or diagnose the question 'Why?'" (*Intention*, §20, p. 31). It is hard to see why placing limits on "Why?" questions will make it impossible to "diagnose the question 'Why?'" The diagnosis is carried out in terms of how *the agent* responds to the question, not to which sort of questions *an observer* might ask about what the agent is doing. Observers can ask whatever they like. Only some of their questions will be given application. Her point is that putting *observers* in the position of privilege does violence to the account of intention that has been emerging through her diagnosis of the question "Why?" A reading that requires *agents* to take on board any true descriptions of what they are doing that are embedded in the observers' questions captures this aspect of the difficulty more clearly, as near as I can tell. In the second place, I think that her phrase—"on pain of being a liar"—is supposed to surprise her reader. The tone of the passage seems to me to be one in which it might not have occurred to the reader that the first interpretation of supposition (*a*) could result in putting agents in this position. If the first interpretation (modified in the suggested way) makes it the case that the question "Why are you A-ing?" cannot be refused application because no one could deny that he was A-ing at the moment the question was posed, then he just *is* a liar if he refuses to give the question application.

I am crossing the street. You ask, "Why are you crossing the street?" Say that I profess ignorance that I was crossing the street when you called out your question. I am either in deep trouble cognitively or psychologically, or else I am telling a lie *so* transparent that it scarcely counts as a lie. Whereas I might profess sincere ignorance if you call out "Why are you crossing Honorary Gertrude Elizabeth Margaret Anscombe Boulevard?" I know that I am crossing the street. I might even know that I am crossing Stony Island Avenue. I may not know that the Chicago City Council had decided to give Stony Island an "Honorary" name to celebrate the achievements of the person thereby honoured. Restricting observers to asking only undeniable questions does no radical violence to the account of intention Anscombe has been working to

6. The Second Interpretation of Supposition (*a*)

We try a different tack. On the new interpretation of supposition (*a*), intention in intentional action "is not a style that marks an action, or an action-in-a-description; for it is possible for a man to think he is doing one thing when he is not doing that thing but another"[33] (as when Jones doesn't know that he's sawing Smith's plank). Moreover, we allow that our man can know that he is X-ing *and* that he is Y-ing, as long as he is Y-ing in X-ing, and this allows for the kind of further intention with which he can act without exceeding the boundaries of the immediate proceedings. So, Jones is sawing and he is dividing the plank into two shorter lengths. In sawing, he is dividing. In this case, he will reach the end of the sawing portion of his time in the woodshop at the same time as he finishes dividing the plank. We could even allow for him to make repeated strokes of the saw, and let him intend sawing in drawing the blade back and pushing it forward. As long as X-ing (drawing the blade back and then pushing it forward) coincides with Y-ing (sawing), we will have stayed within the limits of the immediate proceedings. What does this give us? She writes:

> In this case intentional actions will be marked out as those of which a man has non-observational knowledge, and for which there is a question ["Why did you X?"] whose answers fall in the range (*a*) "I just did," (*b*) backward-looking motive, and (*c*) sentimental characterization.[34]

Our next task has to be to investigate whether this question—the "Why?" question whose answers fall within that range—is the "Why?" question that we have been studying. Is this a *reasons-for-acting-seeking* question "Why?"

Because (*a*) "I just did" is equivalent to "No reason", answers of that sort are not helpful to us. We won't be able to tell, from such answers, whether or not our "Why?" question is in play, since our question sometimes gets such answers too. We don't have forward-looking motive, since we have lopped off thought about the future. We are left with backward-looking motive and a

---

develop. Allowing *any* true description of what I am doing to *become* undeniable once the question is posed does radical violence to the account.
[33] Anscombe, *Intention*, §20, p. 31.
[34] *Ibid*.

fairly impoverished version of interpretive motive that she calls "sentimental characterization". There's the spirit in which the thing is done and there's past good or bad. These can belong to the immediate proceedings no matter what happens next. So our question becomes whether backward-looking motive and this kind of interpretive motive are enough to bring reasons for acting into view, and the answer is, again: no.

It looks as though we might be able to make some headway with this new interpretation of supposition (*a*) because, just as the field of new inquiry opened for us by the reasons-for-acting-seeking question "Why?" is a field in which we criticize a man's reasons, we can criticize *motives*. When Anscombe read a message intended for someone else, thought, "That unspeakable man!" with feelings of hatred, tore the message up and laughed,[35] she acted in anger. We criticize people for episodes of pettiness, petulance, and spite. Perhaps she ought not to have torn the message up.

What is the point of criticizing her under these assumptions?

The answer *can't* be, in order to convince her to develop better self-control in the future, or, in order to convince her to seek out the man, apologize and tell him what his message said (partly with the thought that it is unpleasant to do such things, and this may help her change her ways). Just as she can't have a further, future intention in acting under our suppositions, we, her critics, can't criticize in order to change things in the future. And so, Anscombe writes, "One can argue against motives—i.e., criticize a man for having acted on such a motive—but a great deal of the point of doing so will be gone if we imagine the expression of intention for the future to be absent, as it is in our hypothesis".[36] Basically, our criticism has something of the status of her inward cry, "That unspeakable man!" Her complaint extends to any criticism we might make of backward-looking motive as well.

In short, this "Why?" question is not a reasons-for-acting-seeking question "Why?" And, since the reasons-for-acting-seeking question "Why?" is our device for eliciting intention, we can conclude that we have lost track of intention by confining our attention to the immediate proceedings in the ways we were directed to do by supposition (*a*).

---

[35] *Ibid.*, §11, p. 17.
[36] *Ibid.*, §20, pp. 31–32.

7. Moving on to Supposition (b)

Supposition (b) does away with responses to our "Why?" question that mention backward-looking motive or that give the spirit in which the thing is or was done. We have won the right to do so through the work on supposition (a).

We left the answer, "I just *am*" to one side in considering the second interpretation of supposition (a). *That* answer is equivalent to "No reason". We were trying to discover whether the other answers that were left to us might give reasons for X-ing. There were two of these: backward-looking motive and sentimental interpretive motive. You could tell that neither of them gave a reason for acting because, once we have ruled out talk about the future, we have got rid of the point of criticizing motives. Getting rid of the point of criticism shows us that we are *not* in the field of further inquiry that is supposed to be opened by an expression of intention. We have only one kind of answer that might be an answer to a reasons-for-acting-seeking question left. Could this be the *only* answer to our "Why?"

She points out that the response fails to distinguish between members of the class of acts known without observation. In order to make headway with her argument for this point, it's important to recognize that we are in a world where there is no answer to the question "What for?" The reason that I can't confidently distinguish the inward experience of meaning to make something the case from the inward experience of an involuntary gesture is that the former *is* the experience of future-directedness. If we bracket *that*, since we are bracketing everything *but* the current proceedings (mental, behavioural, what have you), we are left without a principled basis for the distinction. That is her point.

So she tries yet another tack—voluntary acts can be commanded. And here, the problem will be isomorphic with the problem that we encountered in trying to understand pointless criticism of the spirit in which something is done, or an action undertaken in response to some past good turn or injury. Yes—there is a distinction between what can and what cannot be commanded. Sometimes we do things in obedience to some authority. Sometimes we do things commanded by some authority, but not in obedience. But notice that it is not as though we could ask whether an authority ought to be obeyed. You can't use criticism as a technique for changing things, any more than I can use criticism as a spur to self-improvement. Basically, the distinction between what can and what cannot be commanded is useless.

8. A Concluding Remark

I have worked to begin giving readings of §§19 and 20 of *Intention*. Anscombe works to ward off what I called "mind-first" accounts of intentional action in §19. The arguments of §20 ought, I think, to be enough to dispel any concerns that her interest in intentional action marks her as a behaviourist.

The deep concern of both passages is to lay the groundwork for her discussion of what she names the *A–D* order—the means–end structure that informs intention, intentional action and practical reason alike. She takes it that we will fail to understand intention, action, practical reason or practical knowledge if we fail to attend to the nature of intentional action as an unfolding series of doings linked together by and ordered to the end of a larger project or action—that order informs both a mind to do such-and-such and the doing of such-and-such. It's not that we have the class of actions, and, among these, a special sub-class of properly intentional actions, and that action theory is the effort to find the characteristic marks of the privileged sub-class of special, somehow higher, finer, more authentic, or otherwise *better* actions. Her hope is to argue that we cannot even get *action* into view without working out the way that *A*-ing is ordered to the end of *B*-ing, *B*-ing to *C*-ing, *C*-ing to *D*-ing and so on, such that all of these form a unified object of inquiry. Accordingly, "We do not add anything attaching to the action at the time it is done by describing it as intentional", in the sense pointing to the proper operation of some internal element that renders an action intentional, and we do not add anything to an action by marking it as a stage leading to a further, future action. These are already there in understanding an event as an action.

T.A. Cavanaugh

Anscombe, Thomson and Double Effect

1. Introduction

Elizabeth Anscombe introduces double-effect reasoning (double effect, DE or DER)¹ into contemporary Anglophone philosophy in "Modern Moral Philosophy".² More precisely, Anscombe proposes that the distinction between intention (of an end or means) and foresight without intent (of an effect of one's act) can have crucial moral import in the evaluation of consequentially comparable actions (henceforth, the I/F distinction).³

Anscombe maintains that denial (which she attributes to Sidgwick) of the distinction differentiates "old-fashioned

---

¹ Commonly referred to as the "Doctrine of Double Effect" (DDE), I prefer "double effect" (DE) or "double-effect reasoning" (DER). Given DE's Thomistic provenance, "doctrine" suggests to many ears a dogmatic sectarian account, not a reasonable philosophical position. Hence, for many, the name amounts to a dismissal. In Anscombe's first published reference to DE, she writes simply of "double effect". See her 1939 contribution ("The War and the Moral Law") to the two-part pamphlet ("Justice of the Present War Examined") which she penned as a twenty-or-so year-old Oxford undergraduate (along with Norman Daniel who wrote the second part). She re-published this in G.E.M. Anscombe, *Ethics, Religion and Politics, The Collected Philosophical Papers*, Vol. III (Oxford: Basil Blackwell, 1981), pp. 72–81.

² G.E.M Anscombe, "Modern Moral Philosophy", *Philosophy*, 33 (124) 1958: 1–19. Also available in *Human Life, Action and Ethics: Essays by G.E.M. Anscombe*, eds. Mary Geach and Luke Gormally (Exeter: Imprint Academic, 2005), pp. 169–94.

³ I focus on the debate regarding the I/F distinction's moral import in cases typically treated by DE – e.g. tactical bombing/terror bombing and palliative sedation/voluntary active euthanasia (or, PS/VAE). Because Anscombe and Thomson both treat of PS/VAE, I limit my attention to that duo.

utilitarianism" from "consequentialism" (a term she coined in *MMP*, which appellation, needless to say, has taken).[4] She argues that the refusal to acknowledge the distinction's ethical relevance in act-assessment leaves one to count consequences in contrast to the "intrinsic badness of this or that action".[5] Since her introduction of the topic, we find a voluminous literature.[6]

In what follows, I map out neglected contours of a dispute that the deontologist Judith Jarvis Thomson has with Anscombe over DE.[7] Notably, both Anscombe and Thomson oppose consequentialism. Thus, their difference over DE does not reduce to a debate over the merits of that account. Rather, as we will see, it amounts to a difference over the locus of the I/F distinction's moral import. In what follows, I show that this disagreement implicates others—both not expected (such as one involving the possibility of moral dilemmas and how to understand "ought implies can") and those to be expected (such as divergence concerning what constitutes action).

Noting that Anscombe introduces the I/F distinction into contemporary moral theory, Thomson hypothesizes why this supposed error persists (regrettably, in her eyes):

> What I refer to is a failure to take seriously enough the fact—I think it is plainly a fact—that the question whether it is morally

---

[4] Anscombe, "Modern Moral Philosophy", p. 12.
[5] *Ibid.*
[6] DE's intercourse with the larger philosophical world continues to prove prolific. Consider, for example, that Phillipa Foot (1967) first presents the Trolley case in consideration of Anscombe's claim concerning the moral import of the I/F distinction. Regarding Foot, one notes that in her much cited article "The Problem of Abortion and the Doctrine of Double Effect", *Oxford Review*, 5, 1967: 5-15, she denies the ethical significance of the distinction. Years later, in a little-noted book chapter in which she considers the I/F distinction, Foot endorses it, saying: "In 'The problem of abortion and the doctrine of double effect' I argued, (wrongly, as I now think) that the distinction between direct and indirect intention was irrelevant to moral judgement" (Philippa Foot, "Morality, Action and Outcome", *Morality and Objectivity: A Tribute to J.L. Mackie*, ed. Ted Honderich (London: Routledge & Kegan Paul, 1985), pp. 23-38, note 6, at p. 37).
[7] In subsequent treatments of DE, Anscombe displays ambivalence towards it—especially to the abuses to which it has been put. For a more extensive consideration of her thought, see T.A. Cavanaugh, "Abuses of Double Effect, Anscombe's Principle of Side Effects, and A (Sound) Account of *Duplex Effectus*", forthcoming in *Anscombe and Double Effect*, eds. John O'Callaghan and Craig Iffland (Notre Dame, IN: Notre Dame University Press).

permissible for a person to do a thing is just not the same as the question whether the person who does it is thereby shown to be a bad person.[8]

Thomson claims that Anscombe errs in giving the I/F distinction a role in act-assessment in double effect cases. For, according to her lights, it lacks relevance in that arena. Rather, it has import in agent-assessment. (Of course, Anscombe and friends of DE more generally agree on its relevance in agent-assessment.) Let us examine this dispute and the allied matters it implicates.

2. Two Cases: Ambiguous Intent (AI) and Revengeful Intent (RI)

Consider standard DER cases involving a consenting terminally ill patient: palliative sedation (henceforth, PS) and voluntary active euthanasia (henceforth, VAE) (of which both Anscombe and Thomson treat). In PS, a physician administers a palliative-cum-lethal drug (e.g. a barbiturate) with a view to relieving the patient's pain. The barbiturate affects both the patient's pain-receptors and, thereby, relieves his pain and also those nerves responsible for his respiration and, thereby, kills him. In VAE, a doctor administers a lethal drug to an otherwise similarly situated patient as a means of ending pain by killing the patient.[9] While it would not be a typical case of VAE, a physician could employ a lethal-cum-palliative drug such as the barbiturate used in PS to effect VAE.

As Anscombe herself holds, PS is ethically in the clear.[10] Employing the three following criteria of DE, one can discern why. For, PS is: 1) a good act (of pain relief), but for the bad side effect (premature death); 2) the agents involved intend the patient's relief from pain and need not intend the patient's death

---

[8] J.J. Thomson, "Physician-Assisted Suicide: Two Moral Arguments", *Ethics*, 109, 1999: 497–518, at p. 517.

[9] In PS one relieves pain; for the drug palliates. Typically, in VAE and PAS, one ends but need not relieve pain; for the drugs are lethal but not necessarily palliative. I note this difference for the sake of precision, not in order to put weight upon it. In physician-assisted suicide (PAS), a practice allied to VAE, the physician writes a prescription for a lethal drug which the patient fills and takes at her discretion.

[10] See e.g. Anscombe, "War and Murder", in *Ethics, Religion and Politics, The Collected Philosophical Papers*, Vol. III (Oxford: Basil Blackwell, 1981), pp. 51–61, at p. 54.

(either as an end or as a means) while they do foresee it; and 3) the good at issue (relief of agonal pain at the end of life) compares favourably to the bad effect (causing the patient's death earlier than it would have otherwise occurred).[11] Thus, in accordance with DER, a terminally ill patient, his family and physician ethically may treat his otherwise intractable pain with a barbiturate that foreseeably also causes his death.

By contrast (and as Anscombe herself holds), administering a lethal drug to a consenting terminally ill patient in order to kill her and, thereby, end her pain (VAE) is not ethically in the clear.[12] For, while consequentially similar to PS, such an act instances the deliberate killing of a harmless person, and is, thereby, unjust homicide.

Of course, given the comparable consequences and the observable similarity of PS and VAE—as noted above, one could accomplish VAE employing the same drug used in PS—some moralists (including Thomson) find this claim dubious. For how could, e.g., the giving of the same palliative-cum-lethal drug to similarly situated patients be ethically and legally in the clear in PS and be morally and legally out of bounds in VAE if all that differs are the intentions of the agents? More pointedly, how can this make a difference to the legal and moral evaluation of the relevant acts? (For the time being, we will put the law to the side and focus on ethics.)[13]

---

[11] For a more extended consideration of the DER criteria, see T.A. Cavanaugh, *Double-Effect Reasoning: Doing Good and Avoiding Evil* (Oxford: Clarendon Press, 2006), pp. 26–37.

[12] G.E.M. Anscombe, "Murder and the Morality of Euthanasia", in *Human Life, Action and Ethics: Essays by G.E.M. Anscombe*, eds. Mary Geach and Luke Gormally (Exeter: Imprint Academic, 2005), pp. 261–77.

[13] Thomson writes that she knows of no case other than the contrast between PS and VAE in which the law regards two consequentially comparable acts as illegal/legal based on the I/F distinction (Thomson, "Physician-Assisted Suicide", p. 515). Indeed, the distinction proves crucial legally. To provide but one signal example found in U.S. Constitutional law that illustrates the point, consider how to read the first words of the U.S. Constitution's First Amendment:

> Congress shall make no law respecting an establishment of religion, or prohibiting the free exercise thereof; or abridging the freedom of speech, or of the press; or the right of the people peaceably to assemble, and to petition the government for a redress of grievances.

Were a legislator to make a law with the *intention* of establishing or of restricting the free exercise of a religion, etc., such a law would, thereby, by

As noted, Thomson proposes that the I/F distinction contrasts the agents, not the acts. She challenges the I/F distinction's moral relevance in the evaluation of acts by means of two cases, as follows:

> According to PDE [the principle of double effect], the question whether it is morally permissible for the doctor to inject a lethal drug turns on whether the doctor would be doing so intending death or only intending relief from pain. That is just as absurd an idea ... [as to think that a difference in the doctor's intent should make a legal difference, as it, in fact does—Thomson thinks the law errs on this point]. If the only available doctor would inject to cause the patient's death, or is incapable of becoming clear enough about her own intentions to conclude that what she intends is *only* to relieve the patient's pain, then—according to PDE—the doctor may not proceed, and the patient must therefore continue to suffer. That cannot be right.
>
> If a doctor will inject her patient intending his death as an end and, moreover, wants his death only because his death will constitute revenge, then that does matter morally. But we have to be careful about how it matters. I suggest that it has no bearing on whether it is morally permissible for her to act. Whatever her intention may be, the patient, we are supposing, desperately wants her to inject the drug ...
>
> That she will inject for that reason matters morally, not by way of fixing that it is morally impermissible for her to proceed, rather by showing something morally bad about *her*.[14]

We have two cases involving the only available doctor. First, a case in which the physician injects revengefully to kill the patient, not to relieve the patient's pain (which, for ease of reference let us call the case of revengeful intent or RI). Second, a case in which the doctor cannot get clear about her intention being only to relieve the patient's pain and not to kill (which for ease of

---

that very intent, be illegal. Absent such an intent, a law that has the effect of establishing or prohibiting ... etc ... can be legal, other criteria being met (into which I will not here go). For a consideration of U.S. Constitutional casuistry analogous to DER, see Cavanaugh, *Double-Effect Reasoning*, pp. 192-95; see also, Edward Lyons, "In Incognito—The Principle of Double Effect in American Constitutional Law", *Florida Law Review*, 57, 2005: 469-563.

[14] Thomson, "Physician-Assisted Suicide: Two Moral Arguments", pp. 515-16 (emphases in original).

reference let us call the case of ambiguous intent, or AI).[15] Although Thomson puts AI to the side, I address one issue she raises with AI before proceeding to consider RI. Namely, what does one reliant upon DE have to say about the only available physician being unable to rule out intent of the bad as operative in her acting?

To entertain this question, let us further articulate AI along the lines Thomson suggests. We are to imagine a physician who has two morally salient intents, one to relieve her patient's pain and one to kill her patient. Were she to inject the patient with the drug, she knows she would do so with the intent to relieve the patient's pain. However, she cannot conclude that, were she to inject, she would do so only to relieve the patient's pain. She might also inject in order to kill her patient. Given this opacity concerning how operative her intention of the bad would be, Thomson holds that DE tells her not to inject. For she very well may be injecting (in part) with the intent to kill, violating the above-noted second criterion of DER.

I concede what I take to be at least one of Thomson's points made by this case. While DE does not require that the agent have no other intentions besides the good effect, it does require that the agent not intend the foreseen bad effect (either as an end or means). In her use of "*only* to relieve the patient's pain" Thomson focusses our attention on this very requirement—DE's (second) criterion.[16] As Thomson (correctly) puts it, DER requires that an agent can become "clear enough about her own intentions".[17] In other words, she must be able reasonably to judge that she intends the good and does not intend the bad. Of course, an agent may

---

[15] For the sake of clarity, while AI may, RI does not instance VAE (nor does Thomson propose them as instances of VAE). For, as I understand Thomson, in AI the physician injects in order to palliate and may be injecting in order to kill. Since Thomson does not specify why the doctor in AI intends to kill (revengefully or not), I also leave that unspecified. We are not entirely clear why she intends to kill. Does she do so to end the patient's pain? But, the drug will do that and she does intend palliation, so that seems unlikely. Or, does she inject as constitutive of revenge? Whatever the case in AI, in RI the physician clearly injects in order revengefully to kill, not to end the patient's pain. In the paradigmatic case of VAE, the physician (without revenge) injects to kill and, thereby, end pain. Since Thomson uses AI and RI to argue against DER's contrasting PS from VAE, I attend to them.

[16] Ibid., p. 516.

[17] Ibid.

lack such an adequate view. She may not have sufficient clarity about the intentions in accordance with which she acts. Other things being equal, DE—as Thomson suggests—would advise the agent to refrain from acting because she cannot reasonably rule out homicidal intent as operative.

However, are other things equal? No. To see the relevant difference, consider more closely what reasonable judgments the physician in AI can make concerning her intentions. Importantly, she reasonably judges herself as having the intent to palliate her patient's pain. Thus, in this respect, she reasonably judges herself as seeking to act well by her patient. Were she to act, her act would in fact be one of palliating her patient's pain. By contrast, the physician in RI is entirely morally lost. For she lacks the normative intent to relieve her patient's pain while hating her patient. Indeed, were she to act, her act would not even be one of killing in order to end pain; rather, it would be one of revengeful homicide.

Concerning AI, consider the doctor's ethically problematic homicidal intent. She cannot reasonably rule this intent out as operative in her action. Importantly, neither can she reasonably rule it in. It might be operative; but, then again, it might not. This is not the same as reasonably judging herself as intending the bad at issue (as is the case in RI). Were she reasonably to judge herself as intending her patient's death (as the physician in RI must), a moralist employing DE would have to advise her not to act. However, given: 1) her confident judgment that her intent to relieve her patient's pain would be operative, and 2) her doubt concerning how operative her homicidal intent would be, and 3) her being the only available physician, an ethicist employing DE could advise her to administer the barbiturate. (Needless to say, were there a physician not morally compromised as is the physician in AI, the ethicist relying on DE would counsel that he care for the patient.) Thus, closer consideration of AI suggests that it leaves the I/F distinction unscathed. Having addressed the challenge AI poses, let us consider the morally salient intentions present (and absent) in AI and RI with a view to considering the difficulty RI presents for DE.

The important relation between doctoring and palliation (preserved in AI) suggests three questions that point to a substantive issue that Thomson entirely neglects. First, what has led the doctor in AI to have the intention to palliate her patient's pain? Second, and an associated question, what has led the doctor in RI not to have the intent to relieve her patient's pain? Third and finally, what explains the physician's intent revengefully to kill her patient in RI? An investigation into the history of these morally salient intentions (and lack of palliative intent in RI) instanced in these cases suggests that the physician in RI faces a self-imposed moral dilemma. (The physician in AI has compromised herself, but has not put herself into a moral dilemma; she can still act ethically, as argued above.)

Consider the genesis of the physician's intention in AI to relieve her patient's pain. Being a physician involves having such an intention towards one's patient. A physician as a physician purposefully, deliberately or, in other words, intentionally relieves her patient's pain. Indeed, palliative care is a medical speciality. For some physicians, it is all they do. For all physicians, it is one act that, when done, is to be done with that very intent. "Cure sometimes, treat often, comfort always" serves as a medical aphorism indicating the *sine qua non* that palliation represents for a physician. To palliate is to act as a physician *par excellence*. Other things being equal, to palliate instances a physician's office, or, ethically, her professional duty. Thus, our physician in AI has the intention to palliate insofar as she acts as a physician. She comes by the intent honestly as an essential part of her noble profession. Because Thomson does not elaborate upon the intent of the physician in AI to kill her patient (is it to end the patient's pain? is it for the sake of revenge?), let us consider the physician in RI whose intent Thomson articulates more fully.

In contrast to the physician in AI, the doctor in RI lacks the normative intent of relieving her patient's pain. Somehow, at least with respect to this patient, she has lost her orientation towards one of the essential goals of doctoring, palliation. In this respect and towards this patient, she therefore no longer acts as a doctor. For the goal of palliation partially defines her profession. Presumably, her loss of this intent has something to do with her acquisition of a revengeful intent towards her patient. What of a physician's revengeful intention? How does that figure in doctoring?

Thomson elaborates upon RI by specifying that the doctor wants her patient's death in itself, as constitutive of revenge. She speaks of the doctor as injecting the lethal drug "out of hatred".[18]

---

[18] *Ibid.*, p. 517.

That a physician harbours revengeful homicidal intent towards her patient merits comment. Concerning the genesis of this malicious intent, Thomson does not give us much to go on. She does, however, indicate that the revengeful intent shows us something "morally bad about [the physician]"[19] who has it; she is a "bad person".[20] More importantly, in respect of this intent she is a bad doctor. For a doctor as a doctor ought not to seek revenge upon her patient, nor ought she hate her patient. The physician ought not to have this intent towards this patient.

So, let us proceed understanding the physician's revengeful intent as wrongful — as one would reasonably expect.

Accordingly, there is some narrative in terms of which the physician by a previous wrongful act (or acts) came by this intent towards this patient. This history bears on our analysis of the act in question in RI. For in light of the genesis of the malicious intent, one plausibly thinks that the physician has gotten herself into a situation such that she cannot now do the right act; namely, relieve her patient's pain as an act of palliation, not as an act of homicidal revenge. Thomson does not consider this signal possibility.

Rather, she assumes that an agent can always do the right deed. Therefore, she must treat intent as irrelevant in the determination of the deed as right. For, otherwise, the agent in RI would not be able to do the right deed. She would face a moral dilemma. Thomson, however, dismisses the possibility of an agent facing two incompatible oughts (or, in other words, a moral dilemma):

> I think myself that it was not merely odd but patently incorrect to think that
> (3) I ought to give C a banana
> and
> (4) I ought to give D a banana
> can both be true compatibly with my having only one banana; I think we simply do not use the English word "ought" in such a way that this is so. In any case, I will not. I will throughout so use

---

[19] Ibid., p. 516.
[20] Ibid., p. 517.

"ought" that it cannot be the case that I ought to do alpha and ought to do beta where I cannot do both alpha and beta.[21]

Remarkably, Thomson rejects the possibility of incompatible oughts as "patently incorrect" even as not in keeping with English usage (at least one interpretation of "damned if you do; damned if you don't" suggests otherwise). Yet, this offhand rejection of moral dilemmas, although distinct from denying the I/F distinction, instances an allied and implicated disagreement between her and those friendly to the distinction.

Along the lines suggested by Thomson, this particular challenge to the I/F distinction goes by way of an insistence that "ought implies can". Let us turn to consider this objection more fully.[22] How does the moral truism "ought implies can" stand vis-à-vis our physician in RI? If DE is correct, she ought to intend to relieve her patient's pain and ought not to intend revengefully to kill her patient. She has, however, somehow gotten herself into

---

[21] J.J. Thomson, *The Realm of Rights* (Cambridge, MA: Harvard University Press, 1990), p. 86.

[22] W.D. Ross weighs in on the issue, as follows:

That action from a good motive is never morally obligatory follows (1) from ..."I ought"' implies "I can". It is not the case that I can by choice produce a certain motive ... in myself at a moment's notice, still less that I can at a moment's notice make it effective in stimulating me to act. I can act from a certain motive only if I have the motive; if not, the most I can do is to cultivate it by suitably directing my attention or by acting in certain appropriate ways so that on some future occasion it *will* be present in me, and I shall be able to act from it. My *present* duty, therefore, cannot be to act here and now from it. (W.D. Ross, *The Right and The Good* (Oxford: Clarendon Press, 1930), pp. 4–5, original emphases)

Ross uses "motive" to refer to intent of one's end. In the case at hand, it would be the intent of revenge as an end, per Thomson's usage. Ross draws attention to the temporal aspects of an agent's intentions—referring to "some future occasion"—only to neglect the very import he suggests. Namely, that had one in the past cultivated an intent, one would here and now be able to act on it (as one ought). (The same of course holds for not cultivating certain intents.) On this issue of an agent's occurrent inability to control her intentions indicating the unsuitableness of reliance upon intent in act-assessment, see also Jonathan Bennett, *The Act Itself* (Oxford: Clarendon Press, 1995), pp. 195–96, and T.M. Scanlon, *Moral Dimensions: Permissibility, Meaning, Blame* (Cambridge, MA: Belknap Press, 2008), pp. 56–62. Joining Thomson, Bennett and Scanlon both make this move against the I/F distinction's use in act-analysis without any consideration of the history of an agent's intentions and the (presumptive) control she exercises over intention-formation.

such a state that she cannot here and now (occurrently) do so. She can only inject the palliative-cum-lethal drug with the intent of revengefully killing or refrain from doing what she ought to do as a physician (relieve this patient's agonal pain). If ought implies can, then it appears as if the DE moralist errs. For our agent cannot occurrently rid herself of her malicious intent. Nor can she occurrently acquire the intent to palliate required of her as a physician. I concede the point concerning her current inabilities.

One reasonably thinks, however, that while our agent cannot here and now rid herself of the objectionable intent there was a time when she was able to avoid acquiring it. "Ought implies can" applies immediately to that past time and mediately here and now. (The same holds for her loss of the intent to palliate.) Thus, the claim (arising from DE) that the physician in RI faces a moral dilemma does not violate the noted moral truism. It does, however, suggest that we expand our ethical investigations beyond the beguiling putatively all-encompassing "now".

Doing so enables a moralist to acknowledge that an agent can so act in the past as to become incapable of right action now. Considering that past moment, Thomson might reject the attribution of the wrongness to the act, claiming it is applicable only to the agent. Regardless, the preceding establishes that that move would amount to mere assertion. More importantly, it would neglect the historical character of human agency and the attending temporal aspects of "ought implies can".

Our inquiry into the genesis of the physician's intentions indicates a complexity Thomson does not acknowledge. According to the overarching moral theory of which DE serves as a part, the physician in RI faces a moral dilemma of her own making. She can either kill her patient revengefully (an act ruled out of bounds by malice) or forego the obligatory act of palliating her patient's otherwise intractable pain (a violation of a serious obligation). The physician wrongs whether she injects or not. In light of the egregious waywardness of a physician who can palliate only by intending to kill her patient revengefully why would this result boggle one employing a sound ethic? A moralist with a realistic imagination and a sensitivity for the intricacy of the moral life will not find the possibility of a self-inflicted moral dilemma obviously incorrect. Indeed, to take but one example, Aquinas—with whom

DER originates—considers self-imposed moral impasses plausible.[23]

Consider Aquinas who contemplates another instance of an agent doing an obligatory deed but only for the wrong reason:

> there is no inconvenience if something being supposed, a man is not able to avoid wrongful action; just as, supposing the intention of vainglory, he who is obligated to give alms is not able to avoid acting wrongly: for if he gives from such an intention, he acts wrongly; but if he does not give, he violates his obligation.[24]

Concerning the logic of such an act, Aquinas notes:

> just as in syllogisms, given one error it is necessary that others follow; so also in morals, one error posited, from necessity others follow.[25]

---

[23] Aquinas discusses moral perplexity. He distinguishes simple perplexity (the possibility of which he denies) from what we might call conditional perplexity that one causes oneself, the possibility of which he asserts. Hence, I refer to self-imposed moral dilemmas. In Aquinas, see, for example, ST I-II, q. 19, a. 6 ad 3; II-II, q. 62, a. 2, obj. 2; ST, III q. 64, a. 6 ad 3, and *de Veritate*, 17, 4 ad 8. For a thorough consideration of Aquinas's account and a treatment of the (eighteen) texts in which Aquinas addresses moral dilemmas, see M.V. Dougherty, *Moral Dilemmas in Medieval Thought: From Gratian to Aquinas* (Cambridge: Cambridge University Press, 2011), chapter 4. I am not aware of Anscombe addressing moral dilemmas *per se*. An extensive reading of her work in ethics, however, nowhere suggests the denial of moral dilemmas. Her affinity for Aquinas's ethics suggests she would find them possible. More importantly, in a theological text she explicitly asserts that, "sometimes the same thing both ought to be and ought not to be". The "identity of something that both ought to be and ought not to be is not impossible" (G.E.M. Anscombe, "Sin", in *Faith in a Hard Ground*, eds. Mary Geach and Luke Gormally (Exeter: Imprint Academic, 2008), pp. 115-56, at p. 145).

[24] *de Veritate*, 17, 4, ad 8:
> Et hoc non est inconveniens, ut aliquo supposito, homo peccatum vitare non possit; sicut supposita intentione inanis gloriae, ille qui tenetur eleemosynam dare, peccatum evitare non potest: si enim dat ex tali intentione, peccat; si vero non dat, transgressor est.

[25] Aquinas, ST I-II, q. 19, a. 6 ad 3: "sicut in syllogisticis, uno inconvenienti dato, necesse est alia sequi; ita in moralibus, uno inconvenienti posito, ex necessitate alia sequuntur." St. Thomas thinks that (at least in this instance) the individual who got himself into moral perplexity can get himself out; namely, by "dismissing the bad intention" ("potest intentionem malam dimittere"). Hence, we ought not think that a moral dilemma (as Aquinas conceives of it) is entirely inescapable; it is, however, on the supposition of the bad intent.

Given the absurdity of a doctor who can only palliate her patient's pain via a revengeful homicidal intent, other absurdity must follow: to act or not to act wrongs. While Thomson dismisses such a (coherent) judgment, she proposes that the agent in RI merits a negative evaluation. Let us examine this claim more closely to see if it can, as she assumes, comport with her denial of a negative assessment of the related act.

3. Bad Agent

Thomson acknowledges that the agent in RI merits a negative evaluation in terms of the I/F distinction. No doubt, one employing the distinction agrees. The dispute concerns the use of the distinction to evaluate acts, too. Thomson proposes that we should say that the doctor in RI "is bad" while what she does is "morally permissible".[26]

How is the agent in RI bad? Her badness concerns her in a certain respect. Paraphrasing Anscombe's discussion of acts, one might say that an agent is bad (or good) "under some description".[27] She may exercise agency in many capacities: as an employer, a mother, or a pianist. Her badness does not concern these roles. Although nothing hinges on it, having acknowledged that she is bad as an agent, Thomson would presumably also hold her to be bad as a doctor (who ought to seek to relieve her patient's pain and not revengefully to kill). Thus, she is bad as an agent and, specifically, as a physician. (One could make all of the substantive points that follow without reference to her as a physician. It is worthwhile, however, methodologically and substantively to note that agency typically has specificity. One is a good or bad kind of agent, not simply a good agent or a bad agent. Again, one exercises agency, "under some description".) Now, what does it mean to be bad as an agent and as a doctor? What is an agent bad at? What is a physician bad at? Presumably, an agent is one who does acts; a doctor one who does medical acts.

Consider, a potter makes pots; a ballerina dances. In the case of potting we have a product distinct from the activity; in the case of dancing we have the activity. The bad potter makes bad pots and the bad ballerina dances poorly or, if I may so speak, makes bad

---

[26] Thomson, "Physician-Assisted Suicide", p. 517.
[27] G.E.M. Anscombe, *Intention* (Cambridge, MA: Harvard University Press, 2000), section 19, p. 29.

dances.[28] In both instances, the defect in the agent as an agent indicates a defect in the product made or in the act performed. Because defects in the making of actually distinct products (e.g. pots) are not applicable to the acts we consider, put the making of a product case to the side. Let us consider only dancing-like cases.

Curiously and without comment, Thomson asks us to evaluate an agent as an agent negatively while not evaluating the agent's act negatively. Yet, paradigmatically, even analytically, defects in agent as agent suggest defects in acts as acts. For agency is the making of acts. A defective agent implicates a flawed act. Thomson denies the implication; the advocate of DE insists upon it. What of this?

At this apparent impasse, one notes that Thomson holds that while the agent in DR is bad, her act is permissible. For an act to be permissible is for it to be ethically in bounds. It may lack perfection by having some bad-making features, while still being within the boundaries that ethics requires of it. Perhaps Thomson would be willing to concede the analytical point that a negative assessment of an agent makes for a negative assessment of the corresponding act while holding that the negative assessment of the act need not amount to impermissibility. It might, rather, indicate a defect in the act but one that falls short of ruling it out of bounds. If we wish further to advance the conversation, I suggest we take this tack. It directs our attention to the issue of permissibility. Let us consider this criterion.

Roughly, Thomson holds that permissibility of an act is to be understood in terms of claims that individuals have against agents not to be caused harm. In the case of RI, the patient has a claim not to be revengefully killed by the physician while also having a claim to pain relief. Of course, the two claims conflict in the case at hand. For, given this physician's intention, pain relief cannot occur except as coincident upon revengeful killing. The fulfilment of one

---

[28] When it comes to products, the reverse need not hold. As Chaucer shows in *Canterbury Tales*, the worst poem can be the work of the master poet— consider *Sir Thopas*. Of course, as Aristotle famously notes, excellent agency at times excludes acting badly such that the generous person cannot act stingily, nor the virtuous person viciously in respect of that in terms of which he is virtuous (Aristotle, *Nicomachean Ethics*, VI, 5, 1140b24). We, however, move in the opposite direction, looking into the viability of assessing an agent negatively while not assessing the agent's act negatively (at least as far as permissibility).

claim involves the infringement of another. How does Thomson determine permissibility when it comes to the infringement of a claim? She proposes, "It is permissible to infringe a claim if and only if infringing it would be sufficiently much better for those for whom infringing it would be good than not infringing it would be for the claim holder".[29]

In RI, the individual patient is at once the one whose claim is infringed and the one benefitted by the infringement. Regarding such a case, she suggests we determine permissibility in terms of "how bad things are for the claim holder if the claim is infringed"[30] Well, how bad are things for the patient? Which is worse, to be revengefully albeit painlessly killed by one's physician or to die in unrelieved pain? Perhaps most of us would opt for being painlessly but revengefully killed. Regardless, who would in turn say that the doctor's act of revengeful killing is, thereby, *sans phrase*, ethically permissible?

Consider this point from another vantage: if "bad" correctly assesses the physician in RI (as it does), then would not "ethically out of bounds", "wrong", even "impermissible" correctly assess the corresponding act? To consider one a "bad person" as Thomson (rightly) regards the physician in RI amounts to a significantly negative character evaluation. The doctor in RI has serious defects. She both lacks the normative intent to relieve her patient's pain and bears revengeful homicidal intent towards her patient. These are not minor flaws in a physician. Hence, she merits the evaluation Thomson assigns to her, bad. As argued, a defect in the agent implicates a defect in the act. By parity of reasoning, a grave defect in the agent implicates a grave defect in the act. "Bad" as said of an agent would seem to implicate "impermissible" as said of an act.

Thus, if Thomson wishes to maintain the act's permissibility, she needs to lessen the severity of her judgment concerning the physician. Yet, something has gone seriously amiss with the physician in RI; Thomson duly judges the doctor as bad. A less severe character evaluation would err. Hence, Thomson cannot at once assess the agent as bad while not having a correspondingly severe negative judgment concerning her act, such as "impermissible" or its moral equivalent.

---

[29] J.J. Thomson, *The Realm of Rights*, p. 174.
[30] *Ibid.*, p. 175.

By contrast, Anscombe and others who employ the I/F distinction would maintain that, in RI, just as "bad" correctly assesses the agent, so also "malicious", "wrong", "ethically out of bounds", "impermissible" correctly evaluate the agent's act. In any case, we here come to an impasse between the disputants. How shall we proceed? Let us (albeit briefly, due to the extensive treatments each offer as well as a need for brevity) consider their accounts of action, a topic upon which one would expect them to differ, as they do—dramatically.

4. Cause or Agent?

The dispute concerning the I/F distinction (unexpectedly) implicates a difference concerning moral dilemmas and temporal aspects of "ought implies can". Less surprisingly, it involves differences over what constitutes an act. In *Intention*, Anscombe articulates an account of human action as characteristically intentional. In doing so, she stands in a long tradition (that includes, amongst many others, Aristotle, Aquinas, Bentham and Mill).[31]

In *Intention* Anscombe speaks of our "special interest in human actions", or ethics.[32] Because intention defines uniquely human acts, when we do ethics we have a particular interest in an agent's intentions—if only to determine the subject matter of our investigation (actions). One who thinks that intention in part distinguishes what ethics studies (acts) from phenomena associated with humans that ethics does not investigate (digestings, fallings and so on) also reasonably thinks that differences in intention can make for differences in act-evaluation. For as intent makes an act an act, differences in intent make for differences in acts—presumably including evaluative differences. Given Anscombe's extended argument for intention as partially constitutive of action,

---

[31] See e.g. Aristotle, *Nicomachean Ethics*, III, chs. 1-5; Aquinas, ST, I-II q. 1. a.1. For a consideration of how Aristotle's account of action relates to the I/F distinction, see T.A. Cavanaugh, "Aristotle's Voluntary/Deliberate Distinction, Double Effect and Ethical Relevance", *International Philosophical Quarterly*, 54, 2014: 367-78. For a brief consideration of Mill (and Bentham) on intent as defining action, see e.g. John Stuart Mill, *Utilitarianism*, 2nd edition, ed. George Sher (Indianapolis, IN: Hackett Publishing Co., 2001), pp. 18-19, note 2.
[32] Anscombe, *Intention*, section 46, p. 83.

one sees grounds for her acknowledgment of the I/F distinction's role in act-assessment.

While there is a theoretical elegance and immediate plausibility in an account (like Anscombe's) that holds that what makes an act to be an act also plays a role in what makes it to be a good or a bad act (just as what makes an x to be an x enters into an account of what makes it to be a good or a bad x) one could (with argument) hold that intent does constitute an act as an act while not holding that intent serves in the ethical assessment of an act. (Here, for example, Mill appears to diverge from Anscombe.)[33] Rather, one might focus on an intentional act's consequences. Indeed, as noted at the outset, Anscombe claims this is precisely what one would reasonably do if one were (unreasonably) to deny the import of intention in act-evaluation by denying the I/F distinction. This, however, does not instance the approach that Thomson takes. Rather, she has a radically idiosyncratic account of what an act is.

Thomson does not regard intent as crucial to identifying an act as an act. Indeed, she lacks interest in such an identification or in what many would refer to as an "act". Rather, she proceeds backwards, as it were, from, e.g., a harmful effect upon one individual which effect can be causally associated with another individual. She then speaks of the latter individual as an "agent", using the word in a highly deracinated fashion. This salient difference with Anscombe (not to mention Bentham, Mill, let alone Aquinas and Aristotle) in part explains their dispute over the I/F distinction.

At the very end of her book on acts, Thomson (remarkably) speaks of one who would make "animatedness a requirement for agency". Of such a thinker, she goes on to say:

> I suspect that [such a one] ... simply does not find the notion "agency" I have been attending to of interest—what *he* wants is an account of the other notion "agency", the one according to which an event does not have an agent, and is not an act, unless it involves intentionality. Which of the two notions "agency" is of greater interest, I cannot say, and do not now really care.[34]

By "intentionality", Thomson does not mean only fully formed intent, she means psychological elements of human action, broadly, knowing and wanting, or voluntariness. Noting this

---

[33] John Stuart Mill, *Utilitarianism*, pp. 18–20.
[34] J.J. Thomson, *Acts and Other Events*, p. 253 (original emphasis).

alternative account of agency (while not acknowledging its near normative character as the account of agency), Thomson continues, saying:

> I cannot forbear drawing attention to the fact that it is by no means obvious that the notion "agency" I have not dealt with is any more important for ethics than is the notion "agency" I have dealt with. No doubt a great many good acts and a great many evil acts are intentional, and a moral philosopher does need to know something about what intentionality is. But in the first place, what we are responsible for is by no means restricted to what we bring about in a way that involves intentionality. And in the second place, it is a plausible hypothesis that causings will turn out to be central, and intentionality at most peripheral, to a theory of rights — i.e., to a theory about what we have a right to do and why we have a right to do it.[35]

Although her name appears nowhere in Thomson's work on acts, Anscombe is the contemporary thinker who most completely attends to the here curiously named "other notion of agency" (and thus founds the modern discipline of action-theory). Thomson neglects agency to focus on causality. As she tells us above, she does so because her principal interest is a theory of rights in which we have claims upon others, e.g. not to be caused harm (not to have certain effects happen to us which effects are affiliated with others as causes). By focussing on causality and not agency (or human action), Thomson advances a properly legal notion of strict liability. She errs, however, in applying this account broadly to morality.

To see this, consider an example—call it "Parcel"—that Anscombe offers: "Suppose I am a parcel—I mean I've been made up into a parcel—and by sheer accident I get set rolling down a hill in such circumstances that I kill someone by knocking him over into the path of a rapid vehicle—that's not a human action on my part."[36] Anscombe (surely correctly) holds that she does

---

[35] Thomson, *Acts and Other Events*, p. 253, note 1.
[36] G.E.M. Anscombe, "Medalist's Address: Action, Intention and 'Double Effect'", *Proceedings of the American Catholic Philosophical Association*, LVI, 1982: 12–25, at p. 21; also available in *Human Life, Action and Ethics: Essays by G.E.M. Anscombe*, eds. Mary Geach and Luke Gormally (Exeter: Imprint Academic, 2005), pp. 207–26, at p. 210.

nothing morally wrong in Parcel because she does nothing at all. She does not act; therefore, there is no act to evaluate.[37]

Thomson, by contrast, would claim that Anscombe infringes the right of the passerby not to be killed. According to Thomson, what Anscombe does is morally impermissible. Here is Thomson on an analogous case:

> Day's End: B always comes home at 9 P.M. and the first thing he does is to flip the light switch in his hallway. He did so this evening. B's flipping the switch caused a circuit to close. By virtue of an extraordinary series of coincidences, unpredictable in advance by anybody, the circuit's closing caused a release of electricity (a small lightning flash) in A's house next door. Unluckily, A was in its path and was therefore badly burned.[38]

Thomson holds that B (morally) ought not to flip the switch. If B does, B infringes a claim of A's. Her assumption that B's mental states cannot make a difference to act-evaluation leads her to this odd position. She holds it would be "weird in us" to say "Look B, we know something that you don't know. If we tell you, then it will be true to say that you ought not flip the switch, but not if we don't tell you".[39] She does not acknowledge that were B to act with such knowledge, B would thereby perform an act that (now) includes voluntarily burning A. For, as Anscombe more than adequately shows in *Intention*, acts occur under descriptions themselves partially determined by what the agent knows himself to be doing and seeks to do. (Thomson appears entirely innocent of Anscombe's account.)

Concerning the larger issues involving the voluntary and the intentional illustrated in Day's End and Parcel, two points come to mind. First, one must distinguish legal from moral matters. Anscombe might be legally responsible (civilly but not criminally) for the death of the man in Parcel. That is, in many jurisdictions (e.g. in the U.S.) the man's family could legally hold Anscombe financially responsible for the death of their beloved. Indeed, insurance against accidents (personal liability insurance which covers one's non-agential or merely causal effects upon others) serves precisely this purpose. Notably, it does not insure one against the intentional infliction of harm (against one's

---

[37] I here put to the side a complication that is not at issue; i.e. omissions.
[38] Thomson, *The Realm of Rights*, p. 229.
[39] Ibid., p. 233.

performance of criminal acts). Rather, it is, as the name often given to it indicates, insurance against accidents. Emphatically, however, from the standpoint of any sound morality or ethic, Anscombe in the parcel case is not at all responsible for the man's death. For, Anscombe as moral agent (in any tenable sense) did not kill the man; rather, a parcel did. (All the same points hold concerning B in Day's End.)

Second, while it may be true, as Thomson above claims, that an account of causality serves a legal theory of rights, a moralist who relies on such an account mistakes legal relevance for ethical relevance. Concerning Day's End, Thomson entirely misconstrues ethics' subject matter as an individual's causal relationship with salient good and bad effects (as she would were she to employ the causal account of responsibility to Parcel). By contrast, ethics concerns the voluntary—that which one relates to as a knowing willing cause. That which is not voluntary lacks moral relevance. Since the bad outcomes in Parcel and Day's End lack voluntariness, they lack ethical import. For only the voluntary has moral significance. (As Anscombe shows in *Intention*, intent instances especially robust voluntariness.)

Thomson's disregard for ethics' focus upon knowing-willing agency (or human agency) comports with her tendency not to mark much of a distinction between legal rights and moral rights. Here she is, downplaying the contrast:

> Anyone who likes can at the end try to construct an account of what might plausibly be meant by the terms "moral rights" and "legal rights" under which the genus rights can be seen as having species appropriately named in those ways, but what interests us is the genus rights itself—as I will put it throughout, what interests us is people's rights.[40]

Thomson herself sees little reason to contrast legal from moral rights or law from morality. However, law and morality sometimes do differ importantly. For example, as noted, concerning responsibility. Ethics does not have strict liability; it is entirely a legal phenomenon. Because of it, the law—in addition to having an account of criminal liability that attends to the mental elements of human acts (similar to that of morality)—also has an account of

---

[40] J.J. Thomson, *The Realm of Rights*, p. 76.

purely causal responsibility.⁴¹ In terms of its account of purely causal responsibility, the law can hold Anscombe *qua* parcel responsible for the man's death. One errs grossly, however, if one thinks that Anscombe has a scintilla of ethical responsibility in Parcel. (The same holds, of course, for B in Day's End.)

5. Conclusion

The preceding indicates that the dispute between Anscombe and Thomson implicates other matters, particularly a moralist's: 1) stance concerning the possibility of self-imposed moral dilemmas, 2) understanding of "ought implies can", 3) conception of how the evaluation of an agent relates to the evaluation of his act, and, of course, 4) account of action. Concerning each of these matters, reflection shows that the I/F distinction as applied to act-evaluation has much to recommend it. *Contra* Thomson, it is not from "lack of imagination" or a "desire for simplicity" that one acknowledges the I/F distinction's relevance in act-evaluation.⁴² Rather, ethicists who understand the I/F distinction's full import evidence robust imagination coupled with an appreciation for morality's complexity.

I conclude noting Anscombe's apt advice found in "Modern Moral Philosophy": "it is not profitable for us at present to do moral philosophy; that should be laid aside at any rate until we have an adequate philosophy of psychology, in which we are conspicuously lacking."⁴³

---

[41] In criminal law we have the principle "*actus non facit reum, nisi mens sit rea*". The doing does not make the crime without the mental element (*mens rea*); of course, the same holds in ethics.
[42] Thomson, "Physician-Assisted Suicide", p. 517.
[43] Anscombe, "Modern Moral Philosophy", p. 1.

Sarah Broadie

Anscombe and Practical Truth in Aristotle[1]

1. Introduction

G.E.M. Anscombe was apparently the first to puzzle at length over Aristotle's curious notion of practical truth. She published two papers on it: "Thought and Action in Aristotle" (1965) and "Practical Truth" (1993).[2] While both are important, the earlier is better known and has been especially seminal for students of Aristotle's moral psychology. I return to consider and evaluate the plausibility of her interpretation in section 4.

The notion of practical truth occurs only at *Nicomachean Ethics* VI, 1139a26–30 (cf. 18). The main topic of *NE* VI is the intellectual virtue *phronēsis*, practical wisdom. This is the practical analogue of *sophia*, theoretical wisdom. Aristotle elucidates *phronēsis* partly by contrasts with productive expertise (*technē*) and *sophia*, partly by exploring its relation to "ethical" or "moral" virtue. Our text opens

---

[1] I am grateful to Ben Morison for his uncompromising criticism of my earlier paper on this topic, and to Marko Malink and Jessica Moss for improvements to the present one.

[2] G.E.M. Anscombe, "Thought and Action in Aristotle: What is Practical Truth?", in *New Essays on Plato and Aristotle*, ed. R. Bamborough (London: Humanities Press, 1965), pp. 143–58, reprinted in *The Collected Philosophical Papers of G.E.M. Anscombe* (Oxford: Blackwell, 1981), pp. 66–77; "Practical Truth", *Working Papers in Law, Medicine and Philosophy*, ed. J. Dolan, (Minneapolis, MN: University of Minnesota Press, 1993), reprinted in *Logos*, 2 (3) 1999: 68–76, and in *Human Life, Action and Ethics*, eds. M. Geach and L. Gormally (Exeter: Imprint Academic, 2005), pp. 149–60.

by distinguishing two parts of the rational part of soul: one concerned with things whose principles cannot be otherwise, the other with contingent things. Each rational part has its own kind of virtue, i.e. disposition that is best for the part's proper work or function (*ergon*); and the proper work of both parts is truth.[3]

> [1139a15] So we need to understand what the best disposition is of each of these two, since that is the virtue of each, and the virtue relates to the proper work. Now, there are in the soul three things responsible for (*ta kuria*) practical activity (*praxis*) and truth (*alētheia*): perception, intelligence (*nous*), and desire (*orexis*). (But of these perception is not the source of any practical activity; this is clear from the fact that [a20] brute animals have perception but do not share practical activity.) What assertion and denial are in thought, pursuit and avoidance are in desire. So: since ethical virtue is a disposition for decision (*prohairesis*), and decision is deliberative desire, it must therefore be the case that both the *logos* is true and the desire correct (*orthē*) if the decision is a sound (*spoudaia*) one, and [a25] the one must assert (*phanai*) and the other pursue the same things. This (*hautē*), then, is the thought (*dianoia*) and the truth that is practical (*he alētheia praktikē*).[4] In the case of thought that is theoretical and not practical nor yet productive, the well and badly are the true and false, for this is the business (*ergon*) of every intellectual part. But in the case of the part that is practical

---

[3] "Truth", "true" and "asserting truly" occur many times in *NE* VI: 1139a18; 24; 26–31; b12–15; 1140a10; 21; 1140b5; 21; 1141a3; 1142b33; 1143a24. See also *Eudemian Ethics* II, 1221b27–30.

[4] This translation takes *hautē* as subject, *hē dianoia kai hē alētheia praktikē* as complement; thus e.g. Irwin (Aristotle, *Nicomachean Ethics*, 2nd Edition, trans. Terence Irwin (Indianapolis, IN: Hackett, 1999)). An alternative is: "This <kind of> thought, and truth, is practical", taking *hautē hē dianoia kai hē alētheia* as subject and *praktikē* as complement. (On "kind of" here, see M. Pakaluk, "The Great Question of Practical Truth", *Acta Philosophica*, 19, 2010: 145–59.) This may indeed convey Aristotle's thought, but argument is needed, and will be given below, that he recognizes a distinct *kind of truth* that is practical; so I have chosen a translation that is neutral on this score. On this translation, what is the referent of *hautē*? It would be stylistically natural (1) to understand it as the nearest preceding feminine item, i.e. the sound *prohairesis*; many commentators reject this out of hand for philosophical reasons. Alternatively, (2) *hautē* is due to attraction to the gender of *dianoia* and *alētheia*, and refers either (a) to the prohairetic complex true-*logos*-and-right-desire-etc. or (b) to the true *logos* part of that (mentioned at 1139a25). 2b is stylistically somewhat strained. Readings 1 and 2a support proposals A and C below. Proposals B, B* and C* require 2b, or 2a taken as a whole-for-part synecdoche (the complex is referred to in virtue of containing the true *logos*).

and [a30] thinks, <the well> is truth in agreement with correct desire. Decision is a source (*archē*) of action—the source from-which, not the one for-the-sake-of-which—and the sources of decision are desire and the *logos* that says what the end is. Consequently there cannot be decision without intelligence and thought, nor without an ethical nature (*Ethos*). For in the sphere of action doing well (*eupraxia*) and its opposite are impossible without thought and ethical nature. Thought as such moves nothing; what moves, rather, is thought that is for the sake of something and practical. For this <kind of thought> in fact controls productive activity ... Decision is desiderative intelligence or desire that has been thought out (*dianoētikē*), and this kind of source is man ... To sum up (*dē*): truth is the business of both the intellectual parts; so their virtues are those states whereby each part will be truthful (*alētheusei*) to the highest degree. (1139a15–b13)[5]

A question to bear in mind is whether the phrase "truth that is practical" (or "practical truth") expresses a unitary concept or an amalgam of independently intelligible units: <u>truth</u> and <u>practical</u>. The concept is unitary if the truth of practical truth is to be understood as "inherently" practical (this could be cashed in different ways), or if the two sides turn out to be united at source: in any given case of practical truth, whatever legitimates calling it "truth" also legitimates calling it "practical".[6]

I shall consider two kinds of interpretative approach. One, by far the most common, seeks to make sense of "practical truth" in terms of a fairly straightforward and familiar notion of semantic truth. A proposition is semantically true or false depending on whether the facts or realities are or are not as it says. In Aristotle's hands this semantic notion is interpreted in terms of assertion. Anscombe's interpretation of "practical truth", while very distinctive, falls into this category. According to the second type of approach, Aristotle's practical truth is different from assertoric truth although closely related.

---

[5] Cf. *EE* II, 1221b28–30.
[6] Olfert is the first, as far as I know, to make conceptual unity an explicit desideratum for interpretations of "practical truth" (C. Olfert, "Aristotle's Conception of Practical Truth", *Journal of the History of Philosophy*, 52, 2014: 205–31).

2. Assertoric Truth and Theoretical Understanding

A natural starting point is Aristotle's famous definition in *Metaphysics* IV: "To say that what is, is not, or that what is not, is, is false; whereas to say that what is, is, or that what is not, is not, is true."[7] "To say" here surely means "to assert", mentally or in words. I shall not undertake the close discussion that the definition demands.[8] The main point for now is that the definition attaches "true" and "false" (or "being true", "being false") to judgments or assertions rather than to the propositional contents of assertions. See also a few lines down: "For every object of thought and understanding, thought either affirms it or denies it (*kataphēsin ē apophēsin*) — this is clear from the definition — whenever it expresses truth or falsehood (*alētheuē(i) ē pseudetai*)."[9] I shall use "assertion" to cover both affirmation and denial. At the basic level what is asserted are simple sentences (these include negations), which may be existential or predicative, singular or quantified. The truth and falsehood that attach to assertions I shall call "assertoric" truth and falsehood. Truth and falsehood on the semantic or linguistic level are the truth and falsehood of assertions.[10]

On this basis, how should we understand the *NE* VI passage about practical truth? Well, since the practical intellect, there, is compared and contrasted with the theoretical intellect, let us first see how the definition in *Metaphysics* IV lines up with the theoretical side of things. In the *NE* VI passage above Aristotle says that the well and the badly are the true and false, this being the *ergon* of every intellectual part of the soul (i.e. the *ergon* is achieving the true and avoiding the false). So does Aristotle hold that theoretical thought's going well is nothing other than its achieving assertoric truth, and that doing this is the proper business, task or object of the theoretical intellect?

---

[7] *Metaphysics* IV, 1011b25-27.
[8] See P. Crivelli, *Aristotle on Truth* (New York: Cambridge University Press, 2004), pp. 132-36.
[9] *Metaphysics* IV, 1012a2-4.
[10] Crivelli, *Aristotle on Truth*, pp. 86-95; also pp. 7-39 *passim*. "Assertion" here covers any laying down of premises, including ones that are assumed for the purpose of *reductio ad absurdum*. My thanks to Marko Malink for this point.

In a simple or straightforward sense of this question, the answer is "No". This is because the object, for Aristotle, of theoretical intellectual activity is *epistēmē*, scientific knowledge, which involves grasping things on the basis of their causes or principles.[11] We have *epistēmē* in relation to p only if we understand why p is the case—only if we see it as grounded on something more fundamental: its cause or principle. More precisely: *epistēmē* in a field is a disposition for understanding and explaining things in that field. A, who has discovered that p is grounded in q, can teach this to B, i.e. bring B to see p as grounded in the more fundamental q, and hence to understand p. This teaching is an exercise of *epistēmē* by A although we would not expect A necessarily to renew, on each teaching-occasion, her or his own understanding of p by a fresh act of understanding; but we surely do assume that A's ability to get others to understand p springs from A's own prior act or acts of understanding p in terms of q. Such acts of understanding are what *epistēmē* is "all about": it is a disposition defined by such acts, and these acts give value to the disposition. Thus the ultimate object of theoretical inquiry and teaching is the act of understanding. So is the disposition for such acts nothing other than a disposition for making assertions that are true (and none that are false) in the sense explained in the *Metaphysics* IV definition? It does Aristotle no favour to ascribe to him such a view. If "p because q" expresses an act of understanding p, the subject has done more than assert truly that p and that q,[12] and also more than assert truly that p, and that q, and that q is cause or ground of p. For it is possible to do this without understanding or ever having understood p in light of its cause q, or without seeing q *as* cause of p. One could have it on external authority that p and that q and that the latter is cause of the former, yet still fail, oneself, to understand p on this basis. Given a suitable authority K, for any r if K asserts that r then r. So anyone in the circle of adherents could be placed by K in a position to assert truly that p and that q and that q is cause of p. But K has not thereby transmitted understanding of p on the basis of q. In fact

---

[11] At 1141a1720 Aristotle distinguishes the ability to derive, which he calls *epistēmē*, from the grasp of the principles as such, which he calls *nous*; the combination of these he calls *sophia*.
[12] The point is noted by Olfert, "Aristotle's Conception", p. 210.

nothing in this picture guarantees that even *K* understands *p* on the basis of *q*.

So (short of supposing that Aristotle is oblivious to all this): if we still want to explain the theoretical intellect's objective in a way that gives a central role to assertoric truth, we must take a slightly more subtle line. Here is a suggestion. Take the general notion of an intelligent Aristotelian theoretical inquirer. The notion itself implies that the inquirer's aim is to understand something, *p*, in terms of its cause or ground, so that achieving this will constitute success. Then exhibit the understanding as supervening on the moment of the inquirer's coming to possess all relevant assertoric truths. Admittedly, this is idealized. We have to assume an inquirer who, as well as being intent on coming to understand some datum, is undistracted, clear-headed and thorough; but granted this, it seems plausible that access to all the relevant assertoric truths will *ipso facto* result in the "click", the falling into place, that is the act of understanding.[13]

3. Practical Truth

Practical truth is evinced in a sound *prohairesis*, combining a *logos*-factor and a desire-factor which are as they should be: the *logos* true, the desire correct, and in concord.[14] The *prohairesis*, according to Aristotle, is formed by deliberating on what it is good for me to do so as to implement an end *E*. The short answer is "It is good to adopt means *M*". Aristotle tends to focus on the short answer: thus he says that deliberation is *of* the means—i.e. is an inquiry *about* the means—to *E*, and that the eventually reached *prohairesis* is *of* the means, i.e. specifies a determinate answer to precisely that inquiry.[15] Deliberation resulting in the specification of *M* starts from a premise such as "It would be good to get *E*", other

---

[13] The aim here is not to give a non-circular analysis of theoretical understanding but to characterize it for the purpose of clarifying its practical analogue. This sketch also oversimplifies in treating understanding as supervening on the accumulation of all relevant assertoric truths; in fact we often accept a crucial assertoric truth on the ground that the best explanation requires it.

[14] Olfert's helpful discussion of this shows in detail the practical nature of both factors and how they respectively derive truth and correctness from a single standard, i.e. the unqualified human good ("Aristotle's Conception", pp. 219-30).

[15] *NE* VI 1144a8-9; III, 1111b26-29; *EE* II, 1226b9-13; 1227a5-18.

premises being supplied by the particular situation. The fact that deliberation gets its direction from an end-specifying premise does not mean that the deliberator is stuck with aiming for the end E as if it cannot be abandoned (or can be abandoned only if found to be physically unfeasible). Deliberation with a view to E may arrive at specifying M, but what is thereby specified as good to do is M-*as-leading-to-E*. This is the longer answer to the deliberator's question: it says more fully *what* one would be adopting in adopting M. In some cases the only discoverable means to E, given the circumstances, turns out to be simply unacceptable on moral or prudential grounds, regardless of the nature of E. Since M is rejected, E as end is abandoned, anyway here and now. This is analogous to (or is a case of) *modus tollens*: we reject a premise because we reject the conclusion. But often the only available means is not completely unacceptable but is here and now unacceptable because under the circumstances the specified end is not worth the means: it would be disproportionate, hence wrong, to pursue *that* end by *this* means, given the circumstances. This situation may be compared to the one in theoretical inquiry where in attempting to explain p we reject q as a possible explanation even though we grant the truth of q: we reject its claim to be cause of p because it does not fit (e.g. because instances of q are known also to occur in the absence of any instances of p). Similarly, we reject M's claim to be the sanctioned means to E because of lack of practical fit under the circumstances.

What is distinctive about the Aristotelian *prohairesis*, and why it is essentially practical, is that it is an endorsement of some action as good or appropriate *simpliciter*, not merely good from a limited and overridable point of view. It is an *all*-things-considered rational decision, one that represents my sense of how under these circumstances I as a human being should simply *act* or *behave*, or what I should simply *go for*, or what counts as unqualified doing well (*eupraxia*), for me here and now. This is by contrast with what counts as my acting well or doing well as a builder, farmer, money-maker or lover of some type of pleasure. There are two important consequences. First, the *prohairesis* necessarily involves desire to *do* what, through all-things-considered deliberation, the agent has determined would be good to do.[16] Secondly, if truth attaches to the Aristotelian *prohairesis* or

---

[16] *NE* 1139a4–5.

to the *logos*-factor within it, this truth includes truth about what is genuinely valuable in human life. The deliberative conclusion, "It would be good to implement *M*", is part of what Aristotle at 1139a24 calls the *logos*. But the *logos* surely comprises the whole deliberative argument: premises, conclusion, inferences and underlying assumptions, including ones about value and good conduct. If this complex *logos* is as it should be, the *logos* is all true.[17]

From here, detailed interpretation can go in different directions.

Proposal A

> The good *prohairesis* as a whole is an assertoric truth: a true assertion of what it is good to do. Think of the *logos*-factor as supplying the asserted content while the desiderative factor constitutes the assertion of it. (Without assertion there is neither truth nor falsehood.) This would explain very cleanly why Aristotle says that desire is one of the three things in the soul that are responsible for practical activity *and truth*.[18] A good *prohairesis* is true, the bearer of truth, because thanks to desire it is a true assertion. This solution neatly integrates truth with practicality: the very same element, the right desire, both ensures truth, by ensuring assertion of a *logos* that represents things as they are, and ensures corresponding action.

However, there are two objections. First, Aristotle elsewhere distinguishes *prohairesis* from *doxa* (belief, judgment, opinion) on the ground that we differentiate the latter by "false" and "true", the former by "bad" and "good".[19] Secondly, Aristotle says that the sound *prohairesis* involves a *logos* that is true *and* a desire that is correct,[20] and that well-doing for practical intellect is truth *in agreement with* the correct desire.[21] These expressions strongly suggest that the presence of the right desire is somehow additional to the truth of the *logos*-factor. Thus if the latter's truth is assertoric, the

---

[17] See note 32 on truth of arguments.
[18] *NE* 1139a18.
[19] *EE* II, 1226a4; cf. *NE* III, 1111b32–34; VI, 1142b11.
[20] *NE* 1139a24–25.
[21] *NE* 1139a29–31.

truth involved in the good *prohairesis* has already been asserted by the intellect independently of the presence of right desire.

Proposal B

> Truth in the sound *prohairesis* is simply the assertoric truth of the *logos* component, which in itself is a *doxa*: but this *doxa* is practical only if the relevant desire is also present, namely the desire to do what the reasoning has marked out, e.g. *M-for-the-sake-of-E*. Since the desire may not be present (in which case there is no *prohairesis* but just a hypothetical picture of what one would do *if* one were doing what the reasoning showed to be good or appropriate), the truth of the *logos* is only contingently practical: it is truth which is (also) practical, and this is a conceptual amalgam according to the distinction in section I.

Proposal B*

> B can be improved by arguing that, given the assertorically true *logos* (articulated through deliberation and asserted as the *logos* that it is), the absence from it of the relevant desire is not merely a negative fact but a privative one. The desire ought to be present: it belongs with the true *logos*, which was only ever formulated in order to be a reason for *doing* this rather than that. Without the desire, this true *logos* is like a perfectly formed and viable child which never lived because someone smothered it at birth. On this account, surely more Aristotelian than B, the *logos* meets the norm for every *logos*, namely the norm of assertoric truth, but without desiderative support it lacks the opportunity to function as it was meant to function, i.e. by structuring action. Its opportunity is denied if a contrary desire has sprung up, one whose existence and ground in no way undermines the truth of the deliberative premises or the correctness of the reasoning, but which the agent fails to control. This, of course, is *akrasia*, the betrayal of the deliberative intellect through interference from the non-intellectual part of the soul.[22]

---

[22] On this account the *prohairesis* comprises an executive desire for implementation. It follows that the acratic has lost his *prohairesis*. Aristotle seems happy to accept the metaphor of the acratic "jumping out of", "abandoning",

According to B* the phrase "practical truth" does not indicate a mere conjunction of truth with the practicality of desire. Nor does it indicate a special kind of truth, since there is only one kind of truth, namely the truth of assertions that accord with the facts or the nature of things. Rather, "practical truth" points us to the ordinary assertoric truth of a special kind of *logos*, one whose formulation and assertion are pointless—a wasted or not properly exploited work of reason—except in the presence of a fully executive desire to do what the *logos* truly says is good or appropriate. On this account, "practical truth" tells us that the practicality ensured by the right desire is more than the truth of the *logos* if we consider this truth by itself; but the "extra" afforded by right desire is not an external addition, any more than sight to the eyes although a naturally sighted animal might be blind. There is a non-contingent but defeasible connection between the true *logos* and the right desire.

The situation where a true deliberated *logos* is present and the corresponding desire absent might be compared to that of a theoretical inquirer who makes a true assertion of the fact that is the reason or cause of what he seeks to explain, but fails to achieve understanding perhaps because of a false or confused theoretical assumption which has not been cleared out of the way. The assertion of what is in fact the cause meets the norm of truth, but (at least for now) the inquirer is no further forward in the effort to understand than if the assertion had been false. Similarly, the acratically diverted agent who "has" (in some sense) a true deliberated *logos* is for now no better off in a practical way than if the *logos* had been false through empirical ignorance of some circumstance. The truth of the acratic's deliberated *logos* is not only of no practical consequence but of no theoretical consequence either. The information it carries is about contingent things and particulars, which are viewed not theoretically (e.g. as confirming or disconfirming a general physical hypothesis, or constituting a perceptible diagram for the mathematician), but as setting up a

---

his *prohairesis*: NE VII, 1145b11; 1146a18; 1151a1; 20; 26. The acratic's motivational conflict, if there is one, is between the errant appetite and a wish that is, as it were, trying to be prohairetic.

need or practical problem and demanding or suggesting one or another practical response.²³

Neither B nor B* allows for a straightforward reading of Aristotle's statement that desire, along with perception and intelligence, is responsible for practical activity *and truth*. On B and B* one must read this as highly condensed, if not confused. He immediately corrects himself about perception: as such it does not control practical activity, which can be ascribed only to beings of a rational kind. Should he not also have immediately corrected himself about desire here, saying that it as such is not responsible for truth? If he means this latter correction, why does he not state it, given that (a) he does state the one about perception, (b) the one about desire would surely be just as important and (c) the two corrections would mirror each other, one making perception responsible for truth but not practicality, the other making desire responsible for practicality but not truth?

Proposal C

> The proposals so far have assumed that the truth indicated by "practical truth" is assertoric, the truth of an assertion that represents things as they are. We have not yet, therefore, parsed "practical truth" as naming a distinctive *kind of truth*.²⁴ (What, according to B*, was of a "special kind" was the *logos* in the good *prohairesis*, not its truth.) As far as assertoric truth is concerned, it is not clear what it could mean to speak of different kinds of truth. Difference between the subject-matters of true assertions does not make for different kinds of truth. Proposal C, by contrast, introduces a way of conceiving of truth otherwise than as assertoric. On this conception there can be different kinds of truth, one of which would be practical truth.

But before getting to practical truth I consider some passages where Aristotle speaks of *the truth*, using the noun *alētheia*, in a sense that is richer, older and perhaps less neatly definable than

---

²³ Thus it is historically rather misleading to speak, as is often done, of the factual information that features in deliberation as "theoretical truths" (by which is meant that the propositions are non-evaluative and non-normative). From Aristotle's point of view the acratic who has got it right about the circumstances and what he should do in them is not to be congratulated on having at least done well "theoretically".

²⁴ See note 4.

the assertoric sense.[25] "The truth" in this richer sense indicates, simultaneously, actual or possible cognitive achievement in relation to some reality, and the reality itself insofar as it is or might be successfully presented to rational cognition. The truth in this sense may have as its object a thing, a fact, an underlying principle or a whole domain. Aristotle alludes to truth in this sense when, in the context of theoretical inquiry, he speaks of the "study of truth (*theōria tēs alētheias*)" at the beginning of *Metaphysics* II, 993a30 and at *De Caelo* I, 271b5–6; when he speaks of people "philosophizing about the truth" at *Metaphysics* I, 983b2–3[26] and *De Caelo* III, 298b12–13; when he says that philosophy is rightly called "knowledge (*epistēmē*) of the truth" at *Metaphysics* II, 993b19–20; when he speaks of people "philosophically seeking the truth and the nature of what is" at *Physics* I, 191a24–5.[27]

One might say that this is not very different, if different at all, from assertoric truth: "truth" in this so called rich sense makes a reference to the cognitive subject ("the soul"),[28] and so does "assertoric truth" since this assumes a subject who asserts. But there is a difference. Rich-sense "truth" in the passages cited indicates the full achievement of scientific knowledge and understanding, or the corresponding reality as it really is, i.e. as it would present itself to the ideal knower, whereas assertoric truth can attach to true opinions that fall short of being scientific knowledge

---

[25] For assertoric truth elsewhere he uses the adjective *alēthēs* or *to alēthes*, and the verb *alētheuein*. Thus if *alētheia* in our *NE* VI passage means assertoric truth, this is exceptional.

[26] W.D. Ross comments: "Aristotle does not mean either simply that these thinkers tried to reach the truth, as do inquirers in *any* field, or that they studied the nature of truth, as an 'epistemologist' does, but that they studied the truth in general, the ultimate nature of things" (*Aristotle's Metaphysics* (Oxford: Clarendon Press, 1958), p. 128).

[27] See also *Metaphysics* I, 988a20; II, 993b17; *De Anima* I, 402a5; *Physics* VIII, 251a6; *Generation and Corruption* I, 325a17; *Physics* I, 188b30 and *Metaphysics* I, 984b10 on being forced or led by the truth (cf. *Parts of Animals* I, 642a19). See also *Eudemian Ethics* I, 1215b1–2, and possibly 1216b31 and II, 1227a1–2. Other examples may be *Physics* VIII, 263a18; *Magna Moralia* I, 1185b39; II, 1200b23–4. My purpose in making the case that Aristotle sometimes operates with this richer sense of "truth" is not to sell it philosophically (as though Aristotle's patronage is an automatic recommendation), but only to elucidate "practical truth" in *NE* VI. One can concede that what he says in the theoretical passages in terms of rich-sense "truth" could probably have been said just as well in cleaner to us terms like "scientific knowledge" and "understanding".

[28] Cf. *NE* 1139a16–17.

by any standard, e.g. ones that owe their truth to a lucky guess at the facts, and ones that represent incidental combinations like "The doctor is building a boat".

Consider this from *Metaphysics* II:

> It is right that philosophy is called knowledge of the truth (*epistēmēn tēs alētheias*). For the end of the theoretical kind is truth (*alētheia*) and of the practical kind it is a deed (*ergon*).[29] (For practical thinkers, too, investigate how things are: they study [*theōrousin*] — not the cause per se, but — the cause that is relative to something and is *now*.) Without the cause, we do not know a truth. For every <characteristic> *P*, the thing that compared to the others is most *P* is the one whereby the characteristic that has that name is present in other things; e.g. fire is hottest as it is the cause of heat in other things. So that is truest which is cause of the derivative things' being true. Consequently, the principles of eternal things must be maximally true (*alēthestatas*). For they are not true merely sometimes, nor does anything cause them to be: they, rather, cause other things to be (*tou einai*). So, for each thing, the degree to which it has being is also the degree to which it has truth.[30]

However exactly we unpick the metaphysics and epistemology of this, the truth that belongs to things in degrees depending on how ontologically fundamental they are (and therefore how explanatory they are for the scientific inquirer) is clearly not assertoric truth. An assertion that *p* is true as an assertion if and only if the asserter thereby says what is the case, whether what is said is metaphysically superficial or deep. Moreover, the significance of the passage cannot be dismissed by claiming that its degrees-of-truth vocabulary is just an archaic formulation of Aristotle's well known idea that the primary things are the most knowable.[31] This may well be so. But even if degrees-of-truth vocabulary is inter-translatable with degrees-of-knowability vocabulary, what matters for now is that Aristotle conceives of truth in a way that sanctions such translation.[32]

---

[29] It is not clear whether the theoretical and practical kinds here are kinds of *epistēmē* or of philosophy. Note that here Aristotle restricts *alētheia* to theoretical *epistēmē*/philosophy.

[30] *Metaphysics* II, 993b19–31. "True" here is not a just another word for "existent" or "real", since things are said to vary in truth as they vary in existence or reality.

[31] *Metaphysics* I, 982a25–b4.

[32] It is interesting that Aristotle sometimes says that arguments, *sullogismoi*, are true and false, and in some cases for reasons other than assertoric truth or

Proposal C, and its not yet introduced successor C*, build on the good number of passages concerning theoretical inquiry where the noun *alētheia* denotes the full measure of cognitive success.[33] (I say "cognitive success" in general, although our concern is with the intellectual kinds, because at 1139a18 Aristotle also counts sense perception as responsible for *alētheia*.) On this basis, proposal C says that "practical *alētheia*" in our *NE* VI passage marks the culminating intellectual achievement of practical inquiry. Here is the only clear reason I can discern for treating practical *alētheia* as a distinctive kind of truth. Since practical inquiry is a distinctive kind of inquiry, its success is a corresponding kind of intellectual success; and "practical *alētheia*" is a synonym for that success as such.[34]

---

falsity of a premiss or the conclusion (on which see *Posterior Analytics* I, 88a20 ff. and *NE* VI, 1142b21-26). At *Topics* VIII, 162b3-22 he says that an argument is said to be false in four ways: (a) when it is invalid, (b) when it is valid but the conclusion is not the one proposed, (c) when the proposed conclusion is validly reached "but not according to the mode of inquiry appropriate to the case" and (d) when a true conclusion is validly drawn from false premises (see also *Sophistical Refutations* 176b29-33). An argument that avoids all these errors, hence is "true", does not necessarily possess truth in the elevated sense of scientific understanding since it may not be explanatory or even aiming at explanation. But the truth involved seems to be a matter of argumentative success rather than mere assertoric truth.

[33] Cf. the naturalness of "The truth about ..." in titles of *exposés*, e.g. "The truth about the JFK assassination". They promise not merely to substitute assertoric truths for false impressions but to do so by a narrative that makes best sense of all the data.

[34] According to Olfert ("Aristotle's Conception", pp. 208-10; 217), Aristotle treats the different kinds of intellectual truth as *definitive* of different kinds of rational activities, achievement and excellences. Therefore the distinctive character of practical reason should be explained in terms of its distinctive truth. On this basis she objects to interpreters who try to understand what Aristotle means by "practical truth" by (a) treating it as the goal of practical reason and then (b) elucidating this goal by reference to Aristotle's well-known discussions of deliberation and *prohairesis*. The objection rests on a misunderstanding. Grant that inquiry of kind *P* aims at *P*-truth: it does not follow that we should elucidate the nature of *P*-inquiry by first laying out whatever is conveyed by "*P*-truth". Calling *X* a goal does not entail that one must treat *X* as *definitive* of the activity that aims at it. Rich-sense "truth" in the cited theoretical passages is not directly the name of something that explains what theoretical inquiry is or ought to be. Rather, it is an accolade marking the success of such inquiry. What Aristotelian theoretical inquiry essentially is, as we know from innumerable passages, is the search for explanations in the domain of unchangeable facts; and from the *Posterior Analytics* and elsewhere

Thus "practical truth" according to C denotes nothing more nor less than the good *prohairesis* itself, with its true *logos* and its concordant desire.[35] It is not a point against C that a *prohairesis* is not an assertion capable of assertoric truth and falsehood, for practical truth, on this proposal, is not claimed to be assertoric truth. (As to that, we have seen that understanding, the culminating achievement of theoretical intellect, cannot be reduced to a set of assertoric truths. Moreover, some scholars hold that for Aristotle the truth of sense perception, anyway for the special senses, is a non-propositional or non-predicational grasp of a proper sensible.[36] On that view, the truth of perception is also nonassertoric.)

Proposal C avoids one important objection to A, namely that Aristotle distinguishes a *prohairesis* from a *doxa* on the ground that "true" and "false" apply to the latter and not to the former. Presumably this distinction is drawn in terms of assertoric truth and falsehood. But C's claim is that the truth of the good *prohairesis* is truth in a different sense. Furthermore, on C "practical truth" indicates a natural unity, given that truth, the success of intellect, is instanced here by the *prohairesis*, a work of practical intellect.

However, C faces a serious difficulty which also afflicted A. When Aristotle apportions *alētheia* to the practical intellect at 1139a29–31, he says of this *alētheia* that it *agrees with* correct desire. This represents the correct desire as logically extraneous to the *alētheia*. Hence C is mistaken in identifying practical *alētheia* with the good *prohairesis* as a whole: the correct desire is one element of

---

we know how Aristotle fills out the notion of "explanation". None of this substantial information is conveyed or meant to be conveyed by his use of rich-sense "truth". The aim of scoring more goals defines (in part) the game of football, hence "victorious at football" applies to the team which scores more goals; but it does not follow that "victory at football" defines or is meant to define the game — the phrase, unsurprisingly, says nothing of the nature of football. "Practical truth" according to proposal C marks (but does not define the nature of) the success as such of practical reasoning. Certainly Aristotle defines or explains good practical reasoning in terms of something other than itself: this is the good *prohairesis*, which in turn is analysed in terms of the respective truth (ordinary, assertoric) and correctness of the two factors.

[35] This was my interpretation in Aristotle, *Nicomachean Ethics*, ed. and trans. S. Broadie and C. Rowe (Oxford: Oxford University Press, 2002), pp. 362–63.

[36] See e.g. M. Johnstone, "Aristotle and Alexander on Perceptual Error", *Phronēsis*, 60, 2015: 310–38, n. 28. See also Crivelli, *Aristotle on Truth*, pp. 108–09, for discussion and references.

the good *prohairesis*, and *alētheia* is assigned to the other element, the *logos* (identified at 1139a29 as the product of practical intellect). So it is the *logos* and not the whole *prohairesis* that has or is an instance of *alētheia*.

Should we then revert to saying (as in B and B*) that the *logos*'s *alētheia* is simply good old assertoric truth? Not necessarily. We can acknowledge that the *logos*-factor alone is the locus of *alētheia*, and also, of course, that the *logos* is assertorically true (*alēthēs*), without being committed to equating its rich-sense truth with assertoric truth without remainder. We can retain the idea that what belongs to this assertorically true *logos* partnered by correct desire is rich-sense truth, i.e. the culminating achievement of practical intellect. Just as in the theoretical sphere rich-sense truth supervenes when all the assertoric truths are in place, so here rich-sense truth of the prohairetic *logos* can be seen as supervening on its assertoric truth given the presence of concordant correct desire. On this basis we should modify C to C*, as follows.

*Proposal C**

> According to C* the *logos*-factor is assertorically true, but rich-sense truth (indicated by Aristotle's use of the noun) is not excluded from the scene. Rich-sense truth, according to C*, crowns the assertorically true *logos* alone, *but only on condition that it has correct desire at its side*. Apologies to feminist Aristotelians, but this a ceremony where the queen-consort must be compliantly present for the king to receive the crown although his is the only head on which it can descend. C* therefore neatly explains why at the beginning of our passage Aristotle says that desire is one of the things responsible for *alētheia*. If this is understood as assertoric truth, Aristotle has mis-spoken. The acratic has formed a good *prohairesis*, but lacks the correct desire (it is non-executive). Therefore the acratic's *logos* is assertorically true anyway: the right desire, if present, could make no difference to that. But according to C* the latter's presence *is* necessary if the assertoric truth of the *logos* is to count as an unalloyed success of practical reason, i.e. as an instance of rich-sense truth. So correct desire is responsible not only for *praxis* but for *alētheia*. Given an assertoric truth as to what it is good to do, the concordant correct desire is the source of its practical implementation and thereby of its

elevation from being a mere assertoric truth to being an instance of *alētheia*.

4. Elizabeth Anscombe's Interpretation

Anscombe's account is based on the simple and powerful idea that "the description of what [someone] does is made true by his doing it". By "description" here she meant the description under which what is done is done. She concluded her 1965 paper as follows:

> The notion of *truth or falsehood in action* would quite generally be countered by the objection that "true" and "false" are senseless predicates as applied to what is done. If I am right there is philosophy to the contrary in Aristotle. And if, as I should maintain, the idea of the *description under which* what is done is done is integral to the notion of action, then these predicates apply to actions strictly and properly, and not merely by an extension and in a way that ought to be explained away.[37]

This is different from proposals A–C* above. The bearer of practical truth, according to Anscombe, is not the *logos* side of the good *prohairesis*, nor is it the *prohairesis* as such. Practical truth is the fit between the agent's taking himself to be doing so and so and his doing it. Thus the bearer of truth is S's agential assertion "I'm doing F"; it is made true (or makes itself true) *by* S's doing F. Here, the primary source of truth (so I understand Anscombe) is not the event of S's doing F or the fact that S does F: the primary source is an instance of *praxis*, namely the *doing* of F (by S). The event or fact may be called "practical" in that it has an action as a logical constituent (just as a fact is "biological" if its subject-matter is biological), but it is not an instance of *praxis*. The source of truth is the doing of F (by S), which is why the truth here is practical truth.

This spelling out of Anscombe's interpretation is only partial. The other part, which she lays out in detail, follows from the fact that the Aristotelian *prohairesis* embodies an assertion to the effect that doing what it prescribes is a case of doing well *simpliciter*. Thus it expresses the agent's fundamental values. Accordingly, the prohairetic agent's agential assertion "I'm doing so and so" includes the claim "I'm doing what is good or appropriate" *sans*

---

[37] Anscombe, "Thought and Action in Aristotle: What is Practical Truth?", p. 158.

phrase. Depending on the situation, this can take such specific forms as "I'm doing what a just, courageous, wise, generous, etc. person would do". There is only practical truth if the agential assertion is true at every level, so to speak. Hence there is only practical truth if the values expressed, as well as the agent's interpretation of them in the particular situation, are those that a genuinely virtuous person would bring to bear.[38]

Over the last fifty years a fertile philosophy of action has sprung up from and around the thought that action is a self-implementing conception of what one is doing. "What one is doing" is usually cashed in narrow and empirical terms such as "writing a letter", "poisoning the water-supply to that house", "returning a book to the library". Such are the examples in Anscombe's *Intention* (1957). The study of action on these terms is free of contentious meta-ethical assumptions about the truth-aptness of value judgments and ethical ones in particular. Twentieth-century philosophy of action would never have got off the ground had it not detached itself from this millstone of a problem. Anscombe set out to rehabilitate Aristotle's notion of practical truth in the eyes of anyone who thinks that the predicates "true" and "false" are senseless as applied to *what is done*. But her own exegesis makes it abundantly clear that a full rehabilitation, in the eyes of both her contemporaries and ours, would also include an adequate rebuttal of the view that "true" and "false" are senseless as applied to *ethical judgments*.

Anscombe's interpretation has the great merit of making sense of Aristotle's statement that desire is responsible for *praxis* and for truth. Right desire gives rise to Anscombian practical truth by ensuring that the action is done. But if Anscombe is right, it is surprising that our text contains no explicit emphasis on the matter of a good agent's actually *doing* what he takes himself to be doing. Instead the focus is surely on the good *prohairesis* and its factors.[39] Of course, Anscombian practical truth is a close relative to the actual topic, since a *prohairesis* is naturally enacted, and the

---

[38] Here and elsewhere I try to accommodate the fact that goodness of *prohairesis* and the corresponding action is not restricted to possessors of virtue, the latter being a stable disposition for such conduct in a full range of situations (*NE* II, 1105a28–33).

[39] Cf. S. Broadie, *Ethics with Aristotle* (New York: Oxford University Press, 1991), p. 224.

goodness and reasonableness of the action depends on that of the *prohairesis*. But given that practical truth has to do with practical goodness and reasonableness, the direction of dependence just mentioned is an additional reason for restricting "practical truth" to the *prohairesis* itself or one of its constituents.

5. Conclusion

Of the interpretations discussed, B* and C* surely come out in front. One might prefer B* on grounds of philosophical economy and clarity. B* rests on a single, fairly straightforward, understanding of truth as assertoric, whereas C* invokes an additional truth-notion, one that contemporary analytic philosophers would, perhaps rightly, regard as obscurantist and gratuitous. But B* is unable to accommodate Aristotle's difficult remark at 1139a18 that desire (as well as intelligence and perception) is responsible for *alētheia*. C* supplies a natural solution to this problem. B* also fails to explain why, if assertoric truth alone is in play in our passage, Aristotle uses the noun *alētheia*, exceptional for him in this connection. So it seems to me that C* is ahead.

But a supporter of proposal C* must explain why rich-sense truth figures at all in the account of the good *prohairesis*. This question arises because this notion of truth seems quite unnecessary to Aristotle's analysis. The good *prohairesis* is shown to consist in a concordant *logos*-factor and desire-factor which are, respectively, assertorically true and correct. This is all Aristotle needs for explaining the function of practical intellect, and what its virtue is. It is also all he needs for showing how this virtue rests on (or might even be said to subsume) ethical virtue.[40] And it is all he needs for discussing the good deliberation that issues in the good *prohairesis*.[41] So what does rich-sense truth contribute to the doctrines of *NE* VI?

It adds nothing to our analytic understanding of what the good *prohairesis* is, what *phronēsis* is, and what it is to deliberate well. Rather, it presents these things in a certain way. It emphasizes that they are authentically intellectual. Why emphasize this? Suppose that in explaining the achievement of practical reason Aristotle had kept quiet about rich-sense truth: this might well have suggested, to his original audience, a deliberate withholding of the

---

[40] *NE* VI, 1143b18–1145a6.
[41] *NE* VI, 1141b8–1142b33.

accolade. The message would have been that rich-sense truth is available to theoreticians alone.[42] Now, we can all easily agree that the human being is essentially practical, a prohairetic cause.[43] Whether the human being is also essentially theoretical cannot be so easily taken for granted, on which see more below. At any rate, by assigning the goal of rich-sense truth to the practical sphere as well, Aristotle makes it clear that the human being as such—not merely a small and peculiar tribe of theoreticians—is of a nature to seek and attain cognition that deserves praise in the highest alethic terms.

It is important for Aristotle to make this clear because there are considerations pointing in the opposite direction. He wants to resist going in that direction but also to do justice to the considerations. In fact he has reason to be somewhat defensive about the *echt* intellectuality of practical wisdom. In *NE* VI he rejects two models prominent in Plato: practical wisdom as a technical productive expertise, and as expertise in eternal verities about ethical abstractions and the metaphysical foundations of mathematics. To many then, as to us today, these must have seemed absurd intellectualizations of the personal qualities needed to make good decisions in the everyday human context. One natural response would have been to adopt a somewhat crude anti-intellectualism about these very real qualities. Aristotle responds by showing how *phronēsis* in its own way is a genuinely intellectual quality; but doing this involves him in much creative and careful philosophizing. He makes things harder for himself by admitting that the *phronimos* need not have articulate reasons;[44] by mentioning sympathetically (since it suits his purpose in the immediate context) the belief that some lower animals have *phronēsis*;[45] and by implying that *euboulia*, excellence in deliberation, is easy to

---

[42] To anyone brought up on the poem of Parmenides the restriction would have seemed natural. The fact that the domain of *alētheia* is now allowed to include physics, cosmology and pluralistic metaphysics leaves untouched any tendency to dismiss even the best practical cognition as mere "mortal opinions" (Parmenides, fr. 8, 50–51).
[43] *NE* 1139b4–5.
[44] *NE* 1143b11–13.
[45] *NE* 1141b26–28. See e.g. *History of Animals* VIII, 588a24 ff. on animal *sunesis* ("sagacity"); also *Metaphysics* I, 98027–b26. See *Parts of Animals* II, 647b30 ff. and 650b20 ff., for a physiological explanation.

confuse with the non-rational gift of *eustochia*, which hits the nail on the head without knowing how or why.[46]

A lot is at stake, because scepticism about the rationality of practical reason, so called, sends shock-waves through the system. Consider Aristotle's transition from *NE* I's definition of *eudaimonia* in terms of virtuous rational activity[47] to *NE* II's discussion of the ethical virtues. This transition assumes that these virtues are intimately connected to human reason. He defines them by reference to *prohairesis* and *phronēsis*;[48] but these links support the connection to reason only if *phronēsis* is firmly established as an intellectual virtue. If courage, temperance, justice and *phronēsis* itself are only dubiously virtues of the human being *qua* rational animal, the activity expressing them is only dubiously any sort of *eudaimonia*: it is not a clear case of *eudaimonia* at all, even of a second-class kind.[49] So the only undeniable *eudaimonia* is entirely grounded in the only undeniably intellectual part of the soul, theoretical reason, with *sophia* as the only undeniably intellectual virtue. From the point of view of human life, *sophia* is now rather dangerously out on a limb. How to reply to an anti-intellectualist about *phronēsis* who infers that, since the obvious human virtues are not really intellectual, the undeniably intellectual *sophia* is not in fact a virtue of the *human* being as such? Perhaps it is a virtue of the gods alone, and for us just an occasional beautiful contingent ornament, not a flowering of fundamental human nature. Then human individuals and societies are not fundamentally backward or blind to the full range of human good if they make no provision for theoretical activity. This line of thought shows how, if we play down the dignity of practical intellect in human beings, we undermine our ground for holding that the splendours of theoretical intellect represent an ideal for human beings as such. In this dialectical situation Aristotle would have missed a trick in not inserting rich-sense truth into his philosophy of practical reason.[50]

In motivating the study of parts of animals, an ignoble subject-matter compared to the immortal objects of astronomy, Aristotle retails what Heraclitus supposedly said to the guest who found

---

[46] *NE* 1142a32–b6.
[47] *NE* 1097b33–1098a15.
[48] *NE* II, 1106b36–1107a2; cf. VI, 1144b14–28 and X, 1178a16–22.
[49] Cf. *NE* X, 1178a7–22.
[50] This is one of his many intellectualist emphases in this connection.

him in the kitchen: "There are gods here too."⁵¹ In *NE* VI, I have argued, Aristotle laces his account of the good *prohairesis* with the pointed assurance that—as well as *logoi alētheis*—there is *alētheia* here too.⁵²

---

⁵¹ *PA* I, 644b21–645a23.
⁵² In case it seems far-fetched that the virtue-status of *sophia* should piggyback on the rationality of *phronēsis*, note this from the *Magna Moralia*:

Is *sophia* a virtue or not? From this it should become clear that it is a virtue —from *phronēsis* itself. For if *phronēsis* is, as we claim, the virtue of one of the parts that have reason, and *phronēsis* is inferior to *sophia* because its subject-matter is inferior (for the subject-matter of *sophia* is the eternal and the divine, as we claim, whereas that of *phronēsis* is what is useful to the human being)—well, if what is inferior is a virtue, certainly what is superior reasonably <counts as> a virtue: so that it is clear that *sophia* is a virtue. (*MM* I, 1197b3–10)

The topic is evidently *human* virtues. The argument depends on the assumption that *phronēsis* belongs to a rational part of the soul. That this argument exists shows that there was some anxiety about the status of *sophia* as a genuine human virtue. Aristotle feels the need to argue the point at *NE* I, 1103a8–10, and *MM* I, 1197b28–31, shows that someone had suggested that it is not for statecraft to accommodate *sophia*.

Anselm Winfried Müller

Truth as Eternal Norm: Anscombe on Anselm's De Veritate

In several works, Elizabeth Anscombe discusses aspects of the notion of truth.[1] I am here chiefly concerned with the question: what is the notion of truth invoked when one says that *it is true (or: would be true to say) that* ...? Perhaps this was the deepest of Anscombe's own concerns in her works on truth and possibly in her (non-ethical) philosophical thinking generally.[2] In order to address that question, she investigates St. Anselm's dialogue *De*

---

[1] Namely: the idea of truth-makers in "Making True" (*Logic, Truth and Meaning*, eds. M. Geach & L. Gormally (Exeter: Imprint Academic, 2015), hereafter *LTM*, Ch. 10); change of truth-value in "Before and After" (in *Metaphysics and the Philosophy of Mind: Collected Philosophical Papers Volume II* (Oxford: Blackwell, 1981), hereafter *MPM*) and several other publications; the primacy of truth over falsehood and related topics in her *Introduction to Wittgenstein's Tractatus* as well as in "Truth: Anselm and Wittgenstein" – "TAW" (in *From Plato to Wittgenstein*, eds. M. Geach & L. Gormally (Exeter: Imprint Academic, 2011), hereafter *FPTW*, Ch. 7); Aristotle's notion of practical truth in "Practical Truth" (in *Human Life, Action and Ethics*, eds. M. Geach & L. Gormally (Exeter: Imprint Academic, 2011), hereafter *HLAE*, Ch. 11) and "Thought and Action in Aristotle: What is 'Practical Truth'?" (in *From Parmenides to Wittgenstein: Collected Philosophical Papers Volume I* (Oxford: Blackwell, 1981), hereafter *PTW*).

[2] It is prominent, above all, in three papers, "Truth: Anselm or Thomas?" (hereafter "TAT"), "Anselm and the Unity of Truth" ("AUT") and "Truth, Sense and Assertion" ("TSA"). The first and second of these appear in *FPTW*, pp. 51–69, and pp. 77–82; the third in *LTM*, pp. 264–73. A version of the third with additional editorial footnotes appears in *Philosophy*, 91 (1) 2016: 3–14; references here are to the *LTM* version.

Veritate (DV), which she greatly admires.³ The answer she finds in Anselm is this: for a proposition to be true is for it to satisfy a single eternal norm of truth; this deserves to be called truth in a primary sense; and its existence does not depend on that of anything of which truth is predicated.

Does Anscombe herself accept this answer? There are reasons to think that she does: she writes that Anselm's "argument is clearly successful", and sees no good reason "to resist" it. Moreover, she gladly embraces the result: "I was happy to find him of this mind, for I had long thought that propositions didn't have to exist to be true."⁴ Indeed, her interpretation of it in some respects goes beyond what (I will argue) Anselm himself maintains (cf. §3.1 [here and throughout this form of identification is used to refer to sections of the present essay]).

After setting the stage by introducing relevant notions and issues (§1), I will clarify the distinction, already hinted at, between two notions of truth (§2.1-2) and explore its implications (§2.3-5). I'll then present the reasoning regarding eternity (§3.1) and unity (§3.2) of truth that Anscombe finds in Anselm, add some reflexions in support of the unity thesis (§3.3-5), and end by summarizing the most important results (§4).

1. Propositions, Truths and Times

1.1. *The conceptual landscape*

In discussing Anselm's *De Veritate*, Anscombe explains and largely adopts his way of speaking about the topic. I'll follow her in this point, and begin with a brief clarification, largely in her own words, of the relevant conceptual framework.

A) We must first get clear about Anselm's notion of a proposition—the most obvious bearer of truth. As Anscombe tells us, "by a proposition he understands a sentence, vocally uttered or written [...]. He doesn't mean what we nowadays call an 'abstract proposition'. He does regard propositions as liable to have multiple occurrences. In consequence he regards propositions that may

---

³ The translations in the text are Anscombe's own. There is a full English translation of *De Veritate* by Ralph McInerny in *Anselm of Canterbury: The Major Works*, eds. Brian Davies and Gillian Evans (Oxford: Oxford University Press, 1998); the exchanges Anscombe quotes appear there on pp. 153-55.
⁴ "AUT", p. 82.

be true or false [i.e. contingent ones] as changing from true to false or false to true as things change".[5]

"Theaetetus is sitting", for instance, is liable to this kind of change. The time of utterance is *not* considered to affect its meaning — what Anselm calls its *significatio*. So it is indeed the very proposition that can change its truth-value — not just the sentence.[6]

B) Anselm is concerned, primarily, with propositions *qua* asserted. He "says both that the proposition signifies things' being thus and so, *and* that the person using the proposition does so. However, he seems not to notice that a proposition can occur as a subordinate clause [...] and then *there is nothing wrong* with its being false".[7]

This last observation directs our attention to the evaluation of assertoric sentences in terms of their *primary* function. It indicates that the teleology of *propositions* is a complex matter, not simply to be identified with, although to be explained in terms of, the more basic teleology of their use as *assertions*. Like Anscombe, I'll bypass this issue and take it for granted that, to clarify the notion of propositional truth, we shall have taken the essential step when we have given an account of the truth of assertions.

C) Having told us that "the key [to Anselm's account of truth] is the teleology of assertion", a page later Anscombe describes the same key as "identification of truth and rightness".[8] What then is assertion's *telos*; what must it achieve to be right?

> Anselm, the teacher, explains the truth of propositions by a teleological account of [...] assertion. Assertion is for signifying as being so what is so; [...] and truth is explained as rightness of assertion precisely as assertion.[9]

I have more to say about truth as *telos* later on. Here I'll only comment on the qualification "precisely as assertion". An assertion can be defective in various ways: it can be ungrammatical, impolite, premature and so on. But only if it is false does it fail to achieve the *telos* that constitutes it as what

---

[5] "TSA", p. 266.
[6] A *sentence* may of course "vary" in truth-value as a result of constituting different propositions according as, e.g., different bearers are assigned to a proper name. For another case of sentence-ambiguity cf. §2.2.
[7] "TSA", p. 267; cf. "TAT", p. 52.
[8] "TAT", p. 52f.
[9] "TSA", p. 269.

assertion is. Although the *speaker* may use an assertion as a lie, its being an *assertion* depends on its being of a kind to be directed at saying what is the case. Truth is (a kind of) rightness in being achievement of this *essential* task.

D) In the case of a true proposition, Anselm distinguishes two things from its truth: its meaning, or sense, and its verifier.[10] On the one hand, "the proposition does *not* lose its meaning when the fact is no more. So its meaning (*significatio*) is not its truth". On the other, that verifying fact, "the corresponding reality", "what the true proposition tells, the *res enunciata*, is the cause of its truth and not its truth"[11] (cf. §2.2).

E) Anscombe goes along with Anselm in distinguishing a natural from a non-natural truth of a proposition. The latter, which supplies us with the central topic of our inquiry, is what is usually called truth. As Anselm's student says, "when [the proposition] signifies something's being so and it is so, truth is in it and it is true" (*cum significat esse quod est, tunc est in ea veritas et est vera*).[12] But "there are two kinds of rightness and truth: one, to do with what utterances are for, the other to do with their signifying what they do signify. The latter is constant, permanent and natural. The former is variable inconstant, accidental and according to use".[13]

Note that by characterizing non-natural truth as accidental Anscombe is not denying that it is the essential, inherent *telos* of every assertion. The qualifications *non-natural* and *accidental* only indicate that this truth is a *telos* whose *achievement* is *not guaranteed* by what the proposition *is*.

"Theaetetus is sitting", for instance, is naturally true in virtue of being the proposition it is; i.e. by meaning what it is meant to mean (by signifying "what it has had given it to signify") and thereby being what it ought to be. It is, in addition, non-naturally true *whenever* Theaetetus is in fact sitting, in virtue of saying of what is so that it is so (by signifying "what it was created to signify") and thereby doing what it ought to do.[14]

---

[10] *DV* 2.
[11] *Res enuntiata non est in enuntiatione vera. Unde non eius veritas, sed causa veritatis eius dicenda est* (*DV* 2). *DV* 2; "TAW", p. 72; cf. "TSA", p. 265; p. 271.
[12] *DV* 2.
[13] "TAT", p. 53; cf. "TSA", p. 266.
[14] "TAT", p. 53; cf. "TSA", p. 269.

It is of course this second, more stringent, teleology that allows for falsehood and accounts for the asymmetry in "value" between true and false:[15] only when the proposition is non-naturally true is it doing what it is for.[16] Note also that it is non-natural truth that constitutes the central topic of this paper. And that its distinction from natural truth is not to be confused with the distinction between norm and norm-satisfaction that I hope to explain in section §2.

F) The truth whose unity Anscombe wants to understand with Anselm's help is eternal. Whether it should be taken to be omnitemporal or rather timeless is no part of their explorations, and I am not going to deal with the question.

G) The natural truth of propositions is a special case of something totally general: "Truth is a certain rightness inasmuch as something fulfils—i.e. (here) *is*—what it is in the divine mind. That is to say, Anselm thinks that there is truth in objects, and that includes propositions."[17]

Anselm's identification of truth with the mind of God plays a role in what I'll have to say about the causation of propositional truth; apart from this, it is no part of my topic. Similarly, I am not going to examine problems that might be connected with the extension, just characterized in Anscombe's words, of the notion of truth to cover, in particular, what is sometimes called "ontological truth".

In general I am going to use the word "rightness" (*rectitudo*) to express this wider notion, reserve "truth" (*veritas*) for the case of propositions, and call the compliance of propositions with the norm of truth "propositional truth". The reader should however keep in mind that, in Anselm and Anscombe, *truth* and *rightness* are often coextensive.

---

[15] "TAW", p. 73.
[16] Analogously, two kinds of truth are ascribed to rational action. Everything you do is naturally, and necessarily, true in the way that the fire's acts of heating are true. But only by acting well do you achieve non-natural truth (*DV* 5; 8; 12). This idea is one of two non-Aristotelian sources of Anscombe's conception of *practical truth*. The other, tapped by Anselm too, is the Gospel of St. John (3,21).
[17] "TAT", p. 54; cf. p. 56; "TAW", pp. 74–76.

1.2. Ways for truth to be eternal

In "Anselm and the Unity of Truth", the leading question is: does a proposition have to exist in order to be true? As a background, Anscombe observes that things may have properties at a time when they don't exist—as when "Protagoras' monograph on truth is famous but not extant".[18] Truth, however, "is a property the bearer (subject) of which [...] need not have existed either; and it may also never be going to exist. For no one may ever formulate the proposition".[19]

This conclusion is reached by an elaborate route in "Truth: Anselm or Thomas?" Here, Anscombe discusses, *inter alia*, the two philosophers' respective responses to an Augustinian argument. St. Augustine hopes to refute by *reductio* the idea that truth has beginning and end. If truth had begun/were to end, he argues, then *that there is no truth* would at some time (viz. beforehand) have *possessed truth*/would be going to *possess truth* (after the end of truth).

One of the premises he assumes, viz. "There can't be anything true without truth", can be read in a sense in which it is just as toothless (and redundant) as "There can't be anything false without falsehood". On this understanding, the argument would prove the eternity of falsehood no less than that of truth.[20] To save it, one has to find a reading of that premise which gives it bite and secures the eternity only of truth. As we are now going to see, Anselm achieves this by specifying a notion of truth under which truth is *not predicated of* anything. To understand the attraction of this conception, it will help to compare it with the way in which St. Thomas responds to the Augustinian argument.

1.3. Aquinas on the temporality of created truth

What he holds against it is this: "Its being true now to say that the truth of a proposition did not exist before a certain time does not imply that it was true then to say it did not exist then."[21] This is because of a peculiarity exhibited by propositions such as Augustine's. If an ordinary past tensed proposition, say "Theaetetus was sitting", is true *now*, a corresponding present

---

[18] "AUT", p. 77.
[19] "AUT", p. 79.
[20] "TAT", p. 57f; cf. "TSA", p. 265.
[21] "TAT", p. 59.

tensed one, "Theaetetus is sitting", *was* once true; for "they may have their truths caused by that same sitting [even though] it is certainly differently related to them".[22] Analogous considerations cannot simply be applied where the topic is a proposition's having been true. "The truth of 'p' did not exist before there were minds" does not, according to Aquinas, imply that, before there were minds, it was true to say "The truth of 'p' does not exist".

This is because, according to Aquinas, given the truth of any past-tensed proposition, the corresponding present-tensed proposition was true only when there was a *mind* to do the judging. Anscombe comments: "Why, is not clear to me yet."[23] She herself does not see any good reason to deny that *it was true that p* if *it is now true that it was the case that p*. For, just as she agrees with Anselm that it can be true that p even if the *proposition*, "p", does not exist at any time, she would also say that no human *thought* that p needs to exist in order for it to be true that p.

We understand why Anscombe hesitates to go along with Aquinas on this point if we consider that, on her interpretation, he himself distinguishes two kinds of contribution to the truth of propositions: 1) the way things are (*qua* verifying reality); and 2) what might be called topic-neutral notions. The latter are special resources the intellect "has within itself. It works with the present and past tenses and negation, and on the concepts of *truth of a proposition, existence, before,* and *true to say*".[24] These topic-neutral resources are obviously prominent in a proposition such as, say, *"It was the case that there was no life in the universe" is now true.*[25] But if they can *here* function as a "measure of truth", why should they not be allowed to procure the (present) truth also of *"There is no life in the universe" was at some time true* – even if there was no intellect at the time to do the relevant thinking?

---

[22] "TAT", p. 60.
[23] "TAT", p. 62.
[24] "TAT", p. 62.
[25] Indeed, those resources might be said to do *all* the work for the present truth (endorsed by Aquinas) that "at one time the truth of propositions did not exist" ("TAT", p. 63; cf. p. 59). This proposition is not made true by any extra-mental, "objective verifier"; regarding it, "there is no thing to be the measure of the truth in the intellect: this truth is, we might say, a total do-it-yourself job on the part of the intellect working with the present and past tenses and negation [...]" ("TAT", p. 62), it "is an intellectual construct by a mind which grasps the concept of non-existence" (p. 61).

So much for Anscombe's reservations about the doctrine that created, non-eternal truth requires for its existence the simultaneous existence of a created intelligence. She is more than ready, however, to agree with Aquinas that in any case that doctrine is not one that "closes the topic".[26] For "the truth existing in a created intelligence is of a different sort from the truth which is in, and is identical with, an uncreated intelligence".[27] How does this observation bear on the question whether truth can begin and end?

1.4. The eternity of truth in the mind of God

The twofold measure of truth just considered — verifying/falsifying reality plus reflecting intellect — is "intrinsic" to the proposition: implied in what it is. But, much as a pint of beer — this is Anscombe's appealing illustration of Aquinas's explanation — is intrinsically measured by its own quantity and also extrinsically by "a pint pot[, which] is the place of the beer in it" — so a proposition has not only an intrinsic measure of its truth (in the two components just mentioned): there is also "the first truth, from which as by an extrinsic measure a proposition is called true".[28] Without exploring what exactly an extrinsic measure is, we can ask: how does its recognition affect the anti-Augustinian claim that truth had a beginning?

> The explanation must be that the divine knowledge comprises everything, including the not yet existent propositions and truth in human minds. The divine knowledge is the same thing as the first truth [...]. Therefore it was in the first truth: that the later-to-be-framed proposition "At one time the truth of propositions did not exist" was going to be true, and this would imply [divine] knowledge of the non-existence at the time when it did not exist.[29]

In this sense, Anscombe seems to imply, Aquinas does permit us to say (and without inconsistency): Before there was created truth, it was *true from the point of view of the divine mind*, that then there was no created truth. Why is this point of view an *extrinsic* measure? Well, only if the (created) thought *There is no truth (yet)* could then have existed (and of course falsified itself), would there

---

[26] "TAT", p. 61.
[27] "TAT", p. 62.
[28] "TAT", p. 59, quoting *Quaestiones Disputatae de Veritate* 1, 5.
[29] "TAT", p. 63.

have been an *intrinsic* standard to apply to that thought—that standard which the (human) mind itself *includes* in any judgment by *inevitably* intending its truth.

So much then for a first answer to the question whether the truth of propositions and created thoughts had a beginning. On Anscombe's interpretation Aquinas maintains that, yes, created truth did begin with the existence of created minds that were capable of true thoughts; but the uncreated truth in God's mind embraces the previous non-existence of created truth. Having thus, with moderate help from Aquinas, half-salvaged Augustine's argument, she turns to discussing Anselm's "subtler argument" to show that, for human minds, too, "it is impossible even to think of truth as having a beginning or end".[30]

1.5. Two notions of truth?

Here is, in Anscombe's translation, how Anselm formulates the core of that argument:

> Let anyone who can, think when this began or was not true: namely that there will be something; or when this will cease and will not be true: to wit, that there will have been something.[31]

Instead of following the dialectic of Anscombe's discussion of this text, I'll start with a remark of hers that is easily overlooked but apt to lead us straight to the heart of Anselm's approach to his problem: "Unlike Thomas, he did not believe there was such a thing as truth inhering in created things."[32]

At first sight, this claim does not even seem to be borne out by the texts. Thus, to give just one of many examples, when near the beginning of the dialogue the student asks for a definition of truth, the teacher's suggestion is to look at the various things "in [!] which there is said to be truth".[33] But the non-inherence claim will soon prove to be correct—although *not quite* to the extent envisaged by Anscombe.

What she takes Anselm to deny is that a proposition "has to exist in order to be true".[34] Now, we have seen that she attributes

---

[30] "TAT", p. 63f.
[31] *DV* 1; "TAT", p. 64.
[32] "TAT", p. 66.
[33] *DV* 1.
[34] "TAT", p. 66.

such a denial to Aquinas, too (§1.4).[35] What Anselm seems to add is the claim that, even by the intrinsic measure of *human asserting*, a proposition need not exist in order to be true. Strictly speaking, however, his concern is not with actual propositions. Here is what the teacher says:

> When I said "when was it not true that there was going to be something", I did not mean that that expression, saying that there would be something, had never had a beginning or that its [!] truth was God, but rather that it cannot be understood when, if [!] that sentence were to exist, it would [!] have failed to be true.[36]

The claim here implied might be expressed by saying: a proposition type need not exist — i.e. be instantiated by any token — in order for the truth to exist in virtue of which any token of that type *would* be true *if* the type were instantiated. What is this truth, given that it is not to be identified with an actual proposition's being true? It will turn out to be a rightness that is (to quote the chapter title of *DV* 13) "one and the same in all things that are true". The conceptual situation is however complicated by the fact that Anselm's dialogue features *two* ways of speaking about truth.

Having established early on that truth is rightness,[37] the teacher does not merely say that there is *only one* rightness:[38] he also asks his student to consider how that rightness, the highest truth, is "the cause of all other truths and rightnesses".[39] This is naturally taken to imply that different propositions, or different kinds of proposition, or at least different kinds of thing, do in fact exhibit *different* truths, or rightnesses. These truths/rightnesses might then be viewed as features which, unlike that highest truth, do "inhere in" things that are rightly said to be true/right.

A distinction between two notions of truth is also insinuated where the teacher discusses what I am going to call *Anselm's prediction*: the proposition "There will be something". He says that at any time in the past its instantiation would have implied *its* truth (*ista veritas*), and that therefore no beginning attaches to the existence of that other truth (*illa veritas*), viz. "that truth which is the first cause of this one [...]. For the truth of a sentence would

---

[35] Cf. "TAT", p. 62; p. 66.
[36] *DV* 10; "TAT", p. 65.
[37] *DV* 2.
[38] *DV* 13.
[39] *DV* 10.

not be always a possibility, if the cause of its truth was not always there".[40] ("The cause" is here the "highest truth", the "*summa veritas*, which is God",[41] not the verifying reality.)

This is the way in which Anscombe herself reads Anselm when she distinguishes "the truth of the sentence" from "the cause [...] of that truth", which is the *summa veritas*.[42] And also, when she treats a proposition's non-natural truth as "consist[ing] in its signifying what it was given its signification for. This [!] rightness is variable and depends on one's use of it".[43] That truth, by contrast, which causes the proposition to be non-naturally true is in no sense variable.

Do we then have to distinguish the truth that is predicated of propositions that actually exist or have existed—a truth somehow multiplied by inhering in them—from that other truth which is only *one* and "never had a beginning"? I'll try to show that this way of interpreting the dialogue is indeed correct: that the distinction means more than just two ways of speaking about one and the same thing from different points of view, and that Anselm's arguments do in fact involve two notions of truth.

2. Norm-Satisfaction *versus* Norm

2.1. *The dual grammar of true*

Let us read "p1" as "The pyramids will cease to exist". Just as "p1" is true now, it was also true whenever "p1" was used in the past. Now consider the following claims:

1) "p1" was true.
2) It was/would have been true to say that p1.
3) An assertion/occurrence of "p1" would at any time have been true.

Following Anselm and Anscombe, I take (1) to imply that "p1" was actually instantiated. So (1) is not true if no token of "p1" was ever formulated. It can, at least *prima facie*, be said to ascribe a "quality"—which I'll call propositional truth—to (tokens of) "p1".

---

[40] *DV* 10; "TAT", p. 65; cf. "AUT", p. 80.
[41] "TAT", p. 56.
[42] "AUT", p. 80.
[43] "TSA", p. 266.

(1) states a past *fact* that could be specified as: satisfaction by "p1" of the norm that requires assertions to say (only) what is the case.

Unlike (1), (2) is true independently of anyone's ever having formulated "p1". What then does it say is true? If *true* is a predicate as in (1), of what is it predicated in (2)? We can of course *say*: (2) means as much as: "it was true that p1"; so *that p1* is here the "bearer" of truth. But how *this* is to be explained seems more obscure than the meaning of (2) itself, and I'll leave it in this obscurity.

From (3) we learn: the facts are such that, whenever "p1" did occur, *it* deserved the predicate "true". So here, the question "Whose truth?" seems not to raise the problem it raises in the case of (2). Interestingly, however, (3) also seems to be equivalent to (2): they entail each other. Moreover, we may feel that, of the two, it is (2) that supplies the rationale of (3) – and also of (1) – rather than v.v. For (2) is a categorical proposition, (3) a conditional apparently justified by (2); and the correctness of (1) depends on the condition's satisfaction.

Note that the difference between (1) and (2) matches the two ways in which Anselm uses "true" when, on the one hand, he calls *true* the proposition/assertion "which says that something will be the case" and, on the other, he says "it is true that something will be the case".[44]

Only of the truth referred to in the second expression does he say that it has no beginning or end. Is he implying that existence of the first is confined to times at which tokens of the proposition occur? Anscombe warns us *not* to conclude "that the truth of a proposition doesn't exist *unless* the proposition itself exists".[45] But isn't such a conclusion strongly insinuated by the text? Isn't eternity implicitly denied to propositional truth?

Consider *Anselm's prediction*, "There will be something". The teacher tells his student: "It cannot be understood *when*, if that expression were to exist, it would have failed to be true"; therefore its (propositional) truth was *always possible*; and this in turn presupposes that "the truth which is the first cause of this truth [was always actual, and hence] did not have any beginning"[46] (cf. §1.5; §2.4 (B)). But, if the propositional truth of Anselm's prediction *had*

---

[44] *DV* 10.
[45] "AUT", p. 80; cf. "TAT", p. 66.
[46] *DV* 10; "AUT", p. 80.

existed in the *absence* of any token of it, there would be no need for the teacher to speak of the mere possibility of that truth (*ista veritas*) and to postulate the actuality of another, enduring truth (*illa veritas*).[47]

Anscombe does not consistently observe this differentiation. She does embrace, with Anselm, a notion of truth as imposing a *norm* on propositions: "If the rightness *did* pass away with the signifying [...], then the rightness of signifying so would not exist, nor could it be making any requirement [!]."[48] In the argument that follows, however, she forgets about the distinction involved in the idea of a truth which *requires* that truth which *is required* of a proposition. So she ends up saying: "Anselm has come to the conclusion that truth is a property [!] which something can have [...] without ever existing."[49]

This, however, is unwarranted. What Anselm wants to show and, I think, succeeds in showing is the eternity of truth *as norm*, not of propositional truth. The only truth that does not "perish" is the truth *in virtue of which* a true proposition is true, and which *requires* that the proposition do its signifying as it ought (*non existente significatione non perit rectitudo, qua* [!] *rectum est et qua exigitur* [!], *ut quod significandum est, significetur*).[50]

These reflexions confirm what I have said about the example sentences considered above: two uses of "true" are at work in (1) and (3) on one side, and in (2) on the other. The first of these uses predicates truth of any proposition on condition that what it says is the case is the case.[51] To get clear about what can be said about

---

[47] *DV* 10.
[48] "AUT", p. 81.
[49] This phrasing suggests that a proposition need not exist in order to be a subject of the *predicate* true, i.e. to *satisfy* the norm of truth. In this it goes beyond Anselm's doctrine that a proposition does not have to exist for the truth (as *norm*) to exist in virtue of which it *would* be true if it did exist. Likewise, the formulation by which Anscombe represents him as maintaining that "truth is a property which something can have without [ever] existing" ("AUT", p. 82) is, strictly speaking, inaccurate. The truth whose existence is independent of the existence of true propositions cannot—for that very reason—be a *property*. In the same vein, Anscombe errs in attributing to Anselm the view that "truths do not vary through the variations of true things" ("TAT", p. 67). It is *truth*, in the singular, the "first cause" of the *truths ascribable* to propositions, of which he says this.
[50] *DV* 13.
[51] *DV* 2.

the second use and its relation to the first, we may be helped by studying analogies.

2.2. Suggestive analogies

Consider the ambiguity of the sentence "This is a valid chess move". It may either ascribe rule conformity to an actual move, or else amount to something like "Bf1–b5 is a licit (or: valid) sort of move in chess". In the second case the sentence is used to state a norm, in the former, a fact: the satisfaction of a norm.

Again, compare two different ways of applying the word "cost". On the one hand, you may tell us that the guided tour through the exhibition *cost you 10 dollars*. On the other, we may read on a flyer that the tour *costs 10 dollars*. In the first case a fact is stated, in the second a norm. In the first case we learn that 10 dollars actually changed hands, in the second we are informed of a norm that requires them to do so *if* anyone takes a guided tour (which then *costs her/him* 10 dollars). What the flyer says is not verified by anyone's paying 10 dollars for a guided tour, but by the *existence of a specific norm*. The guided tour costs 10 dollars independently of whether it costs anyone 10 dollars.

In much the same way it was always *true to say* that p1 independently of whether anyone ever *said*, or thought, that p1. Indeed, regarding any true proposition "p", it is *true to say* that p even if no token of "p" exists.

Hence, among the propositions discussed above (§2.1), (2) does not predicate truth of anything — much as "Bf1–b5 is a valid move" does not speak about any move made in any players' game of chess, and "The tour costs 10 dollars" is not a statement about anyone's paying 10 dollars for the tour. Like these two propositions, "It is true to say that p" represents, or points to, a norm, it does not predicate truth of anything. "True" does not here function as a predicate, as it does in "'p' is true". Hence, we are justified in speaking of *two notions of truth* invoked by two different uses of "true". We have to distinguish truth as norm from truth as norm-satisfaction.

This clarifies the relationships between the sample propositions considered in §2.1. (1) says of "p1" that it *satisfies* the norm of truth which is represented by (2). What then about (3)? Consider, once more an analogue: "If any chess-player moved a bishop from f1 to b5, they (would have) made a licit move." It tells us how to assess particular moves in terms of the norm that allows

Bf1–b5. Similarly for "If at any time 'p1' was formulated, it was then true". According to this paraphrase of (3), (1) is justified by the norm represented by (2).

2.3. Repercussions of a two-pronged understanding of truth

If we distinguish, as I am arguing we should, between truth as norm and truth as norm-satisfaction, and read both Anselm's doctrine and its exposition by Anscombe against this background, a number of things fall into place.

A) Anscombe's remark that Anselm "did not believe there was such a thing as truth inhering in created things"[52] (cf. §1.5) is vindicated with regard to the way in which "true" occurs in a proposition of the form "It is true/false (to say) that p". On my understanding of Anselm and Anscombe, such a statement identifies the truth-value of possible occurrences of "p" by representing it as instancing satisfaction/violation of a *norm* which applies to any assertion, and thereby, given circumstances, determines concerning any particular proposition (and, in particular, concerning "p" and "not-p") whether it is true or false. If this understanding is accepted, the statement "It is true (to say) that p" can indeed be said to refer to a truth for which there is not anything to inhere in.

B) Recall once more my discussion of the proposition "The pyramids will cease to exist". Abbreviating this as "p1", I considered the following claims:

1) "p1" was true.
2) It was/would have been true to say that p1.
3) An assertion/occurrence of "p1" would at any time have been true.

Now compare what *De Veritate* says about Anselm's prediction. This "expression, saying that there would be something" — like "p1" in (1) — may or may not exist or have existed. But "it cannot be understood when, if [!] that expression were to exist, it would have failed to be true". Here we have, virtually, a conditional that corresponds to (3). And, just as (3) represents (1) — the assertion of a particular proposition's truth — as sanctioned by the norm articulated in (2), so Anselm's conditional — viz. *if at any time the*

---

[52] "TAT", p. 66.

expression "There will be something" existed, it was then true — represents the truth of the expression itself (if this was ever formulated) as sanctioned by the eternal norm of truth: "For the truth of the sentence would not always be a possibility if the cause of that truth did not always exist."[53]

The demand for eternal actuality of *this* truth, as guaranteeing the possibility of "that truth", viz. occasional propositional truth, clearly fits my claim that, for (e.g.) Anselm's prediction to have *satisfied* the norm of truth *whenever* it might have occurred, if it ever did, the *norm itself* had *always* to exist: there cannot be a first time at which *it was true (to say) that* there would be something[54] (cf. §1.5).

C) Anselm's prediction is just an example; innumerable more specific predictions, however trivial, would do just as well. This gives rise to qualms: is it not incongruous (or blasphemous?) to identify a norm that determines the truth-value of such a sentence with God? Well, the identification, I maintain, is Anselm's. Why, otherwise, does he say for instance what he says of that prediction, viz. "I did not mean that [it] had never had a beginning *or that its truth was God"*?[55]

How does God come into it? Well, God *is* the highest truth; and, if my interpretation be granted, this means: he himself is identical with a *norm* of truth that has always existed. He must not, indeed, be identified, or confused, with the truth of (any token of) "There will be something". (*This* truth, we are going to see, began to exist together with that prediction, as "*its* truth", if and whenever there was such a prediction (§3.1).) But Anselm does, by implication, identify God with the eternal truth which, in the *Monologion*, he intends by the phrase "it was true that there was going to be something"[56] — a norm which *requires* that no assertion past or present deny that there will be something. As I hope to show, however, it is one and the same norm that imposes,

---

[53] *DV* 10; "AUT", p. 79. Anscombe comments: "The *permanent possibility* of the truth of that sentence [...] proves the *permanent actuality* of the cause, i.e. the ultimate cause, of that truth" ("AUT", p. 80). The nature of this cause's causality, which Anselm identifies with the highest truth, needs further investigation (cf. §2.5).
[54] Cf. "TAT", p. 65.
[55] *DV* 10.
[56] *DV* 10; "AUT", p. 79.

depending on contingent realities, indefinitely many further requirements on asserting, however trivial its content.

D) We have seen that Anselm's account of truth is a *teleological* one. He defines is as (intelligible[57]) *rightness*.[58] A thing is right if it is and does what it ought, and that is *what it owes (quod debet)* to its design in God's mind.[59] Propositional truth is a paradigmatic form of a thing's rightness. So a proposition is true if it says what, when asserted, it *ought* to say. But the *telos* fixed by this *ought* is supplied by a *norm* that requires assertions to say only of what is that it is. Here we have one of two notions of truth. The other is represented by a proposition's truth as attainment of its *telos* by *satisfying* the norm.

E) One of Anscombe's worries about a basically Augustinian argument in favour of the eternity of truth is the risk that it prove too much, viz. the eternity of falsehood as well as truth[60] (cf. §1.2). How are we to escape the fatal parallelism? She answers: "'There cannot be anything true without truth' is not the harmless redundant premise we have been treating it as; and therefore we cannot allow a parallel construction with 'There can't be anything false without falsehood'."[61] "Truth", that is, must not be viewed as merely naming a universal—the feature we are justified in ascribing to X by having found X to say what, if asserted, it ought to say.

It is not clear to me *how* Anscombe hopes to rule out the "parallel construction". But if my account of two understandings of "true" is accepted, we see why Anselm's argument is not threatened by the same danger as Augustine's. For, it builds on a pertinent *asymmetry* between truth and falsehood. For X to be true, X has to satisfy the norm of truth (and it is this *norm* whose existence cannot be said to be restricted to the time of X's existence). It has indeed always been false (to say) that *the pyramids will never cease to exist* (cf. §2.1). But falsehood is not therefore eternal in the sense of being a *norm* that must exist for that to be false! For X to be *false* is for X *not* to satisfy the norm of

---

[57] This qualification is merely to exclude *rectitudo sensu perceptibilis*: geometrical straightness (*DV* 11; cf. "TAT", p. 54).
[58] *DV* 11.
[59] *DV* 2; 5; 7; 10; 11.
[60] "TAT", p. 57f.
[61] "TAT", p. 58.

truth; *its* eternity is presupposed when the privative predicate "false" is applied to X because X does not do what, *qua* assertion, X ought to do: comply with the norm of truth.

2.4. Peculiarities of propositional teleology

There are different kinds of teleology, and in order to understand the teleology of assertion, we have to attend to the peculiar way in which the norm of truth is related to its satisfaction (cf. also §3.4).

A) The first thing to mention is Anselm's observation that assertion is characterized by a twofold *telos*: natural and non-natural truth. In the present context it is chiefly the latter we have to attend to.

B) *Non-natural* here amounts to *rational*. Now, reason can *give* things a *telos* they would not otherwise have. The rational teleology of judging and asserting, however, is not like that. Judging and asserting are *inherently* or *intrinsically* directed at truth. They are constituted by having that *telos*.

C) There is a danger of misunderstanding this last point. It is often said that judgment and assertion are directed at truth. But this is also true of guesses. What judgment and assertion are really directed at is something rather like knowledge (which of course *entails* truth). Moreover, judgment and assertion aim at the right answer to a *particular question*: the human mind is not a collector of random truths. In both respects the teleology we are concerned with is more modest, and perhaps more basic. By itself, the norm of truth prescribes neither justification nor relevance.

D) This is connected with another aspect of assertion: it is directed at its *telos*, viz. satisfaction of the norm of truth, by *requirement*, not by anything's or anyone's inclination, desire or choice.[62] Anselm makes this point by observing that the rectitude which lasts independently of there being thought and language, "requires" (*exigit*) any propositions there might be to be true.[63] The non-natural truth of propositions, as well as anything's natural truth, is *owed to* the highest truth.[64]

E) The requirement of truth is, moreover, negative rather than positive. In an obvious sense, the norm it represents is not

---

[62] Hence: norm, not: wish. The "value of truth" is not its contribution to success in action or satisfaction of desire!
[63] *DV*, 13.
[64] *DV* 10.

prescriptive but proscriptive. If p, it permits assertion of "p" and forbids assertion of "Not-p". *Qua* norm of *practical* rightness, the eternal truth will indeed, on occasion, require you unconditionally to perform a certain sort of action, possibly including assertion; *qua* norm of *truth*, it never entails a comparable requirement: it is prohibition rather than order.

F) Correspondingly, truth is not a motivating *telos*. You don't think that p in order to think something true. Truth motivates at most in the sense that recognized lack of truth prevents you from judgment and ought to prevent you from assertion. If the truth of "p" supplied you with a motive—an ultimate reason—to judge that p, you would have to become a truth collector of the sort already disposed of (cf. (A)).

G) The distinction between two notions of truth invites the question: how come we use the same word, "truth", for both? Whatever the answer to this question, I can at least say this: we don't understand what truth is without understanding that it is achievement of a proposition's inherent *telos*. In this, *true* differs from a feature such as, say, *airborne*. To be airborne is indeed the *telos* of a kite *qua* kite. But we understand what airborne is without knowing that it is achievement of anything's *telos*. Not so with *true*. Propositional truth is essentially achievement of a *telos*, viz. satisfaction of a norm.

2.5. *Causes of truth*

According to Anselm the highest truth is the cause, *inter alia*, of the truth of propositions,[65] and Anscombe calls it the "ultimate cause" of their truth.[66] How is this to be understood? And how does it relate to the obvious fact that propositions are made true by the way things are? Can their truth be caused by a norm as well?

Neither Anselm nor Anscombe give us much guidance on these questions. Nor do I myself pretend to have an answer to them. Such an answer would presumably have to bring in a considerable amount of natural theology. Perhaps, however, the following considerations will be relevant at least to a sympathetic understanding of Anselm's position.

A) It is in *two ways* that he speaks of a proposition's truth being caused. On the one hand, he respects the "obvious fact": a true

---

[65] *DV* 10.
[66] "AUT", p. 80; cf. "TAT", p. 65.

proposition owes its truth to the reality that verifies it. This reality is expressly called the cause (*causa*) of the proposition's truth.[67] On the other hand, this propositional truth is also "caused" by the highest truth—which I have argued Anselm identifies with the norm of truth: with its being right to assert that proposition, whether it is in fact asserted or not[68] (cf. §2.1; §2.4 (B)).

B) The verifying reality is itself, in its *existence* as well as in *what it is*, caused by God's designing mind (§1.1 (G)). "Nothing will come to be unless it exists in the supreme truth";[69] things are naturally true by being "what they are in the highest truth", i.e. in God's design.[70] So it is in virtue of the *natural* truth of *realities* that *propositions* have their *non-natural* truth.

C) *Ultimately*, therefore, there is only one source of propositional truth: the highest truth. But it is in two respects that God causes propositions to be true. 1) *Qua* designer and creator of propositions and norm of (their) rightness, he brings it about *that*, in virtue of their inherent nature and destination, assertions ought to "say [only] of what is that it is".[71] By doing as they ought they achieve their inherent *telos*. So it is by *final causality* that the highest truth, *qua* norm, is the cause of propositional truth. 2) *Qua* creator of reality as a whole, he brings about *what* it is by saying which any proposition would do what assertions are designed to do. (1) amounts to formal, (2) to material determination of a true proposition's truth.

D) Given simultaneity, any given fact that p secures the truth of any token of "p". I do not deny this. However, the fact does not *by itself* make any proposition true (cf. §2.3). It could not be a *verifier* in the absence of the norm of truth[72]—much as handing

---

[67] *DV* 2. "What is truth in a true proposition, a true 'enuntiation'? Is it the thing enuntiated? No, says the student, the thing it enuntiates is not its truth but the cause of its truth" (*DV* 2; "TSA", p. 265).

[68] *DV* 10.

[69] *DV* 10; "TAT", p. 65; cf. "AUT", p. 80.

[70] *DV* 7.

[71] *DV* 2.

[72] Admittedly, what "p" *qua* kind of speech act *is*, it is in virtue of the norm of truth, which governs its primary use, as assertion, *requiring* it to say what is the case and not what is not; so, in a way, the existence of the norm does not "add" anything to the existence of "p". But this latter existence is contingent, while the existence of the norm of truth is not. Well, doesn't the existence of this norm depend at least on the existence of thought and language in general, even if it does not depend on the existence of "p" or any other particular

over 10 dollars could not be payment of the *fee for a guided tour* in the absence of a norm that fixes this as the *cost* of taking the tour, and moving the bishop from f1 to b5 could not be a licit chess move if there were no game of chess with a rule to allow Bf1–b5.[73]

3. Eternity and Unity of the Highest Truth

3.1. *The eternal truth of tensed propositions*

Anselm's student initially assumes that, in the case of a (tensed) proposition, truth depends on it in the sense that it does not exist when the proposition does not exist or, if asserted, gets things wrong. Consider, e.g., the proposition "Theaetetus is sitting". As Theaetetus changes his posture by getting up, or lying down, the proposition changes its truth-value from true to false. Truth, the student holds, comes and goes like the colour of a body.[74]

The teacher corrects this conception, observing that the truth that is responsible for any token of the proposition's being true is not like that. We already know why: its being true that p does not depend on any occurrence of "p"; i.e. the norm of truth, which wants to be observed by any assertion of "p", exists whether "p" is asserted or not.[75] A colour, he agrees, cannot persist when the body perishes whose colour it is; by contrast, "truth and rightness [do not] depend for their existence on the things that have them".[76] Or, to quote Anscombe, "Destroy the object, and the colour cannot remain"; truth can, or rather: does.[77]

---

proposition? No, says Anscombe, "truth and rightness [do not] depend for their existence on the things that have them" ("TAT", p. 66). The dependence is the other way around: human (assertoric) thought and language only exist in virtue of the *telos* that defines them, and the source of this *telos* is the divine mind, *qua* related as norm of rightness to all things created.

[73] It has to be admitted that the first analogy fails in *this* respect: handing over 10 dollars may *not* come under a norm of payment, whereas any assertion that p is inevitably subject to the norm of truth. In this regard, moving the bishop is a better model.

[74] *Si [...] significetur esse quod non est, vel non esse quod est, aut si nihil omnino significetur: nulla erit rectitudo significationis, quae non nisi in significatione est. Quapropter per significationem habet esse et per eam mutatur eius rectitudo, quemadmodum color per corpus habet esse et non esse* (*DV* 13).

[75] *Non existente significatione non perit rectitudo, qua rectum est et qua exigitur, ut quod significandum est, significetur* (*DV* 13).

[76] *DV* 13.

[77] "TAT", p. 66.

There is, however, a question here, not asked by the student nor addressed by the teacher: how can the truth in virtue of which it would be true to say now that Theaetetus is sitting persist when Theaetetus gets up?[78] The teacher's proof that truth is eternal has been conducted by examining Anselm's prediction, a proposition that would have been true *whenever* formulated. Does the conclusion also hold when we consider a proposition such as "Theaetetus is sitting", which ceases to be true when Theaetetus is no longer sitting?

The first thing to note in answer to this question is of course that truth in the sense of *norm-satisfaction* does *not* persist. When Theaetetus gets up, the proposition "Theaetetus is sitting" *becomes false* (cf. §1.1 (A); §2.1). Hence the *property* of being true, which it had before, gives way to falsehood, just as Theaetetus's sitting gives way to standing, and the car loses its blueness when it is painted green.

It is only the norm of truth that is not affected by Theaetetus's getting up. Only truth as norm does not depend on *things true*, in a sense in which blueness does depend on things blue. (Only of this truth does Anselm say that *because* of it a true proposition is true. There is no comparable *because* that would relate a car's being blue to a norm that required the car to be blue and existed whether or not there was any car to satisfy the requirement!) Hence nothing prevents the *norm* by which a proposition may begin and cease to be true from persisting through such changes.

But even this might be questioned. For, the norm which at first requires one to say "Theaetetus is sitting" seems to *differ* from the norm that later requires one to say "Theaetetus is standing". In order to respond to this challenge, we must explore what Anselm and Anscombe have to say about the *unity of truth*.

---

[78] Anselm says: *Rectitudo igitur, qua significatio recta dicitur, non habet esse aut aliquem motum per significationem, quomodocumque ipsa moveatur significatio* (*DV* 13). What kind of "movement" does he mean? It seems unlikely that *moveatur* refers to a sentence's changing its *meaning* (whereby it would become a different proposition!), or its ceasing to *exist*. So I think, as Anscombe does ("AUT", p. 80), that he is talking about a proposition's changing its signification in the sense of beginning or ceasing to say of what is that it is, i.e. becoming true, or false. So my question is: how can this—a change of truth-value—fail to be matched by a *motus* in *rectitudo*?

3.2. An argument for the unity of truth

Anselm's claim that "the relation of rightness to signifying is *not* the same as that of colour to a body"[79] occurs in a chapter intended to prove not only the independent *existence* but the *unity* of truth.[80] Anscombe summarizes his argument for the unity thesis as follows: there is no such thing as "different kinds of rightness or truth [that would] get their different character from the different sorts of thing that are right and true". For, "*if* they did, and *if* they are of different kinds, then they exist and vary as the different things exist and vary and change. [...] But rightness, truth, is not like that".[81] Well, how does it differ?

Anselm's answer is based on his comparison between the grammar of "true" and that of an ordinary predicate. The structure of his argument seems to be this:

1) For a word like "blue" to be applied correctly, there has to be an object it is predicated of; and the existence of the colour blue is multiplied in accordance with the plurality of objects exhibiting it. When, by contrast, "true" is used in a context such as *It is true (would be true to say) that p*, there is *no* object for it to be predicated of.
2) The existence of this truth is therefore independent of the existence of true objects.
3) Since, then, its being true that p does not depend on the existence of *any* "p", the way in which this truth exists is not affected by a *plurality* of "p"'s occurences either.
4) So there are no grounds for treating this truth as individuated into single tropes of truth.
5) Hence nothing prevents it from being only *one*.
6) Furthermore, by saying that it is true that p, we merely relate the general norm of truth to a particular issue, or question, and to the contingent constitution of reality.
7) It is therefore one truth in virtue of which different true propositions are true.
8) Moreover, and in analogy to (6), that relatively general norm of truth merely relates a maximally general, totally formal, norm of rightness to the case of propositions.

---

[79] "AUT", p. 81.
[80] *DV* 13.
[81] "AUT", p. 81f.

9) It is therefore one rightness in virtue of which true propositions are true and, e.g., a good intention is good.

We are prepared for considerations (1–5) by what has been said before. The concluding steps of this argument, however, (6–7) and (8–9), may strike you as particularly problematic, and they are indeed difficult to understand. For, if (in accordance with §1.2) a norm is represented by "It was/would have been true to say that p", another norm seems to be represented by "It was/would have been true to say that q", etc. To find the unity thesis plausible we have to attend once more to the peculiar normative *teleology* of propositions.

3.3. Infinite import of the norm of truth

Consider this account of truth's normativity: "'p', if true, is true because *it would be true to say that p*. Here, the norm that is satisfied by 'p' is specified by the italicized clause. The 'norm of truth' is just a generalization of particular, specific norms of this form."

To see what is wrong with this, compare the following account of Kelim's compliance with the orders of his Guru: "Every one of these orders is a norm which is satisfied, if Kelim obeys, by its execution. We may also speak of a 'norm of compliance' here, but this is just a generalization of those particular orders."

This does not sound quite right. Why? Because the *import* of the *general* norm, which is open-ended, antecedes and creates the import of any particular order. By being the Guru's disciple (I am assuming) Kelim lives under a norm of obedience to do *whatever* the Guru tells him to do. This general norm is not captured by the collection (complete set) of orders actually given. It is infinite in not being restricted to what the Guru actually happens to order Kelim to do.

In a similar sense the norm of truth is infinite. If it is acceptable at all to speak of specific norms here, their collection must not be thought to exhaust the norm of truth. For they would be determined by what *happens* to be the case, as well as by what *happens* to be at issue, whereas the norm of truth is formal in that it abstracts from any material specificity. It imposes itself on our use of propositions in advance, and as foundation, of any *particular* constraint on what to say. Just as Kelim complies with a general norm of obedience by, say, cleaning the dishes, if and when the Guru orders him to clean the dishes, so truth itself is the norm complied with by an assertion that the cat is on the mat, if and when the cat is on the mat.

But this is not all. "Particular constraints" on assertion ("It would be true to say that p") are created by what I have called *relating the general norm of truth to a particular issue, or question, and to the contingent constitution of reality*. As soon as we try to conceive of them as establishing subordinate *norms*, we realize that the teleology and normativity of truth applies to judgment and the assertoric use of propositions in a way that cannot be expressed by ascribing any *telos*, or requirement, more determinate than truth to particular assertions.

3.4. Truth as formal telos

To see this, suppose you ask yourself whether p. This means: you are aiming at the truth concerning this question — not at the truth of "p" any more than that of "Not-p". An unconscious wish that p, may of course warp your judgment by giving it an extrinsic *telos*, viz. to judge that p, or that not-p. But this does not deprive it of its intrinsic and conscious *telos*, truth; and *this telos*, being impartial as to its being true that p or rather that not-p, can*not* be specified by the phrase *its being true to say that p*. The judgment's *telos* is in this special sense "indeterminate" even where, because p, it is in fact *achieved* by your judging that p, and not by your judging that not-p. It is a formal, non-material *telos*.

We may contrast the peculiar teleology of judgment and assertion with that of an artefact. If your PC misbehaves, its *telos* determines what *it* ought to do instead; if "p" is false, we cannot ask what *it* ought to do instead signifying that p. Or compare judgment with action. When you throw darts, you typically aim to hit the bull's eye. You perform well by *doing* the very thing you *aimed* to do. Judging that p is not like that. The description of what you *aimed at* — "judging truly whether p" — is of necessity *insufficiently specific* to describe the *performance by which* you would achieve that *telos*, viz. *judging that p* or *judging that not-p*, as the case may be. And we cannot articulate a more specific *telos* by the statement that *it would be true to say that p*; for that would be, as it were, *too specific* to be the non-natural *telos* of *an assertion of "p"*.

3.5. No "subordinate" norms of truth

To this characteristic indeterminacy of "p"'s teleology corresponds the inevitable indeterminacy of the norm that requires "p" to do "what it was created to signify".[82] The norm of truth can indeed be said to require *you not to say that not-p when p*; and it requires any *assertion* of yours *to be true*. But there can be no norm that requires any particular *assertion to say that p*. For which assertion could that be: that p?[83] that not-p? that q?

For these reasons the statement "It would be true to say that p" should not be viewed as expressing a "particular norm" that is satisfied by "p"'s being true. What we might say instead is rather something like this: that statement *represents*, or *points to*, a single norm of truth, which is also represented by indefinitely many other statements; it does that by *relating* the norm to one among indefinitely many circumstances, a circumstance characterized by the fact that p.

Here we can again draw on the analogy between *truth* and *cost*. In §2.2 I compared the statement "The tour cost you 10 dollars", which states a past fact, with "The tour costs 10 dollars", which states a norm. But now consider the statement "The tour would cost you 10 dollars", meaning: *If you take it, you are required to pay 10 dollars*. It does *not* express a norm — though it seems natural to say that it *represents* a norm by *relating* it to a particular potential visitor. Analogously, "It is true to say that p" expresses a *conditional requirement*, specifying what may be asserted and what not.

I conclude that the norm you try to satisfy in judging and asserting that p is the norm of truth rather than any more specific "subordinate norm" stating what it would be true to say. This confirms that "there is only one rightness" for everything that is right.[84] Being completely formal, that norm does not by itself, but only *qua* related to circumstances, determine *what* may and what may not be asserted.

This understanding of Anselm's position also allows us to deal with the question (raised at the very end of 3.1) whether the *specific* norm by which it was first true to say that p does not have to differ from that by which it was later true to say that not-p. The answer must be: there is no such specific norm. The same norm of truth was/would have been satisfied first by "p" and later by "Not-p".

---

[82] *DV* 2.
[83] The requirement to say *that p* is satisfied by the *natural* truth of "p"!
[84] *DV* 13.

4. Results and Open Questions

Anselm's dialogue and Anscombe's explanations of it raise questions that I have largely ignored. Here are some: why should "natural truth" be viewed as truth? Can the unity thesis that I have defended for the case of truth be accepted for every form of rightness? Does it apply, in particular, to non-natural rightness in the will and in acting[85] (a question that Anscombe takes up in her papers on *practical truth*)? How do things, including assertions and esp. actions, signify their own rightness?[86] What exactly is meant by the *existencer* of the norm of truth? Is the conviction of God's existence presupposed, or implied, in the idea of eternal truth? If every rightness is eternal truth in God's mind, what about the rightness that apparently guides the person who acts badly but "rightly" by following the rules of, say, duelling?

These questions are challenges that one needs to address in order to advance the work undertaken by Anscombe in clarifying and, possibly, backing St. Anselm's teaching on truth. All I hope to have done myself is throw some light on, and find support for, the rather original conception of truth that she finds expounded in his *De Veritate*. As the most important results of my investigation I consider the following:

A) The account of truth developed in that dialogue is based on a distinction between, on one hand, the *property* that characterizes as right whatever is right (and, in particular, the truth of true propositions) and, on the other, the *norm* by compliance with which that property applies.

B) In the chapters that Anscombe discusses, St. Anselm explores the notion of a bearer-less, eternal truth which he identifies with that norm. His arguments for its eternity and unity can be defended.

C) He also holds that propositional truth (truth as norm-satisfaction), being individuated by the propositions of which it is *predicated*, is *not* eternal.

D) Anscombe follows him in maintaining that, in assertions, such truth is *required* by the eternal norm he identifies with the highest truth.

E) However—perhaps because the notion of propositional truth, once introduced, is of little concern to Anselm himself—

---

[85] *DV* 4; 5; 12.
[86] *DV* 9.

Anscombe tends to pass over the distinction of this notion from that of truth as norm, and to read his observations concerning the latter as an account of truth *tout court*.

My explanations and comments have been concerned with Anselm's texts at least as much as with Anscombe's. But this should not be seen as indicating that I might have arrived at similar explanations without her help. I certainly should not have known and examined and valued the subtle treasures hidden in *De Veritate*, if Anscombe had not sniffed and detected, appreciated and investigated them with her distinctive philosophical nose and characteristic acumen. This is quite typical of a lot of her work: it draws attention to intriguing aspects of great philosophical texts of the past that would otherwise go unnoticed or undervalued.

In the case of Anselm's dialogue the central discovery is, to my mind, the fascinating idea that we understand what it is for propositions to be true—and, indeed, for things quite generally to achieve their *telê*—by understanding that truth, or rightness, is in the first instance not a property predicated of them, but rather a norm that requires them to be as they ought to be—a norm not come about by human institution, and in force independently of the existence of anything satisfying it or even required to do so.

Cora Diamond

Asymmetries in Thinking about Thought: Anscombe and Wiggins

1. Introduction

In what kinds of case may there be no alternative to thinking that so and so? If I think that p, I am quite prepared, usually, to find that others may think the opposite, and indeed that they have what at least appear to be good reasons for what they think. There may be more than one tenable thought about what is in question. And, normally, if I think that p, I recognize that those who disagree (or who at any rate appear to disagree) are not thinking nothing at all. Are there cases, though, in which these symmetries do not hold — that is, in which thoughts do not come along with opposed thinkables? Elizabeth Anscombe allows for some such cases, and so does David Wiggins. I here explore their ideas, beginning with a question to which we are led by Wiggins' views. I then explain Anscombe's quite different approach and some of the wider issues with which it is connected. That will then enable me to consider the relation between Wiggins' approach and Anscombe's.

2. Questions to Which We May Be Led by David Wiggins' Work

When Wiggins writes about the objectivity of ethics, he notes that first-order morality is very unlike elementary arithmetic, but he adds that there is an aspect in which they can usefully be compared.¹ In both cases—in ordinary moral thinking, and in ordinary arithmetical thinking—there are judgments about which we can say, "There is nothing else to think but that so and so". He has used the examples of judging that 7 + 5 = 12 and judging that slavery is wrong. Thus, in the latter case, the idea would be that if you know what slavery is and what "wrong" means, there are considerations that (working together) leave you no alternative but to think that slavery is wrong.² Wiggins calls into question "the insidious presumption of symmetry"—the presumption that, whatever moral view one takes to be true, there are tenable opposed views.³ It is against this presumption, characteristically accepted by non-cognitivists, that Wiggins argues for there being moral questions in response to which there is nothing else to think but that so and so. This is not the claim that there is nothing else for us to think but that so and so, but that there is nothing else to think on this matter. His formulation of the asymmetry here thus goes against the kinds of claim that various relativists may make, that, while there may be nothing else for us to think, a view inconsistent with ours may be taken by those to whom things appear differently.⁴

Wiggins himself is concerned with the role that the truth of your belief can have in an explanation of why you have that belief.⁵ I want to look at a different sort of question. It comes up because, if you say that there is nothing else to think but that so and so, this looks as if it might be taken in two different ways. It

---

¹ David Wiggins, *Ethics: Twelve Lectures on the Philosophy of Morality* (Cambridge, MA: Harvard University Press, 2006), pp. 330-1.
² *Ibid.*, pp. 366-7.
³ David Wiggins, "Moral Cognitivism, Moral Relativism and Motivating Moral Beliefs", *Proceedings of the Aristotelian Society*, 91 (1991): 61-85, at 78. I use "MCMR" as an abbreviation of the title.
⁴ For a discussion of what one might call "the symmetry of opposing appearances" and its relevance to arguments for relativism, see Myles Burnyeat, "Conflicting Appearances", *Proceedings of the British Academy*, 65 (1979): 69-111, reprinted in Burnyeat, *Explorations in Ancient and Modern Philosophy*, vol. 1 (Cambridge: Cambridge University Press, 2012), pp. 276-315. I am very grateful to Sabina Lovibond for bringing to my attention the relation between Burnyeat on philosophical appeals to conflicting appearances and Wiggins on the presumption of symmetry in metaethics.
⁵ Wiggins, "MCMR", *passim*. See also A.W. Moore, "On There Being Nothing Else to Think, or Want, or Do", in *Essays for David Wiggins: Identity, Truth and Value* (Oxford: Blackwell, 1996), pp. 165-84

might mean that if you deny the so and so in question, the relevant considerations will speak conclusively against your judgment. There is, as it were, a thought there—there is a thought opposed to what may be taken to be the only thing that one can think—or maybe there are several candidate thoughts in this region, but they are not thoughts that anyone would actually think if paying attention to the issue and to the relevant considerations. So that is one way of taking a claim that there is nothing else to think but that so and so. The alternative way of taking the claim is as saying that there is no thought there to think. If you say the opposite, there is nothing to what you say but muddle. It is not that you are thinking something and nothing speaks for it, but that there is really no *it*. It might be objected that there is no sharp distinction there, but I am going to take seriously the idea that there is a distinction.[6] But, in any case, there is another objection to the idea that there is no opposed thought. Wittgenstein said once that the negation of nonsense is nonsense,[7] which may be taken to suggest that the negation of muddle is muddle, and that you cannot turn muddle into something thinkable by negating it. But it is not clear what the range of that point should be taken to be. May what has the form of the negation of what one takes not to be an intelligible thought nevertheless be something helpful or illuminating? Or even true?

3. Anscombe on These Questions

In an entirely different sort of context, Anscombe leads us into closely related questions. When she discusses what is wrong with the picture theory, in her *Introduction to Wittgenstein's Tractatus*, one of her complaints is that there are statements which the *Tractatus* counts as nonsensical and which it excludes, although they are illuminating and may be true—indeed, "obviously true".[8] The example on which she focusses comes from her criticism of

---

[6] See also Wiggins, "MCMR", p. 67 n7.
[7] Ludwig Wittgenstein, "Letter to Ramsey", in *Ludwig Wittgenstein: Cambridge Letters*, ed. Brian McGuinness and G.H. von Wright (Oxford: Blackwell, 1995), p. 217.
[8] G.E.M. Anscombe, *An Introduction to Wittgenstein's Tractatus*, 2nd ed. (London: Hutchinson University Library, 1963), p. 85 (p. 68 in corrected 3rd edition published as Part 1 of *Logic, Truth and Meaning: Writings by G.E.M. Anscombe*, ed. M. Geach and L. Gormally (Exeter: Imprint Academic, 2015)).

Antony Flew, who had said that it was part of the logic of the word "somebody", unlike "nobody", to refer to somebody. "If this were so," Anscombe said, "then, on being told that everybody hates somebody, we could ask to be introduced to this universally hated person."[9] Anscombe takes to be obviously true the sort of statement that one might then make in response to Flew: "'Somebody' does not refer to somebody" or "'Someone' is not the name of someone". Such a statement, she says, expresses an insight, the opposite of which is nothing but confusion. The contradictory of the statement, if examined, "peters out into nothingness". So she takes it that there can be statements that are true, but such that there is no opposing thought. The denial of the statement expresses nothing but muddle, not some alternative thinkable thing.[10]

There is in the case as Anscombe describes it a striking sort of asymmetry, which contrasts with two closely related sorts of symmetry. The first sort of symmetry can be seen in discussions of what is truth-apt, where it is usually supposed that if something is truth-apt, it has a truth-apt negation.[11] The second can be seen in Wittgenstein's remark, cited in Part 1, that the negation of nonsense is nonsense—which appears to rule out the kind of asymmetry in which there is nothing but sheer muddle opposed to some intelligible statement.

Thinking about Anscombe's case and her description of it leads into a great variety of issues in philosophy of language, philosophy of mind and ethics. One of these issues is the relation between Wigginsian asymmetry and Anscombean asymmetry, both of which involve cases about which one can say, "There is nothing else to think but that so and so". I shall be focussing first on Anscombean asymmetry. In Part 4, I look at some examples of cases like hers, which I shall call "solo propositions", simply meaning that they do not come in pairs. Solo propositions are then to be contrasted with ordinary propositions as these might, for example, be understood on the basis of the picture theory.

---

[9]   *Ibid.* Anscombe is criticizing the views expressed in Flew's introduction to his *Logic and Language*, 1st series (Oxford: Blackwell, 1951).
[10] I discuss Anscombe's use of the example in her criticism of Wittgenstein in "Disagreements: Anscombe, Geach, Wittgenstein", *Philosophical Investigations*, 38 (2015): 1–24.
[11] On "platitudes" about truth, see Crispin Wright, *Truth and Objectivity* (Cambridge, MA: Harvard University Press, 1992), p. 34.

Ordinary senseful propositions come in pairs, the proposition and its negation, with both members of the pair having the possibility of truth and the possibility of falsity.[12]

One might or might not believe in another kind of proposition that would also come in pairs: one member of the pair expresses something that must be the case, and its negation does not peter out into nothingness but expresses something that cannot be the case. This, then, is a conception of substantial necessities as also coming in pairs: a necessary truth paired with a necessary falsity, where both members of the pair are supposedly intelligible propositions.

There are questions about how to fit tautologies and contradictions into my idea of paired propositions and solo propositions. I am not sure how far Anscombe accepted the Tractarian account of logical propositions; but on that account a tautology does not say the opposite of what you get by negating it since neither the tautology nor the contradiction says anything. What I am after with the idea of solo propositions is a contrast with pairs of propositions, both of which say that something is the case; and you do not have that kind of pairing with logical propositions as understood in the *Tractatus*. A tautology may nevertheless be described as "opposed to" what you get by negating it, in that there is no proposition with a sense that affirms them both.[13] Tautology and contradiction can be taken as an anomalous case or as a limiting case of paired propositions.[14]

When I introduced the contrast between solo propositions and paired propositions, I did not want to imply anything about whether solo propositions may be taken to be true. Anscombe plainly thought they could. Peter Geach, writing about a case like Anscombe's, denied that such propositions would have any truth-value.[15] Anscombe's view is also at odds with the idea referred to above, and accepted in virtually all contemporary philosophical discussions of truth, that truth-apt items come in pairs. To see

---

[12] See Anscombe, "Truth: Anselm and Wittgenstein", in *From Plato to Wittgenstein: Essays by G.E.M. Anscombe*, ed. M. Geach and L. Gormally (Exeter: Imprint Academic, 2011), pp. 71–6.

[13] See Wittgenstein, *Tractatus Logico-Philosophicus* (London: Routledge & Kegan Paul, 1922), 5.1241.

[14] I am grateful to Steven Methven for discussion of these cases.

[15] Peter Geach, "Philosophical Autobiography", in *Peter Geach: Philosophical Encounters*, ed. H.A. Lewis (Dordrecht: Kluwer, 1991), pp. 1–25.

more clearly what is involved in thinking about solo propositions, I turn now to some cases that might be put alongside Anscombe's example.[16]

4. Solo Propositions: Some Examples

To start with, there are cases that resemble Anscombe's. There is, for example, a discussion by Sophie Grace Chappell of Bernard Williams on internal and external reasons.[17] Chappell says that, when Williams argues against there being "external reasons", what he is denying is "only a piece of confusion". Chappell provides a summary statement of Williams' view, but that statement itself has, Chappell says, nothing opposed to it but confusion. There isn't an intelligible thought expressed by the negation. I am not sure whether Chappell would say that the statement she provides of Williams' view is true—so I am not sure whether she would agree with Anscombe on the reasonableness of calling true a statement that has no intelligible negation. But whether or not she would describe Williams' view as true, there is a significant similarity between what she is doing and what Anscombe was doing: they both take there to be a kind of asymmetry between what can be said in response to confusion and the confused statement itself. What they say in response to confusion they take to be not muddle, although their responses (what they are saying in their own voice) are set out in the form of a negation of something they take to be mere confusion.

Another case would be Frege's response to Benno Kerry in "Concept and Object".[18] Frege's response is similar in structure to Anscombe's and Chappell's. Frege takes Kerry's sentence, "The concept 'horse' is a concept easily attained", to embody confusion; and Frege's statement, "The concept horse is not a concept", is part of his response to confusion—and, despite its not being easy to characterize Frege's own statement, it is not itself muddle, or so

---

[16] For more discussion of the examples, see Cora Diamond, "Wittgenstein and What Can Only Be True", *Nordic Wittgenstein Review*, 3 (2014): 9–40.
[17] Sophie Grace Chappell, "Bernard Williams", in *Stanford Encyclopedia of Philosophy*, last modified 2013, http://plato.stanford.edu/entries/williams-bernard/. The quoted words are from Chappell's earlier, 2010 version.
[18] Gottlob Frege, "On Concept and Object", in *Collected Papers on Mathematics, Logic, and Philosophy*, ed. Brian McGuinness, trans. Max Black et al. (Oxford: Blackwell, 1984), pp. 182–94.

I should say. There is then a range of asymmetrically structured cases of responses to confusion: in each such case, the response to confusion is a proposition that is doing some work, but one might say of its negation that it "peters out into nothingness". I should note that it is often not entirely clear how philosophers who are responding to what they take to be confusion conceive what they themselves are doing. A possible example would be David Wiggins' discussion of the confusion of thinking that there are no genuinely benevolent motives because the pleasure the agent takes in achieving his aim is his own pleasure, and thus his pleasure is the point of his action.[19] That, Wiggins says, is muddle; but then what about the summary statements that Wiggins gives of the opposing view? Some of them are structured as negations of what he takes to be mere muddle; but they are not muddle, and he may well take them to be true.

The other kind of case I want to touch on here comes from two readings of the *Tractatus* on mathematical propositions: Michael Kremer's and Roger White's.[20] The basic picture that you get in Kremer's account is that we may do a calculation in the course of working out how to infer from some senseful propositions to a senseful proposition; and we may then make a record of the calculation. Such a record of a calculation can then go on to have a significant kind of use in the language: we can continue using it to guide inference from senseful propositions to senseful propositions. This is then what equations are; so, on this view, an equation is a kind of record of a calculation and serves as a shortcut for us in inferring; it helps us to see what paths in inferring are open. This account of the *Tractatus* view of equations treats them as structures resembling propositions in the narrow Tractarian sense, which have a use as part of the language, and which are not nonsensical. They do not come with negations that have any role in the language, and they are in that sense, then, a kind of solo proposition. Roger White, in his book on the *Tractatus*, gives a similar account of how Wittgenstein understood mathematical propositions. He explicitly takes Wittgenstein to treat mathematical propositions as having the function of rules. While

---

[19] Wiggins, *Ethics*, pp. 41–3.
[20] Michael Kremer, "Mathematics and Meaning in the *Tractatus*", *Philosophical Investigations*, 25 (2002): 272–303; Roger M. White, *Wittgenstein's Tractatus Logico-Philosophicus* (London: Continuum, 2006), pp. 106–11.

mathematical propositions may resemble senseful propositions, their function is entirely different; it is to indicate the ways we can substitute signs for each other. For example, the equation "$7 + 5 = 12$" is a rule that allows us to move from the proposition, "There are 7 books here and 5 there", to the proposition, "There are 12 books here or there". Here, as in Kremer's account of the *Tractatus*, Wittgenstein is read as specifying the kind of use that mathematical propositions have. They are not nonsensical, but provide ways in which we can handle senseful propositions. Understood in this way, they could also be described as solo propositions in my sense. The account White gives of the *Tractatus* on mathematical propositions is quite close to things Wittgenstein in fact says about mathematical propositions later on, in the 1930s, when he compares them with rules and takes them not to be propositions in a narrow sense and not to have significant negations.

It may seem that the first group of examples, responses to confusion, are totally different from the second group, mathematical propositions as understood in the *Tractatus*. But that is not right: there are significant common features, which are the subject of Part 5.

5. Indicating Paths We Can Take, and Paths We Should Not Take: Two Similarities

(1) In the cases of philosophical responses to confusion, there is a path of thought that people have taken, or that someone has taken, and some philosopher or philosophers may bring out why you should not take that path. When they have done that—when they have brought out what the confusion is, or at any rate take themselves to have done so—they may then provide some sort of summary statement of their response, and this is frequently explicitly negative in form, as with "'Someone' is not the name of someone", and "The concept *horse* is not a concept". In the concept-horse case, Frege had been trying to make plain the confusion in what Benno Kerry had said about the concept *horse*, and you could say that Frege wanted to block the road into the confusion. The point of Frege's own statement is, in large part, what it is against, and what Frege shows about how not to get there. I am suggesting that we can think of "The concept *horse* is not a concept" as a kind of road-blocker, blocking a road to confusion. And if we look at responses to confusion as road-blockers, we can bring out also a resemblance to mathematical propositions on the

Tractatus view, which could be described as indicating paths that are open for us to take. I am suggesting then that my two groups of examples of solo propositions can be described as propositions that are indicators of paths: paths for us to take in thinking, or paths not to take. There is an important kind of example that will bring out the similarity I am suggesting—the example of mathematical inequalities. Suppose, for example, we found ourselves frequently multiplying 2 times 24 and getting 46 (perhaps because we tended to slip from multiplying 2 times 4 to adding instead). So in this kind of case, an inequality, "$2 \times 24 \neq 46$", might come in handy. On Kremer's kind of reading of the *Tractatus*, if we wrote down that inequality and kept it handy, it could have a function as an indicator of ways we should not go in making inferences between senseful propositions. What I am suggesting, then, is that an inequality can be used to indicate a path we should not take: it can function as a path-blocker. This is then an account that fits closely with Kremer's and White's readings of the *Tractatus* on mathematical propositions, and that also resembles the account one can give of solo propositions that function as responses to confusion.

(2) There is a further similarity between my two groups of cases: Consider Frege's statement, "The concept *horse* is not a concept". This comes, as I said, from his response to Benno Kerry; but you could not possibly get what Frege is after when he says, "The concept horse is not a concept", if his statement were detached from the account he gives of how Kerry is confused. Or take Anscombe's description of "'Someone' is not the name of someone" as an insight. This comes after she spells out what she takes to be the confusion in what Flew had said about "somebody" and explains how it goes wrong. Detached from her account of the confusion, the statement, "'Someone' is not the name of someone", would not convey the insight which, in context, it can convey. There is a kind of parallel here with the *Tractatus* view as Kremer explains it. An equation, on this view, is a record, a helpful record, of a calculation. On this view, then, we can say that its capacity to indicate an inferential path that we may go on to take depends upon the original calculation. And, again, if someone multiplies 2 times 24 and comes up with 46, you can go over the calculation with the person, and make clear the point at which it goes wrong; you do not merely state or write out the inequality that marks the rejection of "2 times 24 equals 46". The point here is that path-indicators—whether they indicate paths of thought that we should

not take or paths of thought that we can take—go with a story that shows why the path is blocked or that show it to be an open path. That is, the solo propositions that I have considered are associated with a persuasive backstory; and their having such a connection is tied to the kind of use they are meant to have.

In response to the similarities I have noted, it might be said that really what these cases have in common is that they all involve rules, and that rules in general, while they may be expressed in indicative sentences, can be contrasted with genuine propositions. It is not then surprising that they do not come in pairs or that they do not come with significant negations. That is explained by their being rules. An example that might be brought in here is Ramsey's discussion of the kinds of propositions he calls variable hypotheticals—propositions like, "All men are mortal". These sorts of proposition had earlier been taken by Ramsey himself to be genuine propositions, in fact to be conjunctions. In an account based on that of the *Tractatus*, he had taken them to be capable of truth and falsity in the way any other genuine proposition is. In his late paper, "General Propositions and Causality", he presented deep objections to that view and set out an alternative account according to which these "variable hypotheticals" are not genuine propositions. "They are not judgments," he said, "but rules for judging: If I meet a φ, I shall regard it as a ψ." Ramsey added that "[t]his cannot be negated but it can be disagreed with by one who does not adopt it."[21] (This view has some resemblances to the *Tractatus* view of mathematical propositions, as Roger White explains it, and also resembles Wittgenstein's own later view of mathematical propositions.) But the suggestion that solo propositions (like the ones I have looked at) are really rules is less illuminating than it may seem. Independently of any comparison with rules, what we have is the idea that solo propositions may function as indicators of paths that we can take in thinking or that we should not take in thinking. There is not more in saying "Ah they are rules!" than that. It is not as if there were some clear understanding available of a contrast between genuine propositions and rules, and as if we therefore understand these path-indicators better in terms of that existing contrast. Further, there

---

[21] F.P. Ramsey, "General Propositions and Causality", in Ramsey, *The Foundations of Mathematics and other Logical Essays*, ed. R.B. Braithwaite (London: Routledge and Kegan Paul, 1931), pp. 237-55.

are no conclusions one might draw from identifying path-indicators or other solo propositions as rules. Thus, for example, it is not as if you could settle whether solo propositions could be called true by taking such propositions to be rules. Even if we read Anscombe's "'Someone' is not the name of someone" as a rule specifying where we should not go, its being a rule, and there being lots of rules that we might not consider true or false, would leave it unclear whether or not her case was indeed one in which something you could call a rule was something you might describe as true.

6. Pursuing the Issues Here Further

There is another case that is worth considering here. It is an example of a path-blocker, but it is not entirely clear whether it is an example of a solo proposition. The case is that of Brian Davies' defence of the claim that God is not a moral agent subject to moral praise or censure.[22] Davies says that the kind of theology that he is doing "is sometimes called 'negative theology'", and adds that it "puts up 'No Entry' signs ... at the beginning of certain roads down which one might be tempted to wander". One of these roads at which he is posting a warning is the "God is a moral agent"-road. Davies is doing something which is structurally like some of the cases I looked at earlier; that is, he does not just say "Do not go down this road", but explains in some detail what is the matter with it as a road. He does not say that "God is a moral agent" is a false proposition; he says that we have reason for fighting shy of that formula—a very striking remark, partly in that, in speaking of it as a formula we have reason to fight shy of, Davies is avoiding speaking of it as something fully coherent. He does not explicitly say this, but I am going to ascribe to him the view that when people take God to be a moral agent, their thought has gone off the rails in a significant way. (I should add that he thinks you have reason to "fight shy of the formula 'God is a moral agent'" whether or not you believe in God.)

There is a way of connecting what I have just said back to Anscombe. In her work on Aristotle and practical truth, she makes use of a very striking passage in the *Nicomachean Ethics* (1139a

---

[22] Brian Davies, OP, "Is God a Moral Agent?", in *Whose God? Which Tradition? The Nature of Belief in God*, ed. D.Z. Phillips (Aldershot: Ashgate, 2008), pp. 97-122; see especially 111 and 116.

21).²³ This is the passage where Aristotle says that truth is the business of everything intellectual. Doing well and doing badly in thinking are truth and falsehood, whether we are concerned with purely theoretical thinking or practical thought. Here we may ask: might we take it to be—might Anscombe have taken it to be—part of the business of thinking, part of its job, to guide, or to help put back on track, the business of thinking? If you held that that was part of the business of thinking (if you held that part of the business of thinking is to help along the business of thinking), and if you worked with the Aristotelian idea that truth is what you have when the business of thinking is done well—then indeed statements that respond to confusion and that help to put thinking back on track (help it to be done well) could indeed be described as true, even though such a statement might not have an intelligible negation. I do not know whether what I have just suggested was indeed Anscombe's view, but it is constructed with Anscombean material and is meant to fit what she says in response to Flew's confusion.

I have, though, in making this move, changed my description of the cases. The Anscombe case I originally described as a response to confusion, in which the negation of what she puts forward is something that peters out into nothingness. I described the Brian Davies case as reflecting his view that when people take God to be a moral agent, their thinking has gone off the rails— which is not the same as to say there is no thought there that they are thinking. But both of these ways of speaking reflect some notion of failure of thought, and this is not merely a notion of thinking something straightforwardly false. Here I should note something that has been implicit in my talk of "paths of thought". One's thinking may take one from this thought to something else and then to something else, and one can speak of this as a path one's thought has taken. Speaking in this kind of way, one may describe the entire sequence as thinking. But in going down that path, one's thinking may have gone astray as thinking. One may have wound up in sheer muddle, or one's thinking may have

---

²³ Anscombe, "Thought and Action in Aristotle: What Is 'Practical Truth'?", in *From Parmenides to Wittgenstein* (Oxford: Blackwell, 1981), pp. 66-77; also Anscombe, "Practical Truth", in *Human Life, Action and Ethics: Essays by G.E.M. Anscombe*, ed. M. Geach and L. Gormally (Exeter: Imprint Academic, 2005), pp. 149-58.

miscarried in some other significant way. My use of the phrase "a path of thought" does not carry the implication that one is thinking in any full sense as one goes down the path. One's having apparently gone on thinking may nevertheless involve a failure of thinking, as in the case of apparent thinking that "peters out into nothingness".[24]

In my sketch of an Aristotelian-Anscombean conception of guides to thinking, I have worked myself into territory closer to my starting point: David Wiggins' views about ethics, as illustrated by his example of judging that slavery is wrong and of there not being anything else to think but that. But I want to postpone a while longer any attempt to bring questions about ethics or about David Wiggins' ideas into relation with what I have been saying about solo propositions. I need to look first at a kind of conceptual organization that can be found in both Frege and Wittgenstein.

7. Frege, Wittgenstein, and Where We Get by Thinking about Definitions

Frege had the idea that there was a phase in the development of a systematic science, prior to the system's actual use — a phase in which the expressions that will be used in the system are prepared for use. In what Frege speaks of as the propaedeutic, both complex notions and logically primitive elements can be clarified. The clarification of complex notions makes it possible to stipulate the sense of some signs to be used in the system, through definitions which will form part of the system. The proposition used initially to give a definition can then have a distinct and different sort of use as an assertion. Thus a proposition used to establish the meaning of a proper name can be used afterwards to express an assertion about the thing named. In general, if a proposition is used in the preparatory phase or propaedeutic, or if it is used as a definition within the system, it may look as if it is expressing an assertion about things that are named in it, but it may have, at that stage, a quite different sort of use. When Frege explains what he means by "concept", "function" and "object", these explanations belong to the preparatory phase; and I think we can take what Frege says, when he is trying to clear up misunderstandings of his

---

[24] I am grateful to Steven Methven for drawing to my attention the problems in talking of "paths of thought".

remarks about concepts, as also belonging to the preparatory use of language.

Wittgenstein also worked with an idea of preparatory uses of language. In lectures in 1939, Wittgenstein made an analogy between the way definitions set things up for the later use of signs and the way mathematical propositions provide procedures you can use in handling experiential propositions. That was in 1939, but already in the *Tractatus*, he took a view of mathematical propositions that can be understood by connecting it with what he says about definitions. Mathematical propositions are like definitions in being helps to what we do with senseful propositions. So the germ of Wittgenstein's distinction between preparations for the use of language and engaged uses of language can be seen already in the *Tractatus*. There are similarities and differences between what Frege does with the idea of preparatory uses of language and definitions and what Wittgenstein does, but they both held that a proposition used in these ways can also have a different sort of use. They both also held that a proposition used in these ways may be misread, if we take it, or try to take it, as asserting something about the things that are meant by the signs in it. There are, though, extremely significant differences between them on this whole business of preparatory uses of language. For Wittgenstein, many propositions that have this character keep it. Their use continues to be that of enabling other types of uses of propositions. And this is indeed at the heart of his treatment of mathematical propositions. What I have been trying to lead up to here is the importance for Wittgenstein, in many contexts, of thinking in terms of a contrast between kinds of setting out of paths we can take in language, and engaged uses of language where we are taking these or those paths. The notion of preparation of language for its application may then be philosophically useful to us, in that it draws to attention possible ways we may be using language that are not themselves engaged uses, but work as path-indicators and path-blockers for engaged uses. There is a very interesting remark of Wittgenstein about path-blockers:

> Language has the same traps ready for everyone; the immense network of easily trodden false paths. And thus we see one person after another walking down the same paths and we already know where he will make a turn, where he will keep going straight ahead without noticing the turn, etc., etc. Therefore, wherever false

paths branch off I ought to put up signs to help in getting past the dangerous spots.[25]

My suggestion here is that the role of markers of false paths is related to that of equations, thought of as indicating useful paths. Path-indicators — indicators of useful paths on the one hand and paths leading into confusion on the other — belong in the general and varied group of preparatory propositions. And then the point is that propositions with a preparatory use may be misunderstood if one reads them without awareness of their differences from and their relations to the engaged uses of language that they are meant to respond to or to guide.[26]

In Part 8, I shall bring the discussion back to ethics, and then, in Part 9, to the views of David Wiggins and the relation between his views and Anscombe's.

8. Ethics: Indicating and Blocking Paths of Thought

One of the most striking features of practical reasoning is that it is beset with temptations, and this includes practical reasoning when it is philosophically reflective. So a second striking feature of thinking in the region of ethics is that there are responses to practical thinking, responses which come from seeing common kinds of practical reasoning as thought's having gone astray: we have gone down paths of thought that should be avoided but that may be profoundly tempting. Philippa Foot provides a good example of this kind of response. She says, "[S]omething drives us towards utilitarianism. ... We must be going wrong somewhere".[27] There is an easily trodden false path here. What she thinks is indeed that where we are going wrong is in "accepting the idea that there are better and worse states of affairs in the sense that consequentialism requires"; and at the end of her essay, she says that we should accustom ourselves to the thought that there is simply a blank where consequentialists see the phrase, "the best state of affairs".[28] I read this as meaning that, where

---

[25] Ludwig Wittgenstein, *The Big Typescript*: TS 213, ed. and trans. C.G. Luckhardt and M.A.E. Aue (Oxford: Blackwell, 2005), p. 312.
[26] For discussion of Frege and Wittgenstein on preparatory uses of language, see Diamond, "Wittgenstein and What Can Only Be True".
[27] Philippa Foot, "Utilitarianism and the Virtues", in *Moral Dilemmas* (Oxford: Clarendon Press, 2002), pp. 59–77, at p. 59.
[28] Ibid., at pp. 62 and 77.

consequentialists think that there is a thought they are thinking about the significance of the betterness of states of affairs, there is no thought; there is something with a blank in the middle of it. So I see her discussion of this case as a fine example of the significance in ethics of responses to temptation, to the tendencies in practical thinking to go down false paths. Another case of the attempt in ethics to block off paths of thought that may be found extremely tempting is Sabina Lovibond's, which concerns the entertaining (in advance of any actual case) of questions about what we should do if faced with horrific dilemmas.[29] Lovibond was discussing ideas of Elizabeth Anscombe's; and it would be good to mention a quite different sort of example from Anscombe herself—from the speech she gave against the awarding by Oxford of an honorary degree to Truman. In that speech (published as "Mr. Truman's Degree"), she says that "[c]hoosing to kill the innocent as a means to your ends is always murder".[30] In its original context of her speech to Convocation, that statement was meant to indicate a path of thought which her colleagues might not have been aware of, a path to which they might not have been attending as they were deciding whether to vote for the degree. The path she wanted to draw plainly to their attention was the inferential path from "I am going to vote to give Truman the degree" to "I am going to vote to honour a murderer". That is, she wanted to draw to their attention a path of thought that would lead them to see what it was they were doing. It was easy not to see this; it was easy to take the giving of the degree to Truman to be utterly normal and reasonable—hence the value in the circumstances of a path-indicator that might change their conception of what they were doing. My suggestion here is that, in various ways, in practical thinking we may stand in need of, or find useful, many different sorts of path-indicators: both of the kind that block paths of thought we may be tempted to take, and also of the kind that indicate open paths of thought which it may be

---

[29] Sabina Lovibond, "Absolute Prohibitions without Divine Promises", in *Modern Moral Philosophy*, ed. Anthony O'Hear (Cambridge: Cambridge University Press, 2004), pp. 141–58, reprinted in Lovibond, *Essays on Ethics and Feminism* (Oxford: Oxford University Press, 2015), pp. 146–61.
[30] Anscombe, "Mr. Truman's Degree", in Anscombe, *Ethics, Religion and Politics* (Oxford: Blackwell, 1981), pp. 62–71, at 66, see also 64.

important for us to be aware of, but which habits of ease-in-thinking make invisible to us, or enable us to go on not seeing.

Suppose one of the members of Convocation heard Anscombe and realized that voting in favour of the degree would be voting to honour a murderer, and suppose he came to think then that it would be a kind of moral failure to vote for the degree — a failure to take seriously the victims of the bombings that Truman had authorized. We can see what is going on there as having two stages. There is first the stage in which Anscombe's words (her characterization in general terms of what it is to choose to kill the innocent) indicate a significant kind of path for thinking; and secondly there is the stage in which the don who hears the speech takes the path and judges that he should not vote for the degree and that to do so would be a moral failure. I am suggesting that what went on can be conceptualized in terms of the Wittgensteinian contrast between preparation for use of language and the engaged use of what is thus made available. The example is also meant to bring out a further point about truth in ethics. In Part 6, I suggested that we could have a sort of Anscombean-Aristotelian account of truth, based on the idea that it is part of the business of thinking to guide the business of thinking, and that when this guiding is done well, we have truth. This would suggest that there may be importantly different kinds of cases of truth in ethics, depending on whether we have in view the guidance of thinking or engaged thinking that may take or fail to take this or that path of thought.

9. Back to David Wiggins

I began, in Part 2, with David Wiggins' remark that there is an aspect in which elementary arithmetic and first-order morality may be compared: in both, there are judgments about which we can say, "There is nothing else to think but that so and so"; among his examples were "7 + 5 = 12" and "slavery is wrong". The comparison is central in Wiggins' view of the kind of objectivity that moral judgments, understood as he understands them, do have. It is thus also part of his account of moral judgments as capable of truth. His account of moral judgments allows for there being many different sorts of thinking and judging that go on in ethics; but it does not allow for the kind of difference I have wanted to suggest — namely, the difference between ethical judgments that are guides to thinking (indicators of paths that can be taken and paths that should not be taken) and judgments that are not meant as such guides but that are themselves takings of this or that path in thinking about some case, or kinds of case, and that may follow, or may ignore or flout, what one might regard as guides to thinking. I take the absence of attention to that difference to be a significant feature of Wiggins' approach to ethics; I believe it leads to his not getting into focus the structure of the nineteenth-century dispute about slavery. The dispute itself, especially after the cessation of the (legal) Atlantic slave trade, was at least in part a dispute about whether it was a false path in thinking about human affairs to treat such issues (including, in particular, slavery) in an abstract general way. Wiggins invites us to see the nineteenth-century dispute about slavery as capable of illuminating the issue of objectivity in ethics and as helping us to see our way to rejecting the "insidious presumption of symmetry" in ethics. But in order to see the relevance of the dispute to the possibility of objectivity in ethics, we need to understand the kind of complexity the dispute actually had, and the role in it of attempts by pro- and anti-slavery thinkers alike to set up "No Entry" signs to paths of thought taken by their opponents.[31] We can now look at the similarities and differences between the Anscombean approach that I have sketched and Wiggins' view. In Wiggins' remarks about the cases in which there is nothing else to think but that so and so, and in Anscombe's discussion of her example and of related sorts of cases, there are ideas about the normativity of thinking — what it is for thinking to be going as it should, and what it is for it to fail to do so. Their ideas about the normativity of thinking are closely tied, in both cases, to their rejection of familiar sorts of symmetry in philosophical thought about thinking. Wiggins rejects the "insidious presumption" that there is some tenable position opposed to any ethical judgment we take to be true; Anscombe rejects the idea that a thought must have, opposed to it, something that is thinkable. But their treatments of the normativity of thought are nevertheless deeply different. This deep difference arises, I think, out of their different ways of inheriting from Frege and Wittgenstein. Wiggins has his own version of a Davidsonian

---

[31] I discuss the nineteenth-century dispute and its relevance to Wiggins' arguments about truth in ethics in "Truth in Ethics: Williams and Wiggins", in *Reading Wittgenstein with Anscombe, Going On to Ethics* (Cambridge, MA: Harvard University Press, 2019), pp. 271–306.

version of this inheritance, which places great emphasis on the connection between meaning and truth-conditions.[32] He takes it that that connection can be worked up into a general account of linguistic meaning that itself can be elaborated to allow for the plain truth of moral judgments. The account he gives is intended to cover the relation between truth and meaning for declarative sentences in general.[33] Anscombe, on propositions that can only be true, represents a very different understanding of what we should inherit from Frege and Wittgenstein. In particular, she held that there were fundamental insights about truth and meaning in the picture theory—and a big question for her was how far one could keep hold of those insights in the light of Wittgenstein's later work. She took it that there was something basically right in the picture-theory account of the sorts of propositions that have the possibility of truth and the possibility of falsehood, and that there was also something right in the *Tractatus* contrast between such propositions and propositions that can only be true. What she objected to, and thought needed to be changed, was the narrowness of Wittgenstein's conception, in the *Tractatus*, of the second category. One can begin to see what she has in view from her example, "'Someone' is not the name of someone", but that is not an isolated sort of case, and resembles other sorts of responses to what may be taken to be confusion or some other kind of going-wrong of thought. The intelligibility of what we may say in response to confusion, or to other kinds of ways in which thought miscarries, may depend on the context: on the confusions and miscarriages of thought themselves. Anscombe's treatment of her example goes, I think, with rejecting any conception of the semantic uniformity of declarative sentences that would not take deeply enough the distinction between propositions that have the possibility of truth and of falsity and propositions that do not. In allowing for solo propositions, for significant declarative sentences which lack significant negations, an Anscombean approach differs from that of Wiggins on what possible kinds of thinking may be involved in ethics and thus also on what different possibilities

---

[32] See especially David Wiggins, "Meaning and Truth Conditions: From Frege's Grand Design to Davidson's", in *A Companion to the Philosophy of Language*, ed. Bob Hale and Crispin Wright (Oxford: Blackwell, 1999), pp. 3–28.

[33] See Wiggins, "Truth, and Truth as Predicated of Moral Judgments", in *Needs, Values, Truth* (Oxford: Blackwell, 1991), pp. 139–84.

there are for what truth in ethics might be. I have not tried to argue for an Anscombean approach as opposed to a Wigginsean one. I have wanted to show that there are possibilities here; there is a kind of approach—but it is an approach that has had no place in our picture of how we can think about thinking, about language and about ethics.[34]

---

[34] An earlier version of this paper was read at a meeting of the Jowett Society in Oxford. I am very grateful to members of the audience for their questions and comments, to Steven Methven and John Haldane for their helpful suggestions, and to Adrian Moore for his clarification of David Wiggins' views on truth.

Roger Teichmann

The Identity of a Word

1

Does the word "rat" occur in the sentence "Socrates loved Plato"? There is *one* way of taking this question such that the answer to it is Yes, namely the one whereby the answer is No when we replace "rat" by "sausage". But there is another way of taking it such that the answer is No, and where we would say "Only three words occur in that sentence: 'Socrates', 'loved' and 'Plato'".

According to this second reading of the question, and of similar questions, how shall we answer the following: does the word "Plato" occur in "Plato loved if"? Of course the letters p-l-a-t-o occur in that order, but that can't be enough, given that we are denying the occurrence of "rat" in "Socrates loved Plato". There is a gap after "Plato", if we are speaking of the written sentence (or "sentence"); but what if our inquiry concerns speech, rather than writing? Well, if you say those sounds, someone writing down what you say is likely to write "Plato loved if", with just those gaps between the words. But their doing so appears a matter of decision on their part, maybe influenced by precise vocal inflexions. For why not write down "Play toe loved if"?

It's tempting to put the question here, "Did you *mean* 'Plato' or 'play toe' when you said it?" But what would it be for me to have meant "Plato"? "Plato loved if" is after all meaningless. Is the issue one of whether the word, or the man, came before my mind as I spoke? In *that* sense I might mean "rat" when I say "Socrates loved Plato". But we are meant to be construing "Does X occur in...?" in such a way that "rat" does not occur in "Socrates loved Plato". Moreover, nothing relevant may come before my mind when I say "Plato loved if"; or I might have both "Plato" and "play toe" in mind, e.g. if discussing this very question.

I might of course say "Plato loved if" — or rather "Plato, loved, if" — if I am reading out answers to crossword clues, or saying what the first words on pp. 1, 2 and 3 of a book are. In that case I can be said to have meant the word "Plato", in the sense of knowingly and intentionally uttering that word, the name of a Greek philosopher. And if somebody (over)hears me say "Plato loved if", he may well take me to be uttering the three words in some kind of list, the truth-value of his surmise depending on what procedure it was I was actually engaged in. By contrast, if a parrot began calling out what sounded like "Plato loved if", one could not claim that it was saying "Plato" rather than "play toe".

If the question is whether "Plato loved if" can count as an English sentence, in which the words collaborate and are not simply thrown together, it seems we can answer by reference to inferential relations. "Plato loved Socrates" is inferentially related to various other sentences, such as "Plato loved somebody", "Somebody loved Socrates", "Either Plato loved Socrates or I'm a Dutchman" and so on. And this is not true of "Plato loved if". It does not, for example, entail "Plato loved if or snow is white". We can discuss the sentence "Plato loved Socrates" and its inferential relations without considering any actual assertive use of it, though in saying that it e.g. entails some other proposition, we are in part saying what an assertive use of it *would* commit the speaker to, etc. And we assume that the speaker, if asked "What do you mean by that first word?", would be the one who replies, "I mean the Greek philosopher, Plato" — rather than the one who replies, "It's the answer to 7 down: 'Plato'; and the answer to 8 down is 'loved'..." When we said above that "rat" does not occur in "Socrates loved Plato", we made a similar assumption as to what would count as an assertive use of that string of letters or sounds.

Someone might still insist that the name "Plato" occurs in the written string "Plato loved if", regardless of any background activity or practice (such as listing answers to clues). For haven't we put gaps between the words to show what they are? But the rule "Put gaps around all words, and only words, when writing" requires that we *already* discern and distinguish words. The rule can after all be broken, e.g. if I write "Every day language is not always perspicuous". My *decision* to put a gap between "every" and "day" does not result in there being two words, and no such decision will all by itself make it true that there are three words in "Plato loved if". For us to discern the word "Plato" in "Plato loved if" requires justification. Now is it a justification to point out that one who wrote out this string would be likely to know that there exist the three words in question, and to have some purpose in writing them down? We could call that a justification if we wanted to; but this notion of justification would not really go beyond the facts cited (that one who wrote the string would be likely to know, etc.), and would moreover differ significantly from that given for saying that "Plato" occurs in "Socrates loved Plato".

Consider now the following:

(PC) "Plato is the cube root of some rose."

We had to justify saying that "Plato" occurs in the string "Plato loved if"; do we not also need to justify saying that "Plato" occurs in PC? Someone might argue that PC differs from "Plato loved if", for either or both of the following reasons: (i) no special story about a "background activity" (such as listing crossword answers) is needed to justify the claim that "Plato" occurs in PC; (ii) "Plato" is not just an element in some list in PC: it is working in collaboration with the other words, as it does in "Socrates loved Plato" — working as the name of a person.

These two claims are likely to be themselves justified by the observation that PC is at any rate a *grammatical* sentence. But what are the "rules of grammar" it is meant to conform to? Any such rules will pick out certain categories of expression, such as verb, adjective, noun — and it will be alleged that a grammatical sentence is one in which expressions are combined "in the right way", as determined solely by their grammatical categories. Two problems now arise. First, there is more than one way of delineating grammatical categories; to some extent, delineation is stipulation. Secondly, if we take PC to be grammatical, we are assuming that "rose" occurs as a noun in it, rather than as the past tense of the verb "rise"; and what could justify this assumption?

Taking the second problem first, the only available answer seems to be something like, "It *has* to be the noun if the sentence is to be grammatical". After all, won't we say some such thing if asked whether "rose" is a noun or a verb in "He gave her a red rose"? Perhaps there is a sort of circularity involved in calling the latter sentence grammatical: for to do so, we have to assume that "rose" occurs as a noun, not a verb, and this assumption is apparently based on the requirement of taking the sentence to be grammatical. But the circularity is not vicious. For it is a practical necessity involved in language use that someone who has achieved linguistic mastery take a sentence in the most natural way, where this involves both assuming (if possible) that it's grammatical, and being generally in (actual or potential) agreement with others in the linguistic community as to how to understand it. The training that leads to this results in a person's being able to take a sentence or word a certain way without calculation or reasons.[1] If reasons *were* required, the circularity above mentioned would arise and would indeed be vicious, and language use could not get off the ground.

A moment ago I mentioned agreement in how to understand a sentence. Will there be such agreement in connection with PC? Well, understanding a sentence means in part being able to make inferences to and from it, and can't I and others e.g. infer "Plato is a cube root" from PC? It may be asked why this inference is any better than the inference of "Plato loved if or snow is white" from "Plato loved if"; each "inference" seems to be a purely formal manoeuvre. Of course, "cube root" is a noun phrase, and "if" is a conjunction. And it will be said that our rules of inference are framed in terms of grammatical, or logico-grammatical, categories, so that the inference of "Plato is a cube root" from PC is akin to the inference of "Plato is an author" from "Plato is the author of the *Cratylus*", both "author" and "cube root" being nouns/noun phrases.

This brings us to the first problem I mentioned, namely that there are different possible grammars. In one sort of grammar, the word "three", in "I have three cats", counts as an adjective, belonging in the same category as "red", "big" and "non-existent". But if adjectives get explained as words that describe things, we have good reason to exclude "three" (which as Frege showed does not describe any cats, in "I have three cats", nor yet in "My cats are three [in number]"). And there are further reasons for putting numerals into a separate grammatical category, such as that they only "go with" count-nouns – obviously – "There are three heats" being ill-formed. Reasons can also be given for putting "big" in a different category from, say, "red": for "big" functions as an

---

[1] This connects with the fact, as Cora Diamond (speaking for Frege) puts it, that "the rules of the language are in a sense permissions, though conditional ones: to make sense of a sentence is to apply such rules, but it is still a *making* sense, and not a mere recognition of what the pieces are and how they are combined, plus a following of the directions-for-use that have been determined for the individual pieces and their mode of combination". See Cora Diamond, "What Nonsense Might Be", in *The Realistic Spirit* (Cambridge, MA: MIT Press, 1991), pp. 95–114, at p. 111.

attributive adjective (in Geach's sense[2]), so that from "Tim is a big mouse" you cannot infer a self-standing proposition "Tim is big". For "Tim is a small mammal" is also true, and if the inference to "Tim is big" worked, so would an inference to "Tim is small", and we would get a contradiction.

In "A Theory of Language?" Elizabeth Anscombe discusses this issue, writing: "The difference of opinion about what belongs to grammar arises from belief in and practice of a 'formal' science of grammar on the one hand, and a study of what a given use of words amounts to or achieves or tells us on the other."[3] The philosopher who would insist that PC is grammatical has in mind the idea of a formal science of grammar, concerned only with "structure" and "form". It is a formal rule that you can't put a finite verb after "the". But why not say that it is likewise a formal rule that you can't attach a numerical concept to a personal name, as in "Plato is a cube root"? It would seem to beg the question to reply that *numerical concept* is not a grammatical category.

The fact is that the first of the two notions of grammar alluded to by Anscombe cannot be kept utterly distinct from the second. Relatedly, it seems impossible to define "grammatical" in terms of formal rules governing independently graspable categories of expression: the delineation of those categories itself depends to some extent on what we are inclined to call "grammatical" or "ungrammatical", the latter being a close cousin of "nonsensical". Isn't "There were three heats in the house" ungrammatical? How about "London's half-heavy pertinence is buttery"? If the answer is Yes, then there is a case for saying such things as that "pertinence" belongs to a different grammatical category from "horse" (not that simply substituting "horse" for "pertinence" cures that particular sentence). The interdependence between the notion of the grammatical, on the one hand, and the rationale(s) for proposing certain grammatical categories, on the other, is related to that interdependence mentioned above, between the question whether S is grammatical and the question what grammatical category some constituent of S belongs to (e.g. with regard to "He gave her a red rose" and "rose").

---

[2] See Peter Geach, "Good and Evil", *Analysis*, 17, 1956: 32–42.
[3] G.E.M. Anscombe, "A Theory of Language?", in *From Plato to Wittgenstein: Essays by G.E.M. Anscombe*, ed. M. Geach and L. Gormally (Exeter: Imprint Academic, 2011), pp. 193–203, at p. 201.

Given all this, shall we say that the name "Plato" occurs in PC? We can say Yes, on the view I've been considering, so long as PC is grammatical. But in that case we can say Yes or No, depending on how fine-grained our grammar is; for evidently there is a case for having a grammar in which *numerical expression* is a grammatical category, with attendant rules about which expressions can properly be attached to a numerical expression—such a case as we saw hinted at in relation to "three". This does not go for "Plato loved Socrates", since there is no degree of fine-grainedness of grammatical categorization which would justify calling the sentence ungrammatical.

I said that a choice of a grammar depends to some extent on what we are inclined to call grammatical sentences. The sort of inclination I have in mind is one that would be backed up by considerations of "what a given use of words amounts to or achieves or tells us", in Anscombe's words. And our data here include such things as that an assertion of "Plato is the cube root of some rose" would achieve or tell us nothing, in the relevant sense—though it could have various effects on listeners and even aim at such effects. This datum is connected with the fact that we cannot identify the use of "Plato" in this sentence with its use in such a sentence as "Socrates loved Plato": the two sentences do not belong together in a unified or unitary linguistic practice.

The foregoing remarks relate to the question whether a certain word occurs in a given sentence, or "sentence". And of course a word can occur without occurring in a sentence. I can look a word up in a dictionary and find the entry for it, at the head of which occurs the word itself. Assertive uses and inferential relations have nothing to do with this mode of occurrence. But why do we say that e.g. the word "rebarbative" occurs on page 607 of the Oxford English Dictionary, and is the *same* word that occurs in "Henry was being rebarbative"? The answer is that there is a *connection* between these uses, these linguistic phenomena: the first phenomenon is an instance of a convention, a convention with a point or purpose (or points, purposes)—by which e.g. someone who encounters "rebarbative" in a sentence like "Henry is rebarbative" and finds it unfamiliar can read something likely to enable him to understand the sentence, produce similar sentences himself, etc. The convention itself rests on certain background conventions, notably those of spelling and of an alphabetical order.

The fact that "if" occurs in the dictionary unbuttressed by other words, as the head of an entry, is not enough to show that it occurs in similar unbuttressed fashion in "Plato loved if". To repeat our earlier point, what would be needed to show that "if" occurred in some written or spoken production of "Plato loved if" would be a reference to some background activity, practice or convention, sufficiently determinate in its rules for there to be answers to such questions as "What word is that [e.g. pointing to a string of letters]?", where such questions are *not* like "What word did that parrot's squawk remind you of?" Examples of such activities and practices are: reading out quiz answers, listing your favourite words ... and also writing in code. If there were a code in which "if" meant "Socrates", then not only would the string "Plato loved if" include an occurrence of "Plato", but that occurrence would be the same sort of occurrence as the occurrence in "Plato loved Socrates": i.e. as the name of a man about whom one is saying something.

2

In "A Theory of Language?" Anscombe's main goal is to consider two questions: whether it is in principle possible to construct a theory of language, where this means a "micro-reductionist" account of what it is for a sound (or written shape, etc.) to be meaningful; and more specifically, whether Wittgenstein can be read in the *Philosophical Investigations* (hereafter *PI*)[4] as proposing, or pointing towards, such a theory — the nub of the theory being expressed in the statement "A sound is an expression only in a particular language-game".[5] Her answer to the question about Wittgenstein is No, and it seems likely it would be No to the more general question also. Anscombe's argument is difficult and obscure; but one important strand in it is the challenge, for a "micro-reductionist" theory of language, of specifying what it is for the same expression to occur in different contexts.

The basic case we will have in mind is where the same sound occurring in two different contexts counts as the same expression.[6]

---

[4] Ludwig Wittgenstein, *Philosophical Investigations*, ed. G.E.M. Anscombe and Rush Rhees, trans. G.E.M. Anscombe (Oxford: Blackwell, 1953).
[5] This is a fragment of a longer sentence occurring in *PI* 261. See G.E.M. Anscombe, "A Theory of Language?", in *From Plato to Wittgenstein: Essays by G.E.M. Anscombe*, ed. M. Geach and L. Gormally (Exeter: Imprint Academic, 2011), pp. 193–203, at p. 193.
[6] The term "expression" includes words, phrases, exclamations, sentences…

And we will want to say, as above, that the sound "rat" in "Socrates loved Plato" is *not* the same expression as the same sound in "There's a rat in the attic". Anscombe focusses on "Slab", which is of course one of the few words that together comprise the primitive language-game described by Wittgenstein in *PI* 2. We can imagine that language-game being added to and expanded in a variety of ways, and to any extent. If it is so expanded as to include the phrase "This lab work", understood as we understand it, then the word "slab" will not occur in that phrase, any more than did "rat" in "Socrates loved Plato". Anscombe writes:

> Whatever "language-game" you may introduce "This lab work" into, if this is the familiar phrase, the concatenation of the S phoneme with the cluster l-a-b isn't morphemic. — But now, of course, we want to know the criterion for morphemic as opposed to phonemic concatenation.[7]

The reason why this last question is difficult is that it is unclear what the difference is between "mattering for the meaning" and "making a meaning-contribution".

> Shall we say: by itself the phoneme S does not have the kind of role we mean, the role of the sound in the language-game, but only when combined with other phonemes to make the sound "slab"? Only the sequence has that role, and the single phoneme's contribution is that it is part of that sequence. To be sure the individual phoneme matters, witness the difference between "slab" and "slat"; we can't deny that it "matters for the meaning".[8]

We would like to say of cases such as "slab" vs. "slat" that a single phoneme, e.g. B, may "matter for the meaning", but will *not* "make a meaning-contribution"; and Anscombe's challenge (which she goes on to articulate) is for us to explain and justify this distinction. A "micro-reductionist" theory of the English language will have failed if it classifies the phoneme B as an expression; but how is it to avoid doing so, given that B does often matter for the meaning, make a difference to the meaning? How is the sound B to be denied a "role in the language-game"?

---

[7] G.E.M. Anscombe, "A Theory of Language?", in *From Plato to Wittgenstein: Essays by G.E.M. Anscombe*, ed. M. Geach and L. Gormally (Exeter: Imprint Academic, 2011), pp. 193–203, at p. 196.
[8] Ibid.

Anscombe's use of the notions of morphemic and phonemic concatenation is worth remarking upon. It is no doubt motivated in part by the fact that her inquiry cannot be conducted using the simple notions of morpheme and phoneme, as these are usually defined. In particular, the way "morpheme" is usually defined makes it unfit for our purposes. The *OED* definition is: "A minimal and indivisible morphological unit that cannot be analysed into smaller units." "Morphology" in linguistics is defined in the *OED* thus: "The structure, form, or variation in form (including formation, change, and inflection) of a word or words in a language"; and the general notion of *form* or *structure* will not, unaided, allow us to deny that the "rat" in "Socrates" is a morpheme — for it is certainly a structural part of the word "Socrates". (One sort of word-structure, among many, is syllabic structure.) Hence a more useful definition would seem to be Merriam-Webster's: "a word or a part of a word that has a meaning and that contains no smaller part that has a meaning." But again, "rat" has a meaning. What we want to say is that it does not have meaning *as it occurs in "Socrates"* And the standard definitions of "morpheme" do not help us with this idea of "meaning something (or: meaning X) when occurring in such-and-such a context".

Returning to Anscombe: could we perhaps distinguish the word "slab" from the same sound in "this lab work" by reference to those "connections" between uses of language which I discussed earlier, exemplified by inferences, by dictionary entries, by crossword clues and so on? Could we not say that there will be no such suitable connections between uses of "this lab work" and uses of the word "slab"? But this would be to presuppose that we can already identify *uses of the word "slab"*, i.e. occurrences of that sound in morphemic combinations. And doesn't this mean that we would be taking the identities of words as given, something which would undermine micro-reductionist goals?

However, in the basic case, identifying uses of the word "slab" is the same as identifying utterances of the sound "slab" in certain sorts of situations, involving certain human interactions (the bringing of slabs and so on). An explanation of the meaning of "slab" would consist in showing how that sound is used in such situations. Hence, were we to advert to "connections between uses of language", with the aim of distinguishing the word "slab" from the same sound in "this lab work", we need not be illicitly presupposing a criterion (or criteria) of word-identity. We need only presuppose the ability to see certain situations as belonging together: that in which A utters "Slab!" in the presence of B, who then picks up *this* thing and carries it over to A—that in which B utters "Slab!" in the presence of C, who then picks up *that* thing and carries it over to B—etc. And we will claim that a normal human being with this ability will *not* see as belonging with those situations one in which "this lab work" gets uttered (e.g. by someone holding a sheaf of papers, having earlier written on those papers after doing things with test tubes...). The idea of a normal human being is here playing the sort of role which is indicated by Wittgenstein's phrase "form of life".

But now consider those earlier-mentioned additions to and developments of the original language-game involving "slab". Wittgenstein imagines two developments: (1) the addition of "here" and "there", used with pointing gestures, and (2) the addition of "a", "b", "c" and "d", which are used in (as we should say) *counting* slabs, pillars, etc. Does the sound "slab" in "d slab there" mean the same—is it the same word—as the sound "slab" which was being used before the introduction of the new symbols? The uses of the latter sound were utterances of it in certain sorts of situation, situations which a normal human being would see as "belonging together". The sort of situation in which "d slab there" gets uttered are ones e.g. where A utters it in the presence of B, who then carries four slabs, one after the other, to a spot at a distance from A (A's having pointed his finger at that spot). Surely this looks like quite a *new* sort of situation?

Anscombe regards the statement that the same word "slab" is being used both before and after the introduction of the new symbols as a *stipulation*. It is Wittgenstein's describing matters thus that determines that it is so, just as it is Shakespeare's saying that "Horatio" is the name of Hamlet's friend that determines that *that* is so. But it is a permissible stipulation, because of what Wittgenstein's aims are in the opening paragraphs of *PI*. Anscombe sums these aims up thus:

> The "clear and simple language-games" are offered as objects of comparison, not models—to give us the idea of the possible functioning of a word in use, without even invoking that of

meaning. For "it [the idea of meaning] surrounds our considerations with a fog".⁹

It is this contrast between objects of comparison and models that is important for Anscombe's case that Wittgenstein is not in the business of presenting us with a theory of language. Were he offering his "clear and simple language-games" as models of language in general, his remarks about those language-games would appear to point towards a general account of language. But in that context, his statement e.g. that the same word "slab" is being used both before and after the introduction of the new symbols would be "positively fraudulent",[10] because question-begging.

And yet we surely *can* say that a normal human being would, or could, see the new developments of the builders' language *as* developments of it—and not as a distinct set of proceedings. They are still evidently putting up buildings, they are still cooperating in characteristic ways (perhaps they have a foreman with authority over the others), it is still slabs and pillars they are carrying around and placing here and there... It need not even be the same set of builders who are employing what I have called the new symbols; a person coming across a case of the more developed language-game would surely be inclined to see it as a more sophisticated version of the less developed language-game, on account of the human activities in which the two are embedded. And on that account he would surely be within his rights to say that the same word "slab" occurred in both language-games. That verdict need not be *compulsory*, since the idea of one language-game's being a development of another supplies a permissive, rather than a compelling, reason. But the verdict "same word" would be a perfectly natural and intelligible one. If asked "What *determines* the sameness here?" we could reply, "The natural response (=judgement) of the normal human being".

Hence I think Anscombe may be mistaken to speak here of mere stipulation on Wittgenstein's part. Her description of what he is aiming at in the opening paragraphs of *PI* might well, on the other hand, be perfectly accurate. Anscombe could, however, raise the following awkward question: if it is all right to say that the same word "slab" occurs both in the original language-game and

---

[9] *Ibid.*, p. 199.
[10] *Ibid.*, p. 198.

in the more sophisticated one, and is thus the same expression, *what category of expression is it*? We surely cannot talk of "same expression" without being in a position to say "same verb", "same noun", "same imperative" or whatever. But in the context of the "developed" language-game, it is easily imaginable that the utterance of "Slab!" will produce puzzlement, in roughly the way in which an English-speaker's shouting "Slabs!" on a building-site might. The utterance may force such questions as "How many do you want?" and "Where do you want them?", something that was not the case in the original language-game; and in fact it would not be at all clear that the sound "slab", uttered thus in the developed language-game, had any function at all, on its own — let alone the function of an imperative, as we might have hoped. At any rate, it would be unclear that it had any function on its own in the case where the builders *no longer* utter "Slab!" on its own and as tantamount to "Bring me a slab".

There is, however, much to be said against the statement made a moment ago, that we cannot talk of "same expression" without being in a position to say "same verb", "same noun", "same imperative" or whatever. The notion *same expression* is extremely versatile, even protean. In Anscombe's words:

> Language and human capacity are so complex that e.g. different words can come to be counted as in some way the same word. Cf. different *inflections*, as we call them. Or it might be that one used a different sound the next time: "Slab," "Tink," "Noffle" might all be the "same word" — you say "Tink" if *last* time you said "Slab," etc. but otherwise the role is the same. I don't know of any language in which that happens, but it *might*.[11]

"Slab" and "Tink" are evidently the same imperative (if either is to be called an imperative, that is). But consider "She is going", "She goes" and "She will go". These involve different inflections (different tenses) of the same verb, it is usual to say. Does that mean that the words "going" and "go" in the first and third sentences are *not* the same expression as "goes" in the second sentence? For e.g. the future-tensed verb in the third sentence is not "go" — it is "will go". The "go" in the third sentence we might call an infinitive, and an infinitive verb is surely not the very same expression as a corresponding finite verb. Meanwhile, "going" appears to be an

---

[11] *Ibid.*, p. 195.

adjective—unless we take it to be simply a fragment of "is going", not belonging to any part of speech itself.[12] But there surely *is* a sense in which "goes," going" and "go" are all the same expression—or if you like, forms of the same expression?

For certain purposes we may call "goes", "going" and "go" the same expression, while *for certain other purposes* we may call them different expressions. And in the first case, whether we also speak of the same verb, or the same anything, will likewise depend on what purposes we have, i.e. on what use it would be to us to say so.[13] All this, I think, goes also for "slab" as spoken in the original builders' language-game and as spoken in the developed builders' language-game.

A "micro-reductionist" theory of language inspired by the opening paragraphs of the *Philosophical Investigations* will contain statements of the form: "Sound S is meaningful (is an expression of the language) in virtue of its playing such-and-such a role in the language-game." The character of the normal human being, analogous to that of the reasonable person as referred to in legal judgments, is on hand to guarantee that situations in which the expression "slab" is used do not belong with ones in which "this lab work" is used, and that the various situation-groups in which uses of "this lab work" are to be found do not show the sound "slab" as playing a distinctive role. Other sounds occurring in those situation-groups *will* play such distinctive roles, e.g. "lab"; and this is connected with the fact that explanations of meaning can be derived from consideration of the uses of those sounds, but no explanation of meaning for the sound "slab" can be thus derived. The notion of a role in the language-game appears, in this account, to be in the eye of the beholder, the beholder being "the normal human being"—but this should be no objection against the micro-reductionist theory of language, given the Wittgensteinian

---

[12] It of course belongs to the part of speech *present participle*. But although that concept appears in grammar books, someone might still say "But (here) it only functions as a fragment of the genuine grammatical unit, 'is going'. After all, in French that would just be 'va'". The issues here evidently tie in with those mentioned earlier, to do with differences of opinion about what to count as grammatical categories.

[13] A relevant concept here, it might be said, is that of the verb stem. "Goes", "going" and "go" all share a verb stem, viz. "go". But even if the purport of this statement is quite clear, it does not dictate an answer to "Same expression or different expressions?"

equivalence between intersubjectivity and objectivity (to put the matter briefly). The normal human being does provide a standard, and if this standard does not yield concepts with sharp edges, it is no worse for that.

But will the normal human being judge that the original "slab" plays the same role as the sound "slab" in the new sentence "d slab there"? Will she judge that "goes" plays the same role as "going"? What about the English word "in", as it appears in "I have a pain in my foot," "Smith has written a commentary in this book", "They are in a muddle", "They are in a huddle", "John is in London" ...? How many roles are played by the sound "in" in such cases? (We could add "in such cases".) This last question is evidently void for uncertainty, the uncertainty arising from the fact that no *purposes* are specified or understood, relative to which the applications of "same role" and "same expression" might be justified in a given case. The normal human being will be powerless to judge how many roles a sound is playing in the absence of any purpose that might be served by the adoption of one criterion of role-sameness as against another.

And this does seem to spell trouble for our micro-reductionist theory of language. For the theory states that we could in principle proceed as follows: first, detect and classify those sounds which appear repeatedly in contexts of language use; secondly, determine which of those sounds play some role in a language-game. The second task would be the same as: determining which situations, of those in which certain sounds repeatedly occur, a normal human being would see as belonging together in the sort of way that meant that an explanation of the meaning of those sounds could be derived. (Such "derivation" is of course not to be thought of as *proof*-like.) There are two problems: (a) there are indefinitely many different ways of "taking situations as belonging together in the sort of way that means that an explanation of the meaning of the sounds can be derived"; and (b) an explanation of meaning, even if in some sense derived from (consideration of) a certain group of situations, does not on that account delimit what situations in which the sound appears count as ones in which it appears with that meaning.

Problem (b) can be illustrated as follows. An explanation of the meaning of the original word "slab" that works by showing how it gets used on the building-site will not determine for us *in advance* whether the use of "slab" in "d slab there" counts as the same use, or a new one; and indeed either verdict could be given, depending on what our purposes were in adopting the given criterion of sameness.[14] For certain purposes (and here problem (a) becomes relevant), we can take the *totality* of situations, original and later, involving the sound "slab", and see *them* as belonging together in the sort of way that means that an explanation of the meaning of "slab" can be derived. To be sure, the explanation would *look* different from the one we imagined in connection with the original word "slab"; but this is compatible with our regarding the two explanations as explanations of the same word with the same meaning. Remember that explanations of meaning come in all sorts of guises, as Wittgenstein stressed so effectively; cf. the explanation of "game" in *PI* 69: "How should we explain to someone what a game is? I imagine that we should describe [sc. specific] *games* to him, and we might add: 'This *and similar things* are called "games".'" For the sake of the interlocutor who thinks there must be such a thing as *the* ("complete") definition of any expression, he adds: "And do we know any more about it ourselves? Is it only other people whom we cannot tell exactly what a game is?"[15]

3

Anscombe's denial of the possibility of a micro-reductionist theory of language inspired by the opening paragraphs of *PI* thus seems to be right. What about other kinds of micro-reductionist theory of language? All such theories will need to be able to explain why the word "slab" does not occur in "this lab work". And they will face Anscombe's challenge of distinguishing between "mattering for the meaning" and "making a meaning-contribution": they will need to be equipped to say, when it comes to "slab" vs. "slat", that a single phoneme, e.g. B, matters for the meaning, but does not make a meaning-contribution. Finally, they will need to give some sort of account of when two sounds[16] uttered in different contexts count as the same expression, with the same meaning. Such an

---

[14] Thus the present point does not have to do with "rule-scepticism", of the sort associated with Kripke's Wittgenstein; it concerns rather an indeterminacy that is consequent upon *theoretical abstraction* — the doing without reference to those concrete human purposes which alone could provide any determinacy.
[15] Wittgenstein, *PI* 69.
[16] Here as elsewhere, "sounds" is an abbreviation of "sounds, inscriptions, etc."

account may allow for some indeterminacy, some fuzzy cases, etc., but an account there must be.[17]

Jeff Speaks, the author of the online *Stanford Encyclopedia of Philosophy* entry for "Theories of Meaning", writes that there are basically two kinds of theory of meaning, which should not be confused:

> One sort of theory of meaning — a *semantic theory* — is a specification of the meanings of the words and sentences of some symbol system. Semantic theories thus answer the question, "What is the meaning of this or that expression?" A distinct sort of theory — a *foundational theory of meaning* — tries to explain what about some person or group gives the symbols of their language the meanings that they have.[18]

The first sort of theory of meaning, as described, would be tantamount to a dictionary. Is a dictionary a theory? In fact, what Speaks has in mind turns out more to resemble general theories *about* symbol systems, and about types of symbol; hence his taking semantic theories to address such questions as "What sorts of things are contents?" and "What is the relationship between content and reference?" Be all that as it may, the sort of microreductionist theory of language we have been discussing would I suppose be classified by Speaks as a foundational theory of meaning. He divides such theories into mentalist and non-mentalist varieties, the latter including causal theories, regularity theories and social norms theories. An illustration of the sort of thing on offer is the following description of a proposal of David Lewis:

---

[17] David Kaplan proposes a criterion of word-identity that focusses on the speaker's or writer's intention, writing: "The identification of word uttered or inscribed with one heard or read is not a matter of resemblance between the two physical embodiments (the two utterances, the two inscriptions, or the one utterance and one inscription). Rather it is a matter of intrapersonal continuity, a matter of intention: Was it *repetition*?" [i.e. did the person intend to repeat a word, however incompetently?] It is not wholly clear, but it looks as if Kaplan might have to say that if I intend to refer to a sort of animal when I utter the "rat" in "Socrates loved Plato", then I do refer to that animal. See David Kaplan, "Words", *Aristotelian Society Supplementary Volume*, 64, 1990: 93–119, at p. 104.

[18] Jeff Speaks, "Theories of Meaning", *Stanford Encyclopedia of Philosophy*, last modified 23 April 2014, http://plato.stanford.edu/entries/meaning/.

His idea was that the assignment of contents to expressions of our language is fixed, not just by the constraint that the right interpretation will maximize the truth of our utterances, but by picking the interpretation which does best at jointly satisfying the constraints of truth-maximization and the constraint that the referents of our terms should, as much as possible, be "the ones that respect the objective joints in nature".[19]

Lewis is considering what "interpretation" of linguistic phenomena would give the right answer, e.g., to "What does 'slab' mean in this community?" The answer would "assign content" to that expression. What would such an answer look like? Perhaps it would take the form "The word 'slab' has the content C".[20] The expression "C" would presumably be a synonym of "slab"; we are evidently in the (putatively) lexicographical domain of "semantic theories of meaning". Of course even dictionaries do not only assign contents to words by giving synonyms or analyses, as is indeed impossible for vast numbers of words ("the", "akimbo", "sky", "every", "number", "hello", "in" ...). But Lewis can hardly allow for a healthy liberalism as to what shall count as an adequate content-assignment, given that the imagined "right interpretation" must involve our really *pinpointing* the meanings of expressions. "A variety of dog" would be no good, for instance.

All is not lost, however, so long as we "pick the interpretation which does best at jointly satisfying the constraints of truth-maximization and the constraint that the referents of our terms should, as much as possible, be 'the ones that respect the objective joints in nature'". It is to be supposed that most—or most of the important—expressions in our language are referring terms. And the meanings of these building-blocks may be best assigned by assuming that they "respect the objective joints in nature". (We presumably already know ourselves what the objective joints in nature are, having—at some point—perfected our science.) We should like "rabbit" to line up with a certain species of animal, rather than with some weird disjunction of properties. The question will arise *how* "rabbit" comes to line up with the first and not the second.

---

[19] David Lewis, "Putnam's Paradox", in *Australasian Journal of Philosophy*, 62 (3) 1984: 221–236, at p. 227.
[20] It might e.g. read: "The word 'slab' has the content *noffle*." See p. 297, above.

A popular answer to this last question invokes causal origin: if the causal origin of a use (or uses) of "rabbit" is perception of or interaction with actual rabbits, then "rabbit" refers to that natural kind, and not to some weird disjunction of properties. It is suggested that the linguistic theories originally adumbrated by Kripke and Putnam can be extended from the cases of proper names and natural kind terms to the rest of language, or to a sufficiently large chunk of it. How would a causal theory of meaning address some of the questions raised earlier in this article?

The word "rat" does not appear in "Socrates loved Plato". Let us assume that the meaning of some utterance of the word "rat" is down to the causal origins of that utterance; if there is a (non-deviant) causal connection between rats and a given utterance of "rat", then and only then will "rat" mean what it means in "There's a rat in that cage". But what if, in my utterance of "Socrates loved Plato", my production of "rat" is as a matter of fact the effect of previous interaction with rats? This is surely not logically impossible. The philosopher could bite the bullet and say, "In that case you do mean the animal". But this would have to be retracted if my explanation of my words was along the lines of: "I mean that the famous Greek philosopher Socrates, associated with the dialectical method, loved his pupil Plato, author of the *Cratylus*". The philosopher might now allege that since this was my explanation, the causal connection with rats must have been "deviant". But that just shows he is admitting as primary the connection between what a person means and the phenomenon of explanation of meaning (verbal, ostensive or what have you).[21] A causal connection is not in itself deviant or non-deviant. And hand-waving about "the intention to refer to the same thing as the people you learnt the word from" will not help matters.

---

[21] There is no supreme first-person authority in such explanations. I can't sensibly explain my utterance of "Socrates loved Plato" by saying, "I mean that causalism is a philosophical dead end"; or rather, I can't in the absence of some background practice or game, such as a prearranged code. For the default background practice is that of English language-use. The lack of supreme first-person authority here also means that you do not establish the occurrence of the name "Plato" in PC just by laying it down that you would (or could) explain your use of "Plato" in the usual way, i.e. as the name of a Greek philosopher, etc. Despite all this, a person's non-frivolous and sincere explanation of what she means or meant evidently has a default weight.

Of course to interpret "Socrates loved Plato" as involving the name of the animal is anyway ruled out on account of that interpretation's leaving the whole sentence in the lurch. We would have to ask: what then do "Soc", "es", "loved", "Plato" mean here? Perhaps causal origins can be found for all these uttered sounds. But evidently a little holism is necessary: among other things, we do need to be able to point to other situations in which the same sounds occur, with a view to finding those in which the sounds mean the same as in our first situation. The hopeful theorist who claims, in advance, that we'd be able to find (not that we'd ever be able to make the investigation) that what we *want* to call the "same expressions" all do have the same (sorts of?) causal origins invites the Humean query: "And is this a truth of reason? — of experience? — Or is it a product of the imagination?"

Part of the diagnosis of the problem is surely to be found in the phrase which Speaks uses in the above quotation: "the assignment of contents to expressions of our language." There is a strong suspicion that the "theorist" has already got a list of the expressions of a language, and now wants to determine what they mean. But how would one have sorted out, from the jumble of noises and inscriptions that constitute a language, what the expressions of that language are? The expressions are the meaningful bits; is it that we could know that a certain sound was meaningful without knowing its meaning? This might be conceivable for a particular sound, but it seems inconceivable as applied to all the sounds discerned prior to the task of "interpretation". Of course Speaks could respond, for Lewis, that he is indeed assuming that he has a list of meaningful expressions, and that it is no part of his task to sort out, from the jumble of noises and inscriptions that constitute a language, what its expressions are. He takes *that* task as having been done. In other words, the hoped-for foundational theory is not intended as micro-reductionist. This would certainly explain the apparent lack of interest in such questions as whether "this lab work" contains the word "slab"; but it is worth noting that what is referred to as a "foundational theory" turns out to presuppose its own underlying foundations.

4

What, then, can we say about what it is for one sound to be the same expression as another sound, uttered in a different context?

In Section 1, I emphasized how specific forms of this question might be answered by appeal to such *connections* between the uses of the sounds as are exemplified by inferences, by crosswords, by dictionary entries, by codes, and in general by appeal to what can be called *background human practices and activities*. The terminology is obviously, and benignly, vague. By considering the different species of "connections" that we count as such, a philosopher comes to see how extremely versatile and variable is the notion of "the same expression". This is something of which Anscombe is evidently aware, and in Section 2 we saw how problems with the notion of "the same expression" are connected by her with difficulties in explaining the difference between morphemic and phonemic concatenation, and with correlative obstacles to the construction of what she calls micro-reductionist theories of language. She also brings to our attention the interdependence between what we are inclined to take as grammatical categories and what sentences we are inclined to take for nonsense—an interdependence that, once again, constitutes an obstacle for reductionism, in the form of "bottom up" theories of grammar.

The lessons to be learnt are not only in the philosophy of language. You very often hear, in some philosophical discussion, an objection to a line of thought that can be summed up thus: "If you adopt that line, then you're committed to saying that such-and-such expression is *just ambiguous*. But my/our intuition is that it isn't ambiguous. So that line of thought is unpromising." The "intuition" that an expression isn't ambiguous, but has a single sense, should not be allowed to play this sort of judicial role. For the adoption of a given criterion of synonymy, among a plurality of such criteria, is something that depends on a variety of issues, issues that should be brought out into the open. Our intuitions are, or ought to be, quite helpless when faced with such a question as: how many senses does "in" have in "I have a pain in my foot", "Smith has written a commentary in this book", etc. etc.?

One application of this point is to be found in the philosophy of psychology. Consider: does "intend" mean the same in "I intend to go" as in "She intends to go"? Are "intend" and "intends" (forms of) the same expression? These questions concern what is often referred to as the problem of the first-/third-person asymmetry of psychological verbs. The problem arises especially because "I intend..." (e.g.) is typically uttered without grounds and without the need for observation of the person (oneself), and because such an utterance has a special weight or authority—all this being in contrast to "He/she/NN intends..." (These facts are in this context assumed to rule out those brands of behaviourism which allege that observation of behaviour is as necessary for "I intend..." as for "He/she/NN intends...") If the meaning of a word is determined by, or is correlative with, the way the word is *used*, then given the radical difference in how the first-person and third-person verbs are used, doesn't it look as if they must mean something different? On what might be called a Cartesian view, "I intend..." is a report of a privately known inner state, while "She intends..." must be a report of something else, such as bodily behaviour.[22] On a more Wittgensteinian view, "I intend..." is not a report at all, being more like a declaration, while "She intends..." is a report, where the notion of a *mistake* is applicable to reports but not to declarations. On either sort of view, the uses or functions of the first- and third-person forms of the verb appear very different.

But our intuitions tell us that "intend" and "intends" mean the same, are the same expression! So either the idea of some deep first-/third-person asymmetry was illusory, or the picture of meaning as use looks unpromising—or both.

The argument is of course hopelessly swift. The proper philosophical task would be to investigate the ways in which it is *true* that "intend" and "intends" mean the same, and the ways in which it is *false*—relative to different criteria of synonymy and (thus) different purposes. We can certainly say: there are multiple connections between the first- and third-person uses of "intend", connections which allow one to speak of a unified or unitary language-game. The unity of meaning of "intend" is grounded in the unity of that language-game.[23] Against the background of that language-game the point of saying that "intend" and "intends" have the same sense is clear; while if our concern is to highlight the above-mentioned differences in the use of these words—e.g. to

---

[22] On this view, I do not have *grounds* for my belief that I intend to do X, since I am immediately aware of that intention. A Cartesian could attempt to assimilate the first- and third-person uses of "intend" by taking the latter to involve ascription of *the same state* as is reported by "I intend"; the third-personal judgment would then be a species of (unverifiable) inference, from outer behaviour to inner state. Wittgenstein's remarks about "It's five o'clock on the sun" are relevant here; see *PI*, pp. 350–51.

[23] I elaborate this thought further in *Wittgenstein on Thought and Will* (New York: Routledge, 2015), pp. 40–46, 114–119.

show up the implausibility of behaviourism—then the point of saying "different in sense" is likewise clear.

These are remarks about philosophical method, backed up by considerations in the philosophy of language, considerations to do with criteria of identity and difference for *expressions*. This might pique philosophers who wish that the "linguistic turn" had never happened; but that can't be helped. Meanwhile, the non-occurrence of "rat" in "Socrates" proves to be a trickier and profounder business than might at first have been thought.

Index

Abelard, Peter, 41.
Action, 8-9, 14, 67, 73-4, 89, 93, 97, 102, 124, 131, 133-4, 136-7, 139-43, 145-58, 163-4, 166, 168-71, 173, 175-87, 191-4, 196, 201, 205, 207-16, 218, 222, 224, 232-3, 256, 262, 264, 272.
Analysis, 4, 43-9, 52, 55-60, 72-74, 90, 102, 144, 156-7, 172, 186, 203, 234, 302;
See also definition.
Anglicanism, 6.
Anscombe, Alan Wells and Gertrude Elizabeth (parents of Elizabeth Anscombe), 5-6.
Anselm, 5, 7, 10, 238-43, 246-50, 252-60, 263-5.
Aquinas, 5, 7, 20-1, 61, 65-6, 69-71, 79, 84-5, 87, 92-3, 98-100, 103, 105-6, 140, 205-6, 210-1, 243-7.
Arendt, Hannah, 3.
Aristotle, 5, 7, 13, 21, 27, 61, 66, 79-80, 84-5, 87-8, 92, 97, 99, 103, 210-1, 216, 218-24, 226-8, 230-1, 233-7, 276, 278, 282;
Neo-Aristotelian, 121.
Arminian, 135-6.
Assertion, 217-21, 223, 225-8, 230-4, 240-1, 247-9, 252-8, 262-4, 278, 287;
Logic of, 16.

Atheism, 5, 9, 17.
Augustine, 243, 245-6, 254.
Austin, J L, 1-3, 17-21.
Ayer, A J, 1, 3, 9, 20, 58.

Baker, Lynne, 108-12, 116.
Bentham, Jeremy, 4, 15-6, 210-1.
Berkeley, George, 52.
Berlin, Isaiah, 1.
Boethius, 67.
Brandom, R B, 58-9.
Broad, C D, 78.
Brown Book, 27, 30.
Brown, Lesley, 21.
Brute facts, 86, 90, 174.
Bunyan, John, 86.
Burge, Tyler, 94.

Cambridge, 6-8, 22-6, 29-30, 77-8, 80, 86.
Catholicism, 5-7, 10, 17-8, 20, 31, 62, 70, 73-4, 149, 157.
Causality, 4, 8-9, 17-8, 22, 40, 63, 65-6, 70, 85, 93, 133-43, 145, 147, 162, 164, 184, 211-5, 228, 235, 242, 244, 247-8, 256-7, 301, 303-4.
Chappell, Sophie Grace, 271.
Chesterton, G K, 86.
Chisholm, Roderick, 3.
Churchill, Winston, 53, 160.
Consciousness, 50, 75, 81, 84, 105;

Phenomenal, 91;
Self-consciousness, 49-50, 82.
Consequentialism, 8, 14, 86, 196, 280-1.
Contraception, 18.

Davidson, Donald, 3, 27, 94, 134, 136, 142, 151, 153, 175-6, 180, 184, 283.
Davies, Brian, 276-7.
Definition, 4, 43-4, 48, 278-9, 300;
Of causality, 137-8;
Of *eudaimonia*, 236;
Of immaterial act, 102;
Of morpheme, 294;
Of murder, 16;
Of person, 67;
Of truth, 219-20, 246;
Ostensive, 19;
See also analysis.
Dennett, Daniel, 4.
Descartes, 4-5, 7, 68, 70, 75, 79-84, 87-8, 95, 103, 106, 134, 143, 306;
Cartesian Ego, 49-50, 60, 82.
Determinism, 134-5, 137, 139-41, 147.
Dirac, Paul, 40.
Divine law, 14.
Dummett, Michael, 32.

Edwards, Jonathan, 134-7, 141-2.
Emotivism, 1, 16.
Empiricism, 9, 66.
Epistemology, 9, 52, 66, 107, 137, 152, 170, 228.
Extensional vs. intensional, 4, 89-90, 94.

Feferman, Solomon, 35.
Finnis, John, xii, 16, 62.
Flew, Anthony, 165, 269, 274, 277.
Foot, Philippa, 1-2, 5, 8, 17, 176, 184, 280.
Ford, Anton, 173.
Freedom, 65-7, 134-7, 140-2, 145, 147.
Frege, Gottlob, 5, 7, 20-1, 61, 79, 84-5, 87, 271, 273-4, 278, 283-4, 289.

Gardiner, Patrick, 21.
Geach, Peter, 5-7, 10, 17-8, 20-1, 24-5, 31-2, 41, 77-9, 81, 83-91, 93-101, 106, 108, 125, 134, 136, 140, 183, 270, 290.
Gödel, Kurt, 35.
Grammar, 9, 50-1, 53-4, 102, 154, 240, 248, 260, 288-91, 305.
Grotius, Hugo, 12.

Hampshire, Stuart, 1-2, 12.
Hare, R M, 1, 4, 16-7, 21, 164-5.
Hart, H L A, 1-2, 15, 17.
Heraclitus, 236.
Howsepian, A A, 108, 111-4, 116.
Human dignity, 69, 71-2.
Human nature, 62, 65-8, 72, 81, 87, 89, 98, 236.
Hume, David, 4, 7, 46, 48, 61, 84, 138, 176, 304;
Fact/value distinction, 4;
Hume's circle, 46, 48, 59.
Hylomorphism, 97.

Immateriality, 63, 66, 68, 78, 84, 88, 91-2, 94-106, 211.
Intended vs. foreseen consequences, 4, 8, 14-6, 158, 162-6, 168, 170, 195-201, 204, 207, 210-1, 215.
Intention, 8-9, 12-6, 39, 64-8, 72-4, 102, 123-4, 134, 142-3, 145-52, 154-7, 161, 166, 169-

73, 175-95, 198-205, 207-13, 303, 305-6.
Intention, 8-9, 12-6, 27, 70, 72-4, 87, 93, 133, 142, 145, 148-50, 152-8, 168-73, 175-8, 180, 185-6, 190, 194, 210, 213-4, 233.
Intentionality, 18, 51, 53-7, 97, 127.
Intuitionism, 34.

Jackson, F, 58.
Johnson, Samuel, 86.
Just war, 9, 12, 13.
Juvenal, 86.

Kant, Immanuel, 4, 11, 20, 176.
Kenny, Anthony, xiii, 12, 85.
Kerry, Benno, 271, 273-4.
Keynes, John Neville, 78.
Kierkegaard, Søren, 5.
Kneale, William, 21.
Knobe, J, 58.
Kreisel, Georg, 32-8.
Kremer, Michael, 272-4.
Kripke, Saul, 5, 303.

Language-game, 292-3, 295-300, 306.
Lewis, C S, 9.
Lewis, David, 301-2, 304.
Littlewood, John, 35.
Locke, John, 4, 80, 129-30.
Logic, 16, 33-4, 89-90, 137, 143-4, 206, 232, 269, 278;
  of identity, 108-11, 113, 116, 120, 122, 132.
Logical positivism, 2.
London, England, 5-6.
Lovibond, S M, 281.

McDowell, John, 58, 190
Machery, E, 58.
McTaggart, John, 78-9, 91.
Malcolm, Norman, 7.
Marenbon, John, 41.

Materialism, 66, 87, 89-92, 94-6, 99-100, 102-3, 106;
  Scientific, 5.
Merleau-Ponty, Maurice, 3
Metaphysics, 9, 51, 55-6, 66, 68, 78, 85, 87, 99, 104, 108, 118, 126, 130, 132, 137, 146-7, 169-70, 172, 228.
Method, 307;
  Anscombe's, 3-4, 38-9, 42-61, 154-7, 170, 175.
Midgley, Mary, 1-2.
Mill, J S, 210-1.
Modals, 47-8, 56.
Modality, 21, 110.
Molière, 25.
Moore, G E, 78.
Moral psychology, 8, 158, 168, 171, 176, 181, 183, 215-6.
Moral language, 16.
Mortimer, Kate, 21.
Müller, Anselm, xiii, 21, 238.
Murdoch, Iris, 1-2.

Nagel, Thomas, 18.
Natural law, 15.
Naturalistic fallacy, 15.
Nature, 4, 40, 66, 85, 103-5, 111, 137-9, 141, 147;
  See also human nature.
Necessity, 46-8, 55-6, 135, 137-9, 145, 270.
Newton, Isaac, 40, 139.

Obligation, 13-4, 205-6.
Ontological argument, 10;
  Against materialism, 90.
Ordinary language philosophy, 52, 154-5.
Oxford, 1-2, 6, 8-9, 12, 16-7, 19-21, 31, 72, 77-8, 154, 158, 161-2, 164, 167-8, 281.

Pacifism, 160-1.
Pascal, Fania, 27.

Pears, David, 21.
Perception 51-2, 55, 60, 72, 100, 152, 217, 226, 230.
Person, 66-7, 84, 107.
Personal identity, 101, 107-132.
Petraeus, David, 13.
Philosophical Investigations, 7, 28-9, 86, 95, 292-3, 295-6, 298, 300.
Plato, 5, 7, 87, 103, 162-3, 166, 235, 287, 289, 303.
Polkinghorne, John, 40-1.
Practical reasoning, 12, 73-4, 142-7, 151, 170, 180-1, 194, 221-5, 229, 234-6, 280-1.
Price, H H, 17, 20.
Prior, Arthur, 5, 21.
Private language, 19, 180.
Promising, 46-50, 55-6, 59.
Pushkin, Alexander, 28.
Putnam, Hilary, 84, 303.

Quine, W V O, 3-5, 58, 89-90, 122.
Quinton, Anthony, 18.

Ramanujan, Srinivasa, 34.
Ramsey, Frank, 33-5, 275.
Reference, 49-50, 53-4, 56, 83, 89-90, 98, 152, 301-2.
Rhees, Rush, 7, 9, 23, 32-6.
Ricoeur, Paul, 3.
Rothschild, Emma, 21.
Russell, Bertrand, 52, 78.
Ryle, Gilbert, 1-3, 17, 20, 43, 53, 88.

Scepticism, 9, 51, 236;
  Moral, 3.
Searle, John, 18.
Sellars, Wilfred, 3, 58-9.
Skinner, Francis, 23, 25-30, 31.
Smart, J J, 58.
Smithies, Yorick, 7.
Spinoza, 5, 20.

Spirituality, *see* immateriality.
Sraffa, Piero, 29.
Stanford University, 35.
Strawson, Peter, 3.
Suárez, Francisco, 12.
Subjectivism, 1, 3.
Summa Theologiae, 70, 105.
Swift, Jonathan, 86, 162-3.
Swinnerton-Dyer, Peter, 34.

Teleology, 121-2, 127-8, 132, 147, 240-2, 254-7, 261-2, 265.
Thomson, Judith Jarvis, 153-4, 156, 196-7, 199-205, 207-9, 211-5.
Tractatus, 7, 19-21, 268, 270, 272-5, 279, 284.
Trethovvan, Illtyd, 153-4, 156-7.
Truman, Harry, 9, 12, 15, 72, 158-61, 163, 167-8, 281-2.
Truth conditions, 16, 68, 89, 96, 103, 124, 125, 143, 216-65, 269-71, 275-7, 282, 284-5, 302.

Van Inwagen, Peter, 108, 114-7, 120, 125, 126.
Virtue, 8, 13-4, 216-7, 218, 234, 236-7;
  Virtue ethics, 8.

Warnock, Mary, 2.
Weil, Simone, 3.
White, Roger, 272-5.
Wiggins, David, 266-7, 269, 272, 278, 280, 282-5.
Williams, Bernard, 4, 271.
Williams, Glanville, 40.
Wittgenstein, Ludwig, 3-7, 9, 17-21, 23, 25-38, 57, 60, 63, 65, 69, 78-9, 86, 93, 95-6, 101, 106, 154, 268-9, 272-3, 275, 278-9, 282-4, 292-3, 295-6, 298, 300, 306.

World War I, 23, 30.
World War II, 1, 2, 9, 12-3, 23,
    25-7, 30, 72, 159-61.
Wright, G H von, 5, 7.

www.ingramcontent.com/pod-product-compliance
Lightning Source LLC
Chambersburg PA
CBHW071231230426
43668CB00011B/1387